LEFTY & TIM

LEFTY & TIM

How STEVE CARLTON and TIM McCARVER Became Baseball's Best Battery

WILLIAM C. KASHATUS

Foreword by LARRY CHRISTENSON

UNIVERSITY OF NEBRASKA PRESS • LINCOLN

Portions of the book previously appeared in *Almost a Dynasty:
The Rise and Fall of the 1980 Phillies* (Philadelphia: University
of Pennsylvania Press, 2008). Copyright © 2008 University of
Pennsylvania Press. Used with permission.

The University of Nebraska Press is part of a land-grant institution
with campuses and programs on the past, present, and future
homelands of the Pawnee, Ponca, Otoe-Missouria, Omaha, Dakota,
Lakota, Kaw, Cheyenne, and Arapaho Peoples, as well as those of the
relocated Ho-Chunk, Sac and Fox, and Iowa Peoples.

Library of Congress Cataloging-in-Publication Data
Names: Kashatus, William C., 1959– author.
Title: Lefty and Tim: how Steve Carlton and Tim McCarver became
baseball's best battery / William C. Kashatus; foreword by Larry
Christenson.
Description: Lincoln: University of Nebraska Press, [2022] | Includes
bibliographical references and index.
Identifiers: LCCN 2021043219
ISBN 9781496226679 (hardback)
ISBN 9781496232168 (epub)
ISBN 9781496232175 (pdf)
Subjects: LCSH: Carlton, Steve, 1944– | McCarver, Tim. | Pitchers
(Baseball)—United States—Biography. | Catchers (Baseball)—
United States—Biography. | Baseball—United States—History—
20th century. | St. Louis Cardinals (Baseball team)—History—20th
century. | Philadelphia Phillies (Baseball team)—History—20th
century. | BISAC: SPORTS & RECREATION / Baseball / History |
BIOGRAPHY & AUTOBIOGRAPHY / Sports
Classification: LCC GV865.C317 K37 2022 |
DDC 796.357092 [B]—dc23/eng/20211223
LC record available at https://lccn.loc.gov/2021043219

Set in Minion Pro by Laura Buis.

For LC, with great appreciation for his
MLB career and his friendship

CONTENTS

ILLUSTRATIONS

FOREWORD

LARRY CHRISTENSON

Steve Carlton and Tim McCarver are my best friends from Major League Baseball. But fifty years ago I would never have predicted that either one would play such a huge role in my career as a pitcher for the Philadelphia Phillies.

I grew up in the small town of Marysville, Washington, about forty miles north of Seattle. Although I played all sports, basketball and baseball were my favorites, and I excelled at both of them. In June 1972 the Phillies made me their top draft pick, and a few days after I graduated from high school the organization flew me and my family to Philadelphia for a weekend visit.

That Sunday, Steve Carlton introduced himself and congratulated me on being drafted by the Phillies. Later I sat in one of the field boxes and watched him throw a complete-game, three-hit shutout against the Pittsburgh Pirates. The great Roberto Clemente also hit a triple for the Bucs and threw out a base runner at third. Carlton went on to win twenty-seven games for the last-place Phils that season and capture the Cy Young Award.

The next spring I was invited to Clearwater to train with the Major League club. I pitched so well that first-year manager Danny Ozark told me I had made the team. At age nineteen, I was the youngest player in the Majors in 1973. Steve Carlton, who called me "Kid," took me under his wing and protected me from the hazing and other vulnerabilities that young players suffer. Two years later Tim McCarver, who had played for the Phils between 1970 and 1972, rejoined the club, and we became fast friends.

What a great era to have played for the Phillies! We became perennial contenders with Carlton as our ace. Between 1976 and 1983 the
Phillies won five division titles, two National League pennants, and
the club's first-ever World Series. I also learned a lot from Lefty and
Tim. They taught me to stop talking to opposing hitters so those
batters wouldn't be too comfortable with me when they stepped to
the plate in a game. Lefty explained the importance of throwing
pitches to the outside part and edges of the plate and keeping the
ball away from the middle part of the strike zone. Tim taught me
the importance of pitching inside to intimidate the hitter and not
to shake him off when he called for a particular pitch. To this day
Tim still reminds me that his advice allowed me to throw three-
hit and four-hit shutouts on the only two occasions he caught me.

It was also a pleasure to watch Lefty and Tim perform as a battery
and learn how they worked the various hitters in a lineup. Whenever Tim caught, I was put in charge of preparing three Band-Aids
for him so he could wrap them around his fingers before he went
to bat. I think I opened more Band-Aids for McCarver than Carter
has liver pills. Still, I enjoyed the task since it allowed me to eaves-
drop on his discussions with Lefty between innings and learn even
more about pitching.

Lefty, Tim, and I also spent a lot of time together off the field.
Although Timmy transitioned to the Phillies' broadcast booth in
1980, he and Lefty were always there for me. We went out to dinner
together and enjoyed good restaurants and fine food. They introduced me to their former teammates from the St. Louis Cardinals,
including the great Bob Gibson. Those Cardinals became my friends,
too. It's been more than four decades since Lefty, Tim, and I were
teammates, but there is hardly a day that passes that I do not think
of these two Hall of Famers. Timmy, who played in four decades,
became a broadcaster for another forty years and entered the Hall
as a Ford Frick Award winner. When I think of Steve Carlton and
Tim McCarver, I think of their impressive legacies with the Cardinals and the Phillies and their many fans. I think of their character,
their honesty and integrity, and most of all their trust in each other.

I am proud and honored to have been a part of their great careers and grateful for their special friendship, which continues today.

In this dual biography, *Lefty and Tim*, baseball historian Bill Kashatus rekindles many wonderful memories. More important, Bill provides special insight into the careers of Carlton and McCarver that allows the reader to understand how they became such special friends as well as the best battery in Major League Baseball between 1976 and 1979 and one of the best pitcher/catcher tandems of all time. Thank you, Bill, for a book that was long overdue!

ACKNOWLEDGMENTS

This book is dedicated to Larry Christenson, who pitched for the Phillies from 1973 to 1984. Several years ago I asked Larry about the possibility of writing a biography of one of his former teammates and best friends: Phillies Hall of Fame pitcher Steve Carlton. Although LC was very excited about the prospect of such a book, he insisted that Carlton's story could not be told without including Tim McCarver, Lefty's personal catcher between 1975 and 1979.

LC also believed that he could persuade both Carlton and McCarver to do interviews with me, and he approached his former teammates about that possibility on several occasions. McCarver agreed to do three in-depth interviews, but Carlton, after wavering for three years, finally declined, stating that he "chose not to look back on the past, but ahead to the future." While I greatly appreciate Tim's willingness to be interviewed, I am sorry that Lefty refused. Instead, I had to rely on his quotations from contemporary newspaper accounts, Dan Stephenson's brilliant *Lefty: The Life and Times of Steve Carlton* (1989, on DVD), and three extremely rare interviews Carlton did, with Reggie Jackson in 1989, Roy Firestone in 1993, and Tyler Kepner in 2018.

At the same time, I am extremely grateful to Larry for his help. Not only did he make the time for insightful conversations, but he also arranged for photographs, reviewed the manuscript, and wrote a foreword. And he did all of this despite a demanding schedule and caring for family members who were ill.

Special thanks go out to all the individuals who agreed to be interviewed for this book, including Bob Boone, Larry Bowa, Ruly Carpenter, Jerry Crawford, Bill Giles, Gus Hoefling, Larry Jaster, Randy Lerch, Jim Lonborg, Ray Rippelmeyer, Dick Ruthven, Mike Schmidt, Dan Stephenson, Terry Tata, and Bill White. I also relied on interviews I did many years ago while working on other books about the Phillies. Some of those interviews were with Richie Hebner, Tommy Hutton, Greg Luzinski, Sparky Lyle, Larry Shenk, and Rick Wise. Other interviews were with ballplayers, writers, and managers who have since passed away, including Hank Aaron, Gary Carter, Bill Conlin, Darren Daulton, Dallas Green, Frank Lucchesi, Tug McGraw, and Danny Ozark.

I am also grateful to Tyler Kepner, Mike Schmidt, Jayson Stark, and Ray Rippelmeyer, who reviewed the manuscript and wrote endorsements; John Burkhart, who cross-checked the manuscript for any factual errors; John Horne of the National Baseball Hall of Fame and Library, sports artist Dick Perez, and the Phillies' Dave Buck for providing the permission to reprint photographs; Maureen Bemko, who did a magnificent job in copyediting; and Rob Taylor and the staff at the University of Nebraska Press for their support and editorial guidance.

Finally, a special thanks is owed to my family. My parents, who passed away while I was working on the book, always took a special pride in my writing. They were my biggest fans and provided the financial and emotional support for me to become a writer. My sons, Tim, Peter, and Ben, have tolerated my twin passions for baseball and writing all their lives and still seem to love me. I hope that, like their mother, Jackie, they will someday understand. Words cannot adequately describe the love and respect I have for her.

LEFTY & TIM

Introduction

On Saturday, May 1, 1976, Steve "Lefty" Carlton took the mound for the Philadelphia Phillies in the second game of a doubleheader against the Braves at Atlanta's Fulton County Stadium. The Phils, battling the Pittsburgh Pirates for first place in the National League East, won the first game, 3–0, to improve their season record to 9-6.

Winless in his previous three starts, Carlton was struggling to recapture the magic of his extraordinary 1972 campaign. That season Lefty led the NL in wins (27), earned run average (1.97), innings pitched (346.1), and strikeouts (310).[1] The six-foot, four-inch southpaw accounted for nearly half of the last-place Phillies' fifty-nine victories that year. It was one of the most brilliant pitching performances in the history of Major League Baseball, but since that Cy Young Award–winning season Lefty had seemed lost.

Over the next three years Carlton posted mediocre records of 13-20, 16-13, and 15-14, respectively. He abandoned a devastating slider and began to rely on a 90 mph fastball and a long, looping curve as his ERA ballooned to 3.56.[2] Batterymates Bob Boone and Johnny Oates, both talented pitch callers, were unable to help. "When I caught Steve, I felt he was fighting me," Boone said. "He didn't trust my calls and because of his negative thoughts, he would throw poorly."[3]

General manager Paul Owens identified the same problem midway through the 1975 season. Owens had a long history of evaluating players. Since 1965 he had been an instrumental figure in the

1

Phillies' front office. He was either remarkably lucky or extraordinarily smart in signing and trading for talented players. When Owens saw his ace pitcher struggling, he seized the opportunity to reunite Carlton with his old catcher, Tim McCarver, a grizzled, thirty-four-year-old veteran. McCarver, released by the Boston Red Sox in June 1975, was looking for a job in the broadcast booth. Owens told him that the club had no openings there, but he did have one as a backup catcher and pinch hitter. The veteran backstop accepted the position.[4]

Carlton and McCarver had been batterymates on the St. Louis Cardinals from 1965 to 1969 and appeared in two World Series for the Redbirds, in 1967 and 1968, earning rings in '67. McCarver was traded to Philadelphia after the '69 season, and three years later Carlton joined him in the City of Brotherly Love, if only for half a season. Traded to the Montreal Expos in July 1972, McCarver had the opportunity to watch Lefty from the opposite dugout. He noted that Carlton had abandoned the slider in 1973 and struggled mightily because of it.[5] When McCarver returned to the Phillies in '75, he encouraged Lefty to return to the slider, and Carlton obliged.

"I had not just the luxury of facing him [with the Cardinals], but being on a team of guys facing him," McCarver said. "I remember right-handed hitters would come back to the bench and say at least he didn't throw his slider. I tucked that away. I said if I catch him again, that slider is going to be good."[6]

On that May afternoon in Atlanta, Carlton, with McCarver behind the plate, would look like the power pitcher he had been four years earlier. The Phillies gave the left-hander a 1–0 lead in the third when shortstop Terry Harmon drew a walk off Atlanta starter Carl Morton. Carlton sacrificed Harmon to second, and second baseman Dave Cash brought him home with a single to left. The Phils tacked on two more runs in the fourth when left fielder Ollie Brown led off with a double to right. Right fielder Jay Johnstone followed with an infield hit advancing Brown to third. Center fielder Garry Maddox hit a grounder to short, and Johnstone was forced out at second while Brown was held at third, but McCarver followed and singled

Brown home. Harmon then singled to left to drive in Maddox, giving Carlton a 3–0 lead and Morton, an early exit from the game.

Using an effective combination of a high inside fastball followed by a slider low and away, Lefty held the Braves scoreless through five innings. Carlton, who had not been able to go more than six innings in his three previous starts, made only one mistake. After walking Braves left fielder Jimmy Wynn in the sixth, he threw a 3-2 fastball down the middle of the plate to cleanup hitter Earl Williams, who launched the delivery into the left-field bleachers for a two-run homer. That's all the Braves would get, though.

Johnstone added an insurance run in the ninth with a solo homer off Atlanta reliever Roger Moret. Carlton, who gave up 6 hits, walked 3, and struck out 7, shut down the Braves in the bottom of the inning to seal a complete game victory, 4–2, his first of the season.[7]

Lefty went 20-7 that year, and McCarver caught all but two of his thirty-three starts.[8] Those twenty victories paced the Phillies to their first-ever National League East title, as they finished 9 games ahead of the second-place Pittsburgh Pirates and won 101 games, the most in franchise history. The Fightin' Phils also made their first postseason appearance since 1950, when they won the NL pennant. Although the Phillies lost a trio of games to the Cincinnati Reds in the National League Championship Series, Carlton returned to his winning ways in subsequent seasons.

During the next six years Carlton captured three more Cy Young Awards ('77, '80, and '82) with the Phillies, a testament to the special blend of power and finesse that allowed him to be successful on the mound. Fanatical about conditioning, Carlton worked out nearly two hours a day with a personal fitness coach. He also eliminated all outside distractions, believing that the mental aspect of the game was every bit as important as the physical. On the day of a start Lefty rarely spoke with teammates, and he stuffed cotton in his ears when he pitched. He consistently avoided the press and by 1978 was refusing to give interviews altogether. Throughout his career Carlton remained an intense competitor and a seemingly unemotional person, though teammates knew a more supportive and humorous side. When he retired in 1989, Carlton, age forty-four, had amassed

329 career victories, 4,136 strikeouts, and a career earned run average of 3.22.[9] Five years later the great left-hander was voted into the Hall of Fame in his first year of eligibility and with one of the highest vote percentages (95.6 percent) ever accorded a member.[10] Steve Carlton received his due as one of the greatest left-handers in the history of Major League Baseball, but that achievement would not have been possible without Tim McCarver.

Not only did McCarver mentor Carlton as a young hurler with the Cardinals, but the hard-nosed catcher resurrected Lefty's career when they were reunited in Philadelphia. Carlton made 709 starts over the course of his twenty-four-year career in the Majors, and McCarver caught 228 (32 percent) of them.[11] But between 1976 and 1979 Lefty and Tim were the best battery in Major League Baseball. Of the 140 starts Carlton made during that four-year span, McCarver was behind the plate for 128 (91 percent) of them.[12] At one point Tim caught Lefty in 90 consecutive starts. Carlton's record during that stretch was 48-26. With the Phillies overall Carlton was 81-45 when McCarver caught him.[13] Tim also established a close personal relationship with Lefty that allowed the enigmatic southpaw to succeed.

At first glance they seemed like an odd couple. McCarver was old school, while Carlton was new age. Tim did not at the beginning of his career respond well to pitchers shaking him off. He believed that the catcher called the pitches, encouraged the pitcher when necessary, and kicked him in the ass when he deviated from the game plan. Lefty, who pioneered the use of meditation and martial arts in baseball, was stubborn, too. He wanted to control pitch selection, but over time Carlton and McCarver came to think alike because they developed a strong bond off the diamond that allowed them to understand and trust each other. Thus, when Lefty was struggling at the start of the '76 campaign, Tim became his personal catcher. When Lefty refused to talk with the press, Tim became his personal spokesman. When the off-season rolled around, the two teammates went on hunting trips together. In fact Carlton and McCarver became so close that the gruff backstop once quipped, "When Steve and I die, they're going to bury us 60' 6" apart!"[14]

Growing up in Northeast Philadelphia in the mid- to late 1960s and early 1970s, I fell deeply if not madly in love with the Phillies. Unfortunately, aside from 1964, when the Fightins were up six and a half games with twelve remaining and lost ten straight to blow the pennant, there wasn't much to cheer about. Then things got worse. After the 1969 season, my first baseball hero, Richie Allen, a power-hitting first baseman, was traded to the St. Louis Cardinals. I was inconsolable.

The Phillies' key acquisition was a soft-spoken, Gold Glove center fielder by the name of Curt Flood. Like Allen, Flood was an African American ballplayer who had experienced the sting of racial discrimination as a young man. Accordingly, he refused to report to Philadelphia, citing the team's poor record, the dilapidated Connie Mack Stadium, and racist fans. By challenging MLB's reserve clause that bound a player to a team, barring his release, retirement, or trade, Flood, who referred to himself as a "well-paid slave," set in motion a legal process that ultimately resulted in free agency.[15] For myself, however, there was a silver lining to the blockbuster trade, and that was Tim McCarver, who defined for me what it meant to be a catcher.

At age ten I knew that I would have to work hard to become a successful athlete. I did not have much natural ability and envied those who did. I admired those athletes who not only took charge but were intelligent, led by example, and placed team success before their own. McCarver was all that and more. In the mid-1960s the editors of Sports Illustrated considered him to be the archetypal catcher and asked him to write a chapter on that position for a short, hundred-page book that would be published for youngsters. Simply titled Sports Illustrated Baseball, the book contained tips by Major League stars on how to play the game.

In 1970, after McCarver was traded to the Phillies, I was given a copy of the book and paid special attention to chapter 4, in which Tim discussed the responsibilities of the position, the relationship between the pitcher and catcher, which pitches to call, and how to handle them. I was just starting to play baseball at the time and gravitated to the catching position, mostly because no one else seemed to be interested in it. Inspired by McCarver's words, however, I made a virtue out of a necessity.

Tim described the catcher as the "team leader, the guy who shovels the coal into the boiler to make the engine go." He is also the "most active player on defense" because "all the action lies in front of him." Furthermore, "the catcher is the team's thinking apparatus," McCarver stated. "His head is a filing cabinet where all sorts of information about the other team's players and strategy is stored. He is a walking encyclopedia of facts about the hitting habits of every player in the league."

The most exceptional catchers, according to McCarver, are the pitching staff's "best friend on and off the field." The relationship between a pitcher and catcher must be close in order to be successful. Batterymates must be able to put "personality conflicts aside" to "work and live as closely as possible." Throughout a game, pitchers rely on their catcher to get hitters out. Both must have a similar understanding of the situation to develop a coordinated strategy: How many runners are on? How many outs are there? What did the hitter do in his last at bat? What did he do on the last pitch? What pitch should be thrown in a particular count? Who's on deck, and should they pitch around the current batter? By being on the same page, the catcher builds "mutual confidence with the pitcher, and confidence wins ball games." Thus, to be successful the pitcher and catcher must trust each other, and such trust is something that takes years to build.[16]

Between 1970 and 1972, when McCarver was traded to Montreal, I watched him carefully, both behind and at the plate. I was impressed by his integrity; he practiced what he preached. He was the ideal combination of "tough guy" and "thinking man." He was selfless, placing team success above his own. He was excellent at calling pitches, setting up defenses, and blocking balls in the dirt. Although he did not have the strongest arm, he made up for it with a quick release that enabled him to throw out base stealers. McCarver was also the pitchers' best friend, as well as an amateur psychiatrist, knowing how and when to motivate each member of the staff. In addition to his emotional intelligence and defensive skills, McCarver could hit and run just as fast as a middle infielder.

Despite these impressive attributes, Tim, in my estimation, never received the credit he deserved.[17] This disregard was due in part to those backstops who came after him and redefined the position. Catchers like Johnny Bench, Gary Carter, and Carlton Fisk forged their Hall of Fame careers mostly on power hitting and strong arms, though McCarver was every bit as talented at blocking, calling a game, and leading a team. Unlike the previously mentioned Hall of Famers, McCarver also figured prominently in the careers of not one but two immortal pitchers: Bob Gibson and Steve Carlton. Nevertheless, Tim would have to wait to enter Cooperstown and do so as a broadcaster rather than a player.

When I was approached by my editor at the University of Nebraska Press to write a biography of Steve Carlton, I insisted that Lefty's story could not be told fully without including McCarver's. Since Carlton still refuses to speak with writers, there have only been two books written about him and both focus on his remarkable 1972 season.[18] McCarver, a prolific writer, has authored several books, but they include only brief discussions of his playing career.[19] Thus, the literature on the baseball careers of the two men is limited, and any detailed examination of their relationship as batterymates, nonexistent.

Lefty and Tim fills the void by exploring the remarkable association forged by the two men. It is not a biography of either player as much as the story of their success as a battery. Thus, the primary emphasis is placed on the three time periods when Carlton and McCarver were batterymates, first for the St. Louis Cardinals (1965–69) and later for the Philadelphia Phillies (1972, 1975–79). The book is also written in the historical context of the time they played the game. *Lefty and Tim* addresses the tumultuous 1960s, the racial integration of the St. Louis Cardinals, and the dominance of pitching during that era. It also explores the narcissistic decade of the 1970s, dominated by MLB's labor tensions, the arrival of free agency, and the return of the lively ball that followed the lowering of the pitcher's mound in 1969.[20]

Despite all the change, the game in those decades was still simpler and purer than it is today. There were no $100 million salaries. The only metrics used to measure a hitter's value were his batting average and the number of home runs and RBIs he drove in. The best hitters posted averages of .300 or better. The exceptional sluggers compiled thirty-five or more home runs and drove in one hundred runs or more a season and did so in ballparks where the outfield fences could be as distant as four hundred feet or more from home plate. If a pitcher, the player was judged by his win-loss record, number of strikeouts, and earned run average. The complete game was not uncommon, and the best hurlers completed the season with twenty wins and/or ERAs of 2.00 or lower.[21] All of these benchmarks were achieved without the use of steroids, too.

To be sure, the game certainly wasn't perfect. Until 1975 the reserve clause bound a player to one team unless he was traded, released, or retired. The Major League minimum salary was just $5,000 after World War II and had risen a mere $2,000, to $7,000, by 1966. The players had no say in how their pension fund was run. The owners, who refused to bargain collectively with the MLB Players Association, controlled the game's financial structure with the blessing of the commissioner. However, because all the players toiled under the same inequitable conditions, there were closer bonds among them, a sense of team that took precedence over individual achievement.[22] As a result, it was not uncommon for players to remain with one team for their entire career, to play through an injury, to pitch inside or throw at a batter who crowded the plate, or to retaliate on behalf of a teammate who was hit by an opposing hurler.

Steve Carlton and Tim McCarver were both products of that earlier game and catalysts of the dynamic changes that occurred in the national pastime in the 1960s and 1970s. Their examples remind us of a game that was defined by a remarkable work ethic, tremendous pride in performance, and an insatiable desire to win—a game that no longer exists. What's more, *Lefty and Tim* provides a blueprint for pitchers and catchers at all levels of the game. It shows how they must work together if they hope to achieve the common objective of winning. It is a story about what it meant to be the very best in baseball.

1

Always a Catcher

St. Louis, Missouri, is the city of the Gateway Arch, rhythm and blues, and Anheuser-Busch beer. What defines the heart and soul of St. Louis, however, is Cardinals baseball and its die-hard fans. T-shirts, jerseys, and colorful paraphernalia bearing the trademark baseball bat with a red bird at each end can be seen everywhere. Travel the neighborhoods and talk with people, and you'll find it's impossible to have a conversation without discussing the recent fortunes of the Cards. Nowhere else in this country—not even in New York—is baseball more cherished than in St. Louis.[1]

The popularity is due to the team's winning tradition. To date, the Cardinals have won eleven World Series championships, the second most in Major League Baseball behind the widely despised New York Yankees, and the most in the National League. The Cards are also winners of nineteen National League pennants, a record that ranks third in NL history, as well as fourteen division titles.[2] But success did not come easily. It was earned.

Although the Cardinals became a team in 1892, when the old American Association folded and the St. Louis Browns joined the National League as part of the newly reformed twelve-team circuit, the team languished in the second division for twenty years.[3] Branch Rickey, the first manager, laid the foundation for the team's success by establishing a deeply rooted farm system. The first jewel of that system was Rogers Hornsby, who hit .400 three times and won triple crowns in 1922 and 1925. Hornsby replaced Rickey as manager

9

in 1925 and led the Cards to their first World Series title. After the Series, Rickey, then general manager, surprised the baseball world by trading Hornsby to the New York Giants for Frankie Frisch, whose arrival signaled the beginning of the "Gashouse Gang."[4] This collection of hard-nosed, slightly offbeat characters had gained renown as much for their crazy antics as for their baseball talent. The group included Pepper Martin, Leo Durocher, Joe Medwick, and the Dean brothers, Dizzy and Daffy.

The Gashouse Gang won pennants in 1930 and 1931 and met the powerful Philadelphia Athletics in both World Series. They lost in the 1930 Series but won the rematch, with Martin hitting .500 and driving in five runs. Three years later the Cards won a close pennant race against the Giants and defeated the Detroit Tigers in seven games.[5] When the Gang began to run out of gas, the Cardinals' farm system produced a new generation of Hall of Fame talent. While Johnny Mize and Enos Slaughter provided the offensive firepower and shortstop Marty Marion anchored a dependable defense, Stan Musial was the franchise player who would go on to record 3,630 hits, seven batting titles, 475 home runs, and three Most Valuable Player Awards. With this talent, the Cardinals won three World Series titles (1942, 1944, 1946) and four pennants (1942–44, 1946).[6] While St. Louis fielded competitive teams in the 1950s, it was an infusion of talent late in that decade that paved their return to the Fall Classic during the 1960s. Among the players was a hard-nosed catcher by the name of Tim McCarver.

McCarver was destined to become a catcher for the Cardinals. Growing up in Memphis, Tennessee, in the 1940s and 1950s, he couldn't help it. Memphis, 290 miles south of St. Louis along the Mississippi River, was a hotbed of Cardinals baseball. McCarver spent many a hot summer's afternoon listening to Harry Caray's grandiloquent radio voice broadcasting Redbird games on KMOX. Caray's ebullient style and his signature "Holy cow!" became so ingrained in the youngster's mind that he imitated the announcer while doing play-by-play of his neighborhood stickball games. No doubt Timmy, who struggled with a speech impediment until age seven, was every bit as colorful as his broadcasting idol.[7]

McCarver was a huge baseball fan. When he was a student at St. Thomas Grammar School, the youngster sold peanuts and popcorn at Russwood Park, home of the Southern Association's Memphis Chicks. The job provided him with not only some spending money but an opportunity to watch professional baseball players develop their craft.[8] His parents encouraged the passion, probably to keep him out of trouble. They lived in Lamar Terrace, a tough, socially diverse neighborhood where some kids went "straight from high school into prison," he recalled. "I don't want to give the impression that I went from rags to riches," Tim explained many years later, "but by any legitimate social measurement, [our family] rated just a smidgen less than lower middle class."[9] The McCarvers belonged to an Irish Catholic minority in a largely Protestant city where the Black residents barely tolerated white residents and vice versa. To survive in Lamar Terrace, Tim had to know how to defend himself, and he quickly learned to become a "dues-paying roughneck." One time a neighbor pulled his father aside and warned, "If your son don't change his ways, he's going to wind up squatting in an electric chair!"[10]

Ed McCarver, a Memphis cop, was a no-nonsense parent. He understood well the dangers that lay ahead if his three sons didn't walk the straight and narrow. With a meager salary of $417 a month, he also realized that he could not afford to relocate his family to a safer neighborhood. Accordingly, Ed taught his boys to channel their aggressiveness into sports.[11] From age ten on up, the only squatting Tim McCarver did was behind home plate. "I was always a catcher," he recalled in an interview. "I was born and bred to play that position."[12]

James Timothy McCarver was born on October 16, 1941, in South Memphis to G. E. "Ed" McCarver and his wife, Alice. He was the next to youngest of five children, four boys and a girl. Surprisingly, Tim credits his sister, Marilyn, for his early development as a ballplayer by turning him into a left-handed hitter and working with him on fielding. Marilyn would take her three-year-old brother out to the backyard, get down on her hands and knees, and roll ground balls to him, preparing him to become an expert at blocking errant pitches. Because Tim was a natural right-hander, she taught him to hit lefty. "Everybody hits right-handed," she told him. "Why don't you hit from the other side?"[13] Whether the suggestion was made to cultivate independence or to give her little brother a distinct advantage on the ball diamond is not known. But Marilyn McCarver achieved both objectives, as Tim would become a reliable hitter from the "other side" of the plate as well as his own man behind it. Their father also did his part to encourage baseball.

Whenever Ed umpired in the local ten- to twelve-year-olds' Rotary League, he took his four sons along with him. The older boys, Grover, Pat, and Dan, played for the Bemis Bag Co. Bums, and Timmy, for the Oliver Finney Co. Candy Kids, a less competitive club. His initial appearance was the result of necessity. Lacking a ninth player, the coach allowed eight-year-old Tim to play right field to avoid a forfeit. After the game the youngster was given his own uniform and played with the team for the next two years, before he was officially eligible. At age ten Tim joined the Bemis Bums and, under the tutelage of coach Joe Etzberger, became a catcher. "No one wanted to catch," McCarver recalled, suggesting that he took up the position more from necessity rather than personal inclination. "Either their parents discouraged it, or they just weren't interested in the position," he said.[14] But Etzberger recognized some natural ability in the youngster and encouraged him to catch. Tim agreed. After all, Etzberger was a legend in Memphis, having won many amateur championships. One year the coach rewarded his players with a trip to St. Louis to see the Cardinals play. "I don't remember anything about the game," McCarver said many years later, but he did remember staying in a tenth-floor hotel room, where "it was too tempting not to drop water balloons."[15]

In the 1950s McCarver attended Christian Brothers High School, one of Memphis's most respected parochial schools. Juggling an early-morning newspaper route with school proved difficult for the teen. "I had a hard time staying awake in algebra class," McCarver admitted, but he did develop a love of books and for reading, an interest that became a passion as he grew older. Tim was more successful on the athletic field, where he competed in football, basketball, baseball, and track, but his favorite sport was football. On the gridiron McCarver distinguished himself as an all-state linebacker on an outstanding team that won twenty straight games. "I played bang-'em-up, hard-nosed football in high school," said McCarver. "Eventually I had at least forty colleges knocking on my door and wanting to talk about football scholarships."[16]

The most persistent suitors were Tennessee and Notre Dame. "General Bob Neyland, the legendary coach at the University of Tennessee, wanted me," recalled McCarver. "He sent Johnny Majors, the great Tennessee running back, to recruit me. Moose Krause, the Notre Dame athletic director, invited me and a teammate to go to South Bend for their game against Purdue. After the game, Moose gave each of us $10 to go to a movie, probably a violation of NCAA rules!"[17]

The attention from such illustrious college football programs must have been flattering to a seventeen-year-old. But McCarver was just as good, if not better, at baseball, and he knew it. Tim, the starting catcher for Christian Brothers all four years at the school, had a career batting average of .412 by the time he graduated. He also captained the team his senior season, when he was named all-state. In addition, the teenaged catcher hit .390 for an American Legion team that won state and regional championships.[18] With that kind of ability, he realized that professional baseball offered an immediate opportunity to earn an income. "Money was the deciding factor, plain and simple," Tim admitted.[19]

Baseball clubs sought out the teenager, and the New York Yankees had been early suitors. In 1958, when McCarver was a junior, Bill Dickey, the Yankees' Hall of Fame catcher, came to scout him. Dickey was so impressed by Tim that he called him "a Yankees-type player" and told the teen, "We want you, Tim."[20] After the workout the Hall of Famer gave McCarver some advice he would never forget: "Be a pitcher's friend." When Tim asked if "this meant always telling the pitcher he's right," Dickey explained that it was "being a tough friend when the pitcher needed that or being a reassuring friend if that's what the pitcher needed."[21]

The Yankees offered McCarver a $60,000 signing bonus, and

Dickey told him, "If you sign with the Yanks, I'll take you along with me on a two-week fishing trip. We'll talk about catching inside and out." Dickey also asked McCarver to let him know before signing elsewhere if another Major League scout gave him a better offer.[22] But Buddy Lewis, scouting for the Cardinals, was more relentless in his pursuit of the seventeen-year-old backstop, believing that McCarver was the "best young catcher he'd ever seen." Lewis, a former big league catcher with the Cards and Braves, scouted Tim for four years. He also "spent many an afternoon at the McCarver home, talking baseball, catching and lastly, but not least, telling the St. Louis Cardinals story."[23]

St. Louis farm director Walter Shannon sealed the deal. Outbidding nine other Major League clubs, Shannon offered McCarver a $75,000 signing bonus—the largest given by the club to that date—and a guaranteed annual salary of $6,000 per year for five years.[24] It was too good to turn down.

At 1:45 a.m. on June 8, 1959, Tim, accompanied by his parents, signed with St. Louis. The reason for the early hour was that Ed McCarver, who had to sign for his son because he was not yet twenty-one, had been recently promoted to police lieutenant and worked the early shift. "I am too excited for words," Tim told the *St. Louis Post-Dispatch*, "but I am happy that Mr. Lewis was the scout signing me, and I am thankful for the confidence expressed by the Cardinals."[25] Many years later McCarver admitted that the huge signing bonus wasn't the only factor in his decision. He was also swayed by the fact that St. Louis was "only 290 miles away" from home and that the Cardinals had also given him "a take-it-or-leave-it deal," which "scared [him] to death."[26]

"I was just seventeen years old at the time," recalled Tim. "My family had never seen $75,000 before. So when the Cardinals said 'take it or leave it,' my father, who was acting as my agent, wasn't about to call their bluff. That's why I never called Bill Dickey back, and I regret that."[27]

Assigned to the Cardinals' Class D Minor League affiliate at Keokuk, Iowa, in the Midwest League, McCarver made his professional debut in the second game of a doubleheader at Waterloo,

Iowa, on June 14, 1959. "The fans will love this kid," Keokuk manager Frank Calo said after watching McCarver hit. "Just wait until they see this kid." In sixty-five games, Tim hit .360, but he also committed fourteen errors at backstop. In August, when Rochester catcher Dick Rand dislocated a right index finger, McCarver was promoted to the Class Triple-A International League club to replace him. He hit .357 for Rochester in seventeen games and made no errors. Because of their financial investment in the young catcher, the Cardinals' front office kept close tabs on McCarver. Pleased by his considerable development, McCarver was promoted to the Cardinals in September, just three months after he had graduated from high school.[28]

"When I arrived that first time, I was nervous enough," McCarver recalled. "I didn't know these guys and I wanted to impress them." Unfortunately, he failed to do so on September 10, 1959, when Tim, starstruck, joined the Cardinals on the road in Milwaukee. Stan Musial, a boyhood hero, was now a teammate. Hank Aaron, another idol, was just across the diamond on the opposing team. "When Hank came to bat for the first time that day," McCarver said, "I leaped from my perch in the Cardinals' dugout and did what I always did when I listened to the Braves play the Cardinals. 'Come on, Henry,' I yelled. 'Come on, Henry.' The action seemed natural to me, but some of my teammates weren't amused." One teammate was more vocal. "Around here, kid," snarled a fellow Redbird, "we root for *our* guys, not theirs."[29]

McCarver got the chance to atone for his indiscretion in the ninth inning. With two outs, a runner on second, and the Cardinals trailing by three, manager Solly Hemus sent the youngster to the plate. "There I was, younger than Musial's own son, picking up a bat and advancing to the plate," said Tim. "As I stepped in to face Don McMahon, a veteran right-handed relief pitcher with a commanding fastball, my knees literally shook with fear."[30]

McCarver's Major League debut as a pinch hitter was short and sweet. He swung at an 0-2 curveball and lifted it to right field, where the game-ending catch was made by Aaron.[31] The following day seventeen-year-old Tim got his first big league start at catcher. On the mound was twenty-year-old Bob Miller. Together they formed the youngest battery in Major League history.[32] As lead-off batter, McCarver went 1-for-3 against the Chicago Cubs' Glen Hobbie, who defeated the Cards, 8–0.[33] Tim played in eight games for the 1959 Cardinals, hitting .167 (4-for-24) before returning to the Minors.

In 1960 McCarver was invited to the Cards' spring training camp in St. Petersburg, Florida, where the Redbirds shared Al Lang Field with the New York Yankees. While white fans could sit wherever they pleased in the seven-thousand-seat facility, Black fans were confined to the "colored" section down the right-field line, unprotected from the scorching sun. Despite the 1954 Supreme Court ruling mandating the integration of public schools, southern states like Florida clung to Jim Crow laws that upheld segregation in schools, restaurants, hotels, railway cars, restrooms, and other public places. "Separate but equal" accommodations were noticeably different, as was obvious in the unshaded seats at Al Lang Field.[34]

Like the Reverend Martin Luther King Jr.'s Southern Christian Leadership Conference, which was organizing nonviolent protests against segregation in the Jim Crow South, young Black ballplayers training in Florida launched their own protests to desegregate public facilities, especially the hotels where their teams stayed. One of those African American ballplayers was Bill White, a Cardinals first baseman who was raised in racially diverse Warren, Ohio. White, who had been a premed student at Hiram College, arrived at his first spring training at St. Pete in 1959 in a taxi assigned to "colored" customers. When he tried to check in at the Cardinals' hotel, the clerk informed him that he would be staying across town in the "colored section" with a widow who rented rooms to "colored" players.

White was infuriated by the second-class treatment. "I was called words I had never even heard before," he recalled. "Having to sit on the team bus while the other guys went into a restaurant to eat. Not being able to go into a gas station to use the bathroom, not being able to stay in a decent hotel. It was a bitter experience for me. You don't forgive those things when people treat you like dirt—*worse* than dirt."[35] St. Louis wasn't much better.

White and his wife purchased "a nine-hundred-square-foot home in the suburb of Rock Hill" and became the "first black family on the block." When the Cardinals' first baseman moved in, his white neighbor "refused to speak with me." Although the two men later became friends, the sting of racial discrimination stayed with him for many years. De facto segregation was not limited to housing. According to White, Black players "knew there were restaurants and hotels and other places where they weren't welcome."[36]

For the growing pool of African American baseball players, St. Louis was not an attractive place to play let alone live. Historically, the Cardinals drew most of their players from places where Jim Crow reigned. Cardinals fans shared the same racist attitudes as some players raised in the South and Southwest. KMOX, the radio station that broadcast the team's games, had listeners throughout the South. For most white, working-class men from Alabama, Mississippi, and Arkansas, KMOX was their connection to the team, and they listened to Redbirds broadcasts religiously. Many would make the all-night drive to St. Louis on a Friday after work to catch a Saturday game at Sportsman's Park, where the seating was segregated. Some even stayed for a Sunday doubleheader before driving through the night to return home. Predictably, the Cardinals' front office had been hesitant to challenge the racial prejudices of their players or to alienate the fan base by signing Black athletes.[37] There also wasn't any pressure to do so because the Cards already enjoyed the best farm system in baseball and could rely strictly on white talent.

The team's refusal to sign African American players finally faced challenges in the 1950s. Financially strapped, Cardinals owner Fred Saigh put the team up for sale in 1953. August Anheuser "Gussie" Busch Jr., president of a St. Louis–based brewing company, persuaded Saigh to sell the club to him for $3.75 million, less than what he was asking.[38] Shortly afterward Busch bought Sportsman's Park from the American League Browns, who were moving to Baltimore.[39]

Gussie Busch's enthusiasm and money reinvigorated the Cardinals. After renaming Sportsman's Park for himself—Busch Stadium—the new owner refurbished the ballpark, reducing the seating capacity to 30,500. To inspire greater enthusiasm among the fans, Busch installed an illuminated eagle atop the scoreboard, and every time a Cardinal hit a home run the lights flashed and made the eagle "flap" its wings.[40]

He also made a genuine effort to sign Black players. Stunned to learn that he had purchased an all-white team, the new owner vowed to correct the problem immediately. Since Budweiser sold more beer to Black consumers than any other brewing company in the country, Gussie feared that an all-white team would result in Black customers boycotting both his beer and his baseball franchise. To his credit, Busch also believed that it was morally wrong to exclude Black players from baseball, especially when his personal fortune depended on it.

"How can it be the great American game if blacks can't play?" he asked his manager, Eddie Stanky.

The silence was deafening.

"Hell," he added, "we sell beer to everyone!"[41]

Within months of taking over, Busch ordered general manager Frank Lane to find Black ballplayers for his team. When Lane bungled the assignment by signing marginally talented Black players, Busch fired him and in 1957 replaced him with Vaughan Pallmore "Bing" Devine.[42] Unlike Lane, who was ruthless in making his own deals, Devine was a soft-spoken, modest man who sought and received a lot of input from others. He was largely responsible for integrating the Cardinals. The cornerstone of Devine's success was a young African American pitcher by the name of Bob Gibson, who would make the Cardinals a perennial contender in the 1960s.[43]

Gibson was a complex young man. He could be intimidating, or soft-hearted. Intensely competitive, or unconditionally loyal. Scarred by racial discrimination as a youngster, Gibson became somewhat of a loner with a deep skepticism toward white society. One of seven children of a poor family, Gibson was raised in the housing projects of Omaha, Nebraska, by a widowed mother. His father, a mill worker, had died before he was born. Stricken as a child with asthma, rickets, and rheumatic heart disease, Gibson overcame those afflictions to become a talented and graceful athlete. But until his senior year at Omaha Technical High School, he was banned from playing baseball because of his race. Instead, Gibson turned to basketball, became his high school's first Black player, and demonstrated so much potential that he hoped to go to Indiana University on a hoops scholarship. Denied that possibility because of racial quotas, Gibson accepted a basketball scholarship from Creighton University, where he broke every school scoring record.[44] Undecided over whether to pursue baseball or basketball, Gibson signed with the Cardinals in 1957 for $4,000 and also played with the Harlem Globetrotters in the winter months. Although he compiled a pedestrian 23-22 record in the Minors, Gibson eventually chose baseball and made the Majors in July 1959. He started his first Major League game on July 30 at Cincinnati and blanked the Reds, 1–0. It was the first of fifty-six shutouts he would record over the course of a seventeen-year Hall of Fame career.[45] But manager Solly Hemus was hardly encouraging.

Hemus, who operated on negative motivation, alienated his Black players by calling them "n——s." He told Gibson that he wasn't big league material and suggested that learning the strengths and weaknesses of opposing hitters was beyond his intellectual capacity.[46] "Either he disliked [the Black players] deeply or he genuinely believed that the way to motivate us was with insults," Gibson said.[47] Hemus refused to pitch the youngster on a regular basis, giving him just nine starts despite a 3.33 ERA. Gibson finally had enough and decided to quit. He was packing his gear when coach Harry Walker convinced him to stay with the club, insisting that Hemus "will be gone long before you will."[48]

Bob Gibson was not only an extremely talented athlete; he also handled the racial situation with a level of maturity and honesty rarely seen in baseball at that time. It allowed him to develop a close friendship with McCarver, who was six years younger than Gibson and much more naïve in terms of race relations. Tim did not make a good first impression when he met Gibson at spring training in 1960.

During an early practice that spring a Black youngster jumped the fence and tried to run off with a foul ball. McCarver went after the boy, calling him a "little n——." Gibson, never one to back down from the courage of his convictions, heard the epithet and got in the young catcher's face. "I told him what I thought of his language, his mother, his hometown, his catching ability and anything else I could think of," said the pitcher who would later become the ace of the St. Louis Cardinals.[49]

Gibson admitted that there was an "air of racial tension" between himself and the young catcher during that first year, but he used humor to transcend it. Later that spring, after an exhibition game, McCarver boarded the team bus licking an ice cream cone and sat down across from Gibson.

"Hey, Tim, can I have a bite of that cone?" asked the pitcher, intending to rag him.

McCarver cringed. He gazed at Gibson's face to see if he was serious, and then at his ice cream cone. Pausing to consider the situation, the catcher finally mumbled, "I'll save you some."

Gibson laughed so hard that he nearly fell out of his seat.

"By that time, I could see that Tim was already changing," Gibson said years later. "Ultimately, he did a 180-degree turnaround in his racial attitude. It was the first time I saw a white man change."[50]

McCarver admitted that Gibson intimidated him, not only because he was older but also because he wore "a scowl on his face." His very presence was "forbidding" for a kid from Memphis who did not associate with any African Americans when he was growing up. "When I was signed by the Cardinals in the late Fifties, I had never played against a black man, much less with one," recalled Tim. "I heard racial slurs all the time when I was a kid. It was a substantial thing to overcome all of that. I went to that first spring training with many of the prejudices that were related directly to my birthplace. I hadn't formed any opinions of my own. Gibby, more than any other black man, helped me overcome whatever prejudices I might have had."[51] McCarver and Gibson would develop a close friendship over the next decade, one that would enable both teammates to realize success at the Major League level.

Tim started the 1960 campaign with the Memphis team of the Southern Association, and he batted .347, second in the league. The performance earned him another late-season call-up. Appearing in ten games for the Cards, McCarver batted .200 with 2 hits in 10 at bats. In 1961 Tim played for San Juan/Charleston of the International League before another promotion to St. Louis, where he appeared in twenty games and batted .239. He also hit his first home run, on July 13, a solo shot to right field off Tony Cloninger of the Braves. Returning to the International League in 1962, McCarver hit .275 with 11 homers and 57 RBIs for Atlanta. Because Atlanta made the playoffs, Tim remained in the Minors, thus missing the September call-up.[52]

These were rebuilding years for the Cardinals. Between 1959 and 1962 St. Louis contended just once (in 1960), when the club finished in third place, nine games behind the league-leading Pittsburgh Pirates.[53] General manager Bing Devine was tasked with rebuilding the farm system while trying to jump-start the parent club. By 1962 Devine had landed on the hot seat, having failed to produce a pennant in the four years since he had been hired. Gussie Busch was not the most patient owner.[54] Having purchased the Cardinals in 1953, Busch had become frustrated with a decade of losing. To improve the fortunes of his club, Gussie hired Branch Rickey as a senior consultant on October 29, 1962. In that consulting capacity, Rickey, who had presided over the most successful period in franchise history, would exercise considerable authority in the front office.[55]

At first glance Rickey and Devine appeared to be ideal for each other. After all, Rickey had left St. Louis for Brooklyn in 1942 to realize his dream of integrating baseball. Devine was just as committed to integrating the Cardinals as his track record demonstrated. On December 5, 1957, Devine engineered a trade that brought Curt Flood, an extremely talented outfielder, to St. Louis from the Cincinnati Reds.[56] Just over a year later, on March 25, 1959, Devine acquired another African American, Bill White, from the San Francisco Giants. White, a first baseman, would blossom into one of the team's most reliable power hitters.[57] However, Devine's greatest catch came on June 15, 1964, when he fleeced the Chicago Cubs of Lou Brock, another hugely talented outfielder who would forge a Hall of Fame career in St. Louis.[58] Just as important, Flood, White, and Brock, like Gibson, also handled the racial atmosphere with maturity and honesty.

Despite their mutual commitment to integration, Rickey and Devine locked horns almost immediately. Rickey, who was eighty-one in 1962, did not have much respect for Devine, who had been a low-level staffer when Rickey ran the Cardinals in the 1930s and early 1940s. Devine knew that Rickey didn't respect his abilities as general manager and tried to undermine his authority. Thus, the two executives engaged in a power play that was often personal.[59] The initial conflict was over a trade for shortstop Dick Groat, who had fallen out of favor with the Pittsburgh Pirates. Devine engineered the deal because he was uncomfortable with the rookie Julio Gotay, who had played the position during the '62 campaign. Gotay was the weakest link in a Cardinals infield that featured Ken Boyer at third, Bill White at first, and Julián Javier at second. While Boyer and White were virtual All-Stars, Javier showed signs of greatness. But Devine wanted a veteran shortstop to mentor and play alongside his young second baseman. He believed that Groat, the 1960 National League Most Valuable Player, was the perfect fit. Rickey, on the other hand, disagreed on principle; never trade a young player for an older one was his view. After several weeks of haggling, Devine went over Rickey's head to Gussie Busch, who approved the deal. Infuriated, Rickey seized every opportunity to undermine the general manager's authority.[60]

There was also instability on the field with manager Solly Hemus, a fiery cuss who baited umpires and had difficulty tolerating players who exhibited less intensity. A former Cardinals shortstop, Hemus ingratiated himself with owner Gussie Busch. Shortly after he was traded to Philadelphia in 1955, Hemus wrote Busch a letter gushing about how much he appreciated the Cardinals organization. Busch remembered that letter when he was seeking a new manager in 1959, but Solly wasn't the right man for the job. He intimidated his players.[61] His gruff, authoritarian manner disturbed the younger players, especially Black players, including pitcher Bob Gibson and outfielder Curt Flood, both of whom considered the manager racist.[62] Nor did Hemus endear himself to the veteran players when he benched Musial two months into the 1960 campaign.[63] Hemus's Cardinals struggled to play .500 ball during most of his three-year tenure. Finally, on July 6, 1961, Hemus was fired and replaced by coach Johnny Keane.[64]

Keane, who had the weathered appearance of a sea captain, was the ideal manager for the rebuild. He had been the top manager in the Cardinals' farm system, developing many of the prospects who were now playing for the Cards. Patient, likable, and highly respected in the organization, Keane exhibited undying confidence in McCarver, Flood, and first baseman Bill White, all of whom he made everyday players. He also gave unwavering support to Gibson, who would become the undisputed ace of the team.[65] Under Keane's leadership, the Cards soon became pennant contenders. His cultivation of the young players and their blend of personalities allowed the Cardinals to develop a special camaraderie that transcended racial differences.

The Redbirds enjoyed themselves and each other. Veteran third baseman Ken Boyer provided leadership for his teammates, both on and off the field. On the field he led by example. Between 1958 and 1964 Boyer averaged 26 homers and 100 RBIs a season. During that seven-season span, he compiled a .302 average, appeared in six All-Star Games, and won five Gold Glove Awards, as well as the 1964 Most Valuable Player Award. Off the field Boyer made sure that no one was excluded from a team activity. Everybody went out to dinner or to a movie together.[66] "When Kenny took over as captain of our team, he was the boss, the guy everyone looked up to," recalled McCarver. "It was understood that Kenny took care of all the players coming into the organization. He took people under his wing and proved to be a pillar of strength in the organization."[67]

Stan Musial, winding down his Hall of Fame career, was also an indispensable part of the team. "The impact of a man like Musial on a bunch of ballplayers can't ever be exaggerated," said McCarver. "Year in and year out, it was more than his seven batting titles that made an impression on us. He was a person of good character and decency. He tried to lead by example. He wasn't much of a talker, a special pleader, or a clubhouse lawyer. He was just a good man."[68] Musial was one of the very few Cardinals from an earlier era who accorded Black players the same respect as white teammates. "I never hesitated to ask Stan about hitting," said Bill White, who as one of the Cardinals' first African American players was a man with a strong appreciation of the racial struggles that existed in baseball during the 1960s. "He is helpful to anyone who asks him. More important is his cooperative attitude toward anyone—white or Black—who approaches him. It doesn't make any difference to him. He's that kind of man. He's always congenial, always ready to share."[69] In fact, "Stan the Man" inspired his teammates to such epic proportions that some believed "nothing bad could happen to them if he was around," whether it be on the playing field or traveling in an airplane between cities.[70]

There were also natural comedians on the team, like backup catcher Bob Uecker, who performed hilarious impressions of teammates, the manager, and even owner Gussie Busch. Not to be outdone, McCarver revealed a hidden talent for a dead-on impersonation of Frank Fontaine, the always-inebriated character "Crazy Guggenheim" of the popular *Jackie Gleason Show*'s "Joe the Bartender" skits. Once, McCarver and pitcher Ray Sadecki, inspired by a late-night horror movie, purchased Halloween masks and donned them in the clubhouse. McCarver showed up as a Quasimodo-like figure and Sadecki as a wolfman. Gibson loved the idea so much that he got himself a Frankenstein mask. "Pretty soon we had a whole squad of freaks," recalled Gibby. "We wore the masks on airplanes and on buses to the ballpark."[71]

The Cardinals were a rare team. They hung out together. They joked around with each other. They talked baseball all the time—in the dugout, over dinner, on planes, at hotels. Not only did they believe in each other, but they genuinely liked each other. "As a team, we would simply not tolerate any sort of festering rancor between us, personal or racial," said Gibson. Usually that kind of chemistry occurs *after* winning a pennant or a World Series. This combination of veterans and youngsters, however, developed the affinity *before* they won anything.[72]

To be sure, the Cardinals had the nucleus of a championship

team in place in 1963. The lineup featured a solid blend of power, speed, and timely hitting. Bill White (.304, 27 HRS, 109 RBIS) and Ken Boyer (.285, 24 HRS, 111 RBIS) provided the power. Musial came off the bench in his final season to contribute another 12 homers and 58 RBIS. Second baseman Julián Javier and center fielder Curt Flood provided the speed, stealing a total of 18 and 17 bases, respectively. Shortstop Dick Groat (.319, 43 doubles) and Flood (.302, 34 doubles) provided the timely hitting. The pitching was just as formidable. Gibson (18-9, 204 SO, 3.39 ERA) and Ernie Broglio (18-8, 145 SO, 2.99 ERA) topped the rotation. Curt Simmons (15-9, 127 SO, 2.48 ERA), Ray Sadecki (10-10, 136 SO, 4.10 ERA), and Ron Taylor (9-7, 91 SO, 2.84 ERA) provided flexibility pitching out of the bullpen as well as starting.[73]

McCarver was also a part of the championship nucleus, though Branch Rickey did not give him much credit early on. During spring training the senior consultant sat on a perch high above the old batting cages in St. Petersburg and observed all the players. What he saw of the young catcher did not impress him. "McCarver needs to improve his footwork on his throwing," Rickey wrote in a memo to owner Gussie Busch. "He doesn't need to take two steps before he throws to second base." Nor did Branch like what he saw of McCarver's swing, and he embarrassed him before the entire team when he critiqued it. "There is a player I watched in batting practice," Rickey began. "I don't want to mention his name, but he's a young fellow who should know better. He didn't take the bat back far enough. He'll never hit a fastball like that."[74] According to McCarver, Rickey "didn't have to mention my name because everyone on the team knew" that the senior consultant was criticizing him.[75]

Despite Rickey's negative opinions, Devine and Keane not only promoted McCarver to the Cardinals in 1963 but also dealt starting catcher Gene Oliver at the trading deadline for pitcher Lew Burdette of the Milwaukee Braves.[76] The trade officially anointed McCarver as the starting catcher, and he responded well both behind and at the plate. Although young, he demonstrated exceptional leadership skills. He worked hard to familiarize himself with the strengths and weaknesses of the pitching staff and used that knowledge effectively in his game calling. He knew when to take charge of a game and, just as important, when to defer to the veterans. He also made a substantial contribution to the offense.

Although McCarver batted eighth in the lineup, he displayed rare speed for a catcher. On June 9 he hit an inside-the-park grand slam off Larry Bearnarth, thus helping the Cards to a 10–4 victory over the Mets in the second game of a doubleheader at New York's Polo Grounds.[77] He also delivered in the clutch. On July 16 he laid down a squeeze bunt scoring Bill White with the winning run in a ten-inning, 5–4 victory over the Reds in Cincinnati.[78] Similarly, on August 19 McCarver singled home Julián Javier with the winning run, breaking a 7–7 deadlock against the San Francisco Giants for an 8–7 Cardinals victory.[79]

With McCarver behind the plate, the Cardinals hit their stride during the stretch run, making a strong bid for the pennant. On August 29 the Redbirds, seven and a half games behind the league-leading Los Angeles Dodgers, defeated the Phillies, 11–6, in Philadelphia. The victory marked the beginning of a streak in which the Cards won nineteen of their next twenty games. During the winning streak, Cardinals pitching held opponents scoreless for more than thirty consecutive innings. By September 15 the Cards had reduced the Dodgers' lead to just one game. But by September 29, when "Stan the Man" played in his final game, the Cardinals had folded, finishing in second place, six games behind the Dodgers and their remarkable pitching tandem of Sandy Koufax and Don Drysdale.[80]

McCarver ended the '63 campaign with a .289 average, 4 homers, 7 triples, and 51 RBIs.[81] Tim's impressive rookie year performance reminded Wally Schang, of the old Philadelphia Athletics, of a teammate who later entered the Hall of Fame as a catcher. "The kid reminds me of Mickey Cochrane," said Schang. "I don't know if McCarver will hit like Cochrane, but he's got Mickey's same aggressiveness and speed. And as a kid, McCarver's a pretty good hitter right now."[82]

Branch Rickey was also effusive in his praise. Comparing McCarver to Bill DeLancey, the catcher for the 1934 Cardinals' Gashouse

Gang, Rickey told the St. Louis sportswriters that DeLancey "had the stronger throwing arm, but Tim's arm is strong enough." Furthermore, "McCarver's a solid .280 hitter," he said. "He could hit .300 and he can run faster than DeLancey could. He has the same aggressiveness and baseball intelligence." Then, in a dramatic reversal of his opinion of the young backstop, Rickey boasted, "If we had 25 McCarvers on this team, we would win many pennants."[83]

The 1964 season proved to be one of unexpected twists and turns as the Cardinals overcame adversity to capture their first pennant and World Series title since 1946. The Cards began the season playing so well that they were just one game behind the league-leading San Francisco Giants on May 22. But then the team suffered a devastating slump in which they dropped seventeen of twenty-three games. By mid-June they had fallen seven games behind the front-running Philadelphia Phillies.[84]

Bing Devine tried desperately to find help as the trading deadline approached. He set his sights on a young outfielder who played for the Chicago Cubs: Lou Brock. Devine finally acquired Brock on June 15, trading Cardinals pitchers Ernie Broglio, Bobby Shantz, and outfielder Doug Clemens. Initially, Cards fans criticized the trade because Broglio, age twenty-eight, was a proven pitcher with seventy career wins to his name, and Shantz, age thirty-eight, had pitched well for the Redbirds since his acquisition from Houston two years earlier. On the other hand, Brock was viewed as a one-dimensional player who could do little more than steal bases. Within weeks, however, Brock proved his naysayers wrong, batting at a .340 clip. At season's end the new Cardinals outfielder was hitting .348, with 12 home runs and 33 stolen bases.[85]

With Curt Flood hitting lead-off and Brock batting second, the Cardinals had an effective top of the order. Not only could Brock steal bases, but he could bunt and use the hit and run to protect Flood. Together the two Black outfielders were among the best lead-off combinations in the game and were instrumental in clinching the pennant during the final weeks of the season.

In mid-August the Cardinals were 63-55 and languishing in fifth place, nine games behind the league-leading Philadelphia Phillies.

Owner Gussie Busch was so unnerved by his team's poor performance that he fired his general manager, Bing Devine, and replaced him with Bob Howsam, who had been president of the American Association in the 1950s before becoming owner of the National Football League's Denver Broncos. Rickey orchestrated both moves, but that did not dismiss the fact that Devine had pieced together a winner over the course of his six-and-a-half-year tenure. In fact, Devine had been so popular among the players that his firing served as a catalyst for an incredible comeback.[86]

With two weeks remaining in the season, the Cardinals overcame a six-game deficit to unseat the Phillies, who suffered a devastating ten-game losing streak that coincided with the Cardinals' winning spree. It began on September 22, when the Cards defeated the lowly New York Mets, 2–1. On September 27 the Cards completed a five-game sweep of the Pirates in Pittsburgh, while the Phillies continued to lose. The Cincinnati Reds, who had just completed a doubleheader sweep of the New York Mets, were now in first place, with the Cards just a game and a half out.

Returning to St. Louis for a three-game series against the Phillies, the Cardinals were greeted by five thousand cheering fans as their plane landed at Lambert Field. The Redbirds rose to the occasion and swept the Phillies by scores of 5–1, 4–2, and 8–5. When Pittsburgh knocked off the Reds, 1–0, in sixteen innings on September 30, the Cardinals held sole possession of first place.

The Cards lost their next two games at home to the Mets but still entered the final game of the regular season on October 4 tied for first with the Reds and a game ahead of the Phillies. The Redbirds started Curt Simmons against the Mets' Galen Cisco. Simmons lasted only four and a half innings before he was relieved by Gibson, who was pitching on just one day's rest. The Cards took a 5–3 lead in the fifth with three runs and never looked back. White hit a two-run homer in the sixth, and Flood added a solo shot in the eighth to complete the scoring. In the top of the ninth, with Met runners on first and third and two outs, Ed Kranepool hit a pop foul down the third base line. McCarver located the ball, tossed off his mask, and made the catch for the final out in the 11–5 victory.

The Phillies eliminated Cincinnati by walloping the Reds, 10–0, and gift wrapping the pennant for the Cardinals.[87]

St. Louis faced the heavily favored New York Yankees in the '64 World Series. It was the fifth straight American League pennant for the Bronx Bombers, who had finished the regular season with a record of 99-63 under first-year manager Yogi Berra, a St. Louis native. The Fall Classic opened on Wednesday, October 7, before a crowd of 30,805 at Busch Stadium. Trailing 4–2 entering the bottom of the sixth inning, Cardinal Mike Shannon tied the score at 4–4 with a one-out, two-run homer. Two more runs scored on a double by McCarver, a pinch single by Carl Warwick, and a triple by Curt Flood. Ray Sadecki allowed four runs on eight hits in six innings, but he received credit for the victory as the Cards defeated Whitey Ford and the Yankees, 9–5, to capture Game One.

New York evened the Series the following day. Mel Stottlemyre held the Cardinals to three runs on seven hits. Bob Gibson, who started the game for St. Louis, limited the powerful Yankee offense to two runs through six innings. But New York added two more runs in the seventh and erupted for an additional four runs off relievers Barney Schultz and Gordie Richardson in the ninth to win the game, 8–3.

The Series shifted to New York on Saturday, October 10. A crowd of 67,101 packed Yankee Stadium to watch a pitching duel between Jim Bouton and Curt Simmons. Simmons pitched masterfully, allowing the Yanks just one run on four hits in eight innings of work. The Cardinals' only run came in the fifth, when McCarver led off with a single and ended up on second when the ball got passed to center fielder Mickey Mantle. A groundout by right fielder Mike Shannon advanced McCarver to third, and he scored when Simmons's hard shot to third was knocked down by Yankees third baseman Clete Boyer (Ken's brother) but couldn't make the play. Simmons was lifted in the ninth when Yankees manager Johnny Keane elected to send Bob Skinner to the plate to pinch-hit with two runners on and one out. But the Cards failed to score, and reliever Barney Schultz was summoned from the bullpen to pitch the bottom of the frame. The first batter Schultz faced was Mantle, who promptly deposited the reliever's first pitch into the upper deck in right field to seal the win for the Yankees, 2–1.

The Cardinals fought back in Game Four on Sunday, October 11, to even the Series at two games apiece with a 4–3 victory. Although the Yankees scored three runs in the first inning off starter Ray Sadecki, St. Louis's bullpen saved the day. Roger Craig went four and two-thirds scoreless innings, surrendering just two hits. Ron Taylor followed with four hitless innings. Ken Boyer accounted for all four Cardinal runs with a one-out grand slam off Al Downing in the sixth.

McCarver was the hero the following day as the Cards won Game Five. Gibson started the game and took a 2–0 lead into the ninth. After registering his thirteenth strikeout of the game for the first out in the bottom of that frame, Gibby surrendered a two-run homer to Tom Tresh to tie the game. In the top of the tenth Bill White walked and Ken Boyer beat out a bunt to set the stage for McCarver. After working a full count off Yankees hurler Pete Mikkelsen, Tim belted a three-run homer, giving the Cards a 5–2 advantage. Gibson came in to close the victory in the bottom of the inning as the Redbirds pulled within one game of a World Series championship.

Back in St. Louis on Wednesday, October 14, the Yankees and Jim Bouton forced a seventh game by defeating the Cardinals, 8–3. The contest was knotted at 1–1 until the sixth, when Mantle and Roger Maris blasted back-to-back homers off Curt Simmons. Joe Pepitone sealed the victory with a grand slam off reliever Gordie Richardson in the eighth.

Game Seven pitted Gibson against Stottlemyre, both pitching on just two days' rest. The Cards scored three runs off the Yankee starter in the fourth, with one of the runs scoring on a double steal. McCarver was on third and Mike Shannon on first with one out and the Cardinals ahead, 1–0. With Dal Maxvill at the plate and Mel Stottlemyre pitching, Shannon broke for second base. Yankees catcher Elston Howard threw to second, trying to nail Shannon, who eluded Bobby Richardson's tag. Meanwhile, McCarver dashed for home, beating Richardson's return throw to Howard.

Tim's steal of home would be his only stolen base in twenty-one World Series games.

The Cards added another three runs off reliever Al Downing in the fifth, the first tally coming on a solo homer by Lou Brock. Mantle cut the Cardinals' lead in half with a three-run homer in the sixth. Ken Boyer hit a solo shot in the bottom of the seventh to increase the Cards' lead to 7–3. Gibson surrendered solo homers to Clete Boyer and Phil Linz in the bottom of the ninth but hung on to secure the 7–5 victory, earning the Cardinals their seventh World Series title.[88]

Gibson was named Most Valuable Player for his two wins and for 31 strikeouts in twenty-seven innings of work. But the award could have just as easily gone to McCarver, who played in every game of the '64 World Series and hit .478 with 5 RBIs and a game-winning home run. Not only did Tim record the highest batting average by a Cardinals regular since Pepper Martin hit .500 in 1931, but he became just the seventh catcher to hit .400 or better in a Fall Classic and one of just three catchers to hit a double, a triple, and a home run in a single World Series.[89] McCarver also compiled a .552 on-base percentage, stole home, and led the Cardinals in hits (11) and walks (5) and fielded flawlessly (no errors in sixty-three innings) while helping the Cardinals' pitching staff navigate a Yankees lineup that included the era's most prominent power hitting duo: Mickey Mantle and Roger Maris.[90]

One of the greatest tributes to McCarver's ability came after the World Series. When *The Sporting News* asked Stan Musial for his impressions of the Cardinals' young catcher, he replied, "He is a pretty sound hitter with a fine swing for a young fellow. He also is a tough-fibered player. He plays hard and took an awful lot of work in his first two years at the difficult position of catcher."[91]

Tim McCarver had come a long way since September 10, 1959, when he first donned a St. Louis Cardinals uniform and sat, starstruck, in the same dugout as Musial, his boyhood hero. McCarver had proven himself at the highest level of Major League Baseball, earning the respect of his teammates, his team's manager, and one of the game's greatest players. The future looked bright. There were no limits.

2

Odd Couple

Steve Carlton made his first appearance for the St. Louis Cardinals in a 1965 spring training game at Al Lang Field in St. Petersburg, Florida. The lean rookie had rocketed through the Redbirds' farm system the previous year, winning a total of fifteen games at the Single- and Double-A levels. The remarkable achievement earned him an invitation to the big league camp. Now he was ready to prove that he belonged in the Majors.

On that sun-drenched afternoon in St. Pete, Carlton went four innings, surrendering 2 runs on 5 hits; it was hardly an impressive performance. But he refused to accept blame for the poor showing. Afterward, in the Cardinals' locker room he approached his catcher, Tim McCarver, while he was shaving.

"Hey," began the brazen young hurler. "You've gotta call for more breaking pitches when we're behind in the count."

McCarver couldn't believe that a rookie had the gall to tell him how to call a game. He was, after all, a veteran and the club's regular catcher. Just five months earlier, he had hit .478 in the World Series and smacked a three-run homer in Game Five to help the Cards clinch the championship against the storied New York Yankees. The Redbirds catcher was a bona fide Major Leaguer, and yet here was a rookie questioning his judgment.

"You son of a bitch!" McCarver exploded, appalled at the young pitcher's brashness. "Who the hell do you think you are, telling me that? You've got a lot of guts. What credentials do you have?"

Unimpressed by the tirade, Carlton simply shrugged and walked away.[1] McCarver realized that he had gotten off to a bad start with the brash rookie. He also remembered what Hall of Fame catcher Bill Dickey had told him as a high school junior about a catcher's responsibility to "be a pitcher's friend" and that "the seeds of that relationship are planted as soon as the two teammates meet."[2] Feeling remorseful, McCarver apologized to Carlton the next day, but the rookie brushed him off again. Looking the veteran catcher straight in the eye, Carlton said, "I wasn't listening anyway."[3]

"McCarver had been in the Majors for about five years before Carlton arrived," recalled shortstop Dal Maxvill, who joined the Redbirds in 1962. "Timmy was also a big part of our 1964 World [Series] championship team, so he was well respected by teammates and opponents. He was also pretty headstrong. But Carlton took it to another level when it came to stubbornness. That created some friction between them initially."[4]

Carlton and McCarver were an odd couple. Both were fierce competitors who took control of a game, but the similarities ended there. McCarver was six feet tall and 180 pounds, with a solid frame and rugged features that gave him a commanding presence. Carlton, at six feet, four inches and 185 pounds, still needed to grow into his body. His most dominant physical feature was a protruding Adam's apple, which, along with his lanky frame, earned him the nickname "Ichabod Crane," the protagonist of Washington Irving's "The Legend of Sleepy Hollow."[5] There were other differences, too.

McCarver, at age twenty-four, was a hard-nosed veteran with a garrulous personality, while Carlton was a brash twenty-year-old rookie with an aloof disposition. McCarver was candid to a fault. Carlton was a perfectionist who would eventually make a living by deceiving hitters.[6] Somehow the two men adjusted to each other's idiosyncrasies and became a winning combination for the Cardinals.

Steven Norman Carlton was born on December 22, 1944, in Miami, Florida, the only son of Joe Carlton, a maintenance worker for Pan Am World Airways, and his wife, the former Ann Laurie Powers. Raised in a small Truman-era rancher on 144th Street in North Miami, the youngster grew up on the edge of the Everglades and spent hours in the swampy green wilds.[7] One of his boyhood friends, Fred Hannum, recalled that the ruins of a Seminole village were located behind the Carlton house and that the two boys "were always getting into the old burial mounds." He recalled that they would "find animal bones, pottery and arrowheads" and that they "kept some, and took the rest over to the local museum where they'd give us a buck or two."[8]

On other occasions the two friends would seek adventure in the local swamps. Scrounging an eight-by-four-foot metal pan used by construction crews to mix cement, Carlton and Hannum would "float down the mangrove swamps out to the bay." Then the boys would "bait a line with live shrimp and catch big snapper and ladyfish," explained Hannum. "Toward evening, we'd start hollering and fighting and pushing each other out of the pan. We were sort of saltwater Huckleberry Finns. We'd swim awhile and then we'd wind up carrying that big heavy pan back a mile or two to where we found it."[9]

Initially Steve shied away from organized sports. He quit Little League Baseball after a single practice, saying that the game was "no fun."[10] But he eventually returned to the sandlot after he discovered how much he enjoyed pitching. "Steve was always a frail kid," recalled Hannum. "He was almost a hypochondriac with his arm. He was always complaining about how sore it was, but he'd never tell our coach because he always wanted to pitch. Just give him the baseball and he'd throw like hell."[11]

At age fourteen Steve began lifting weights to build muscle on his thin frame, though he claimed the reason was because he "had the arms of an 8-year-old girl."[12] Two years later Carlton took a job as a pool boy at the Waikiki Resort Motel in Miami Beach. He quickly developed a reputation as a comedic diver, and one time he even jumped off the roof of the pool shack to rescue a little girl from drowning.[13] But Steve preferred to hunt. Once, while he was tracking a rabbit in the Everglades, his rifle jammed. Refusing to be denied his prey, he picked up a rock and from ninety feet away hurled it at the creature's head, killing it instantly. On another occasion Carlton flung an ax toward a quail that had taken refuge between the branches of a tree. With extraordinary precision, he decapitated the bird.[14]

At North Miami High School Steve proved to be an exceptional athlete. He could throw a football seventy-five yards, although he did not compete on the gridiron. In basketball he was a dominant forward who could out-rebound most centers.[15] "Carlton was a phenomenal athlete," recalled Bill Cave, who coached varsity football. "I wanted Steve to play for me in the worst way. He had the skills. He could have played any position, even quarterback. He was also one of the finest basketball players you would ever want to see. He was so fluid and effortless. What someone else could work a lifetime to achieve, Steve could walk out onto the court and make it look easy."[16]

Fred Hyrne, the varsity basketball coach, was just as impressed with the tall, gangly teen. "Steve was a good rebounder," Hyrne remembered. "He was a good corner shooter, too. Underneath the basket, he could shoot with either hand because he had such great coordination. I thought he was going to be one of the best basketball players we ever had." But Carlton dropped basketball after his junior year because the season extended into the beginning of baseball. "In Florida, baseball coaches are notorious for practicing at Christmastime, especially with pitchers and catchers," Hyrne explained. "I knew Steve loved baseball, so there were no hard feelings when he left the team. Besides, I couldn't get mad at him. He was just a super kid."[17]

To be sure, Carlton had realized his future was in baseball by his junior year, when he pitched a no hitter in the first round of the Florida state playoffs.[18] In 1963, his senior year, Carlton teamed up with Richie Mehlich, a right-hander, to lead the Pioneers to the state semifinals. Mehlich, who posted a perfect 9-0 record that season, was a better hurler than Steve, who went 4-1. But the skinny southpaw was a power pitcher even at that young age.[19] The local newspapers dubbed him "King Carlton" because of his ability to dominate hitters with his fastball.[20]

"I alternated them that season," recalled Jack Clark, North Miami High's head baseball coach. "Richie, the right-hander, and Steve, the lefty. Carlton had a better fastball, but Mehlich had much better control, and a lot of heart. At just 145 pounds, Richie didn't have the size or the arm that Steve did. Steve was the one with pro potential.

"I remember the day Steve tried out for our baseball team. He was a 10th grader, a big, tall, skinny kid with long arms and legs. I had no idea who he was. But when I first saw him pitch, I said, 'That kid should be able to throw a hundred innings and never come up with a sore arm.' He had such a loose, free motion.

"The only problem I had with Steve is that he wanted to do too much. I can remember him taking a window sash bar, tying it to a cord, tying the other end to a stick, and rolling it back and forth with his hands to strengthen his forearm. Another time he took a pair of roller skates apart, put the wheels on a board, and fastened them together. He pushed himself with one leg all over North Miami with that homemade skateboard. Then he'd switch to the other leg. When I asked him about it, he told me that he was trying to strengthen his legs."[21]

The unorthodox training practices would follow Carlton into the Major Leagues and figure prominently in his success on the mound. They also reflected a creative mind.

According to Paul Duncan, the assistant principal at North Miami, Steve "would have gotten a scholarship had he continued in basketball, and he would have earned a college degree." Furthermore, "he had a good mind," said Duncan, "but you'd never know it by the way he carried himself. Steve, 'the student,' was not a talkative person. He kept to himself. It was kind of, 'Don't bother me, and I won't bother you.' He was on the quiet side, not boisterous as many jocks are."[22]

In June 1963, after Carlton had graduated from high school, Demie Mainieri, the head baseball coach at what is now Miami Dade College, offered him a $300 scholarship. But Carlton had other plans and turned down the offer.[23] While pitching for North Miami's American Legion team that summer, the gangly left-hander attracted interest from the Pittsburgh Pirates and the St. Louis Cardinals, thanks to his American Legion coach, John Buik, who scouted on the side.[24]

"I wanted Carlton badly," recalled Rex Bowen, who scouted for the Pirates. "On the basis of what he showed in high school, you couldn't blame the scouts who walked away. He didn't throw hard enough." What had caught Bowen's eye was Carlton's "free and easy delivery" and the "rotation on his pitches."[25]

But Pittsburgh hesitated to offer the young southpaw a contract. Meanwhile, the Cardinals expressed greater interest. Chase Riddle, the Redbirds' scout, arranged a tryout at Norwood Field, located at 196th Street and Twelfth Avenue in Miami.

"I threw as hard as I could and as well as I could, but I don't think I threw fast enough for them," Carlton recalled years later. "They were looking mostly for that hummer."[26]

On the contrary, Riddle was impressed by Carlton and continued to monitor his progress.[27]

In late August, Steve contacted Mainieri again to see if the scholarship to Miami Dade was still available. "By that time, I had committed all my scholarship money," recalled Mainieri. "But Steve still enrolled and pitched for us in the fall of '63."[28] Again Carlton found himself in the shadow of a more accomplished pitcher: Gerry Greenside. Discouraged by his prospects for making the Falcons' spring squad, Carlton asked for Mainieri's advice.

"In fairness to Steve, I felt it was essential that he pitch enough innings in order to develop his potential," said the Miami Dade head coach. "I also told him that if he felt he wouldn't be making our rotation it might be wise to sign."[29]

Carlton took the hint and contacted Riddle, who gave him a plane ticket to St. Louis, where he would throw for Cardinals pitching coach Howie Pollet. "I liked Steve's sneaky fastball and I felt his curve was good enough to take a gamble for $5,000," Pollet said. "I figured he could improve with more experience."[30] Pollet was a three-time All-Star and the left-handed ace of the 1946 world champion Cardinals. It took him just five minutes to determine that Carlton had the makings of an exceptional pitcher. "I remember when Steve came up to St. Louis to throw for Pollet," said Dal Maxvill, who became one of Carlton's closest friends. "He was around 6 foot 3 about 160 pounds and skinny as a rail. He looked more like Ichabod Crane than a bona fide athlete. But Pollet told [Cardinals general manager] Bing Devine to sign him right away. His potential was that clear."[31]

Carlton signed with the Cardinals and began his professional career the following spring at low-A Rock Hill, South Carolina, in the Western Carolina League. It was not the last he would see of Mainieri, though.

In March 1964 Eddie Stanky, the Cardinals' director of player development, invited Miami Dade to play Rock Hill at the Cardinals' Minor League complex in Homestead, Florida. Mainieri's squad, which would capture the Junior College World Series at Grand Junction, Colorado, three months later, roughed up a succession of Rock Hill pitchers. Carlton was the last to take the mound against his former team. When the score reached 19–0, Stanky called the game, saying, "This skinny kid isn't going to get anybody out."[32]

Mainieri went on to become the first junior college baseball coach to win a thousand games, in an illustrious thirty-year tenure at Miami Dade. Thirty of his former players made it to the Majors, including Bucky Dent, Kurt Bevacqua, Warren Cromartie, Mickey Rivers, and Mike Piazza. Another seventy were drafted or signed by pro teams.[33] But years later he still regretted Carlton's decision to leave Miami Dade. "Had Steve stayed with us, maybe we would've gone undefeated for a year or two," he chuckled.[34]

Carlton would also realize success while still only a teenager. Rock Hill was just his first stop in 1964. While there, he compiled a record of 10-1 with an ERA of 1.03, and he struck out 91 batters in seventy-nine innings. In midseason the lanky left-hander was promoted to advanced Class A Winnipeg of the Northern League, where he made twelve starts, won four more games, and posted a 3.36 ERA. Before the '64 campaign was over, Carlton had earned himself another promotion, this one to Double-A Tulsa, where he would start three games, win one, and record a 2.62 ERA for the Texas League club. Overall, he won fifteen games and earned an invitation to the big league camp the following spring.[35]

On April 12, 1965, Carlton made his Major League debut against the Chicago Cubs at Wrigley Field. Bob Gibson started the game and was lifted after surrendering five runs in 3.1 innings. Carlton entered the game in relief in the eleventh inning of a 10–10 tie. The Cubs had Ron Santo on second base with one out. Red Schoendienst, the Cards' rookie manager, went to Carlton to face George Altman, a left-handed-hitting slugger and former Cardinal. The twenty-year-old southpaw walked Altman on five pitches and was lifted for Bob Purkey, who got out of the jam without allowing a run. The game was called because of darkness, ending in a tie. Carlton continued to pitch one or two innings in relief for the rest of the month, mostly in mop-up roles in games the Cards were losing by four runs or more.

At the end of April, Carlton had pitched just five innings in as many games, surrendering 2 earned runs on 4 hits, including a homer, for an earned run average of 3.60. The rookie left-hander also recorded 4 strikeouts, 3 walks, and 3 wild pitches. Finally, on Monday, June 14, Steve got his first start of the season. It came against the Pittsburgh Pirates at St. Louis's Busch Stadium. He went 4.1 innings, surrendering 2 earned runs on 7 hits. One of those hits was a solo home run that came in the first inning off the bat of lead-off hitter Bob Bailey. Carlton left the game in the fifth inning with the score tied at 2–2. He was relieved by Ron Taylor, who recorded the win in a 5–2 Cardinals victory.[36] It was hardly an auspicious beginning.

Steve was given one more start in '65, and it came the following week, on June 23 against the Chicago Cubs. But he never got out of the third inning after walking the bases loaded. When the southpaw returned to the mound in late August, he was used strictly as a late-inning reliever to close out games that were out of reach. In fact, Carlton was kept on the Cards' roster that season only because St. Louis didn't want to lose him in the draft of players with only one year's experience. He threw just twenty-five innings in fifteen appearances, including two starts.[37]

"I would have been better off pitching regularly," Carlton said. "I figure I really lost a year."[38]

McCarver, who broke a finger in spring training and missed the first week of the regular season, caught Carlton in eight of his fifteen appearances. Backup catchers Bob Uecker and Dave Ricketts were behind the plate for the other seven.[39]

The next season was just as disappointing for McCarver and the Cardinals. Tim battled injuries throughout the '65 season, limiting him to 113 games. Somehow the Redbirds' catcher still managed to hit .276 with 11 homers and 48 RBIs.[40] There were other injuries, too.

Second baseman Julián Javier missed seven weeks with a broken finger. Third baseman Ken Boyer struggled with back and hip injuries all season, batting just .260. And there were subpar performances. Starting pitchers Ray Sadecki and Curt Simmons, who recorded a combined 38-20 record the previous year, slumped to 15-30. Right fielder Mike Shannon hit just .220, forty points below the previous year's average. First baseman Bill White drove in 73 runs, his lowest total in six years.[41] Johnny Keane, who had managed the Cards to a World Series championship the year before, was gone. Fed up with Gussie Busch's constant criticism, Keane had resigned after the World Series to take a more lucrative job as manager of the New York Yankees.[42] His replacement, Red Schoendienst, the Cards' former second baseman and a future Hall of Famer, was unable to right the ship, and the Cardinals slumped to a seventh-place finish. The Los Angeles Dodgers, led by the brilliant pitching of Cy Young Award winners Sandy Koufax and Don Drysdale, filled the vacuum, winning the first of two straight pennants.[43]

St. Louis improved only slightly in 1966, finishing in sixth place. At least Cardinals fans enjoyed a new venue; Gussie Busch's dream for a new state-of-the-art stadium came to fruition that season. Known as Busch Memorial Stadium, the new ballpark was located just south of the downtown shopping district on an eighty-two-acre site that was once dominated by warehouses, cheap hotels, greasy spoons, and strip joints. It was part of an urban renewal program that included construction of an eight-hundred-room hotel, office buildings, stores, restaurants, and shops. While Anheuser-Busch contributed $5 million to the construction of the stadium, the lion's share of $21 million was raised by the Civic Center Redevelopment Corporation, headed by James P. Hickok, president of First National Bank of St. Louis; Sidney Maestra, board chair of Mercantile Trust Company; and Preston Eslep, president of Transit Casualty Company. The Civic Center Redevelopment Corporation owned the new stadium, leasing it to the St. Louis Cardinals and their NFL counterparts.

Bounded by Broadway, as well as Seventh, Walnut, and Spruce Streets, Busch Memorial Stadium was one of the first multipurpose "cookie cutter" sports facilities built in the United States between the early 1960s and the early 1980s. Four tiers of 46,068 red seats surrounded the natural grass playing field. Spacious outfield dimensions made the park favorable to pitchers. The left- and right-field foul poles were 330 feet from home, and the power alleys of left-center and right-center were an ample 372 feet from the plate, with dead center being the deepest part of the park at 402 feet. There was also a $1.5 million scoreboard located behind the outfield fence in left-center, with an electronic cardinal that chirped.[44] Unfortunately, the grand opening of the stadium was delayed by more than a month due to labor strikes. When the Cards finally played their first game at Busch, on May 12, they were buried in eighth place due to an anemic offense. Still, the Redbirds managed to pull off a 4–3 victory over the visiting Atlanta Braves. A month later, St. Louis hosted the All-Star Game, which featured three Cardinals on the National League squad: McCarver, Gibson, and Flood.

Nearly fifty thousand fans packed Busch Memorial Stadium to watch the midsummer classic despite the blistering 105-degree temperature at game time. The American League took a 1–0 lead against Dodgers ace Sandy Koufax in the second, when Oriole Brooks Robinson hit a one-out liner to left and wound up with a triple when the ball slipped past outfielder Hank Aaron of the Atlanta Braves. Robinson scored a few moments later on a wild pitch, but the National League tied the game in the fourth when pitcher Jim Kaat of the Minnesota Twins surrendered singles to Willie Mays, Roberto Clemente, and Ron Santo. With the score deadlocked at 1–1 in the bottom of the tenth, McCarver began a game-winning rally. After singling off the Washington Senators' Pete Richert, Tim was sacrificed to second by the Mets' Ron Hunt and scored the game-winning run when Dodger Maury Wills singled to right for the National League's 2–1 victory.[45]

Carlton, who spent the early part of the '66 season at Triple-A Tulsa, returned to the Cardinals on July 25 to pitch in an exhibition game during the Hall of Fame festivities in Cooperstown.[46] Facing the defending American League champion Minnesota Twins, Carlton pitched a 7–5, complete-game victory, striking out ten. The game was played in just two hours and four minutes. Carlton demonstrated poise, confidence, a devastating fastball, and a sharp overhand curve. The impressive showing earned him a start against the defending world champion Dodgers on July 31. In four innings of work the twenty-one-year-old southpaw struck out one, walked two, and gave up two runs.[47]

Carlton made his next start on August 5 against the Mets at Shea Stadium in New York, where he earned his first Major League victory. Alternating a 90 mph fastball with a changeup and a curve, Carlton tossed a 7–1, complete-game victory. "Up here you need that third pitch, especially when you're having trouble with either your fastball or your curve," Carlton said afterward. "I wasn't getting my curve over this time, so I relied more on the change-up."[48]

When asked how he felt about his first Major League victory, Steve, who grew from six feet three and 178 pounds as a rookie to six feet four and 200 pounds in his sophomore season, said glibly, "Maybe the bubble gum cards will get my height and weight right now!"[49]

Carlton's first victory came in the middle of a Cardinals hot streak in which the team won fifteen of eighteen games. The win streak was highlighted by the brilliant pitching of ace Bob Gibson, who went 21-12 that season despite a sore elbow that kept him out of the rotation for two weeks.[50]

"Carlton, Nelson Briles, and me were the young guys on the pitching staff," recalled starter Larry Jaster in a 2020 interview. "Steve and I were given the opportunity to start that season because the Cardinals needed left-handers in the rotation, and we were the only lefties." Jaster made a favorable impression by hurling five shutouts against the Los Angeles Dodgers, tying a record for the most shutouts against one team in a single season. "I was a fastball pitcher," said Jaster. "Steve was more durable and had the breaking stuff, but he was not what you would call a 'power pitcher' back then."[51]

Carlton posted two more victories during the '66 campaign: a 3–0 shutout against the Astros at Houston on August 22 and a 7–4 win against the Atlanta Braves on September 1. He completed the season with a 3-3 record and a 3.12 ERA. McCarver was behind the plate for seven of the nine starts, including the three victories.[52] He also established himself as one of the best catchers in Major League Baseball in 1966.

When free of injuries, McCarver was a workhorse behind the plate, catching 148 games that season and making his first All-Star Game appearance. "Tim was an excellent catcher," said Jaster. "He worked well with all of us because he made the time to get to know us on and off the field. Tim's greatest strength was knowing the weaknesses of opposing hitters. He knew how to work a hitter, both in terms of location and pitch calling."[53] McCarver also batted .274 with 12 home runs and 68 RBIs and set a Major League record for catchers with a league-leading 13 triples.[54] Tim, who also had a reputation for being a cerebral player, took an active role in the MLB Players Association, which would eventually become a double-edged sword during his time in St. Louis.

In 1966 McCarver and veteran pitcher Bob Purkey represented the players in a dispute against management over the lack of financial compensation for appearances on pre- and postgame broadcasts. The union wanted the players to be paid $25 for radio and $50 for television appearances. But management balked at the demand, pointing to the small print in the standard contract stipulating that players agree to cooperate with the club and participate in any and all promotional activities of the club and league. Gussie Busch was not pleased with either McCarver or Purkey for their involvement in the meeting, but the Cardinals' owner realized that Tim was a popular player in the clubhouse and an important part of the organization's future. Purkey, on the other hand, was a thirty-seven-year-old veteran who alternated between spot starting and relief pitching. He was dispensable. As a result, Busch sold the pitcher's contract to the Pittsburgh Pirates a few days after the dispute took place. Four years later McCarver would also be traded, partly because of his ongoing role as the team's player representative.[55]

The 1967 season was Carlton's first full one in the Majors. Entering the campaign, manager Red Schoendienst planned to use him primarily as a reliever and occasional spot starter. But Carlton had other plans. "My goal this season is 20 victories," he told Bob Broeg of the *St. Louis Post-Dispatch* in spring training. "But I won't be greedy," he added with a smile. "I'll settle for 10 or 12."[56]

As the season unfolded, Carlton became a vital part of the Cardinals rotation. Making his first appearance on April 16 at home against the Houston Astros, Steve entered the game in relief of Bob Gibson in the seventh inning and pitched three frames, earning the save in the Cards' 11–8 victory. Leading the Cardinals' attack was Lou Brock, who hit two homers and two singles for the second straight game.[57]

Carlton's first start, however, did not come until April 26, against the Astros at Houston's Astrodome. He pitched eight innings and surrendered just 2 earned runs on 5 hits while striking out 9 for the 7–2 win. In May, Steve was made a full-time starter. In five games he went 2-1 with 19 strikeouts and a 3.0 ERA.[58] Although he did not fare as well in June, going 2-4 in 35.2 innings of work with a 3.89 ERA, the Cardinals remained locked in a battle for first place against the Chicago Cubs.[59]

Carlton proved to be indispensable after July 15, however, when ace Bob Gibson went on the disabled list for fifty-two days. Gibson had suffered a stress fracture in his right leg when a line drive off the bat of Pittsburgh's Roberto Clemente felled him in the fourth inning of a 6–4 loss against the Pirates at Busch Stadium.[60] Nelson Briles took Gibson's place in the rotation and reeled off nine straight victories. But Carlton also picked up some of the slack, going 9-4 after the All-Star break. His best performance came in September, when he recorded a streak of twenty-eight scoreless innings, including shutouts against the Pittsburgh Pirates and Cincinnati Reds.[61] In the four games he started that month, Steve averaged almost nine strikeouts a game, the most exceptional performance coming on September 20 in a 3–1 loss against the Phillies when he struck out sixteen batters. "He had a great fastball, a good overhanded curve and a good change-up," said Phillies outfielder Don Lock. When told that Carlton was just twenty-two years old, Lock exclaimed in disbelief, "I'd like to trade places with him right now!"[62]

When Neal Russo of *The Sporting News* asked Carlton about his performance on the mound, the hurler confessed that he "didn't even know he was close to a record until he heard [Phillies catcher] Gene Oliver and the plate umpire talking about Bob Feller and Sandy Koufax holding the record with 18."[63] In fact, what was then the Major League single-game strikeout record was 19, set by Charlie Sweeney of the Providence Grays in 1884.[64] Carlton attributed his success to a fastball that was "jumping all over the plate" and to his curve, which was "working fine, too."[65] But some credit is also due to Cardinals pilot Red Schoendienst, who let Carlton bat in the eighth inning with the Redbirds trailing so he could have a shot at the record.[66]

Carlton completed the '67 season with a 14-9 record, 168 strikeouts, and a 2.98 ERA. Of the twenty-eight starts he made, McCarver was behind the plate for nineteen of them, including nine of the fourteen victories. Six of the nine wins were complete-game victories, too.[67] The battery of Carlton and McCarver was beginning to gel.

Together with the remarkable pitching, the Cardinals' offense saved the season. First baseman Orlando Cepeda hit .325, with 25 homers and a league-leading 111 RBIs, earning him a nod as the National League MVP. Right fielder Roger Maris, acquired in the off-season from the New York Yankees, was a quiet but influential presence who led the team with 18 game-winning hits. Second baseman Julián Javier (.281, 14 HRS, 64 RBIs) and left fielder Lou Brock, who hit .299 with 65 extra-base hits, 76 RBIs, and a league-leading 52 stolen bases, also added to the Cardinals' attack. McCarver, who was batting .348 at the All-Star break, tailed off to .295, but he still finished with career highs in home runs (14) and RBIs (69). He also made his second and final appearance in the All-Star Game.[68] But the catcher's true value came in holding together a young pitching staff in the wake of Gibson's injury, something he did in spite of the extraordinary fatigue he experienced at times.[69]

"There were nights when he was doing reserve duty in the army, that he got virtually no sleep," explained manager Red Schoendienst. "He'd get off duty just in time to get to the ballpark and then rise early the next morning. I don't know how he did it."[70]

Gibson returned to the rotation in time to pitch the pennant clincher on September 18 in Philadelphia. He surrendered just one run on three hits in the 5–1, complete-game victory over the Phillies. With eleven games remaining, the Cardinals had a thirteen-game lead over the second-place San Francisco Giants, mathematically eliminating the West Coast team from the postseason.[71]

The Cardinals faced the "Impossible Dream" Boston Red Sox in the World Series. Boston, which finished ninth the previous year, had prevailed in a four-team pennant race. Rookie manager Dick Williams guided the BoSox to their first pennant since 1946, finishing one game ahead of the Detroit Tigers and Minnesota Twins. Boston's offense was led by triple crown winner Carl Yastrzemski (.326, 1.040 OPS, .418 OBP, 44 HRS, 121 RBIS). First baseman George Scott (.303, .839 OPS, .373 OBP, 19 HRS, 82 RBIS), right fielder Tony Conigliaro (.287, .860 OPS, .341 OBP, 20 HRS, 67 RBIS), and shortstop Rico Petrocelli (.259, .750 OPS, .330 OBP, 17 HRS, 66 RBIS) provided the additional firepower. Rookies Reggie Smith (.246, .704 OPS, .315 OBP, 15 HRS, 61 RBIS) and Mike Andrews (.263, .699 OPS, .346 OBP, 8 HRS, 40 RBIS) also added speed and defense.

Other key contributors were Ken Harrelson, released from the Athletics earlier in the season, who replaced the injured Tony Conigliaro in right field, and catcher Elston Howard, picked up from the Yankees in a midseason trade. Although Howard only batted .147, he was extremely effective in handling a talented pitching staff headed by "Gentleman Jim" Lonborg (22-9, 246 SO, 3.16 ERA). Gary Bell (12-8, 115 SO, 3.16 ERA), José Santiago (12-4, 109 SO, 3.59 ERA), and Lee Stange (8-10, 101 SO, 2.77 ERA) rounded out the starting rotation with John Wyatt (20 saves) as the closer.[72]

The Series opened at Boston's Fenway Park on Wednesday, October 4. The Cardinals, brimming with confidence, boarded their team bus and went to the ballpark early. Curt Flood could not help but rip the BoSox. "Well, it's a great thing for baseball that the Red Sox won," he chirped sarcastically. "A great thing for a great game in a great town.

"They should put up signs on every great church saying, 'God bless the California Angels,'" added Flood, referring to the team that had knocked off the second-place Detroit Tigers on the final day of the season to give the Red Sox the American League flag.[73]

Bob Gibson, who was scheduled to pitch the first game of the Series, sat alone at the front of the bus, thinking about how much he hated the Red Sox. Gibson said very little on days he was schedule to pitch. But even he could not resist the temptation to join in the bantering.

"Flood, that's the park up there," he exclaimed as the bus neared Fenway. "That's the pawk," he continued in his best Boston accent. "Fenway Pawk!" When three mounted police officers pulled alongside the Cards' bus to discourage a crowd of youngsters from hanging on to it, Gibson hollered, "Giddyap! Spread the word. The Redcaps are coming; the Redcaps are coming!"[74]

Although St. Louis smacked nine hits in the first six innings off Boston starter José Santiago, they were only able to produce one run. Instead, Santiago tied the score in the bottom of the third with a solo home run, and the Red Sox held on, turning a double play in the first and another in the second. Yastrzemski preserved the 1–1 tie in the fifth with an extraordinary backhanded catch. The winning Cardinals run came in the seventh on an infield groundout by Roger Maris, who had also knocked in the Cards' first tally on a groundout in the third. Gibson pitched a complete game, striking out ten batters to give the Cardinals Game One, 2–1. When asked after the game about his two RBIs, Maris downplayed the feat, saying, "You're supposed to get the man in from third any way you can when there's less than two outs."[75]

The Red Sox evened the Series the following day. Boston's ace, Jim Lonborg, took the mound on three days' rest. For inspiration, the tall right-hander wrote on his glove "$10,000," the anticipated player's share for winning the Series. Lonborg took a perfect game into the seventh, when he walked Curt Flood with one out. He lost his no-hitter the following inning, when Julián Javier doubled with two outs. Still, Lonborg preserved a one-hit, 5–0 shutout.[76]

The next three games were played in St. Louis. Nelson Briles won Game Three, 5–2, before a crowd of 54,575 who came to watch the first-ever World Series game played at the new Busch Memorial Stadium. The Cards started the scoring in the bottom of the first, when Lou Brock led off with a triple. Flood followed with an RBI single off Red Sox starter Gary Bell. McCarver opened the second inning with a base hit and scored on Mike Shannon's line-drive homer to left field, extending the Cardinals' lead to 3–0 and sending Bell to the showers. In the sixth Brock beat out a drag bunt and advanced to third when BoSox pitcher Lee Stange threw an errant pick-off to first. Brock scored on a Roger Maris base hit, and Cepeda followed with a double to score Maris with the final St. Louis tally.[77]

Before Game Four, Maris was asked to compare the Cardinals with the Yankees teams he had played on from 1960 to 1966—teams that won five pennants and two World Series titles. "We have speed and power, and we have guys who know what they are doing," he explained. "With the Yankees we had much more muscle and played for the big inning. Here, we get what we get and we know how to go about getting it.

"One of the things that sometimes bothers us is that people are in such a hurry to compare us with the Gas House Gang of the 1930s," added Maris. "We're 'El Birdos' because Cha-Cha [Orlando Cepeda] named us that, and that is how we want to be remembered."[78]

Game Four belonged to Bob Gibson, who threw a five-hit, complete-game shutout. The 6–0 victory gave the Redbirds a 3-to-1 advantage and set the stage for Steve Carlton to clinch the Series in front of the hometown fans the following day.[79] But Red Sox ace Jim Lonborg had other plans.

Game Five was Carlton's World Series debut. He struck out 5 batters and surrendered just 3 hits, 2 walks, and a single unearned run in six innings of work. The only run off the young lefty came in the third inning, when Boston's Joe Foy hit a hard drive up the middle that went through Carlton's legs into center field. Harrelson later drove Foy home with a single. "I'm not the best fielder in the world," Carlton admitted after the game. "I come off the mound in a poor position to get a ball hit up the middle and sometimes it hurts me."[80]

Cards manager Red Schoendienst pulled Carlton after the sixth, though he later admitted that the southpaw "certainly pitched well enough to win because he had a good change-up to go with his great curve and fastball."[81]

The score remained 1–0 in favor of the Red Sox until the top of the ninth, when Cardinals reliever Ron Willis walked George Scott, and then Reggie Smith followed with a bloop double into the left-field corner. Willis loaded the bases with an intentional walk to Rico Petrocelli. After throwing ball one to Elston Howard, Schoendienst brought in Jack Lamabe from the Cardinals' bullpen. Howard singled to right, driving in Scott and Smith and extending Boston's lead to 3–0. The lone Cardinals run came on a solo homer by Roger Maris in the bottom of the ninth, but it wasn't enough; the Red Sox won, 3–1.[82]

When the Series shifted to Boston for the final two games, Carl Yastrzemski told Red Sox Nation, "You don't have to worry about us. We're going to win." Manager Dick Williams added that Gibson was the only Cardinals pitcher who impressed him. McCarver was livid. "We have respect for the Red Sox, but they don't respect us," he grumbled. "I haven't heard anything like this before. When we played the Yankees in the '64 World Series, nothing was said. We had respect for each other."[83] But before the Series was over, the Cardinals would earn the respect of Boston's manager and their star player.

On Wednesday, October 11, Boston forced a seventh game by defeating the Cards, 8–4, at Fenway. Redbirds hurler Dick Hughes became the only pitcher in World Series history to surrender three home runs in one inning. The gaffe came in the fourth, when Yastrzemski, Smith, and Petrocelli blasted homers, giving Boston a 4–2 lead and sending Hughes to the showers. The Cards tied the game, 4–4, in the top of the seventh on a two-run homer by Lou Brock. But Boston put the game on ice in the bottom frame with another four runs, setting the stage for a deciding Game Seven.

Gibson and Lonborg faced off in the finale, pitching on three and two days' rest, respectively. Gibson prevailed, striking out 10 batters while surrendering just 2 runs on 3 hits. "Gentleman Jim," on the other hand, was running on empty. In six innings of work he surrendered 7 runs on 10 hits. The Cardinals' attack was led by Javier, who went 2-for-4 with a home run and 3 RBIs. Brock also went 2-for-4 with 3 stolen bases. Maris went 2-for-3 with an RBI, and Gibson contributed a home run.[84]

After the game McCarver enjoyed the taste of champagne and

sweet revenge. "You just don't say things in the newspaper," he quipped, referring to BoSox manager Dick Williams's earlier insult. "You don't knock the other guy. We weren't angry. We wanted to win very badly, though. We wanted to win for the prestige of being world champions."[85]

3

Learning Curve

Steve Carlton's early success as a pitcher was due in part to impeccable timing and good fortune. To pitch for the St. Louis Cardinals in the mid- to late 1960s was to be part of a baseball dynasty that won two world championships and three National League pennants over a five-year span. Redbirds pitchers enjoyed ample run support from a lineup that included Lou Brock, Curt Flood, Roger Maris, Tim McCarver, Mike Shannon, and Orlando Cepeda. Cardinals hurlers also benefited from an excellent defense. Flood and Brock possessed the remarkable speed to chase down long drives in the spacious outfield of Busch Memorial Stadium, while the superb double play combination of Julián Javier and Dal Maxvill killed the offensive rallies of many opponents. McCarver, widely considered the league's best catcher, was the maestro of the pitching staff. He was exceptional not only at pitch calling and setting up the hitter but also at motivating his batterymates.[1] While Carlton benefited from both these offensive and defensive advantages, he also gained valuable experience with the introduction of the four-man starting rotation.

Prior to the 1960s, Major League teams employed a five-man rotation, with managers relying on their most effective hurlers to pitch against the best opponents in the league. But in the 1960s teams embraced four-man rotations with a spot starter, or fifth pitcher, who would be skipped occasionally when there were more off days in the schedule. The introduction of the four-man rotation dramatically increased the number of pitchers who made 20 percent or more of their team's starts, making it easier to start as many as forty games a season without risking injury to the arm.[2] When Carlton was first promoted to the Cardinals in 1965, he was primarily a reliever and spot starter. Of the twenty-four games in which he appeared in 1965 and 1966, Carlton started fewer than half.[3]

Beginning in 1967, however, the young southpaw was slotted into the back end of a four-man rotation that included right-handers Bob Gibson and Ray Washburn and southpaws Larry Jaster and Carlton. "Gibson, Washburn, Carlton and me did the brunt of the starting pitching between 1967 and 1968," said Jaster. "Dick Hughes, a twenty-nine-year-old rookie, went 16-6 as a spot starter in '67, but he hurt his arm near the end of the season and didn't pitch much after that. Gibson was the strikeout pitcher. He threw gas. Washburn was a fastball-slider pitcher who was fairly successful. He averaged ten or eleven wins over that two-year period before an arm injury ended his career. I was third in the rotation and relied on my fastball, probably too much. Midway through the '68 season I injured my arm and that ended my career.

"Steve came up as a reliever but was added to the back end of the rotation in '66 and remained there for good. I know he experimented with the slider, but he mostly used his curve to get hitters out. Steve really wasn't a strikeout pitcher in those days. He started piling up the strikeouts when he added the slider and that was after he left the Cardinals," Jaster said.[4] At the end of the '67 season Carlton boasted a record of 14-9 and a 2.98 ERA, and he had established himself as the team's number-two starter.[5]

Other changes also shifted the balance of power from the hitter to the pitcher, making the 1960s the golden era of pitching. One change was the enlargement of the strike zone. Anything thrown between the hitter's shoulders and knees was called a strike. Pitchers were better coached. Many were able to master the slider, a more deceptive pitch than a curveball because it's thrown harder and has spin that more closely resembles that of a fastball, though it doesn't create as much overall movement. Relief pitching became more reliable, and managers called on their relievers more readily.[6] Many teams boasted starters who were stunningly dominant.

The New York Yankees rode the arm of Whitey Ford to six World Series titles and eleven American League pennants during a brilliant fifteen-year career that included two world championships and five pennants in the 1960s. Ford was the best pitcher in Major League Baseball in terms of consistency between 1950 and 1966. Excepting his rookie season and final year, Ford, sometimes called "Chairman of the Board Ford," won at least ten games each season. His highest ERA was 3.24 in 1965, one of only four seasons in which he rose above 3.00. Ford lost ten or more games only twice (1959, 1965) and had two twenty-win seasons.[7]

Other AL teams also boasted some remarkable starters. Mickey Lolich was the all-time strikeout leader for the Detroit Tigers, registering a total of 1,336 strikeouts during the 1960s and averaging 7.87 strikeouts per nine innings for the decade. In 1969 he averaged 8.69 strikeouts per nine innings. Lolich struck out 200 or more batters in a season seven times in his career (twice in the 1960s), with a career best of 308 in 1971. He is the only Tiger ever to reach the 300 mark.[8] Teammate Denny McLain's incredible 1968 season produced Major League Baseball's last thirty-game winner. McLain's 31-6 record was achieved with a 1.96 ERA. He led the league in winning percentage (.838), games started (41), complete games (28), and innings pitched (336). He also struck out a career-high 280 batters. His exceptional performance earned McLain both the Cy Young and Most Valuable Player Awards.[9]

The Cleveland Indians had Sam McDowell and Luis Tiant. McDowell was the AL's most proficient strikeout pitcher during the decade; "Sudden Sam" finished just behind the Dodgers' Sandy Koufax in average strikeouts per nine innings with 9.41. He led the AL in strikeouts four times during the 1960s and topped 300 strikeouts in a season twice. Altogether McDowell struck out 1,663 batters for the Cleveland Indians in the 1960s.[10] Tiant pitched only six seasons during the 1960s and struck out only 1,041 batters during the decade, but he averaged 7.81 strikeouts per nine innings, the sixth-best average among Major League pitchers during the decade. In both 1967 and 1968 Tiant averaged 9.2 strikeouts per nine innings, both years fanning more than 200 batters.[11]

In the National League, Sandy Koufax teamed with Don Drysdale to form the game's most dominant starting duo in the early 1960s. The brilliant tandem led the Los Angeles Dodgers to world championships in 1963 and 1965. Koufax averaged 9.51 strikeouts per nine innings pitched, the highest average among all Major League starting pitchers that decade. He finished third in total strikeouts for the decade, with 1,910, though he retired after the 1966 season. Koufax led the National League in strikeouts four times and struck out more than 300 batters in a season three times. Koufax also tossed four no-hitters during the 1960s, the last being a perfect game against the Chicago Cubs on September 9, 1965. In that perfecto, the Dodgers' southpaw registered 14 strikeouts, the most ever in a perfect game.[12] Drysdale was the right-handed workhorse of the Dodgers' pitching staff from 1957 through 1965. He won the Cy Young Award in 1962 with a 25-9 record and won eighteen or more games over the next three seasons, including a twenty-three-victory campaign in 1965. Drysdale also led the NL in strikeouts twice in the 1960s, totaling 1,910 strikeouts for the decade, to tie for third with Koufax. The Dodgers' right-hander averaged 6.54 strikeouts per nine innings during the 1960s and had six seasons with 200 or more strikeouts in his career, which spanned from 1956 to 1969. In 1968 Drysdale broke Walter Johnson's Major League record of 56 consecutive scoreless innings with a streak that reached 58.2 scoreless innings, including six consecutive complete-game shutouts.[13]

The San Francisco Giants boasted an ace in Juan Marichal, known for his high leg kick, pinpoint control, and intimidation tactics. Marichal posted 191 victories during the 1960s, more than any other pitcher in the Majors. He led the NL twice in shutouts, throwing ten of them in 1965 and striking out 200 or more batters in a season six times, amassing a total of 1,840 strikeouts for the decade with an average of 6.49 strikeouts per nine innings. Marichal also finished in the top ten in ERA seven consecutive years, starting in 1963 and culminating in 1969, when he led the league in that category.[14] The Philadelphia Phillies had Jim Bunning, one of the decade's most resilient starters. A 224-game winner during a seventeen-year Major League career, Bunning was a 20-game winner only once. But he recorded 19 wins in four separate seasons and was a 17-game winner three other times. Bunning was the first pitcher to win 100 games in both the NL and the AL. He was also the first to strike out more than 1,000 batters in each league. As a member of the Detroit Tigers, Bunning topped the AL with 201 strikeouts in both 1959 and 1960, and with the Phillies he led the NL in strikeouts with 253 in 1967. Altogether Bunning struck out 200 or more batters in a season six times in his career, and during the 1960s he tallied 2,019 strikeouts, second only to Bob Gibson. He averaged 7.02 strikeouts per nine innings during the 1960s. Finally, Bunning was the first pitcher to hurl a no-hitter in each league. His second no-hitter was the high point of his career. Pitching for the Phillies on Father's Day in 1964 at New York's Shea Stadium, Bunning struck out 10 of the 27 he faced in the 6–0 perfecto.[15]

St. Louis was also blessed with one of the very best pitchers of the era: Bob Gibson. With a total of 2,071, Gibson recorded more strikeouts during the 1960s than any other pitcher. He averaged 7.62 strikeouts per nine innings and struck out 200 or more batters in a season seven times during the 1960s. Gibby's finest season was 1968. That year he posted a win-loss record of 22-9 and led the National League in strikeouts (268), earned run average (1.12), and shutouts (13). He was also the decade's best strikeout pitcher in the World Series, fanning 92 batters in eighty-one innings, including a record 17 in the first game of the 1968 World Series.[16]

Gibson's influence on Carlton's career cannot be overstated. To pitch in the same rotation as the Cardinals' ace was to enjoy the advantage of learning from one of the very best pitchers in the game's history. At the beginning of the 1967 season Gibson, age thirty-one, approached his younger teammate to offer some wisdom and was rebuffed. "Steve was a very promising and extremely confident pitcher, whose style was similar to mine," recalled Gibson. "Since I was the veteran of the staff, I thought he might benefit from my experience and relative wisdom. But when I approached him in that vein, it seemed that he had little respect for either."[17] Instead, Carlton learned mostly from observation.

"I was so wrapped up in watching Gibson pitch that season," said

Carlton, who at age twenty-one was still one of the youngest players on a team of established veterans.[18] One of the most valuable things he learned was how to pitch inside. "When I was young, I was afraid to throw inside," Carlton admitted in a 1994 interview. "I was afraid to hit guys. But then I watched Gibson do it and I knew I wanted to pitch that way." McCarver encouraged Steve to follow Gibby's example. "Timmy always reminded me to brush back a hitter if he was really hurting us," added Carlton. "Sometimes he'd even set up behind the hitter and I couldn't see him, so I had to throw inside."[19]

Gibson, who was infamous for knocking down hitters, believes that he was never given as much credit as he deserved for his pitching repertoire. "It was said that I threw basically five pitches—fastball, slider, curve, change-up and knockdown," he explained. "I don't believe that assessment did me justice, though. I actually used nine pitches—two different fastballs, two sliders, a curve, change-up, knockdown, brushback and hit-batsman."[20] The remark was made partly in jest. But Gibson's penchant for knocking down hitters was no laughing matter. Dick Allen (formerly known as Richie Allen) of the Phillies once said that the Cards' ace would "knock you down and then meet you at the plate to see if you wanted to make something out of it."[21]

To dismiss Gibson as a "headhunter" is too simplistic, though. Ironically, the Cards' ace was so dominant because he was a *control* pitcher. That is, Gibson staked claim to the inside two inches of the plate and the outside two inches, rarely throwing into the thirteen-inch zone in between. Those thirteen inches belonged to the hitter. If the hitter encroached on the inside two inches by crowding the plate, Gibson staked his claim by throwing a knockdown pitch. The concept of dividing the plate between the pitcher and the hitter was arguably the most important lesson Carlton learned from Gibby because it ensured his subsequent success. Years later Steve admitted that when he was with the Cardinals he began "visualizing the inside and outside lanes" of the plate as "pre-game preparation." Thus, "if I concentrated on those two lanes," he explained, "I was able to eliminate the middle of the plate [the hitter's zone] altogether."[22] Carlton, one of the first pitchers to use the visualization technique, looked for any edge that would enable him to win, just like Gibson.

"I never saw anyone as compelled to win as Bob Gibson," swears McCarver. "Gibby hated to lose, and because of that he hated the opposition. *Hated* them. I was driven to succeed, but not like him, nor with his intensity. Gibson's desire to win influenced all our teammates. It was one of the reasons we revered him."[23] Not only was Gibson the most dominant force on the successful Cardinals teams of the 1960s, but he was also the most competitive and most feared pitcher of his era. He viewed the duel between pitcher and batter as a simple act of survival. With Gibson, winning—and especially losing—was personal. Never would he allow an opposing hitter to show him up, even if he had retired them on a grounder or a fly ball. If, for example, a hitter happened to cross over or behind the mound when he was pitching, Gibson would make a mental note and deck him the next time up. Even Pete Rose, the ultracompetitive lead-off hitter for the Cincinnati Reds, respected Gibson's wishes. With other pitchers, Rose purposely ran across the mound after being retired, just to rankle them. He *never* did that with Gibson, though.[24] Carlton saw that and demanded the same kind of respect from opponents.

"That's the way I should handle myself," he told McCarver. "That's what I'm going to do." He summed up his view by saying, "No one is going to come into my office," referring to the mound as his domain.[25]

"Bob Gibson was the ultimate competitor," Carlton said in 1989 after he retired. "I think anybody who wants to be a starting pitcher should posture himself after Gibson. He was intimidating. He was hard-nosed. He was dedicated to winning. He was a hard worker. He pitched quick. He never talked to opposing hitters, which I think is a flaw in a starting pitcher because opposing hitters like to feel comfortable around you so they always try to buddy up to you. Gibby would never talk to an opposing hitter. That unsettled hitters. It also got them to back off the plate. He used everything he had mentally, emotionally and physically to help himself to win. I thought he was a master at it."[26]

In fact, all the qualities Carlton admired in Gibson were the same ones he developed during his time in St. Louis and demonstrated when he became the ace of the Phillies in 1972. There were two other traits that both pitchers shared. Neither one was by nature, or intention, friendly to the writers or to the fans. In St. Louis, Carlton, when he was a young pitcher, saw that Gibson did not like baseball writers, although he usually answered their questions, nor was he very gracious to fans, who were put off by his stern demeanor. If approached for his autograph, Gibson might or might not sign. "Do you want to know why I get surly and bitter sometimes?" Gibson asked Bob Addie of the *Washington Post*. "Take a look at some of the hate mail I get," he said, flinging a letter that read, "Why don't you and the other blackbirds on the Cardinals move to Africa where you belong?" Essentially, Gibson believed that he owed the press and the public "just one thing—a good performance."[27]

McCarver, who became close friends with both hurlers, also recognized the similarities. "Steve learned more from Gibson than he did from anybody," he said. "The way he conducted himself on the mound, the way he went about his independent selection of pitches. His refusal to listen in meetings [with the catcher or manager] because he believed that nobody could pitch like he could. Steve could be matter-of-factly obstinate and not know it."[28]

Despite Gibson and Carlton having a very similar approach to pitching, McCarver had a very different relationship with each of them. Since he had caught Gibson longer and proved his worth on two world championship teams, in 1964 and 1967, Tim was respected by the Black hurler and considered himself on "equal footing" as a teammate. "Gibby is one of my closest friends," McCarver said in 2019. "He's very intelligent, very funny. He also knows a bullshitter from the get-go and he'll call you on it, too. Just tell the truth, and you'll get along with him."[29] But sometimes even being truthful wasn't enough.

When Gibson stepped onto the mound, he was all business. Fiercely competitive, the Nebraska-born hurler gave no quarter to opposing hitters. He threw hard and fast. He intimidated batters by pitching inside and often decking them, and he did not appreciate distractions, even from his own catcher. Gibson worked quickly and had no patience for mound visits. Sometimes when McCarver trotted out to talk, Gibson would be staring off in the distance, focused on how he should pitch to the next hitter.

"Bob! Oh, Bob! Remember me?" McCarver would say facetiously. "I'm Tim, your catcher. I believe we've met."

Gibson, annoyed by the disturbance, proceeded to insult McCarver. If Tim reminded him that there was a runner on first, Bob replied, "I know goddamn well there's a man on first because I put him there."

Pausing for effect, Gibson added, "What difference does it make? If he tried to steal, you couldn't throw him out anyway!"

McCarver, sensitive to the fact that he did not possess a strong throwing arm, ignored the insult. Instead, he instructed Gibby on how to pitch to the next hitter.

"Get your ass back there [behind the plate]," Gibson snapped. "The only thing you know about pitching is that it's hard to hit."[30]

But McCarver could be just as stubborn. He prided himself in knowing his batterymates, not only as pitchers but as human beings. He also realized that Gibson carried a big chip on his shoulder when it came to his craft and to his racial identity. To his credit, McCarver was careful in choosing his battles and, just as important, when and how to address them. One of those difficult moments came on Friday, April 4, 1968, when the Cardinals, still in spring training, learned that the Reverend Martin Luther King Jr. had been assassinated in the catcher's hometown of Memphis. At a time when Black consciousness was sweeping the United States, the assassination of the Black civil rights leader sparked riots in cities across the nation. Although Gibson did not join in the self-expression or protests that were features of the Black Power movement, his racial anger was palpable. Growing up in the projects of Omaha with a widowed mother and six siblings, he had experienced the sting of discrimination. Like millions of other African Americans, Gibson admired King, and his death struck him especially hard.[31]

"It was a very disorienting time in many respects," recalled McCarver long after his playing career had ended. "It all began with John Kennedy's assassination five years earlier. Then Reverend King was shot. Then it was Bobby Kennedy just a few months after. There was so much trying to drive people apart at that time. . . . Bob and I had a very serious discussion in the clubhouse the morning after Reverend King's death. He was very emotional, and initially he turned his back on me. Probably the last person he wanted to talk to that morning was a white man from Memphis, of all places. But I confronted him on that. . . . I told him that I had grown up in an environment of severe prejudice, but if I were any indication, it was possible for people to change their attitudes. . . .

"He really didn't want to be calmed down and told me in so many words that it was plainly impossible for a white man to completely overcome prejudice. I said that he was taking a very nihilistic attitude and that just because some white people obviously maintained their hatred for Blacks and considered them inferior, it was senseless to embrace a viewpoint that would lead nowhere.

"I found myself in the unfamiliar position of arguing that the races were equal and that we were all the same. It was a soul-searching type of thing, and I believe that Bob and I reached a meeting of the minds that morning. I think about our friendship now, and how race never built a wall between us. That bond was created in all the turbulence of the 1960s and has now lasted a lifetime."[32]

McCarver was probably the only white teammate who could speak to Gibson so candidly. The Black hurler listened, too, because he respected Tim. Both teammates understood that they had been thrust into leadership roles, whether they wanted them or not. McCarver's leadership stemmed from his playing position. Effective catchers have encyclopedic minds. They must remember the strengths and weaknesses of the opposing hitters because catchers not only call the pitches but set the infield and outfield defenses, as well as confer with the manager and coaches on strategy. Tim also led by example. If not the hardest worker on the team, McCarver was among the top two or three. He was also passionate. He could wear his emotions on his sleeve, especially when an umpire made a bad call or a pitcher needed to be reprimanded. On the other hand, Tim praised a masterful pitching performance as loudly as he criticized the ineptitude or laziness of a teammate. Gibson's leadership was different.

"Generally speaking," said Tim, "pitchers are not leaders on ball clubs because they don't play every day. But Gibby was the uncontested leader of those Cardinal teams, not only by what he did, but by the way he did it."[33]

Like his friendship with Gibson, McCarver's relationship with Carlton evolved over time. During their early years together, the two batterymates tended to tolerate rather than support each other. "McCarver had a knack for getting close to pitchers, especially young ones," recalled Mike Shannon, who played third base and right field for the Cards. "But Tim and Steve had their run-ins. When Carlton made up his mind to do something, he did it. He didn't deviate very much. And McCarver was the same. So, you had two hard heads knocking against concrete."[34] There were times that McCarver admired Carlton's stubbornness, though.

"Most young pitchers who are a little wild want to throw fast balls when they get behind on a hitter," McCarver noted. "Not Steve. He'd tell me to call for the curve if that was the right pitch. He had that 'killer instinct' that a successful pitcher needs."[35]

Entering the 1968 season, Carlton had reason to be confident. He was coming off his first solid year as a starter, having posted a 14-9 record, 168 strikeouts, and a 2.98 earned run average. In the off season he had added fifteen pounds to his six-foot, four-inch frame, the result of a regimented but mild weight-lifting program, along with shoulder and back exercises. The program, according to Carlton, was designed to "increase muscle tone, strength and endurance without becoming muscle bound."[36] When asked in spring training how many games he would win, the tall left-hander replied, "I hope to better myself every year so I can win 20 games."[37]

But Carlton did not get off to the start he had anticipated. He was 4-1 with three no-decisions in his first eight games of the '68 campaign. McCarver believed that part of the problem was that Steve needed another pitch and not just any pitch but the slider. The slider, when thrown correctly, has a lateral motion. The pitch would complement Carlton's four-seam fastball, which had considerable velocity but little lateral movement, and his curve, which dropped straight down in a twelve-to-six-o'clock motion. Since Gibson threw a sharp, 92 mph slider that handcuffed hitters, Steve begrudgingly approached him to ask about the pitch.[38]

Gibson told Carlton that his success with the pitch was due to "timing" and that the "pitch really doesn't break that much." He explained that "it's just really hard to hit," reasoning that it was "because I throw it out of the same three-quarter arm slot as my fastball." By the time the hitter had made the distinction, the pitch was by him. But Gibson also told Carlton that his arm was "sore all the time" because he threw the slider with "a stiff wrist that placed a great stress on the elbow."[39]

Instead, Steve began experimenting with the cut fastball, a hybrid of the fastball and the slider. The grip is almost identical to a four-seam fastball, but the fingers are moved slightly to the right and more pressure is placed on the ball with the middle finger. There is no wrist snap. To the hitter, the cutter looks identical to a fastball, if thrown out of the same arm slot. The pitch gave Carlton the two-plane movement—first cut, then drop—he needed to complete his repertoire.[40] He experimented with the cutter throughout the '68 campaign, believing that he had discovered his out pitch.

Gibson also struggled at the beginning of the 1968 season, going 3-5 with two no-decisions in his first ten starts. At one point he had not won a game in three weeks.[41] The Cardinals' offense was in a slump, unable to give either starter the run support they needed to be successful. Once, when Gibson tried to encourage Carlton by offering some pitching advice, Steve snapped, "How the hell are you going to help me? You're three and five!"

"Maybe [the Cardinals'] inability to score runs was making everybody a little testy," Gibson said. "But just to play it safe, I left Carlton alone after that. He had his own problems, I suppose—mainly with the press. He didn't want to say something that might embarrass him when it appeared in print."[42]

On May 29 the defending world champion Cardinals lost to the San Francisco Giants, 2–1, at Busch Stadium. It was their eleventh loss in the last thirteen games, dropping St. Louis three games behind the first-place Giants.[43] The next day, when the Cards helped Carlton to a 6–0 victory, Gibson put his teammates on notice. "If you guys don't get some runs for me, there's going to be a fight," he said, with tongue in cheek. "I'm going after Carlton because he's been getting all the runs lately."[44]

In retrospect, the Memorial Day victory triggered the Cardinals' turnaround. Between May 30 and August 1, St. Louis went 49-15 and entrenched themselves in first place with a commanding fifteen-game lead.[45] Gibson led the charge, pitching five straight shutouts—one shy of the Major League record—in the month of June. During that span, Gibson allowed 21 hits, walked 5, and struck out 35 in forty-five innings of work.[46] By the end of the regular season, Gibby had made thirty-four starts and completed twenty-eight of them. He was 22-9 with thirteen shutouts and a fifteen-game winning streak and led the National League in strikeouts with 269 and a minuscule 1.12 ERA, the lowest ever by a Major Leaguer with at least three hundred innings pitched.[47]

Gibson was just as impressive in the World Series against the Detroit Tigers. He started three games and posted complete-game victories in Games One and Four. In Game One, Gibson faced thirty-one-game-winner Denny McLain and threw a 4–0 shutout, striking out a Series record 17 batters. In Game Four, Gibson gave the Cards a 3 games to 1 lead when he struck out 10 batters en route to a 7–3 victory. Gibby continued his brilliance in Game Seven, until the seventh, when he surrendered 3 runs on 4 straight hits. The Cards could only muster a single run on Mike Shannon's solo homer in the ninth, and Gibson took the 4–1 loss against Mickey Lolich, who pitched a complete-game victory.[48] The Cardinals, who had stormed out to a 3-games-to-1 lead in the Series, were stunned by the Tigers, who mounted a comeback and took three games in a row to win the world championship.

Carlton's quest to become a twenty-game winner in '68 began to unravel in midseason. Having posted an 8-4 record at the end of June, Steve was named to his first All-Star team. But he struggled during the season's second half. Between July 5 and September 28, Carlton started seventeen games, winning just five while losing seven and recording five no-decisions. At season's end he was 13-11 with 162 strikeouts and a 2.99 ERA. Carlton's fortunes did not improve in the World Series, where he pitched just four innings in relief, giving up 3 earned runs and 7 hits.[49]

McCarver also struggled during the season. He saw his batting average dip 42 percentage points, from the previous season's average of .295 to .253, but he atoned for it in the World Series, batting .333. Among his 9 hits was a 3-run homer in the fifth inning of Game Three off the Tigers' Pat Dobson, which put the Cards ahead and spurred them on to a 7–3 victory.[50]

It turned out that 1968 was the last year of a great run for the Cardinals, who captured their third pennant in five years. In a meeting with his players after the World Series, club owner Gussie Busch warned the team about getting "fat, greedy and selfish" and scolded them for backing union leadership he considered "disrespectful" to management.[51] Stunned, the players had expected that Busch would've shown some gratitude for their having achieved back-to-back pennants. Instead, they were demoralized after being told they needed to do a better job of conforming and representing the organization. Years later many of the players cited the owner's lecture as a turning point in transforming the Cardinals from winners to losers. St. Louis would not return to the World Series until 1982.[52] Carlton's career, on the other hand, began a steady trajectory that would lead to one of the most remarkable single seasons of any pitcher in Major League history. The key to his success was adopting the slider.

After the '68 campaign, the Cardinals went on a tour to East Asia and competed in several exhibition games against Japanese All-Star teams. While the Cardinals viewed the games as a noncompetitive, goodwill event, the Japanese took it much more seriously. "They came out swinging," recalled Carlton in a 2019 interview with Tyler Kepner, the national baseball writer for the *New York Times* and author of *K: A History of Baseball in Ten Pitches*. "They were trying to kick our ass."[53]

Carlton decided to test his slider against the greatest player in the history of Japanese baseball, Sadaharu Oh. Oh had already homered twice off of him, so Steve felt he had nothing to lose. After the second home run, he approached McCarver to reconsider his pitch selection, saying, "Timmy, I gotta break out the slider against Oh because I can't move him off the plate." Oh, a left-handed power hitter, stood at home plate like a flamingo. He would lift his right leg high into the air as the pitcher released the ball, and in the process he would crowd the plate. The next time Oh came to bat, Carlton threw a slider that nearly struck him in the ribs. "When I threw him that slider, he backed away and the ball was a strike," recalled Carlton. "That's when I knew I had something."[54]

Confident in his ability to throw the pitch, Carlton informed Cardinals pitching coach Billy Muffett during spring training that he intended to add the slider to his repertoire. Muffett did not give his immediate approval. He wanted to think about it because the pitch placed greater strain on a hurler's arm than either the fastball or curve. But after Carlton lost four of his first six decisions of the '69 campaign, Muffett gave approval to use the slider as long as the pitch did not strain his arm or detract from the effectiveness of his curve.[55]

With the slider added to his arsenal, Carlton won ten of his next twelve starts with a 1.65 ERA. He only got better after that. Between June 27 and July 16, Carlton yielded a total of five runs, getting wins in all five games he started. In Chicago he struck out twelve Cubs en route to a 3–1 victory two weeks later, and he recorded the same number of strikeouts in a 5–0 whitewashing of the Phillies. That stretch boosted Steve's record to 12-5, earning him the National League starting pitching assignment for the All-Star Game.[56] Together with Gibson, Carlton kept the Cardinals better than respectable despite an anemic offense. That was no easy feat.

With Major League Baseball expanding and splitting each league into two divisions, run production was up. There were two new teams in the National League (Montreal and San Diego), thus giving Major League jobs to at least twenty more pitchers. That meant that the number of experienced hurlers declined, giving an advantage to hitters. The offensive explosion was also aided by the lowering of the pitcher's mound from fifteen inches to ten. Now those hurlers who relied on an overhand curve no longer enjoyed the vertical drop through the strike zone they once had. All these changes enabled NL teams to score an average of 139 more runs than they had in 1968. The Cardinals, on the other hand, scored only 12 more runs than they had the previous year. They finished tenth in the NL in run production, ahead of only the two new expansion clubs.[57]

Ironically, Cards general manager Bing Devine believed that he had strengthened the lineup during the off-season by acquiring Vada Pinson from Cincinnati to replace the retired Roger Maris in right field and by trading the oft-injured Orlando Cepeda to the Atlanta Braves for Joe Torre. While Torre knocked in 100 runs, the rest of the offense struggled. Pinson suffered a broken foot and was out for a month. Curt Flood's batting average dropped to .300 for the first time in three years. Mike Shannon's batting average slipped by more than 12 percentage points, to .254, and shortstop Dal Maxvill hit just .175. Although Lou Brock turned in another impressive season, hitting .298 with 12 homers, 47 RBIs, and a league-leading 53 stolen bases, and Julián Javier (.282, 10 HRS, 42 RBIS) and McCarver (.260, 7 HRS, 51 RBIS) contributed solid performances, it wasn't enough to kick-start the offense.[58]

A perfect example of the Cards' offensive woes came on September 15 at Busch Stadium, when Carlton struck out a modern Major League record 19 hitters in a nine-inning game against the New York Mets and still lost, 4–3. Carlton fanned the side in the first, second, fourth, and ninth innings and retired 12 of the first 15 Mets on strikeouts. New York scored all 4 runs on a pair of 2-run homers by Ron Swoboda, in the fourth and eighth innings.[59]

Carlton said that Swoboda's first home run was on a fastball "right in his wheelhouse" and that he "hung a slider" on the second.

"I felt so good until that second home run," Carlton said. "I threw four fastballs and really had him set up for the slider. I figured he'd be as tense as I was, thinking about me hanging it."

But Swoboda disagreed. "You can't call that [slider] a mistake because it could have been a foul ball or a double play ball," said Swoboda. "He threw worse pitches that I didn't hit."[60]

Those "worse pitches" were probably recognizable at the time they left Carlton's hand, though. What made the slider so effective was that it could not be distinguished from the fastball until it crossed the plate. Carlton also attributed the effectiveness of the pitch both to the guessing game it created in the hitter's mind and to his ability to control the slider. "Now a batter can't come up to the plate knowing he has to guess only curve or fastball," he explained. "He has to think about the slider, too. The right-handed batters can't just sit and wait for the fastball outside. And the slider is easier to control than a big, sweeping curve. It's why I've been throwing [the slider] about 25 percent of the time."[61]

An examination of the pitch breakdown from Carlton's September 15 gem supports his assertion. Of the 152 pitches he delivered, 96 were fastballs (63 percent), 34 were sliders (23 percent), and just 22 were curves (14 percent). The pitch breakdown also reveals that Carlton's success came just as much from his fastball, which he used as his "out pitch," or the pitch he used to strike out the hitter. Of the 106 strikes Steve threw, 66 came off fastballs, 24 off sliders, and just 15 off curves.[62]

"Steve struck out nineteen Mets that night because he was able to throw a *heavy* fastball that stayed on the same plane," said McCarver, who caught the game. "That kind of pitch is an anomaly," he added. A heavy fastball is gripped along two seams and either tails or sinks. A *light* fastball, on the other hand, is a four-seamer that remains on one plane or might have some movement at the last second as it enters the hitting zone. According to McCarver, Carlton's fastball was both "heavy" and "stayed on the same plane" that night, making it extremely difficult for the hitters to drive. "Pitchers aren't supposed to be able to throw a hybrid like that," McCarver said. The feat was also rare for Carlton. "Almost every other time I caught Steve," McCarver added, "his fastball was too light to be his out pitch, which became his slider when he was traded to the Phillies."[63]

In fact, Carlton, who struck out sixteen in a losing effort against the Phillies in 1967, admitted that he was not aware of how many strikeouts he had recorded until the eighth inning, when the scoreboard announced that he had just tied his old record. McCarver remembers Carlton telling him before the game, "Something strange is going on. The ball is just exploding out of my hand."[64]

The Cardinals' southpaw went out to the mound in the ninth with the intention of striking out the side in order to set the new single-game strikeout record.

"I decided to go for [the record] after the eighth," he admitted after the game. "I wanted that record so bad. There's no reason to go out there if you're just going to tie it.

"I was so nervous," he added. "I just reached back and fired. You can't finesse out there. I would rather have had the guy get a hit than foul out or ground out just so I could get the strikeout."[65]

In striking out nineteen Mets, Carlton broke the modern Major League mark for strikeouts in a nine-inning game, which was eighteen. Bob Feller, Don Wilson, and Sandy Koufax had all accomplished the eighteen SO feat, and Koufax had done it twice.[66] Carlton also broke the Cardinals' team record of seventeen strikeouts in a nine-inning game, a record set by Dizzy Dean in 1933 and matched by Bob Gibson in the 1968 World Series.[67]

Carlton's Major League strikeout record was tied by Tom Seaver of the Mets in 1970 and Nolan Ryan of the California Angels in 1974 before Roger Clemens of the Boston Red Sox struck out twenty batters in 1986. Clemens also struck out twenty in 1996, and Kerry Wood of the Chicago Cubs matched the feat in 1998. Randy Johnson of the Arizona Diamondbacks fanned twenty hitters in the first nine innings of an eleven-inning contest in 2001. But Carlton's nineteen strikeouts feat remains the Cardinals' team record.[68]

Although in 1969 St. Louis finished in fourth place in the National League's new East division, thirteen games behind the "Miracle Mets," who would go on to stun the baseball world and capture the World Series, that season was Carlton's best so far. He won seventeen games, lost eleven, and made his second All-Star team. In thirty-one starts, Steve surrendered an average of just over 2 runs per game and fewer than 6 hits per start. He recorded 210 strikeouts in 236⅓ innings of work. Carlton also lowered his ERA from 2.99 the previous season to 2.17 and thus ranked second in the National League behind only Juan Marichal of the Giants (2.10) and just ahead of Cardinals teammate Bob Gibson (2.18). In addition, Steve's WAR (wins above replacement) was a remarkable 6.8.[69]

Some of Carlton's success must be attributed to McCarver, though. During Steve's first five years in the Majors, he started 104 games and posted a win-loss record of 47-34. Of the 104 starts, Tim caught 77 percent of them. When McCarver was behind the plate, Carlton won 80 percent of his games, sporting a record of 38-22.

Under McCarver's tutelage, Carlton had become one of the best young arms in the game. He was being compared to Sandy Koufax, widely considered the best left-handed pitcher of the modern era.[70] Like Koufax, Steve was a power pitcher who intimidated batters with a rising fastball and a sharply breaking curve. Unlike Koufax, Carlton threw the slider, the pitch that would define his Hall of Fame career.

4

Moneyball

On October 7, 1969, Tim McCarver was dealt to the Philadelphia Phillies. It was a seven-player transaction in which the Cardinals sent McCarver, Gold Glove center fielder Curt Flood, relief pitcher Joe Hoerner, and outfielder prospect Byron Browne to the Phillies for the exceptionally talented slugger Dick Allen, infielder Cookie Rojas, and pitcher Jerry Johnson.[1]

"I really hate to use the old cliché, but this is just 'one of those things' that happen to any baseball player sometime in his career," the veteran catcher told the *St. Louis Post-Dispatch* at the time, seeming to take the trade philosophically. McCarver had "prepared" himself, believing that "if there would be a deal at all involving [him] it would be this winter."[2]

McCarver had become expendable. Although Tim batted .260 with 27 doubles during the '69 campaign, he had trouble throwing out runners. He allowed the most stolen bases (64) of any National League catcher that season. "There is nothing wrong with my arm," McCarver insisted. "My technique got fouled up this season because I was pressing." With catching prospect Ted Simmons waiting for playing time, though, the Cardinals were willing to part with the veteran backstop.[3]

"Simmons was a young, switch-hitting catcher with some power," explained Cardinals shortstop Dal Maxvill, who became the team's general manager in the mid-1980s. "He may not have been as strong as Tim defensively, but Simmons was ready to take over behind the plate. That coupled with the fact that our offense just wasn't scoring a lot of runs at the time led to the trade. Tim, Curt Flood, and Joe Hoerner were also seasoned veterans who were making good money. Trading them to the Phillies allowed [team general manager] Bing Devine to free up some salary."[4]

St. Louis had been McCarver's baseball home since his rookie year in 1959. He was a core player of a Cardinals team that had won three National League pennants and two World Series titles. Tim had invested himself so completely in the Cardinals organization that the trade couldn't have been anything less than devastating for him. In fact, McCarver years later admitted to the hurt he felt after the Cards traded him. When the team's general manager at the time, Bing Devine, broke the news to the veteran catcher, he confessed that "it hurt him to make the deal." But Tim didn't buy it. "That's like a father dangling a razor strap in front of his 4-year-old son and saying, 'This is going to hurt me more than it'll hurt you,'" he said of Devine's remark. "Bullshit! It hurt me a lot more."[5] The trade also marked the end of the Cardinals' special chemistry.

"I was sickened by the thought of McCarver and Flood leaving us," wrote Gibson in his 1994 autobiography. "Those two guys struck right at the heart of what the Cardinals had been about for the past decade. I loved the Cardinals, was proud to be one, and recognized that Tim McCarver and Curt Flood were two of the biggest reasons why. With them gone, being a Cardinal would never mean quite the same thing."[6]

Although no one knew it at the time, the October 7, 1969, trade that sent McCarver to the Phillies also altered the history of Major League Baseball itself. It proved to be the catalyst of a fiercely contested "moneyball" battle between the owners and the players, one that would eventually lead to free agency. At issue was the reserve system, a medieval-like institution that tethered a player to his team unless he was sold, traded, or released.

The opening salvo was fired by Flood, who refused to report to Philadelphia. Not wanting to relocate his family or his business interests, the disgruntled outfielder wrote to Commissioner Bowie Kuhn, informing him that he "did not feel . . . he was a piece of property to be bought or sold irrespective of [his] wishes." Furthermore, he wrote, "I believe that any system which produces that result violates my basic rights as a citizen and is inconsistent with the laws of the United States." Flood closed the letter by declaring his "desire to play baseball in 1970," but he added that he wanted to "consider offers from other clubs before making any decision" to accept the Phillies' contract offer.[7]

Kuhn feigned ignorance, insisting he did not understand how Flood's "rights as a human being" applied to the reserve clause and stating further that if the former Cardinal refused to report to Philadelphia, he could not play at all.[8]

Flood regarded Philadelphia as "the nation's northernmost southern city" because of the Phillies' poor history of race relations.[9] Some believed that Flood's decision was based on monetary considerations, a notion that McCarver quickly dismissed. "Curt was a man of conviction," he insisted. "Nobody was going to talk him out of his decision to challenge the reserve clause. [Phillies general manager] John Quinn offered Curt a salary in the neighborhood of $110,000. That was a considerable amount of money at that time. But Curt still turned it down out of principle."[10]

In addition to refusing to report to the Phillies, Flood filed a $3.1 million damage suit against the Cardinals and took his case all the way to the Supreme Court. Although he eventually lost the battle, Flood's action set in motion a chain of events that led to the 1975 arbitration ruling that granted players the right to free agency.[11]

Flood's refusal to accept a trade to the Phillies, as well as the ensuing litigation, deeply angered Busch, who felt he had no other alternative but to defend his principle—that he was the owner of the club and had the final say on policy, no matter how unpopular it might be. Thus, when Steve Carlton asked for a sizable raise in salary, from $26,000 to $50,000 for 1970, Busch stood his ground.

Carlton, who posted a 17-11 record with 210 strikeouts and a 2.17 ERA in 1969, believed that he had earned a reputation as one of the game's elite pitchers.[12] In fact, Carlton was among the National League's leaders in only two categories that season: ERA (second behind Juan Marichal of the San Francisco Giants) and strikeouts per nine innings (7.997), which made him eighth behind Houston's

Tom Griffin and Don Wilson, Sam McDowell of the Cleveland Indians, Bob Moose and Bob Veale of the Pittsburgh Pirates, Mickey Lolich of the Detroit Tigers, and Dick Selma of the Chicago Cubs.[13] Nevertheless, Carlton believed that he should be paid like one of the game's premier pitchers and asked the Cardinals for a $50,000 contract. That would have made his among the top five salaries on the team. Bob Gibson was the highest-paid Cardinal, with a salary of $125,000, followed by field players Dick Allen ($85,000), Lou Brock ($85,000), Joe Torre ($85,000), and Mike Shannon ($50,000).[14]

When Busch offered to increase Carlton's salary to $32,000, the southpaw countered with a $40,000 figure. Busch held firm, and Steve refused to report to spring training. "I don't give a damn if Steve Carlton never pitches another ball for us," fumed Busch to the press on March 9 at the Cards' St. Petersburg training complex. "He got a 25% increase with a club that finished way down in the standings. I only hope that some of the other owners have the guts to take the stand I have, and return things to normal."[15]

Busch was prepared to take the hard-line position. His million-dollar payroll was already the highest in baseball, and he was put off by an aggressive players' union, which had threatened to strike the previous year over a dispute with owners on the percentage players would receive from television revenue.[16] "Player representatives make all kinds of derogatory statements about the owners," he snapped. "We suddenly seem to be their greatest enemies. Last season they threw down all sorts of challenges, threats and ultimatums. Personally, I don't react well to ultimatums."[17]

To counter Carlton's holdout, the Cardinals on March 11 enacted a unique provision of the controversial reserve clause allowing the club to renew his contract under the same terms as the previous one for a period of one year. The renewal clause protected ownership from free agency and allowed the team to supervise the rebellious player as he got into shape for the upcoming season. Carlton was now "legally obligated" to report to spring training or face a considerable fine.[18] The impetuous hurler also realized that unless he signed a contract, he wouldn't be eligible for additional pension plan benefits, nor would he be covered by the players' insurance plan if injured. "With the generous pension fund the players have," said Busch, driving the point home, "I don't see how Carlton can say we're tightfisted. We've been so fair with these players. You have no idea. I'm no attorney, but if you ask me, this is another challenge to the reserve clause."[19] Despite the tough talk, Busch relented, and Carlton signed a two-year contract worth $40,000 a year.[20]

Having missed three weeks of spring training, Carlton never got on track in 1970. During the first two months of the regular season, he went 2-6 in nine starts, including a 4–3 loss at Philadelphia on May 21 in which he struck out sixteen batters.[21] Things didn't get much better during the summer.

Between May 27 and September 3, Carlton started twenty-one games and won only six of them.[22] Of the thirteen losses he suffered, the worst came on a muggy Sunday afternoon, July 26, against the Reds at Cincinnati's Riverfront Stadium. He surrendered 10 earned runs on 9 hits in just four innings of work. The offensive barrage began in the first inning, when Johnny Bench hit a Carlton fastball over the right-center field wall for a 3-run homer. The very next inning Bench hit a slider for a 2-run home run to left. True to form, Carlton retaliated by firing a brushback pitch at the next batter, Lee May, sending him sprawling to the dirt. Reds starter Wayne Simpson got even the next inning, hitting Carlton in the right calf with a pitch. Tensions escalated in the bottom of the third, when Simpson came to the plate and Carlton threw inside. The two pitchers exchanged words, but home plate umpire Lee Weyer interceded before a fight broke out.[23]

"Carlton throwing at [Lee] May is just baseball," Reds manager Sparky Anderson told the *St. Louis Post-Dispatch*. "Still[,] I don't like anybody throwing at my hitters," he added. But Cardinals manager Red Schoendienst defended his pitcher: "A pitcher doesn't have a chance anymore. There's the lively ball and the AstroTurf and the smaller strike zone. If you're a pitcher, you have to brush back those hitters."[24]

Bench struck again in the fifth inning, belting a Carlton fastball over the left-field fence for his third home run of the game. He had been a one-man wrecking crew, going 4-for-5 with 3 homers, 7 RBIS, and 3 runs scored as the Reds coasted to a 12–5 victory.[25]

Carlton was infuriated. "Lefty and I commiserated over dinner and a little wine," said Joe Torre, Carlton's catcher and roommate on road trips. "I guess we had more than a little wine," he admitted. "When we got back to our hotel suite, I think we broke every stick of furniture in the room. When we awoke in the morning and realized what we had done, we tried to glue everything back together.

"When we left the suite, we had to make sure we didn't close the door too hard because we were afraid the noise would cause everything to fall apart."[26]

Carlton made four starts against the Reds that season and lost every one. In 25.1 innings against the Reds, Steve yielded 24 runs and 35 hits, posting a 7.82 ERA. In those four games Johnny Bench hit .467 against Carlton, with 4 home runs, 2 doubles, and 9 RBIS.[27] Steve would eventually learn that he couldn't "let Bench key in on [him]" because the power-hitting catcher "covers more of the plate than any other hitter [he'd] seen." To be successful, Carlton would have to "keep him guessing with off-speed stuff."[28] Still, Bench would prove to be the left-hander's greatest nemesis over the course of their Hall of Fame careers.

Carlton completed the '70 campaign with just ten victories, a 3.73 ERA, 103 strikeouts, and 109 walks. He also led the National League in losses (19).[29] There are conflicting accounts as to why Steve pitched so poorly. One belief is that the strain on his arm from throwing the slider had forced the lean left-hander to abandon the pitch, making him rely too much on his fastball. Another account maintains that Cardinals pitching coach Billy Muffett discouraged him from throwing the slider for fear it might hurt his curveball.[30]

Carlton could have scapegoated his poor performance on his new catchers. After McCarver was traded to the Phillies in October 1969, Joe Torre, a veteran backstop who had been acquired from the Atlanta Braves, split the catching for the Cardinals with rookie Ted Simmons. Torre caught Carlton in twenty games in 1970, and Simmons was his catcher in fifteen.[31] Simmons would have been an easy target considering his lack of Major League experience. But the first time Carlton and Simmons started a regular-season game together was June 2, 1970, when the Cardinals won, 12–1, versus the

San Francisco Giants at St. Louis. Carlton pitched a four-hitter, and Simmons had a single, a triple, and a walk, scoring twice.[32] Instead, Steve blamed himself for his problems.

"Holding out really hurt me," Carlton said, ruminating about his poor season. "I worked out on my own, but I really missed the first part of spring training. That's when you stretch your arm out and loosen up the muscles. When the season started, I just wasn't ready." He also stopped throwing the slider. "It didn't feel right," he explained. "The few times I threw the slider it hurt my arm so I quit on it altogether." What made matters worse, Carlton wasn't getting much run support from the Cardinals offense. Five times he pitched a complete game and still lost. On four other occasions, he was shut out. "I lost 19 games because I got wrapped up in self-pity," he said. "But I learned a lot about mental attitude. If you want to be a winning pitcher, you have to have a positive attitude."[33]

Carlton credited a night watchman by the name of Briggs with pointing out the necessity of a positive mental approach and better concentration when he was on the mound. Briggs, concerned about Carlton's lackluster performance, began sending him four or five letters a week midway through the 1970 season. According to Carlton, the night watchman was much more than a baseball fan. He was a "spiritual guide" who understood that the key to successful pitching was to develop a mind free from distraction. Briggs's letters contained snippets of writings from Friedrich Nietzsche and Arthur Schopenhauer—German philosophers who stressed the importance of mind over matter. With Briggs's encouragement, Carlton began to apply the theories of the two philosophers to baseball.[34]

Determined to improve his performance in 1971, Carlton began doing martial arts training in the off-season to improve his concentration and mental approach to the game. He also lifted weights and did stretching exercises. Although Steve bulked up to 225 pounds, he was able to retain the flexibility and strength needed to become a power pitcher. The rigorous training paid off, and Carlton produced his first twenty-win season in '71. He also made his third All-Star team. And he did it all without throwing the slider.[35]

Gibson, with sixteen wins, had the second-best record among the starters. Due to a pitiful June, however, the Redbirds finished second in the National League East, seven games behind the pennant-winning Pittsburgh Pirates. The Cards entered the month of June in first place, with a two-and-a-half-game lead over Pittsburgh. Then Gibson went down with an arm injury and spent three weeks on the disabled list. The bullpen was overworked and the defense slumped. As a result, St. Louis had an 8-21 record for the month, which virtually knocked them out of the pennant race. Carlton was the one bright spot on a Cardinals pitching staff whose 3.85 ERA was the second worst in the National League.[36]

Between April 7 and June 22 Carlton won eleven games and dropped just three. Among the most outstanding games were a 7–1 victory on June 3 against the Pirates in Pittsburgh in which he struck out 9 batters; a 6–5 win on June 22 against the Dodgers in Los Angeles in which he struck out 12 hitters; and a 5–2 victory on September 28 against the Mets in New York.[37] Since the Cardinals had shifted Torre to third base, Ted Simmons was the club's regular catcher and caught thirty-three of Carlton's thirty-seven starts that season.[38] The September 28 game was the most noteworthy, not only because Steve had earned his twentieth win of the '71 campaign but also because the contest would be the last game Carlton would pitch for St. Louis and the last game Nolan Ryan, the opposing starter, would pitch for the Mets.

Although Carlton and Ryan would go on to have Hall of Fame careers, both pitchers were considered underachievers at the time.[39] Like Carlton, the twenty-four-year-old Ryan clearly had talent but too often disappointed. He began the '71 season with an MLB career record of 19-24. Entering the September 28 game against the Cardinals, Ryan had won just two of his last thirteen starts and had a season record of 10-13. His lack of command showed in the very first inning, when Ryan walked Lou Brock, Ted Sizemore, Matty Alou, and Joe Torre, forcing in a run. When Ted Simmons followed with a single to right, scoring Sizemore and Alou, New York manager Gil Hodges lifted Ryan. Carlton fared better.

The Cardinals scored twice in the second inning after Carlton ignited the offense with a lead-off single. Spotted a 5–0 lead, Steve clamped down on the Mets. He pitched a 7-hit, complete-game victory, striking out 8, as St. Louis won, 5–2. The victory made Carlton a twenty-game winner for the first time in the big leagues and the first Cardinals left-hander to achieve the feat since Ray Sadecki in 1964.[40] He finished the Cards' 20-9 season with eighteen complete games, 172 strikeouts, and a 3.56 ERA.[41]

McCarver, on the other hand, did not fare as well with the cellar-dwelling Phillies. When he arrived in the City of Brotherly Love, Tim was optimistic. "To go to a club that hasn't won for a long time is a good challenge," he remarked. "I think I can help the Phillies become a live team again like I helped the Cardinals in 1964. St. Louis hadn't won a pennant for a long time before that."[42]

McCarver began the 1970 season as the starting catcher, but on May 2 in a game against the San Francisco Giants he fractured his right hand on a foul ball off the bat of Willie Mays. Later that very same inning, backup catcher Mike Ryan suffered a similar injury while tagging Willie McCovey as he was sliding into home plate. Both catchers were shelved for a good part of the season, and manager Frank Lucchesi was forced to use a platoon consisting of coach Doc Edwards and three unproven rookies. "Well, they claim I'm the 'leader type' on the field, and I guess I proved it," quipped McCarver. "After I went out and got hurt, so did the other catchers!"[43]

When Tim returned to the lineup in September, he batted second and hit .316 with 4 homers and 14 RBIs, but he was hampered defensively by the fourth finger he'd fractured on his right hand, as it did not heal correctly. As a result, his throws to second became more erratic, lessening his ability to cut down base runners.[44]

McCarver's performance improved in 1971. He appeared in 134 games, hitting .278—three points better than his career average—with 8 round-trippers and 46 RBIs. Tim also demonstrated his ornery side in a September game against his former Cardinals teammates.

The incident began when McCarver dropped a pop-up near the St. Louis dugout. With the slow-footed Joe Torre on first base, Cardinals players began riding Tim, yelling, "There he goes!" The implication was that McCarver's throwing problems would not even allow him to catch a lumbering base runner like Torre. To retaliate, Tim called for two straight brushback pitches when Redbirds outfielder Lou Brock was at the plate. When Brock angrily objected, the two former teammates began to scuffle. Umpire Al Barlick ejected McCarver.

Tensions remained when the two teams met again the following week. Brock was on third this time when Torre lifted a shallow fly ball to right field. Brock tried to score, but Phillies outfielder Willie Montanez's throw easily beat him to the plate. That left Brock no choice but to bowl over McCarver. For a moment it appeared as if the previous week's fight would resume. But Brock eased the hostility by picking up McCarver's hat and handing it to him.[45]

The highlight of the veteran catcher's season came on June 23, when he caught Rick Wise's no-hitter against the Reds at Cincinnati's Crosley Field. While McCarver also collected two hits in three plate appearances, Wise hit a couple of home runs and collected a trio of RBIs in the 4–0 win.[46]

Tim hoped to have an even better season in 1972. He had good reason to believe that the Phillies were committed to winning when general manager John Quinn approached him in spring training and asked, "We have a chance to get Steve Carlton. What do you think?"

McCarver, ever the comedian, asked, "For what franchise?"

"No, I'm serious," replied Quinn. "We can get him from the Cardinals for one player."

Stunned, Tim didn't think there was anyone on the current roster who was Carlton's equal. "Is there a phenom in the farm system?" he asked.

Quinn took a quick glance over his shoulder to make sure no one else could hear, then replied, "They're willing to take Rick Wise."[47]

Even after McCarver had been traded to Philadelphia, he maintained close ties to Carlton. During the off-season they went hunting together. "I went on many of those trips," recalled Dal Maxvill, the Cards' shortstop. "Carlton was the ultimate outdoorsman, and Tim wasn't sure which end of the rifle to shoot from. Needless to say, we followed Steve's lead on where to go and what to hunt."[48]

One time the trio traveled to Canada. Flying first to Montana, they drove from there to Alberta, then boarded a seaplane to Lac La Ronge in northern Saskatchewan. When they got off the plane, they looked for a guide among the indigenous residents who were standing nearby. McCarver singled out one. Dressed in bearskin, the guide spoke in a gruff voice and was communicating with his friends in their native language.

"That's the guy we have to get!" exclaimed Tim. "He looks like he's experienced. He'll know where to take us."

Tim assumed the Indian couldn't speak English, and after trotting over to the man, he introduced himself using Hollywood "Indianspeak," with equally offensive mannerisms.

Without missing a beat, the guide responded, "Hi, guys! I'm Ray Mackenzie, Harvard class of '66. How the fuck are ya?!"

Carlton, who had been in a bad mood up to that point, roared with laughter. "Gee, Timmy," he said, "you sure handled that real well!"[49]

McCarver was aware that Steve was asking the Cardinals for a $25,000 increase in salary, a raise from $40,000 to $65,000. Tim also knew that Gussie Busch had refused the request and was determined to hold the line this time. But the catcher didn't think Phils general manager John Quinn would pay that kind of money either. "Quinn pinched pennies harder than any general manager in baseball," McCarver said in a 2018 interview. "He was intimidating when you sat across the desk from him to negotiate your salary. Quinn refused to pay a dollar more than he thought you were worth, and he lowballed everyone."[50]

What McCarver did not know was that the Phillies' general manager had been pursuing a trade with the New York Mets for pitcher Nolan Ryan and using the veteran catcher as the bait until Carlton became available.[51] Tim also did not realize that, like Carlton, Rick Wise was also embroiled in a similar salary dispute with the Phillies. Wise had posted seventeen wins, including a no-hitter, in 1971 and was asking the Phillies for a $20,000 increase in salary, from $45,000 to $65,000.[52] Phillies owner Bob Carpenter refused the demand, telling Quinn to offer an additional $10,000 and no more. When Wise and Carlton held out in February 1972, they became expendable. Carpenter and Busch would use the pitchers as examples in an effort to intimidate the MLB Players Association.[53]

Labor relations between the owners and players had become

increasingly antagonistic as the March 31, 1972, expiration of the 1969 Basic Agreement neared. Initially, Marvin Miller, the players' negotiator, had taken a cautious approach. Hired by the players' union in the mid-1960s, Miller, once a negotiator for the United Steelworkers, was a patient man. Instead of immediately challenging the reserve system, he secured limited but winnable objectives in order to earn the players' confidence. Over the course of five years Miller improved both the players' salary scale and their working conditions. The minimum salary was raised from $6,000 to $10,000 and the maximum pay cut reduced to 20 percent. Spring training expense money was raised from $25 to $40 a week, and players began to receive first-class travel and hotel accommodations. These achievements might sound modest by today's standards, but players' salaries and working conditions hadn't improved since 1947.[54]

By 1970, however, Miller had become much more aggressive. He pressed for a structural change in the Basic Agreement. This change was called "grievance arbitration," whereby a player, if he believed his contractual rights were being violated and the union supported him, could take the matter to an independent arbitrator who would serve as a mediator between labor and management. Under the existing system the MLB commissioner remained the absolute authority in disputes between players and teams, as well as between leagues and among teams.[55] Miller also wanted a 17 percent increase in the owners' annual contribution to the pension plan, which would match the previous three years' inflation; it amounted to an annual payment of $6.5 million. Naturally, the owners rejected both proposals, publicly portraying Miller as a "labor boss who dictated terms to the players." In private they referred to the player negotiator as a "Jew bastard."[56] Still, Miller persisted. To ease the owners' out-of-pocket costs, he proposed that the $800,000 surplus accrued from the pension plan be applied to the benefits increase, thus drastically reducing the cost to clubs. Surprisingly, the owners, led by Gussie Busch, rejected the proposal and decided to take the union on.[57]

Busch and the other owners believed that the Players Association was still weak and could be broken. This cohort of team owners belonged to an era when players and owners were bound to each other by a mutual love of the game. While the players hadn't been well paid, the owners showed their appreciation by giving them job security and perks that would reinforce personal commitment and loyalty. In 1972, while the players and their agents were trying to drive salaries up to the $125,000 range, only six players were earning a salary at that level: Frank Robinson, Carl Yastrzemski, Frank Howard, Willie Mays, Hank Aaron, and Bob Gibson. These players were an elite group who compiled league-leading statistics year after year. Now there was emerging a new breed of ballplayer who demanded to be paid for his services, whether or not he turned in a consistent performance. Busch saw players like Steve Carlton as the crux of the problem. When Carlton, who had never had a twenty-win season before 1971, asked for $65,000, Busch told his general manager Bing Devine, "Give him fifty and if he won't play for that, get rid of him!" Phillies owner Bob Carpenter viewed Rick Wise the same way and refused the pitcher's demand for $65,000.[58]

On February 25, 1972, Carpenter and Busch decided to show the Players Association that the owners still ruled the game. They did so by trading the two rebellious front-line pitchers for each other. It was a new tactic in labor-management relations that had little to do with salary demands or improving the quality of their teams. Carlton and Wise were almost mirror reflections of each other. Carlton, age twenty-seven, had compiled seventy-seven victories in seven seasons with the Cardinals. He was asking for $65,000, but St. Louis refused to give him more than $57,500. Wise, age twenty-six, had posted seventy-five wins in seven seasons with the Phillies. He was asking for $65,000, but Philadelphia refused to pay him more than $55,000. Yet after they were traded, each pitcher was paid essentially the same salary he had asked his former club to pay him.[59]

When Wise learned of the trade from Phillies general manager John Quinn, he was elated. "It's a great opportunity," he told the press. "You get tired of being a .500 pitcher when you've been with a second division club. The Cardinals just gave me a raise bigger than all the combined raises I ever got from Philadelphia."[60] Years later, however, Wise admitted that he was "stunned" by the deal since he had "grown up in the Phillies organization" and that it "hurt to be traded." Ultimately, he said, "I learned that the trade was all about money and the power that management exercised to control the lives of the players. What it came down to was, 'If you're not going to sign the contract we offer you, you're gone.' Then Steve and I signed basically for what we had asked for to begin with."[61]

Carlton, on the other hand, was in shock after learning of the trade. In fact, the day before the trade was made Steve had confided to a close friend, Cards shortstop Dal Maxvill, that he was going to end his holdout, fly down to spring training, and accept the Cardinals' $57,500 offer.[62] He never had the opportunity to do so. Now he was heading for a perennial cellar dweller.

Carlton considered the Phillies an "awful team" and didn't want to pitch for them. "I was devastated," Steve admitted years later:

"The Phillies were a last-place club at that time and the Cardinals were always competing for first place. I thought, 'Oh my God, there goes my career.' In those days being traded was more of a negative thing than it is today. When they traded you back then, it was because they thought you were no good, or they were just trying to get rid of you.

"I thought the Cardinals were trying to bury me by trading me to the Phillies, who were a last-place organization. After I thought about it, I called [Cards general manager] Bing Devine back and asked if I could change his mind. I told him, 'I'll take the money you offered me. I'll take anything.' But it didn't matter because it was a done deal by then."[63]

At the time, Devine insisted that the trade had been provoked by Carlton's stubborn negotiating tactics two years earlier and that the Cardinals could "sense a similar situation developing."[64] Years later, however, Devine admitted that Carlton wasn't traded because he "wanted too much money." He was traded because the pitcher's "relationship with Busch had soured" and the Cardinals' owner "wanted him gone."[65]

Shock soon turned to anger for Carlton, who expressed his displeasure to the *New York Daily News*. "I'm mad," he admitted. "The Cardinals kept telling me that they couldn't pay me until I won 20 games. Well, in 1971, I won 20 games and they still wouldn't give me what I was asking, so they traded me. I came up through the Cardinals organization and I didn't have anything to say about it. I thought we were working things out. Then, all of a sudden I'm traded cold turkey. If you ask me, the reserve clause is unconstitutional."[66]

Carlton refused to go quietly. He telephoned Marvin Miller and asked what the players' union could do to help him. "You have two alternatives," replied Miller. "You can play or you can quit."[67] Only then did the southpaw pull in his horns. It was clear that the reserve system was the stumbling block in baseball's labor relations.

Near the end of spring training the MLB Players Association, seeking a cost-of-living increase in pension benefits, voted to go on strike unless the owners agreed to submit the dispute to arbitration. Determined to fight the demand, the owners refused. "We voted unanimously to take a stand," declared Gussie Busch, who emerged as the owners' leading voice. "We're not going to give the players another god-damned cent! If they want to strike, let 'em!"[68] On April 1 the players walked out of their spring training camps, marking what *The Sporting News* called "the darkest day in sports history."[69] Days later, as Busch and most of the other owners settled in for the long haul, Phillies owner Bob Carpenter softened his position and allowed his striking players to work out at the team's spring training fields in Clearwater, Florida. The Chicago White Sox and Pittsburgh Pirates did the same for their striking players. Having broken with each other, the owners, after thirteen days, finally agreed to the players' cost-of-living increase. They also sustained the financial losses of the eighty-six games that had been canceled, while the players agreed to forfeit their pay for their time away. The strike was over, but the owners' hold on the game was beginning to weaken.[70]

Two months later, on June 19, the Supreme Court of the United States rejected Curt Flood's challenge to baseball's reserve clause. The court, by a vote of five to three, ruled in favor of baseball and its exemption from antitrust laws, keeping the reserve clause intact. But the decision was hardly an endorsement of the reserve system. In handing down the ruling, the court admitted that baseball's exemption was "an aberration" and insisted that it was "time for Congress—

not the Court—to remedy the problem."[71] Although Flood lost his bid to eliminate the reserve clause, his challenge turned public opinion to the players' side. Shortly after the Supreme Court rendered its decision, a national poll revealed that fans opposed the reserve clause by an 8-to-1 margin.[72] Congress also began to pay closer attention. "Even if I believed the solemn predictions of the pro sports industry spokesmen, and I don't," said Senator Sam Ervin of North Carolina, who would become famous two years later for his role in chairing the Watergate hearings, "I would still oppose a system that demands lord-like control over serf-like hired hands."[73] Fearing that the reserve clause might be taken from them, the owners announced that any player with ten Major League seasons to his credit, including five seasons with his current team, could veto any trade he didn't approve.[74] It was a last-ditch effort to avoid the inevitable dissolution of the reserve system.

In Philadelphia, Steve Carlton adopted a wait-and-see attitude after Phillies general manager John Quinn agreed to his salary demand of a one-year contract at $65,000. "The transition was tough," Carlton admitted many years later. "It was going from the Cardinals who could win 95 games to a team that wasn't winning a lot. But I had to play the hand. It took me a week to change my whole thinking about the trade."[75]

The Phillies' brain trust was optimistic, convinced they had received the better end of the deal. Quinn was adamant that Carlton had "what it takes to become a great one."[76] Nor was the Phillies' general manager the only one who entertained that belief. According to Ruly Carpenter, the son of the Phillies' owner, "My father, farm director Paul Owens, and me all recommended that we acquire Carlton. We were fortunate that Dad and Gussie Busch were close friends because we were given the first chance to get him. I know if Busch offered Carlton to any other club, they would have grabbed him before us."[77] Phillies manager Frank Lucchesi was ecstatic when he learned about the trade. "It was the best deal we'd made in years," he recalled many years later. "Carlton was a winner, a real competitor. You could tell by the way he conducted himself on the mound. We'd been trying to trade for him for three years. John Quinn offered the Cardinals *two* pitchers for him. They wanted Chris Short—and we agreed to trade Short—but Bing [Devine] wasn't interested in our other offers. And we really tried. I know we offered them one of four different guys to go along with Short—Woodie Fryman, Joe Hoerner, Barry Lersch, and Dick Selma. But they just weren't interested in any of them, so the deal was never made."[78]

Phillies fans were less enthusiastic about the trade, though. Wise had been the club's pitching ace, having won forty-five games the previous three seasons. In 1971 he hurled a no-hitter in which he blasted a pair of home runs and was the team's only All-Star. Perhaps Wise had caused headaches with his recent contract demand, but he still managed to win with a second-division team. Carlton, on the other hand, had presented ongoing problems in contract negotiations, and if he allowed as many runs in Philadelphia as he had with the Cardinals, there were doubts that he'd win as many games for the Phillies.[79]

When Rick Wise went to St. Louis and won his first five decisions, Phillies fans were convinced that they had gotten the worse end of the deal. But it wasn't long before they realized they were wrong. "Wise was a good pitcher, but he was no Steve Carlton," said McCarver. "For a lousy $10,000, the Cardinals traded away a guy who would win 251 games for the Phillies; become the second-winningest left-hander of all time behind Warren Spahn; the fourth leading strikeout pitcher in baseball history behind Nolan Ryan, Randy Johnson, and Roger Clemens; a four-time Cy Young Award winner; and a Hall of Famer.

"During his time with the Phillies, Lefty won five division titles, two pennants, and one World Series. Meanwhile, St. Louis finished second twice and third a bunch of times. For the Cardinals, that trade would turn into one of the worst in baseball history."[80]

At the time of the trade, however, Carlton was justified in his concern about the Phillies. The lanky southpaw had grown accustomed to winning in St. Louis. The Cardinals gave their pitchers the run support needed to win games. Redbirds scouts had a knack for identifying and signing amateur talent, thus feeding an already rich farm system. General manager Bing Devine was adept at trading washed-up veterans for the budding stars of other teams, and until recently owner Gussie Busch had retained his star players by paying them well. As a result, the Redbirds made two appearances in the World Series during Carlton's seven years with the club, winning the championship in 1967. Despite two straight fourth-place finishes, in 1969 and 1970, St. Louis returned to winning form in 1971 by finishing second, so the future looked bright for the Cardinals.[81]

Philadelphia, on the other hand, was cursed with a losing tradition. No other Major League team had suffered more losses in its history, including a record twenty-three-game losing streak in 1961.[82] No other team had had as many last-place finishes; by '61 they had racked up twenty-two.[83] No other team had blown a pennant with a six-and-a-half-game lead and just twelve games left to play in the regular season. But the 1964 Phillies somehow managed to do that by dropping ten straight and finishing in a tie for second place.[84] More than any other team in Philadelphia sports history, the '64 Phillies saddled the city with a reputation for being a "loser." Even when victory seemed certain, Philadelphia always found a way to lose. Between 1965 and 1969, losing became a self-fulfilling prophecy. Injuries, poor trades, and personal conflict among the players prevented the Phillies from finishing any higher than fourth place. Thus, a team that had the potential to contend for the next five seasons became tailenders for the balance of the decade.[85]

Phillies fans came to demand a lot from the team, but deep down they expected very little. While the silent majority of the fan base possessed a good understanding of the game, acted respectfully at the ballpark, and tended to suffer in private when the Phillies lost, the defining spirit of the team's fandom—for better, but mostly worse—was the vocal minority of clock punchers and blue collars known as "Boo Birds." Boo Birds went to the ballpark to seek refuge from the disappointments in their lives. They relied on the Phillies to provide an imaginary escape from a rotten job, a lousy marriage, or ungrateful children. When the team failed—as it so often did—the Boo Birds became vindictive. Sitting up in the cheap seats, the cantankerous bunch rained down their venom on the hometown players. They were like pigeons that built nests under the rafters and crapped on unsuspecting victims. Truth be told, the Boo Bird was to be pitied. He was either a disillusioned idealist, one who truly believed the Phillies had the potential to contend each and every season and who thus showered the players with boos when they didn't, or a fool who was delusional enough to think that if handed a bat, glove, and uniform he could perform much better than the players themselves.

With a perpetually disgruntled fan base and no hope of contending, owner Bob Carpenter began a rebuilding process in the early 1970s. This time, however, he relied on his son, Robert Ruliph Morgan Carpenter III, nicknamed "Ruly," and farm director Paul Owens. In fact, Owens understood that he was to mentor Ruly and prepare him to assume the presidency of the club in the near future. Together Owens and his protégé overhauled the farm system. They fired half of the scouting staff, hired more competent evaluators, and began signing more talented prospects.[86]

One of those prospects was Larry Bowa, a fiery shortstop who scratched and clawed his way up to the big leagues in 1970. Greg Luzinski, a two-hundred-pound slugger who stood six feet one and could hit to all fields with power, was another talented prospect. Nicknamed "The Bull" because of his tremendous power, Luzinski was promoted to Philadelphia for good in 1971, becoming the team's cleanup hitter for the next decade. Another prospect who played a significant role in the fortunes of the Phils during the 1970s and early 1980s was Bob Boone. Signed by the Phillies as a third baseman, Boone, a graduate of Stanford University, where he had majored in psychology, was shifted to catcher. His innate intelligence for the game, a remarkable ability to handle pitchers, and a physical toughness that belied his calm exterior enabled Boone to become the anchor of the Phillies pitching staff during the team's glory years, as well as a voice of reason as the National League's player representative during acrimonious strike negotiations in 1981. Mike Schmidt was the most talented of all the prospects signed by the Phillies. An All-American shortstop at Ohio University, Schmidt, a natural power hitter, would be moved to third base, where he would forge a Hall of Fame career.[87]

Frank Lucchesi was chosen to mentor the young prospects. He was a congenial man with tremendous patience and an unconditional loyalty to the organization. "I don't bleed red," he remarked on September 26, 1969, the day he was hired to manage the team. "I bleed *Phillies* red." Lucchesi had certainly paid his dues, having spent nearly twenty years as a Minor League manager. Although he was fair to his players, he did not coddle them. "There's only eighteen inches between a pat on the back and a kick in the butt," he loved to say.[88] The team seemed to respond to him, too. After finishing in fifth place in the National League's new East division in 1969 with a record of 63-99, Lucchesi's Phillies finished fifth again in 1970 but improved their record to 73-88.[89] It was perhaps only a slight improvement but an improvement nonetheless at a time when reversing the dismal fortunes of a club took many years to achieve.

Carpenter's plans to rebuild the Phillies organization also included the construction of a brand-new multipurpose stadium in South Philadelphia. Connie Mack Stadium had seen better days. Once located in a white working-class enclave in North Philadelphia, the neighborhood had by 1970 become a community of poor minority residents living in the old row houses vacated by Irish, Polish, and German immigrants. The factories that had once been the lifeblood of the community, such as Exide Battery, Baldwin Locomotive, Budd Manufacturing, and Philco, had all left the run-down area. Several patchwork additions over the years made the Connie Mack Stadium look like the abandoned factories. The final game at the old ballpark was on October 1, 1970, and the Phillies surprised their fans by defeating the last-place Montreal Expos, 2-1.[90]

The new Veterans Stadium was dedicated on April 10, 1971, when the Fightins opened the gates to 55,352 fans who came to watch the hometown team defeat the Expos again, this time by a score of 4-1. Outside, the "Vet," as it quickly came to be known, looked much like the other multipurpose structures of the era, including Busch Stadium in St. Louis, Riverfront Stadium in Cincinnati, and Three Rivers Stadium in Pittsburgh. Constructed of eighty-seven thousand cubic yards of concrete and nine thousand tons of steel, the massive structure cost $52 million and rose 135 feet above street level. Designed in the shape of an octorad, the stadium had a façade punctuated by a series of concrete ramps supported by steel cables.[91]

Inside, the Vet was a state-of-the-art facility. Twin hundred-by-twenty-five-foot animated scoreboards were situated above the green outfield wall. An $800,000 "home run spectacular," especially designed for the youngest fans, was located in center field. Whenever a Phillie hit a home run, "Philadelphia Phil," an animated character dressed in colonial garb, would swing his bat against a replica of the Liberty Bell. The loud sound of a clapper could be heard as a light flashed from the bell and another animated character, named "Philadelphia Phyllis," pulled a rope that set off a cannon. Green-colored "dancing waters" would then spurt up from behind the outfield fence as a Betsy Ross flag unfurled across the center-field wall. Together with the animated scoreboards and the "home run spectacular," the orange, red, brown, and yellow theater-type plastic seats gave the Vet a circus-like atmosphere designed to appeal to families with young children.

With a seating capacity of 56,371, the Vet was the largest of any stadium in the National League. Fans could sit in a field box seat for a reasonable $4.25 or climb to the "nosebleeds" for just fifty cents. There were sixty concession stands, with a picnic area for groups, as well as private, air-conditioned luxury boxes on the press level that were leased for five-year terms at an annual rental fee of $12,000 to $15,400. For those fans who wanted to dine before or during the game, the Vet offered a stadium club with a two-hundred-foot-long bar and seats for four hundred diners.[92]

The field surface was 146,000 square feet covered with green AstroTurf, with the exception of the base cutouts and the brown, rubberized warning track. Unlike the idiosyncratic dimensions of Connie Mack Stadium, the Vet's measurements were more symmetrical; it was 330 feet from home plate to both the left- and right-field fences and 408 to straightaway center field. Just as noteworthy were the new "Fillies." These were shapely young women dressed in white sleeveless blouses, high white boots, and fire-engine red miniskirts. They would chase foul balls along the warning track, direct fans to their seats and, at the lower levels, serve food and beverages.[93]

Veterans Stadium was much more than a ballpark; it was a striking new showplace designed to attract thousands of new fans. To fill the seats, Bob Carpenter hired Bill Giles as vice president of marketing operations. Giles was especially adept at luring young families with children by arranging creative pregame ceremonies, special events, and promotional giveaways.[94] But the attraction of the new stadium and all the showmanship would only last so long, and Carpenter knew it. His young group of talented prospects would have to deliver at the Major League level if the Phillies were to keep their turnstiles moving. They would also need a proven star and veteran leadership to propel them out of the second division. Steve Carlton would answer both of those desperate needs.

5

Reunited

When Steve Carlton reported to the Phillies' spring training camp at Clearwater, Florida, he considered himself a fastball pitcher. He had abandoned the slider, believing that his inability to throw the pitch consistently for strikes resulted in his nineteen-loss season two years earlier. On the other hand, in 1971, when Carlton relied on his fastball and curve, he recorded the first twenty-win season of his career.[1] If he could win twenty games for the Cardinals, he genuinely believed he could win twenty-five for the Phillies, no matter how anemic their offense, if he relied on the same two pitches.[2] But pitching coach Ray Rippelmeyer had other plans.

On Carlton's first day in camp Rippelmeyer asked the former Redbird to throw a few dozen pitches. After some warm-up tosses, the lanky southpaw proceeded to throw his fastball and curve. "Rip," as the coach was known among the hurlers, was impressed. But he wondered why Carlton wasn't throwing the biting slider that he'd seen back in 1966, when Rippelmeyer was the pitching coach for the Phillies' Triple-A club at San Diego and Carlton was dispatching hitters with ease for the Cardinals' Tulsa farm club.

"The Cards didn't want me to throw that pitch because I'd end up losing my curve ball," Steve explained to the coach.

"I've heard that theory before and I disagree with it," replied Rippelmeyer. "The only reason a pitcher loses his curve when he starts throwing a slider is because the slider becomes an easier pitch to throw for a strike and he stops throwing the curve. Look, I'd like to see that slider of yours."

Carlton threw a series of sliders, alternating it with his fastball. His arm slot remained the same, making the two pitches almost indistinguishable, that is, until the slider entered the strike zone, where it cut inside and dropped dramatically. After ten pitches, Rip said, "Young man, if you don't use that slider in the Majors, it would be a crime!"

"What are you talking about?" a confused Carlton asked, having already made up his mind to abandon the pitch.

"That slider of yours is the best breaking pitch I've seen in my two years as a Major League pitching coach. If you start throwing it again, I will make sure you don't lose your curveball."[3]

Rippelmeyer was true to his word. He was aware that other pitchers who had experienced success with the curveball abandoned the slider, believing that they would lose the feel for staying on top of the curve. Those pitchers were also told that the slider places undue pressure on the elbow and could cause serious injury. In fact, the two beliefs became so firmly entrenched in the Dodgers organization in the 1970s and 1980s that it refused to allow the team's pitchers to throw it.[4] But Rip believed that Carlton could use both pitches without risking injury.

"The curve and the slider are two completely different pitches in terms of wrist and fingertip action," Rippelmeyer explained in a 2019 interview. "When Steve threw the curve, he wrapped his wrist. But he threw the slider with the same grip as a fastball with his fingers on top and no wrist action. Because he was so strong and he did not break his wrist when he threw the slider, Steve was able to avoid any elbow problems.

"Using both the curve and the slider also gave Steve a change of pace," he added. "Steve's slider was sharp and quick, about 10 mph faster than his curve, which was big and slow. The curve essentially served as his change-up."[5]

To prevent Carlton from losing his curveball, Rippelmeyer throughout the '72 season made sure to call for that pitch when-

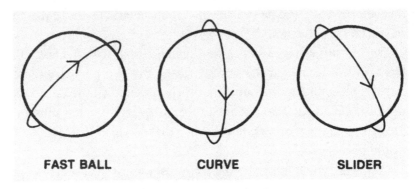

| FAST BALL | CURVE | SLIDER |

Spin rotation of Carlton's pitches. The arrow shows the direction of rotation.
(Illustration by the author)

ever the southpaw's arm slot began to drop during a game. The curve forced Carlton to elevate his arm slot in an over-the-top motion that enabled him to throw his fastball and slider effectively. Together with the fact that opposing batters could not distinguish between Carlton's fastball and slider, the use of the curve and slider would be the keys to Carlton's success in 1972.[6] But winning twenty-five games? That sounded unrealistic given the Phillies' inexperienced lineup.

Sports Illustrated predicted "another year of development" for manager Frank Lucchesi's Phillies and a "franchise trying to alter its losing image." There were some bright spots, though. The outfield was young and promising. Center fielder Willie Montanez, age twenty-four, was runner-up for Rookie of the Year voting in 1971, when he hit 30 homers and had 99 RBIs. Twenty-one-year-old outfielders Mike Anderson and Greg Luzinski were promoted from the Triple-A team in Eugene, Oregon, where each hit 36 home runs. Although veteran Roger Freed was a huge disappointment (6 HRS, 37 RBIs) in 1971, he did hit .346 in the month of September. The infield also showed potential. Larry Bowa, age twenty-six, had emerged as the best defensive shortstop in the National League over the previous two seasons, with a .987 fielding percentage. Third basemen Don Money, age twenty-five, and John Vukovich, age twenty-four, provided excellent defense at the hot corner. Tommy Hutton, recently acquired from the Dodgers, was an outstanding defensive first baseman. If veteran slugger Deron Johnson (34 HRS, 95 RBIs) faltered, the twenty-six-year-old Californian was ready to step in. The second base platoon of Denny Doyle and Terry Harmon provided steady defense up the middle. Catcher Tim McCarver, age thirty, provided veteran leadership and hit .278 in 1971, three points above his lifetime batting average.[7]

"We were optimistic going into the '72 season because we had a core of young players who were gaining experience," recalled Bowa in a 2020 interview. "The fans knew us even before we got to the big leagues because most of us played nearby at [Double-A] Reading [Pennsylvania]. In the Minors we won every year, so there was a reason to expect we'd do the same when we got to the Majors."[8]

The big question mark was the pitching. Carlton was the ace, but after that the starting rotation was questionable. Southpaw Woodie Fryman had averaged ten victories a season since arriving from the Pittsburgh Pirates in 1968. Chris Short, also a left-hander, won twenty games for the Phillies in 1966 and another nineteen in 1968, but since then he had been hampered with back problems and averaged five wins a season over the previous three years. Besides, if Fryman and Short joined Carlton in the four-man rotation, the Phils would be top-heavy with left handers.

Lucchesi was banking on young right-handers Wayne Twitchell, Billy Champion, and Lowell Palmer. Barry Lersch, another righty, had been used as a spot starter during the 1971 campaign, but his eleven-game losing streak eliminated him from consideration. Of the other right-handed prospects, only Champion had pitched well enough during spring training to be considered for a starting role. Thus, Lersch, Twitchell, and Palmer would begin the regular season in the bullpen with veteran relievers Joe Hoerner, Darrell Brandon, Billy Wilson, and Ken Reynolds and rookie Mac Scarce. Dick Selma, another veteran righty, had been a starter with the Chicago Cubs and New York Mets, but Lucchesi had used him strictly as a reliever the previous two years. With such a dearth of experienced pitching, though, the Phillies' skipper slotted Selma for a starting role. Thus, the Phillies opened the '72 season with a four-man rotation of Carlton, Fryman, Selma, and Champion.[9]

Carlton, being the most experienced—and successful—starter,

became an unwitting role model. The youngsters on the pitching staff were immediately impressed by the professionalism with which he conducted himself, as well as his obvious talent. On the mound he was an intense competitor with tunnel-vision focus. When he wasn't pitching, Carlton did his running in the early morning and without complaint. When asked for advice, he accommodated his younger teammates, who were also awed by his appearance. Standing six feet, four inches and weighing 210 pounds, twenty-seven-year-old Carlton was a striking physical specimen.[10] His matinee-idol looks were accentuated by wavy, dark-brown hair, fashionably long sideburns, and deep hazel eyes. Both in appearance and conduct, Carlton was a proud man who quickly assumed a leadership role on the team. His younger teammates readily deferred to him, as did some of the veteran hurlers. When Phillies publicity director Larry Shenk approached Darrell "Bucky" Brandon and asked if he would give up his uniform number (32) because Carlton would "like to wear the same number he wore in St. Louis," the thirty-one-year-old reliever replied, "Well, he won twenty games. He can have it."[11]

Carlton realized that the Phillies were "young" and would "not compete for a couple years," but he did believe that the starting rotation was "just a veteran pitcher away" from being successful. He was also unconcerned that the Phillies offense had not given their pitchers much run support the previous year. "The Cardinals never had a history of scoring runs either," he insisted. "I was over there in lean years. If we had scored more runs, I would have had a better season [in] 1969 when I won 17 games. That year my ERA was 2.17, second best in the league, but I should have won 20 or more games.

"Besides," he added, "we have guys like [Deron] Johnson, [Greg] Luzinski and [Willie] Montanez who are going to hit 30 home runs, possibly more. We have some good ballplayers over here. I can see the nucleus of a pretty good club. We will score runs and it's up to me to keep the game close, even if I have to pitch a shutout. And if we do win, well, I'm going to get some of the credit. I get the chance to be a leader over here."[12]

Carlton had reason to be optimistic. In St. Louis he had been overshadowed by Bob Gibson. He did not have the opportunity to pitch every fourth day because manager Red Schoendienst was a firm believer in the five-man rotation and the cycle began with his ace, Gibson, who needed the extra day of rest.[13] The Phillies' four-man rotation would give Steve more starts and thus more opportunities to win. Carlton was also excited to be reunited with his former batterymate, Tim McCarver.

"Timmy knows the hitters better than any other catcher in the league," said Steve. "We worked together well when he was in St. Louis." Carlton admitted that he had had some difficulties throwing to the Cardinals' young backstop Ted Simmons the previous two seasons because he "didn't have the experience Timmy has." According to Steve, "You know, sometimes a pitcher gets lazy and stops thinking." Carlton explained: "He calls a pitch in a situation where he shouldn't be throwing that pitch. In St. Louis there was more responsibility on the pitcher to make sure that the sequence of pitches was correct. Timmy won't let that happen. He knows the hitters too well."[14]

McCarver was just as enthusiastic about the reunion. "That spring Lefty threw a new fastball," he recalled. "There was vengeance in that fastball. He had something to prove. We both did. Honestly, that spring Steve threw his fastball harder than I have ever caught it before."[15]

The Phillies opened the 1972 season on a cold Saturday afternoon, April 15, at Chicago's Wrigley Field. They sent their new ace to the mound, while Cubs ace Ferguson Jenkins took the mound for Chicago. The two starters were cut from the same mold. They were so fiercely competitive that neither would give an inch. Predictably, the game was a pitcher's duel through eight innings. The Cubs scored a run in the bottom of the third, but the Phillies tied the game on a solo homer by Luzinski in the next inning. In the seventh the Phils added another run to make the score 2–1. But Chicago answered with another run in the eighth. Carlton, armed with a vicious fastball, a deceptive curve, and a biting slider, allowed just six base runners in those eight frames, surrendering two earned runs on four hits before leaving the game in the hands of the bullpen.[16]

"Carlton was tough," recalled Jenkins years later, after both pitchers had been inducted into the Hall of Fame. "That game was the first of many when we faced each other. I think the only other pitcher I faced more was Bob Gibson, and I beat him quite a bit. With Carlton it was different. I beat him and he'd come right back and beat me the next time we faced each other."[17]

With two outs in the top of the ninth and the score deadlocked, 2–2, Lucchesi sent outfielder Ron Stone to the plate to pinch-hit for Carlton. Stone stroked a base hit to right. Bowa followed with another base hit, putting Phillies runners on first and second. The Cubs brought in left-hander Steve Hamilton to face McCarver, who hit a high fly ball to deep right field. José Cardenal got a late jump on the ball and misjudged it, allowing two runs to score and giving the Phillies a 4–2 lead.[18]

Lucchesi sent reliever Joe Hoerner in to pitch a scoreless ninth and secure the victory for his old Cardinals teammate. After the game Hoerner joked, "Carlton's not that good. He's just lucky. He just pitches on days the other team doesn't score."[19]

Carlton was even better four days later when he faced his former team, the St. Louis Cardinals, at Veterans Stadium. It was a gorgeous night for baseball. The temperature was in the upper seventies, unseasonably warm for April. But the competition between Carlton and his former mentor, Bob Gibson, was much hotter. The game was scoreless until the bottom of the sixth, when Deron Johnson's RBI single drove in Willie Montanez, who had tripled. It was the only earned run Gibson surrendered on 11 hits over eight innings of work.[20] Carlton was even better, striking out 5 while surrendering just 3 hits.

Since both starters were quick workers, the game was played in just over ninety minutes. "It was unbelievable," said Phillies third baseman Don Money. "That game began around 7:30 p.m. and it was over just after 9:00 p.m. Neither of those guys wasted any time on the mound. There were very few deep counts. It's one of the reasons we loved playing behind Steve. He was a quick worker, and he threw strikes. When you have a pitcher like that, the fielders are on their toes."[21]

After the game Ray Kelly of the *Philadelphia Bulletin* asked Carlton if he felt any additional incentive to beat his old team. "The incentive is to win," replied the Phillies' ace. "Pitching against Bob Gibson is all I need to get the juices flowing. He is such a competitor."

"But don't you feel any vindication?" asked Kelly in the follow-up.

"Forget about the Cardinal thing, okay?" Carlton snapped. "[Cards owner] Gussie Busch is a gentleman. I'm kind of sorry that he took some of the contract negotiations personally. It was nothing personal.

"Tonight," he added, "it was just me against the Cardinals for the first time, and I gave them my best shot."[22]

While Carlton sounded diplomatic, he must have felt some satisfaction in defeating his former team because of Busch's shabby treatment of him. But outfielder Greg Luzinski, who played behind Carlton for nine seasons, insisted that that first victory over the Cardinals "didn't mean anything more to Steve than defeating anybody else.

"Sure, he and Gibson were teammates in St. Louis and Gibson was the ace when he was there," said Luzinski. "But I really don't think that stuff bothered Steve. He was just a fierce competitor who was able to block out all the other things that didn't involve the game itself."[23]

The Phillies kicked off their first West Coast road trip on April 25. Carlton faced Juan Marichal and the National League West champions, the San Francisco Giants, at Candlestick Park. "It was freezing that night," said McCarver. "Worst playing conditions imaginable. But it didn't bother Steve. Nothing bothered him."[24]

Impervious to the elements, Carlton surrendered a base hit to lead-off hitter Chris Speier and then shut down a Giants lineup that included sluggers Bobby Bonds, Willie McCovey, and Dave Kingman. Alternating between his fastball, curve, and slider, the Phillies' ace struck out 14 hitters, tying a club record, in the 3–0, single-hit victory. More impressive, Carlton threw just 103 pitches in the hour and forty-seven minutes it took him to dispatch the Giants for his second consecutive shutout.[25] Both of those statistics were exceptional, considering the average pitch count was 120 deliveries and most games lasted at least two hours.

"My slider's a great pitch," Carlton mused after the game. "My rhythm was excellent, and from the standpoint of quality and location, it's the finest game I've ever pitched."[26] McCarver agreed, insisting that his batterymate had such "exceptional control" of the pitch that he called for the slider on the "inside edge of the plate to righthanded hitters," which he usually didn't do. "That slider was unhittable tonight," he boasted. "Sometimes it came in on the hitter, other times it came down and in. Either way, no one could touch it."[27]

Pitching coach Ray Rippelmeyer was just as effusive in his praise. "Steve can get any hitter in the world out with his fastball," he gushed. "At his age, he still has to think of himself as a fastball pitcher. But that slider was great tonight. His fastball, curve and slider are all A+. It's the first time I've ever rated a pitcher excellent on all three."[28] In fact, of the twenty times Carlton used his slider in the game, he threw seventeen for strikes.[29] He used the pitch whenever he got behind in the count or needed a strikeout, though he didn't throw the pitch nearly as often as he would in later years.

Although Carlton lost his fourth start, 4–0, against the San Diego Padres, the Phillies ended the month of April with a doubleheader sweep of the Padres thanks to Billy Champion and Barry Lersch, who had recently replaced Dick Selma in the rotation.[30] With a record of 9-5, the Phils were tied for second with the New York Mets and just a half game behind the division-leading Montreal Expos. Surprisingly, the fast start was due to the team's starting pitchers, who boasted remarkably low earned run averages: Carlton (1.59), Fryman (0.82), Lersch (1.20), and Champion (2.57). The starters allowed an average of just 2.9 runs per game, while the Phillies' offense was producing an average of 3.7 runs per game to support them.[31]

General manager John Quinn realized that those impressive performances—with the exception of Carlton's—were an anomaly. Even before the season began, Quinn was trying to deal for more experienced starters. At the top of his wish list was Juan Marichal, the thirty-four-year-old Giants hurler, and Clay Kirby, who was just twenty-four but had won fifteen games the previous season and looked like a solid starter for years to come. But Quinn had nothing more to offer than cash, and both teams turned him down.[32]

For better—but mostly worse—the Phils would have to rely on the pitching they already had.

On May 7 at the Vet, Carlton struck out 13 Giants en route to an 8–3 victory and improved his record to 5–1.[33] Then the Phillies went into a tailspin, losing twenty-two of their next twenty-five games. Not even Carlton could stop the bleeding. On May 13 the Phillies' ace surrendered just 2 earned runs and struck out 6 in seven innings of work but still lost to Claude Osteen and the Dodgers, 3–1. Carlton lost again on May 17 to the Cubs, 3–2. His third straight loss came four days later against Tom Seaver and the Mets, 4–3. He lost again to the Pirates, 6–4, on May 26. All four games were hard-luck defeats. The only blowout came on May 30—a 7–0 whitewashing by the New York Mets. It was Carlton's shortest outing of the season as he surrendered 6 earned runs on 8 hits and 3 walks in just five innings. The Mets' Rusty Staub, who hit Carlton extremely well over the course of his career, went 4-for-4 with 4 RBIs, and rookie Jon Matlack tossed a 3-hitter.[34]

When the dust settled, Carlton was 5–6 with a 5.89 ERA. Phillies fans began to question the trade again. Although Steve could have blamed the Phillies' poor offense, which scored only ten runs and stranded a total of forty-eight base runners in those five starts, he assumed complete responsibility for the defeats.[35] The Phils' ace attributed his slump to "losing rhythm," which prevented him from making his pitches. His mechanics were also off. "I had trouble staying on top of the ball," he explained, not realizing that he had inadvertently slid the ring finger of his left hand to the outside of the baseball, creating drag. By doing so, Carlton was throwing a "three-finger fastball" with very little movement.[36] Opposing hitters made him pay. Fortunately, Rippelmeyer identified the problem and corrected it.

Someone had to pay for the Phillies' prolonged losing streak, though. General manager John Quinn took the fall on June 3, when owner Bob Carpenter fired him. "My only regret," said Quinn in parting, "is that I haven't been able to produce a pennant-winner for two fine gentlemen—Bob Carpenter and his son, Ruly. I still think the organization has great potential, both here and in the farm system."[37]

The Carpenters promoted farm director Paul Owens to replace Quinn. Nicknamed "Pope" because of his uncanny resemblance to Pope Paul VI, Owens had paid his dues toiling in the Minor Leagues for more than two decades. Signed as a first baseman with the St. Louis Cardinals in 1951, Owens eventually became a player manager and later worked as a scout before being elevated to farm director. During his six years in that last position, Owens had signed and developed Larry Bowa, Greg Luzinski, and Denny Doyle. He also mentored Ruly Carpenter, preparing him to one day take over for his father.[38] Owens was a no-nonsense baseball lifer and a savvy judge of talent. He knew the art of deal making so well that in the future he would fleece other teams by exchanging the Phillies' lesser-valued players for another team's late-blooming prospects and/or seasoned veterans considered washed up by other teams. When he became general manager, Owens's greatest challenge was in evaluating the Major League club and determining which players were worth keeping and which needed to move on from the organization. Although he told the sportswriters that "no one was untouchable," Owens had no intention whatsoever of dealing his ace pitcher.[39]

In early June, Carlton went on perhaps the most remarkable run by a starter in modern history. He did not lose a game for nearly three months, winning fifteen consecutive decisions. During that span, Carlton had fourteen complete games and five shutouts with an ERA of 1.67. The streak began on June 7 against the Houston Astros at Veterans Stadium. Carlton faced Jerry Reuss in a pitcher's duel through the first five innings. But in the sixth the Phillies broke the scoreless deadlock when Luzinski's 2-run double knocked in Bowa and Money to give Carlton all the run support he needed. The lean lefty struck out 11 while scattering 5 hits and 3 walks in seven innings of work.[40] Four days later in Atlanta, Carlton defeated the Braves, 3–1, for his second straight victory.[41]

"Mentally, I was the best I've ever been that season," recalled Carlton in a 1993 interview on ESPN. "I don't ever recall throwing a pitch down the heart of the plate. The pitches were always on the corners and the balls were breaking outside of the strike zone.

"Timmy was leading the way," he added. "He had such a great ability to set up hitters. He was a bridge player and remembered sequences and batters and how we set them up and got them out in different situations. He was just phenomenal at it. When you have a catcher like that it's a real asset."[42]

Unbeknown to Carlton, McCarver would soon be traded. Owens had been involved in serious discussions with half a dozen clubs about a right-handed starting pitcher and/or a veteran power hitter. One trade rumor had Luzinski going to Houston for slugging outfielder Jimmy Wynn. Another rumor had Bowa being shipped to Pittsburgh for power hitter Bob Robertson. Owens was also interested in Pirates outfielder Gene Oliver and infielder Rennie Stennett. He had made inquiries about right-handers Don Sutton of the Dodgers, Larry Dierker of the Astros, and Carl Morton of the Expos.[43] But when the June 15 trading deadline passed, the only deals Owens had made were sending reliever Joe Hoerner and first base prospect Andre Thornton to the Atlanta Braves for right-handers Jim Nash and Gary Neibauer and swapping McCarver for utility catcher John Bateman of the Montreal Expos.[44]

The McCarver trade was surprising because the gregarious catcher had such great chemistry with Carlton. Although no one could have predicted that the Phillies' ace would be embarking on fifteen-game winning streak at the time of the trade, most general managers would be hesitant to interfere with such a successful battery. But McCarver insists that Lucchesi forced Owens's hand.

"The reason I was traded to Montreal in June of '72 was Frank Lucchesi, the manager," Tim said in a 2019 interview. "We didn't get along from the moment I arrived in Philadelphia. He was a phony. Lucchesi did not know baseball, and he knew that I knew it."[45]

Steve Bucci and Dave Brown have confirmed McCarver's belief. According to the two authors, in September 1971 Lucchesi was standing next to the batting cage before a game and talking with a team employee when he hinted that McCarver had to go. The Phils' manager was gushing with enthusiasm over recent call-ups Greg Luzinski and Mike Anderson as he watched them hit. "These guys are going to make us better," Lucchesi told the employee. "But we've still gotta make some changes around here, and the first place we have to make a change is right here," he added, pointing emphatically to the catcher's box behind home plate. The employee, who wished to remain anonymous, immediately understood the reference. "Lucchesi hated McCarver," he said. "Timmy thought he wasn't a good big-league manager. That he was a minor league guy. They hated each other."[46]

Lucchesi was jealous of McCarver's popularity, too. Tim had been the leader of a small clique of veteran players. His blithe manner and good-natured needling endeared him to them. Each night after the game McCarver would gather the vets at a table in the west end of the clubhouse and hold court. After discussing the game over a few beers, they might play a game or two of cards before calling it a night.[47] But McCarver's departure became a fait accompli in May, when the Phillies were struggling through a horrific ten-game losing streak. Lucchesi, irked by the veterans' playful banter after a loss, registered his disapproval by banning the customary two cases of beer on a charter flight from Montreal to Pittsburgh. When the team arrived at their hotel, McCarver buttonholed the Phils' skipper in the lobby and told him that the "players would like to be treated like adults" and that "cutting off the beer ration would prove nothing." Embarrassed that the catcher had raised the subject within earshot of the other players, Lucchesi, without responding, turned abruptly and headed for the elevator.[48]

When asked about the incident years later, the former Phillies manager insisted that "Tim and I had our differences, but I respected him and his catching ability." He went on to add that "the reason he was traded was because he wasn't hitting. We needed more offense from that position, and we thought we could get it from [John] Bateman."[49]

There is some truth to Lucchesi's assertion. At the time of the trade McCarver was hitting .237, but Bateman, who was hitting .241, certainly wasn't much better.[50] And McCarver was a better pitch caller and defensive catcher than Bateman, who had been a backup to John Boccabella in Montreal. "The people who have been saying the Phillies could get nothing for McCarver were right," wrote Bill Conlin of the *Philadelphia Daily News* in his June 15 column. "Last night," he continued, "they got nothing for McCarver when they traded him to Montreal for an overweight, 29-year-old plough horse named John Bateman."[51] Tim would make Conlin eat his words four years later when he returned to the Phillies to become Carlton's personal catcher, helping him to resurrect a floundering pitching career.

McCarver, one of the most respected veterans in the National League, wasn't even given the courtesy of being informed of the deal by the Phillies until late in the process. Baseball protocol requires that players involved in a trade be informed by their own club. That responsibility fell squarely on the shoulders of Paul Owens as general manager. Not only did Owens fail to inform Tim, but he handed the task to Lucchesi, who delivered the message *after* Montreal manager Gene Mauch broke the news to McCarver.

But Mauch, still stinging from his firing by the Phillies four years earlier, wanted to embarrass his old team. At 6:15 p.m., on Wednesday, June 14, shortly after the trade was made, he telephoned McCarver in the Phillies clubhouse and asked, "What would you think about playing third base for me?"

"What?!" exclaimed Tim in disbelief.

"If Mike Shannon [McCarver's former teammate with the Cardinals] can do it, you can," replied Mauch. "I'll get back to you," he added before hanging up. Thirty minutes later, just before the press was briefed, Lucchesi summoned McCarver to his office. "I guess you heard?" asked the manager, not even bothering to look up from his desk.

"Yeah, I did," answered Tim, stunned.

"Well, I just wanted to make it official," said Lucchesi. "We traded you to the Expos."

"For whom?" asked McCarver.

Lucchesi hesitated momentarily. "John Bateman," he said finally.

"And?"

"Well, there'll probably be another Minor Leaguer involved," Lucchesi lied. Both he and McCarver knew it was a one-for-one trade made simply to get Tim out of Philadelphia.

"If you didn't get any more for me than Bateman, you got fucked!" snapped McCarver before stomping out of the office.[52]

Years later Lucchesi insisted that the gaffe was an "innocent mistake" and that Mauch had "no right to call Tim." Mauch "should've followed protocol and waited for us to tell him," explained the former Phils manager. "It was bush league. Mauch was still sore at the Phillies for firing him a few years before. But that still doesn't excuse it."[53]

McCarver, on the other hand, maintained his professionalism. When asked by the press if his "poor relationship with Lucchesi" was the reason for the trade, Tim insisted that he had "always gotten along with Frank." Quickly changing subjects, he praised the fans. "I've been very happy in Philadelphia," he said. "I'll miss the fans a lot. The way they support this club when it's losing is exceptional. There's no telling what they'd do with a winner."[54]

But the trade still hurt. "Being traded was something I acclimated to, but it would have been easier to accept if the people being traded and their families were treated with respect," he admitted many years later. "Two things bothered me about that trade," Tim added. "One is that I never heard from Owens, and the other was that I had just put $1,000 down on an apartment in Philadelphia and had to uproot myself."[55]

Although McCarver denies it, his role as the Phillies' player representative might also have led to the trade. The Players Association, under the leadership of Marvin Miller, was becoming increasingly confrontational with the owners. The dispute over player pensions during spring training in 1972 was the most recent incident in an ongoing battle between the two sides. During the work stoppage, Phils owner Bob Carpenter met with McCarver on several occasions and told him that the relationship between the union and the owners had "always been successful before Miller became president." Carpenter also suggested that the union "push Miller aside and get back to doing business the old-fashioned way." When Tim reported the remark to the union chief, he told McCarver to end his meetings with Carpenter because they can "only do more harm than good."[56] The snub did not go unnoticed by the Phils' owner. Tim was one of the sixteen player representatives who were traded or released during or shortly after the 1972 season.[57]

McCarver's time in Montreal was brief, lasting just half a season. But for the first time in his Major League career Tim played other positions besides catcher. He appeared in seventy-seven games: forty-five behind the plate, fourteen as an outfielder, six as a third baseman, and fourteen as a pinch hitter. He also hit .251 with a .309 OBP and a .652 OPS—stats that are fairly impressive for a part-time player with twelve years of playing experience. Most of those seasons were spent behind the plate, where McCarver caught more than a hundred games a season, something that wears a man down, especially his back and legs. Yet Tim could still hit and, remarkably, run.[58]

Fortunately, the McCarver trade did not disrupt Carlton's impressive performance that season. Bateman quickly adapted to the left-hander's fast-working tempo. The new batterymates were so much in sync with each other that Carlton was able to sustain almost robotic perfection when he took the mound. On June 16 he pitched ten scoreless innings against Houston at the Astrodome, striking out 12 and allowing just 6 hits. Unfortunately, the Phillies' offense stranded thirteen base runners. Dick Selma, pitching in relief, lost the game in the eleventh on a solo home run by Jimmy Wynn. Carlton took the no decision in the 1–0 loss. It was the first of three extra-inning contests he pitched that season.[59] Steve recorded another no-decision against the Atlanta Braves on June 21, when he lasted only five innings, but the Phillies bullpen managed to pull out a 9–7 victory.[60] He returned to his winning ways four days later against the Expos at Montreal's Jarry Park.

It was a quiet game for the first three innings. In the fourth, Montreal starter Ernie McAnally plunked outfielder Joe Lis on the arm with a fastball. Carlton retaliated by beaning shortstop Tim Foli, the first batter he faced in the bottom of the frame. "Yes, I threw at him," Steve admitted after the game. "You have to retaliate in that situation, and I did. I'm not ashamed of it. But I didn't mean to hit him in the head. I was trying to get him in the ribs. The ball just got away from me."[61]

Expos manager Gene Mauch didn't waste any time. Bolting from the dugout, Mauch made a beeline to the mound, intending to deck the Phillies' ace. But by the time he arrived, both benches had emptied, setting off a full-scale brawl. "Mauch tried to blindside me," said Carlton. "I saw him at the last minute and grabbed him by the collar. I was about to punch him when five of our own guys jumped on top of him and got in my way."[62]

Those five teammates were Pete Koegel (6'6", 230 pounds), Jim Nash (6'5", 215), Roger Freed (6'1", 200), Don Money (6'1", 190), and Joe Lis (6'0", 180), a pretty formidable bunch. Needless to say, Mauch emerged from the pileup bloodied, limping, and complaining that the punch he tried to land had "missed that motherfucker, Carlton."[63]

"We knew we could count on Steve to retaliate if one of us got hit, and he knew we had his back if anyone charged the mound," said Don Money. "We might not have won many games, but we sure didn't lose many fights. With the size of our players, it was just plain dumb for another team to take us on."[64]

The game was decided in the next inning, when John Bateman, the newest member of the Phillies, hit a solo home run. That's all Carlton needed, as he scattered 4 hits and struck out 8 for his eighth victory of the season.

Carlton notched his ninth win of the season—and the fourth victory of his fifteen-game winning streak—on June 29, defeating the New York Mets, 9–4, at the Vet. The Mets held early leads of 1–0 and 3–1, but Steve overcame some control problems to limit New York to a single run after the fourth inning. Don Money and Bill Robinson, recently promoted from Triple-A Eugene to replace a slumping Mike Anderson, hit solo homers as the Phillies belted out seventeen hits to come from behind.

Although Carlton surrendered 4 earned runs on 7 hits, he struck out 13 in the 9–4 victory. He also threw 171 pitches. "I just couldn't find the plate until the fourth inning," he said, explaining why he threw so many pitches. "I went out there and tried to throw too hard. By the fifth I was tired and couldn't throw as hard. After that, I had better concentration. I felt great."[65]

"Steve had tremendous focus," recalled Larry Bowa in a 2020 interview. "That's why he was such a fast worker. When he got on the mound, he didn't fidget with his cap, or play with the resin bag. He looked down, got the sign, and threw the pitch." Carlton's focus was so intense, according to Bowa, that he "never allowed things that he couldn't control [to] affect his pitching.

"We had a real bad baseball team. We were young and he had no control over that. But every fourth day when Steve pitched he elevated everybody's play. We knew if we scored just one or two runs, we had a good chance to win. He told us that, too.

"Steve would walk into the clubhouse on days he pitched and say, 'Today is *win* day.' And you believed him. It didn't matter if we lost eight in a row before that. We really felt we could win when he took the mound. At the same time, you stayed away from him on days he pitched. He was in a zone. He didn't want to talk with anybody."[66]

Bowa quickly learned to respect Carlton's space, too. Once, when the Phillies' ace got into a jam, manager Frank Lucchesi motioned to the shortstop to go out to the mound to offer some encouragement. When Bowa got there, Carlton glared at him and snapped, "What do you want?!"

"I just came in because Frank wanted me to talk with you," replied the shortstop.

"Okay, you talked to me," Carlton rejoined. "Now get the hell out of here and don't ever come out to the mound again when I'm pitching!"[67]

Carlton also made it clear to Bowa that he didn't appreciate the shortstop's penchant for antagonizing teammates, whether he was scheduled to pitch that day or not. Bowa loved to agitate. Sometimes he did it as negative motivation, other times simply to heckle teammates. But he didn't mess with Carlton. "I made Bowa fear me," explained Steve. "I watched his act in the clubhouse, and I didn't feel like being pestered by him. One day I grabbed his face and said, 'Stay away from me and we'll be just fine.' It was done in jest, but he didn't know whether I was being serious or not. Still, he got the message."[68]

When in a 2020 interview Bowa learned of Carlton's ploy, he laughed. But he also admitted, "I was smart enough to know who I could mess with, and Lefty wasn't a guy to mess with.

"I knew about his intensity level," explained the shortstop. "He set that example in 1972. *Nobody* said a word to him on the day of a start, and definitely not while he was pitching. He was all business.

"Even between starts, I didn't mess with him," added Bowa. "He was just too strong. He'd give you that stare and you knew to stay away from him."[69]

On July 3 Carlton won his tenth game of the season, against the San Francisco Giants at the Vet. The Phillies managed just 5 hits but scored 4 runs in the first inning off Don Carrithers to give Carlton all he needed for the 4–2, complete-game victory. The win halted a three-game losing streak that dropped the Phils' record to 24-45.[70] The tall left-hander extended his win streak to six games four days later in the first game of a doubleheader against Mike Corkins of the San Diego Padres. Scattering 9 hits, Steve surrendered just 2 runs. But those runs came on solo homers in the fourth and fifth to put the Phillies in a 2–0 deficit. The Fightins went ahead in the sixth, 3–2. The big blow was a 2-run single coming off the bat of John Bateman. The Phillies added an insurance run in the eighth, and Carlton cruised to his eleventh victory of the season. He also struck out 8 Padres hitters to raise his season total to 174, which was tops in the Major Leagues.[71] Carlton's victory was the only bright spot in a four-game series against San Diego. When the Phillies dropped three of the four games against the Padres, who were the cellar dwellers of the National League West, Owens felt he had to take matters into his own hands.

With the Phillies buried at the bottom of the National League East, Owens fired Lucchesi on July 10 and named himself the team's new manager.[72] "It's the same old story," said a teary-eyed Lucchesi at the press conference announcing his dismissal. "You can't fire the troops, so you have to fire the general."[73] Years later Lucchesi admitted that he "still didn't know why they made the change." He had always been under the impression that the team was in a rebuilding process, and he knew his young players—both in the farm system and on the parent club—well enough to supervise the process. "I wasn't mad, just hurt because I loved the Phillies," he said. "I thought I was going to be there quite a few years."[74]

Lucchesi had been popular with the Philadelphia press, who roundly criticized his firing and questioned Owens's motives for naming himself as the replacement. Frank Dolson, a veteran sportswriter for the *Philadelphia Inquirer*, called the firing "cruel, unhuman," and "not what a good guy like Lucchesi deserved." In Dolan's opinion, "what he deserved was a better team." Instead, Owens "repeatedly lied to him, telling the manager his job was not in jeopardy."[75]

Dolson was right about one thing—Lucchesi was a "good guy." He loved the Phillies. He'd paid his dues in the Minor Leagues. He had an abundance of patience with his young players. He was active in the community and hugely popular with the city's Italian American fans.[76] But to paraphrase Leo Durocher's aphorism that "nice guys finish last," the Phillies were heading for a second straight season as cellar dwellers when Lucchesi was let go. He had to be fired if the club was going to move forward. Owens knew it. He would later admit that by "going into the dugout," he "found out who we could build around and who needed to go."[77] And the players knew it too.[78]

6

Drinking Coffee with a Fork

Few baseball executives have the confidence to assume the responsibilities of field manager. The day-to-day demands of the position are draining and can easily distract from the broader administrative duties that must be addressed in the front office. But if members of the press believed that Paul Owens's decision to name himself manager was based purely on ego, they were wrong.

No one else in the Phillies organization at that time commanded as much respect among the players as Owens did. He had signed and developed most if not all the young talent and would not hesitate to make them accountable. "Not everyone can make the transition from the front office to field manager," said Ruly Carpenter, who would soon take over as the team president. "But Paul was able to do that because the players had a tremendous amount of respect for him. They knew he [had] played professionally and, of course, he had signed many of them. Nor did we expect that things would go smoothly. Paul didn't have a problem chewing their asses out when they didn't perform. He wasn't afraid of anybody. We also knew that as field manager, he would find out which guys really wanted to play and which ones didn't. You can only do that by being with the team on a daily basis."[1]

Owens said as much on the day he announced his dual responsibilities. "I took over with the idea of learning our personnel and the personnel around the league," he explained, "and I thought I could do that better as manager than I could from the general manager's office."[2]

Indeed, Owens was determined to find out who could play. Frank Lucchesi had operated in the past with a set lineup that only changed when a regular got hurt or traded. An examination of the box scores for the first half of the season reveals a strong consistency among the starting field players and their positions in the batting order:

Larry Bowa, shortstop
Tim McCarver, catcher
Willie Montanez, center field
Greg Luzinski, left field
Deron Johnson, first base
Don Money, third base
Mike Anderson, right field
Denny Doyle, second base[3]

But after Owens became the field manager, he platooned players and called up prospects from the farm system to see what they could do. For example, Denny Doyle and Terry Harmon platooned at second base. Tommy Hutton, Deron Johnson, and on a few occasions Greg Luzinski alternated at first base. In right field Owens rotated Roger Freed, Oscar Gamble, Bill Robinson, Joe Lis, and occasionally Tommy Hutton. With the exception of Carlton, pitchers alternated between starting and relief roles. In September, Owens called up several prospects, including catcher Bob Boone, infielders Craig Robinson and Mike Schmidt, and pitcher Dave Downs. The batting order also changed depending on which hitters were doing the best at any given time.[4] The shuffling was necessary in order to determine which players were worth keeping for the future.

Meanwhile, Carlton continued his masterful season. For three-day stretches the Phillies were an awful team. But on the fourth day, when their ace left-hander took the mound, they became almost unbeatable. Even when he didn't win, Carlton's competitiveness taught opponents that the Phillies should not be taken lightly. On July 15, for example, Steve lasted only five innings against the San

Francisco Giants at Candlestick Park, surrendering 4 earned runs on 5 hits. But before he exited the contest, he taught the Giants to respect the last-place Phillies. The lesson came in the bottom of the first inning, when Bobby Bonds led off with a solo home run. Garry Maddox, the on-deck hitter, greeted Bonds at the plate, where the two teammates slapped hands, gripped thumbs, touched elbows, and played patty-cake. Angered by the showboating, Carlton threw the first pitch at Maddox's head when he stepped to the plate. "I didn't think Maddox was going down on the first pitch," said Owens. "But I knew he was going down."[5]

After the game Bonds insisted that he was "not trying to show Carlton up." Instead, "we just do that routine because the fans like it," he explained. "We did the same thing after my homer last night and nobody threw at us."[6]

But Carlton was watching from the bench the night before, and it irked him then, too. He considered the routine disrespectful, not only to the Phillies but to the game itself. He swore that he'd seek retribution if Bonds and Maddox did it when he was on the mound.

"If I want to watch Flip Wilson," said Carlton, referring to a popular Black comedian of that era, "I'll turn on the TV. They showed me up, so Maddox had to go down. I should have decked Bonds, too. Nothing personal. I just don't like being shown up."[7]

The Phillies got Carlton off the hook by scoring a season-high eleven runs in the top of the seventh inning to win, 11–4, and preserve their ace's consecutive-game winning streak.

The next week Danny Murtaugh, manager of the defending world champion Pittsburgh Pirates, named Carlton to the National League's All-Star squad. It was the fourth time he had been selected for the All-Star Game, and this time he was the Phillies' lone representative. His numbers certainly warranted the selection, too. At the halfway point in the season, Carlton boasted a win-loss record of 12-6 with a 2.65 ERA, having allowed just 52 earned runs in 176 innings of work. He also led the Majors with 187 strikeouts.[8] He would pitch only one hitless inning in the National League's 4–3 victory over the Americans during the Midsummer Classic, played in Atlanta on July 25. By that time Carlton had already chalked up another two victories, to increase his total to fourteen and extend his winning streak to nine straight. The first was a 3–2 win over the Padres in which he surrendered 7 hits and 4 walks but struck out 8.[9] The second victory came against Tommy John and the Dodgers, a 2–0 shutout in which Carlton won his own game with a 2-run triple in the seventh.[10]

On July 28 Carlton posted his fifteenth win of the season, against Milt Pappas and the Chicago Cubs at Veterans Stadium. The 2–0 gem also extended his streak of scoreless innings to twenty-seven straight. The Phillies gave their ace all the run support he needed in the bottom of the fourth, when Willie Montanez hit a two-run homer. In winning his tenth straight game, Carlton eclipsed the Phillies' club record of nine consecutive victories shared by Robin Roberts (who achieved the feat in 1952), Ken Heintzelman (1948), and Grover Alexander (1915).[11]

"I remember that fifteen-game win streak," said pitching coach Ray Rippelmeyer in 2019. "Steve was unhittable in July. In fact, I could have told you that he was going to win those games because I watched him loosen up. His fastball had pop, his curve was breaking, and his slider had that bite. When I saw that all three pitches were working, I just knew he was going to have a great game. And I saw the same thing before every one of those fifteen wins."[12]

Carlton continued his remarkable winning streak through most of August. On the first of the month he defeated Jerry Koosman and the Mets, 4–1, in the nightcap of a doubleheader to give the Phillies a split.[13] Four days later he beat the Cardinals in St. Louis, 5–0, to notch his twelfth straight victory and his seventeenth win of the season. In so doing, Steve tied Curt Simmons's club record for shutouts by a left-hander in a single season with six. It was also the Phillies' fifth straight victory, the longest winning streak of the season.[14] As usual, Carlton did things his way. In the fourth inning, with Redbirds runners at the corners and two outs, Willie McGee stepped to the plate. Owens trotted out to the mound and told his ace not to throw any curveballs to McGee, who feasted on breaking balls. After Owens returned to the dugout, Carlton proceeded to throw the Cardinals batter three straight curveballs, striking him out.[15]

Mechanics of Carlton's slider. (1) By gripping the seam, Carlton was able to pull hard on the ball when he released it. (2) Lefty threw all his pitches over the top. This allowed him to disguise his slider, which he threw out of the same arm slot as his fastball. (3) When Carlton threw his slider, he kept the back of his hand on top of the ball—never under the ball, which causes stress and possible elbow injury. Thus, the ball approached the plate with the same velocity as his fastball but broke suddenly in almost a straight plane. The sudden break made his slider extremely difficult to hit.

(Illustration by Dick Perez)

Apparently, Owens didn't care about the transgression. When asked after the game how much he was willing to pay to re-sign Carlton, the Phils' manager told Bruce Keidan of the *Philadelphia Inquirer*, "Steve can have anything he wants within reason. He will probably be the first $100,000 ballplayer in club history and he's worth every cent of it."[16] Indeed, Carlton *was* worth "every cent," if you asked Willie Stargell, the Pittsburgh Pirates' future Hall of Famer.

On August 9, after the Phillies' ace had dispatched the defending world champions at Pittsburgh's Three Rivers Stadium, 2–0, a frustrated Stargell told the press that facing Carlton was like "trying to hit [Sandy] Koufax, which is like drinking coffee with a fork."[17] When Steve learned of Stargell's remark, he humbly admitted, "If I had to choose between Koufax and myself to start one game, it would be Koufax. He had better stuff."[18] Maybe so, but Carlton's "stuff" was just as overpowering as Koufax's when he pitched for the Dodgers in the mid-1960s.

In recording his eighteenth win of the season—and fourth shutout in five games—Steve used a wicked fastball, sharp curve, and devastating slider to strike out twelve Pirates hitters, five of whom were hitting .300 or better. Just as impressive, he surrendered just three hits to a Pirates team that had been batting .278 entering the game, thus extending his streak of consecutive scoreless innings to fifty-four. It was also Carlton's thirteenth straight victory in a winning streak that had captivated Philadelphia.[19] When Bruce Keidan of the *Philadelphia Inquirer* asked after the game about his most recent masterpiece, Steve remarked that he was simply "playing an elevated game of catch" with his batterymate, John Bateman. "My vision was limited to the catcher," he explained. "A man on base is merely a variable. I see the batter only. I don't care if he's Willie Stargell or Rennie Stennett up there. Either can hurt you. But neither can if I'm doing my job."[20]

Carlton extended his winning streak to fourteen games on a muggy Sunday afternoon, August 13, against the Montreal Expos at the Vet. Facing Ernie McAnally in the first game of a twin bill, Steve held Montreal hitless until the top of the fourth, when Bob Bailey homered. "It was a good fastball," Carlton said of the pitch, "but it was down and over the plate and that's where Bailey loves it." The homer would prove to be the Expos' only run of the game as Carlton went on to hurl a three-hit gem, striking out eight to break Chris Short's 1965 record for most strikeouts by a Phillies left-hander in a single season. The Phillies scored both of their runs in the bottom of the first, when Willie Montanez drove in Denny Doyle with a double. Luzinski followed with a run-scoring single to give Carlton all the offense he needed. Still, after the game Steve insisted that he "didn't have good stuff" and that he was "lucky to get away" with the victory.[21]

Despite his impressive pitching performance that afternoon, Carlton was overshadowed by one of marketing wiz Bill Giles's most death-defying promotions. Intent on drawing more families to the Vet, Giles had hired Karl Wallenda, the patriarch of a world-famous family of high-wire performers, to walk a two-inch-wide steel cable, 640 feet long, from foul pole to foul pole across the top of the Vet. Wallenda performed the stunt at a height of 140 feet and without a safety net. Midway across the stadium, the sixty-seven-year-old entertainer stopped and did a headstand while hovering over second base. The feat, which had never been attempted before in a Major League stadium, took seventeen minutes and was greeted with a boisterous standing ovation by the more than thirty thousand fans on hand.[22]

The Phillies paid Wallenda $3,000 for the performance and had to take out an insurance policy from Lloyd's of London. "It was a little nerve-wracking for me," admitted Giles. "I was worried that he might fall. As I watched him walk across the high-wire, I became more confident, figuring he had done this plenty of times before. But when he came down from the roof and asked for six martinis, I knew he was scared."[23]

Wallenda admitted it was the toughest walk he had ever attempted. "I had a bad feeling during the walk," he told Kathy Begley of the *Philadelphia Inquirer* as he nursed one of the martinis. "It was the loosest rope I ever walked on," he added, referring to the four-foot play in the wire.[24] The only damper that afternoon came in the second game of the doubleheader, which the Phillies dropped, 8–3.[25]

Carlton's twentieth victory came on August 17 against Cincinnati's Big Red Machine at the Vet. The 9–4 complete-game win was Steve's first victory against the Reds since 1967, when he pitched for the Cardinals. Deron Johnson spotted Carlton an early lead with a two-run homer in the bottom of the first. But the Reds answered with three runs in the top of the third, when Bill Plummer's double scored Dave Concepción. Pete Rose followed with a single, and Joe Morgan hit a two-run double for a 3–2 Cincinnati lead. The Phillies tied the game in the bottom of the fifth on Don Money's sacrifice fly and went ahead, 5–3, when Willie Montanez followed with a two-run homer. The Phils added two runs in the six and two more in the seventh to pad the lead and give their ace his fifteenth straight victory.

Carlton was not overpowering, but he was good enough to prevail, holding the Reds to a single run in the final six frames. "I had a tendency to go with the breaking ball, and I was getting hurt by it," he admitted after the game. "I didn't have great location, either. So after the third I told [catcher John] Bateman, 'Let's stay with the fastball the rest of the way.'"[26]

The fans refused to leave the stadium until Carlton had answered their curtain call. As the lean lefty emerged from the dugout to tip his hat, the electronic PhanaVision scoreboard in right-center field lit up with the words "Super Steve." It would become Carlton's moniker until the mid-1970s, when Tim McCarver returned to the Phillies and started referring to his batterymate as "Lefty."

"I was excited," said Steve of his most recent win. "We were all excited. It was a combination of things—all the people who came out to support me, the twentieth win, the streak, and the Reds." That victory made Carlton the Phillies' first twenty-game winner since Chris Short went 20-10 in 1966. When asked about the milestone, Carlton said that his twentieth victory together with his fifteen-game winning streak were "the greatest things that ever happened to me in baseball" and that "there's been nothing even close."[27]

Super Steve's winning streak ended on August 21 against the Atlanta Braves at the Vet. It was a heartbreaker, too. With the score tied, 1–1, in the top of the eleventh, Carlton retired Braves lead-off hitter Félix Millán on a pop-up. He struck out Hank Aaron looking for the second out, and then his luck ran out. Dusty Baker stepped to the plate and stroked a double to center. Carlton decided to intentionally walk catcher Earl Williams to get to utility outfielder Mike Lum, who had struck out in the ninth. The move backfired. Lum reached for a slider low and away in the strike zone and flared a broken-bat single over Larry Bowa's head and into center field to drive in Baker. Phil Niekro retired the Phillies in order in the bottom of the eleventh to give the Braves a 2–1 victory and hand Carlton his first loss since May 30.

"It was a pitcher's pitch," explained manager Paul Owens to the media after the game. "Lum did what a good lefthanded hitter has to do to stay alive up there. He got the bat on the ball and found a hole."

Catcher John Bateman was more blunt in his assessment: "Lum hit the fuckin' ball right on the end of the fuckin' bat, and we got fucked!"

Carlton, who recorded ten strikeouts, took the loss in stride, though. "I wish I could have won the game for a lot of reasons," he told Bill Conlin of the *Philadelphia Daily News*. "For the fans, the record books, the streak. It's the kind of game you want back. I didn't make many bad pitches. [The streak] was fun while it lasted, though. I guess I'll have to start another one, right?"[28]

During the winning streak, Carlton started nineteen games and completed fifteen of them with only four no-decisions. He recorded fifteen wins, including five shutouts, posted a WHIP (walks and hits per inning pitched) of 0.932, and struck out 8.2 batters per nine innings.[29] It was the kind of performance Phillies fans would come to expect of their ace in the future, as unrealistic as those expectations might have been.

Four days later Carlton returned to his winning ways, outdueling Jim McGlothlin of the Reds at Cincinnati's Riverfront Stadium, 4–3. The Phillies gave their ace an early lead in the third when Bowa singled, advanced on a fielder's choice, and scored on an RBI base hit by Greg Luzinski. The score remained 1–0 until the sixth. Luzinski led off with a walk. Don Money followed with a bunt and reached base safely when Reds pitcher Jim McGlothlin made an errant throw to first. A fielder's choice advanced Luzinski to third and Money to second. With first base open, McGlothlin intentionally walked Bateman before Carlton singled, driving in Luzinski. Denny Doyle followed with a sacrifice fly, increasing the Phillies' lead to 3–0.

Cincinnati narrowed the Fightins' lead to one run in the bottom of the eighth, but the Phillies added an insurance run to make it 4–2 in the top of the ninth. Carlton started the bottom of the frame but surrendered another run on a single by Dave Concepción, a double by Bill Plummer, and a pinch-hit single by Julián Javier. Pitching coach Ray Rippelmeyer called time and ambled to the mound along with catcher John Bateman.

"Are you tired?" Rippelmeyer asked Carlton.

"What the fuck do you think?!" snapped an incredulous Bateman. "It's over 100 degrees out here. He can't breathe and you're asking him if he's tired?!"[30]

Owens went to his bullpen and brought in Mac Scarce. With runners on first and third and nobody out, Scarce would have to face the top of the Cincinnati order, beginning with the always dangerous Pete Rose. Scarce fell behind Rose, three balls and one strike, before throwing him a slider. Rose, expecting a fastball, hit a slow roller to second. Doyle fielded the ball and threw it home to nail the slow-footed Plummer, who was out by six yards. Now there were runners on first and second and one out, with Joe Morgan at the plate. Scarce uncorked a wild pitch, and the runners advanced with the winning tally at second. Somehow the young Phillies hurler managed to keep his composure and fanned Morgan as well as Bobby Tolan to preserve the 4–3 win for Carlton.[31]

Steve lost his final start of August, 5–3, to Jerry Reuss and the Houston Astros.[32] But he rebounded in early September to dispatch the Atlanta Braves with an 8–0 whitewashing for his twenty-second victory of the season.[33] Super Steve notched win number twenty-three four days later on September 7. The 2–1 victory marked his one hundredth career win and came against the St. Louis Cardinals in an ironic twist of fate. Carlton struck out 9 batters in the contest, to increase his season total to 272. By this point in the season, the Phillies' ace was setting new club records—and personal bests—with nearly every start. This particular victory set two new Phillies records: (1) most wins in a single season by a left-hander, breaking Eppa Rixey's mark of twenty-two wins set in 1916; and (2) most strikeouts in a single season by a Phillies pitcher, breaking Jim Bunning's record of 268 set in 1965.[34]

Carlton was also within striking distance of another, more impressive record: specifically, becoming the first National League pitcher to record thirty victories in a single season since Dizzy Dean of the Cardinals accomplished the feat in 1934. Predictably, the Philadelphia sportswriters began asking the Phils' ace what he thought about breaking the record. After all, Steve was within two victories of achieving the twenty-five-win goal he had set for himself at the beginning of the season. With seven starts remaining, how difficult would it be to win five more games? Carlton knew thirty wins was possible but not probable. He was approaching three hundred innings pitched after his twenty-third victory, and his body was feeling the exhaustion that inevitably accompanies that kind of workload. "A lot of things will have to happen," he told Bill Conlin of the *Philadelphia Daily News*. "It's a pretty tough schedule and I don't want to get greedy. My legs are also tired and when that happens my pitches tend to be high. I depend on my legs to carry the arm."

The thought of thirty wins had also crossed Owens's mind. "If Steve keeps winning and he still has a shot at 30, maybe we can help him," the Phillies' manager told Conlin. "We could bring him in in a tie game to face one hitter and we score a run in our half. It's Steve's arm and his career though, so I won't ask him to do anything he doesn't want to do."

But Carlton nixed the possibility of pitching in relief. "I don't throw at all between starts, so it would be tough for me to pitch in relief," he admitted to Conlin. "I prefer to stay in the rotation and see what happens."[35]

On September 11 Carlton lost his ninth game of the season, 4–2, against Jerry Koosman and the New York Mets. New York's offense was powered by catcher Duffy Dyer, who went 3-for-4 with a home run, a triple, and a single and drove in three of the Mets' four runs. After the game Dyer said that both the homer and triple were hit off high fastballs and that Carlton "wanted the ball down both times." But Steve disagreed with the analysis.

"Dyer's a high fastball hitter," noted Carlton, "and that's what I threw him all night. It's not that those pitches were up in the zone, it's that my fastball kept sliding back over the plate. That's what hurt me."[36]

On Wednesday, September 13, Super Steve broke precedent and agreed to throw a few pitches for Philadelphia TV talk show host Mike Douglas. Arriving at the KYW-TV studio, Carlton was greeted by the producer, who was lugging two dozen baseballs. He asked the Phils' ace to stand thirty-five feet away from a tank of water and to throw at a target with a trigger mechanism. If he hit the target, Douglas's cohost, Ron Carey, who was seated above the tank, would fall into the water.

"I had to throw pretty hard even though it was only 35 feet," Steve admitted. "Besides, I can't hit anything if I'm throwing easy."

When Carlton hit the target a few times and nothing happened, Douglas interceded. "I saw it!" shouted the TV host. "He hit the target!" And then Douglas pushed the trigger, dunking his cohost.[37]

Between warm-up tosses, a practice run, and the show itself, Carlton wound up throwing sixty pitches, which amounted to half a game's workload.[38] But he was also enjoying himself. For the first time in his career, Steve was taking time away from the game to make public appearances. He was extremely accommodating to the press, as well as to the local and national broadcast media. It was a generosity he would eventually abandon altogether.

To show their appreciation, the Phillies held "Steve Carlton Night" on September 15 when they hosted the Montreal Expos. More than twenty thousand fans flocked to the Vet to honor Super Steve in a pregame ceremony. Pitching great and future Hall of Famer Robin Roberts served as master of ceremonies, and Carlton's wife, Beverly, and his parents were in attendance. Among the many gifts the organization presented were a brand-new 1973 Chrysler Imperial, golf clubs, a color television, luggage, hunting rifles, and savings bonds for the couple's two sons.

Unfortunately, Steve was not so super when the game began. He surrendered a solo homer to Coco Laboy in the top of the second. But the Phillies tied the game in the bottom of the inning when Don Money lifted a sacrifice fly to shallow right field to score Willie Montanez. Carlton surrendered another pair of runs in the third by loading the bases and giving up sacrifice flies to Bob Bailey and Hall Breedon.

Bateman realized that his batterymate's fastball was hanging, so after the second inning the catcher approached Steve and said, "Let's go with the slider outside." The catcher's reasoning, Conlin reported, was that "since [Carlton] already throws a lot of fastballs outside," then "why not throw the slider out there?" After all, Carlton's fastball and slider were indistinguishable until the ball crossed the plate. The hitters might give up on a slider outside thinking it was a fastball, and when they did, the slider would break back over the plate for a strike. It was a great strategy. Carlton did not surrender another run for the remainder of the game.

Meanwhile, the Phillies tied the game, 3–3, in the bottom of the third when Montanez singled home two runs. Luzinski hammered a solo homer to center in the bottom of the sixth to give Carlton a 4–3 lead, and the Phils added an insurance run in the bottom of the next inning when Montanez walked with the bases loaded. Carlton surrendered 4 runs on 10 hits and 3 walks with only 4 strikeouts, but his effort was good enough to pick up his twenty-fourth win of the season.[39] His twenty-fifth win would be more memorable.

On September 20 Carlton faced Rick Wise, the pitcher for whom he had been traded. It was the first and only time the two hurlers faced each other that season, and they had experienced very different fortunes with their new teams. While Carlton entered the game at 24-9, Wise's record was an even 15-15 and there was some indication of bitterness over that fact. When an Associated Press photographer asked the two starters to pose for a pregame picture, the Phillies' ace agreed, but Wise snapped, "Absolutely not!"[40]

The game was a pitcher's duel and was played on a very hot, humid night at St. Louis's Busch Memorial Stadium. Wise gave up a run in the first inning on a double by Denny Doyle, who advanced to third on a sacrifice and was singled home by Tommy Hutton. But the Cardinals got the run back in the bottom of the frame when Lou Brock doubled, stole third, and scored on a Ted Sizemore base hit. After that, Carlton did not allow another Redbirds hit until the sixth, when Brock and Joe Torre collected singles. By that time the Phillies had already scored their second run. Then Hutton doubled, advanced to third on a fielder's choice, and scored on a Greg Luzinski single to right. Wise, who allowed both Phillies runs on six hits, was lifted after the seventh inning but suffered the one-run defeat.[41]

Despite his refusal to pose with Carlton for a pregame photo, Wise seemed humble after the game. "The trade's been good for Steve and it's been good for me," he told Bill Conlin of the *Philadelphia Daily News*. "I feel I've pitched well here. Tonight, I pitched well enough to lose another one-run game."[42] But forty years later it was still difficult for Wise to accept the results of that season.

"I pitched in seventeen one-run games that year, and I lost twelve of them," he said in a 2015 interview, still disappointed by the memory. "That's got to be some kind of record. Still, I had twenty complete games that season and won sixteen. But I go 16-16 with a fourth-place club and Carlton goes 27-10 with a last-place club. Go figure."[43]

Indeed, Wise was a hard-luck loser in 1972. Seventeen of his thirty-five starts were decided by one run, and he lost twelve of them: six by scores of 3–2, three by 2–1, two by 4–3, and one by 1–0. His record was 15-16 after the loss to Carlton. Wise would start two more games that season, winning one to even his record at 16-16.[44] "Rick could've easily won 20 by now," said Cardinals manager Red Schoendienst after the game. "We just didn't score him any runs. He hasn't had the kind of super year Carlton is having, but how many guys pitching for a last-place team ever have that kind of season?"[45]

Having recorded his twenty-fifth victory, Carlton achieved his preseason goal, but it was anticlimactic. Steve was not only a perfectionist but also unapologetically ambitious. Once a goal was achieved he rarely spent time celebrating. Instead, he quickly moved on to the next objective. "I try never to lose sight of a goal," he explained after the game. "But now that I've won 25 games, I really don't feel anything. I've known for sometime that I was going to reach that goal. Then everybody started raising the possibility that I could win

30 and that stayed on my mind. I guess winning 30 kind of super-seded my desire to win those 25 games."[46]

On September 24 Carlton suffered his tenth and final defeat of the season. It came against Tom Seaver and the New York Mets at Shea Stadium. Although Steve didn't walk a single batter and struck out 9, he did surrender 2 earned runs on 7 hits. Seaver, on the other hand, allowed a single run on 5 hits and 2 walks while striking out 6 through eight and a third innings before yielding to closer Tug McGraw, who retired the Phillies in order to save the 2–1 victory.[47] Four days later, on Thursday night, September 28, Carlton made his last home start of the season. Facing Bob Moose and the Pittsburgh Pirates, Steve hurled a 2–1, complete-game victory. Second base-man Denny Doyle's throwing error in the second inning led to an unearned run for the Pirates, but that was all Pittsburgh scored. The Phillies picked up both of their runs in the fifth when Don Money hit a lead-off single, advanced on a fielder's choice, and scored on Carlton's double to right-center field. Doyle followed with an RBI single, which proved to be the game-winning run. An estimated crowd of 12,216 fans were on hand to see Super Steve strike out 9 to increase his NL-leading total to 303 on the season.[48]

By today's standards the game attendance seems low. But the Phillies were a bad baseball team in 1972, and considering that the game was played on a weeknight, the Phillies would've been lucky to draw 2,000 fans if Carlton hadn't pitched. In fact, whenever the Phillies' ace took the mound at the Vet, there were between 20,000 and 30,000 fans in the stands. To be more specific, Carlton made twenty starts at the Vet in 1972, and a total of 484,595 fans came out to see him pitch. That's an average of 24,230 fans per start. That aver-age increased to 33,510 fans in July and August, when he was in the middle of his fifteen-game winning streak. Conversely, when Carl-ton was not pitching, the average attendance was below 18,000.[49] Bill Giles, who kept close tabs on the attendance figures, believes that Carlton attracted "nearly half of the Phillies' total attendance that season."[50]

Steve's final start of the season came at Wrigley Field against the Chicago Cubs on October 3. Chicago fielded a lineup dominated by rookies, while the Phils stayed with their regulars. Predictably, the Phils battered the Cubs' pitching, hammering six home runs—two apiece by Greg Luzinski and Don Money and one each by Bill Robinson and Terry Harmon. Carlton took nothing for granted, though. "The game didn't feel that easy because I didn't know any of the hitters," he said. "But I didn't waste pitches, either. I just threw everything for a strike."[51]

When it was over, the Phillies had an 11–1 win and Carlton had pitched a complete game, surrendering a single earned run on 9 hits and 1 walk while striking out 7. The victory also improved his season record to 27-10, tying Sandy Koufax for the modern NL win total for a left-hander.[52] He also snagged pitching's triple crown, posting league-leading marks in wins, strikeouts (310), and ERA (1.98). But those statistics were just the tip of the iceberg.

Carlton's 1972 season was one of the most—if not *the* most—extraordinary pitching performances in the game's modern era. In addition to his league-leading twenty-seven wins, 310 strike-outs, and 1.98 ERA, Steve also led the National League in starts (41), complete games (30), and innings pitched (346). If MLB had had metrics for walks and hits per innings pitched (WHIP) or wins above replacement (WAR) in the 1970s, Carlton would have led the National League in those categories as well, with a WHIP of 0.993 and a WAR of 12.1. Third baseman Don Money posted the second-highest WAR on the club, a paltry 1.9.

But Carlton's most impressive statistic, the one for which he will always be known, is that he did all this for a last-place club. The Phillies finished with a record of 59-97, making them the cellar dwellers in the National League East, thirty-seven and a half games out of first. Aside from Carlton, the Phillies' pitching staff was a disaster. Of the seven other pitchers who started games that season, Darrell Brandon (7-7, 3.45 ERA) had the second most victories. Of the forty-two appearances Brandon made, all but six were in relief of Carlton, including two of his seven wins. Wayne Twitchell (5-9, 4.06 ERA) made forty-nine appearances and earned three of his five victories as a starter before the All-Star break. Billy Champion (4-14, 5.09 ERA) won his first three decisions and had only one more victory after that. Woodie Fryman made seventeen starts in twenty-three appearances and went 4–10 with a 4.36 ERA before he was traded to the Detroit Tigers on August 2. Barry Lersch made eight starts in thirty-six appearances and posted a 4-6 record with a 3.04 ERA. Ken Reynolds (2-15, 4.26 ERA) made twenty-three starts in thirty-three appearances, and Dick Selma (2-9, 5.56 ERA) made eight starts in thirty-six appearances. The remaining four pitchers on the staff were used strictly as relievers: Billy Wilson (1-1, 3.30 ERA, 23 appearances), Mac Scarce (1-2, 3.44 ERA, 31 appearances), Chris Short (1-1, 3.91 ERA, 19 appearances), and Joe Hoerner (0-2, 2.08 ERA, 15 appearances). Thus, Carlton, with twenty-seven wins, was responsible for 46 percent of the team's fifty-nine victories.[53] No other pitcher in MLB history ever won close to that many of his team's games, especially hurling for a club that scored an average of just 3.1 runs per game, as the '72 Phillies did.[54] These singular honors made Carlton the unanimous choice for the 1972 National League Cy Young Award and fifth-place runner-up in the MVP voting behind Cincinnati Reds catcher Johnny Bench.[55] The Phillies' ace also rewrote the history of Phillies pitching. Among the slew of single-season club records he established were the following:

Record	Former holder
Wins by a left-hander (27)	Eppa Rixey (22), 1916
Winning percentage by a left-hander (.736)	Curt Simmons (.680), 1952
Shutouts (8)	Curt Simmons (6), 1952
Innings pitched by a left-hander (346)	Chris Short (297), 1965
Starts by a left-hander (41)	Chris Short (40), 1965
Complete games by a left-hander (30)	Eppa Rixey (25), 1925
Strikeouts (310)	Jim Bunning (268), 1967
Consecutive victories (15)	Charley Ferguson (12), 1886[56]

Carlton attributed his success to the four-man rotation. "The big thing is having the opportunity to pitch every fourth day," he said at season's end. "I needed the work. It made me more consistent by giving me more rhythm, better control, and more confidence. The Phillies gave me the opportunity to pitch every four days, so being traded here was a blessing in disguise. The fans have also treated me wonderfully. It was great to go out and pitch when the stands were full, and it inspired me more."[57]

Pitching every four days also gave Carlton greater focus. "Mentally, I was so locked in that I hardly ever threw a ball over the heart of the plate," he said shortly after being inducted into the National Baseball Hall of Fame in 1994. "I never made a bad pitch. I could feel the pitch coming off my fingers. I could see where it was going to go in the strike zone. I never really saw the hitter. To me, it was like an advanced game of catch. I'd just see the ball reaching the catcher's mitt.

"For a pitcher to be successful," he added, "he can't throw to the hitter. He has to throw by the hitter."[58]

Bruce Morgan, author of *Steve Carlton and the 1972 Phillies*, and Steve Bucci and Dave Brown, coauthors of *Drinking Coffee with a Fork: The Story of Steve Carlton and the '72 Phillies*, insist that Carlton's 1972 season ranks at the top of all single-season pitching performances in the modern era of baseball. All of the writers identify four other single-season pitching performances as comparable: Sandy Koufax's 1965 season (26-8, 2.04 ERA), Bob Gibson's 1968 season (22-9, 1.12 ERA), Dwight Gooden's 1985 season (24-4, 1.53 ERA), and Ron Guidry's 1978 season (25-3, 1.74 ERA). But they also point out that all of these hurlers were pitching for pennant contenders and enjoyed much greater run support than Carlton did while toiling for a last-place team.[59] Morgan concludes that Super Steve's 1972 season would be "tough to duplicate" and "still stands as one of the most incredible single season performances ever."[60] Similarly, Bucci and Brown insist that "by any standard, Carlton's final numbers for 1972 were mind-boggling," but "for a last-place team, they were otherworldly."[61]

It is difficult to dispute that Carlton's 1972 pitching performance was the best ever in the game's modern era when it is viewed in the context of a last-place club that averaged just 3.1 runs per game. But here's another fact that makes Carlton's '72 performance so unique among even the greatest single-season records: Carlton won at least three of his own games at bat as well as on the mound. On April 19 he had two hits off his mentor and former teammate Bob Gibson as the Phillies beat the Cardinals, 1–0. On July 23 the Phillies beat the Dodgers, 2–0, on a two-run triple by Carlton. And on September 28 Steve had a single and an RBI double as the Phillies defeated the Pittsburgh Pirates, 2–1.

Although Carlton only hit .197 that season, he collected 28 hits, including 3 doubles, a triple, a home run, and 8 RBIs.[62] Some of those hits helped to determine the outcome of the game, especially when they were decided by a one-run margin. Thus, as impressive as the single-season performances of Koufax, Gibson, Gooden, and Guidry were, none of those pitchers had to win their own games in the batter's box as well as on the mound.

7

Sphinx of the Schuylkill

On January 16, 1973, the Phillies made Carlton the highest-paid pitcher in Major League Baseball by signing him to a one-year, $165,000 contract. There was also an additional $2,000 in incentives if the Phils' ace made the All-Star team or led the National League in wins, ERA, and/or strikeouts. Carlton's agreement was $15,000 more than his former Cardinals teammate Bob Gibson's, which had been the previous top salary for a hurler.[1]

Ruly Carpenter, the club's new president and CEO, believed that Steve deserved to be not only "the highest paid pitcher in the game based on his spectacular performance in 1972" but also the first Phillie "to break the $100,000 barrier." Paul Owens, who drafted the contract, admitted that he not only "took into consideration what Steve could do for the club in 1973, but the leadership he can provide in the future."[2]

When the sportswriters asked Carlton about his goals for the '73 campaign, he replied, "Thirty wins."

"How many starts will you have to make to achieve that goal?" asked Gene Courtney of the *Philadelphia Inquirer*.

"Thirty," answered Carlton with a devilish grin.

"Pretty confident, aren't you?" asked another writer.

"No, seriously," insisted Steve. "I got forty-one starts last year because I was able to pitch every fourth day. I did not have that chance in St. Louis. If I have the same opportunity this season, I think I can win thirty."

"So, you think the Phillies are a better club than last year?"

"Sure we are," said Carlton, citing the recent acquisitions from the Milwaukee Brewers of pitchers Jim Lonborg, who was a former American League Cy Young Award winner, and Ken Brett. "Lonborg can win fifteen to eighteen games, and Brett will give us another twenty wins," explained the Phillies' ace. "We also kept the nucleus of a good club that can compete. But we're gonna have to work on scoring more runs this spring."[3]

If Carlton intended to win thirty games in 1973, he was relying on a very productive spring training. The southpaw did not believe in throwing during the off-season. "I really don't have to throw," he explained. "I stay in shape by walking five, six miles a day and go quail hunting. I don't use my arm until spring training[,] when I get all the work I need. Once the season starts, you remain consistent when you pitch every fourth day."[4] It's also doubtful Super Steve would have found the time to throw with the hectic pace he kept in the off-season.

Carlton spent most of the winter capitalizing on the success of his Cy Young Award–winning season. He hired David Landfield of Athletes Financial Services to handle his income, from both baseball and endorsements. Landfield also managed Carlton's investments; negotiated various contracts; purchased securities, real estate, and businesses for him; paid his bills; and calculated his income tax. In return, Steve paid the agent 5 percent of his annual income, plus 2 percent for any expenses the agent incurred on Carlton's behalf.[5]

When Landfield realized that his star client was hesitant to do product endorsements, he made the appearances more palatable by negotiating television commercial contracts for as much as $5,000 each. Among the more profitable deals he landed for Carlton in the off-season were those with MAB Rich-Lux house paint and Pontiac. There was also a shaving cream company whose marketing department asked the Cy Young Award winner to shave off his long mustache because prospective customers "preferred to buy their product from men who shave their entire face."[6] Upon learning of the request, Carlton said that "the mustache is only a distraction." But, he added, "I hate distractions. I just want to go out there and pitch and win. I can always grow a mustache. I can't always win thirty games."[7] Off came the mustache.

Steve was also in huge demand as a banquet speaker. Although he was basically a shy person, Carlton spent most of the off-season eating rubber chicken and leather-tender roast beef and speaking on such topics as "winning" and "clean living." Between the endorsements and the speaking appearances, the Phillies' ace rarely saw his wife and their two sons, Steven Jr., age five, and Scott, age three. When asked about the demanding schedule, Carlton initially dismissed it as "something that is expected of people who are in the public eye."[8] But when the appearances began to cut into his off-season conditioning, Steve became noticeably agitated. "Everybody and his brother want to give me an award, so I've been going to these banquets all winter," he told Maury Levy of *Philadelphia Magazine*. "But if I had my way, I wouldn't go to any of them. I really don't enjoy speaking at those things. Usually, I'd spend the offseason with my family and exercising. Instead, I had to go wherever they wanted me to go. I didn't have a chance to work out all winter. Now here I am in spring training in not such great shape. That upsets me."[9]

Bill Conlin, a beat writer for the *Philadelphia Daily News*, criticized Carlton when he showed up at the Phillies' Clearwater, Florida, spring training site "badly out of shape after an ambitious winter on the banquet circuit." Pointing out that the left-hander also suffered a "severe case of bronchitis" that forced him to miss several weeks of camp, Conlin went on to lambaste Steve for "trying to throw too hard, too soon," which resulted in "shoulder tendonitis."[10] It was the opening salvo in a one-sided battle Conlin would wage against the Phillies' ace that season, one that would eventually result in Carlton's decision to stop talking to the media completely.

Despite the setbacks, Steve started the regular season with a 4-2 record. After losing to the Mets, 3–0, on Opening Day, April 6, in New York, the left-hander rebounded to post back-to-back victories against the Montreal Expos, 7–5, and the Mets, 7–3.[11] On April 18 Carlton suffered a hard-luck loss against Montreal when he surrendered two first-inning runs on an infield single, a ground ball single, and a Texas leaguer. They would be the only runs he gave up all day as the Phillies lost, 2–1.[12] Steve won his next two contests. They were complete-game victories, one over St. Louis, 4–2, in the first game of an April 22 doubleheader, and one over the Big Red Machine, 3–1, in Cincinnati.[13] Then his season went south.

Carlton went 1-5 with two no-decisions in his next eight starts. He completed only two of those contests and surrendered an average of four runs per game as his ERA ballooned to 3.94.[14] During the losing streak Steve was getting raked by hitters he used to dominate. Those same hitters were just as bewildered after they were able to make solid contact, especially with the slider that used to make them look so foolish at the plate. Carlton's worst outing came on May 5, when the Atlanta Braves throttled him, 7–0, in just six innings of work. Frustrated, Carlton threw a fastball at Atlanta third baseman Darrell Evans's head before he exited. It was the first time Steve was yanked for a reliever all year, and he was insulted by it. After the game the Phillies' new manager, Danny Ozark, admitted that he was "worried about *any* pitcher who gets beat that badly," especially one who "gets fined $50 for headhunting."[15] Carlton's next outing wasn't much better.

On May 9, 1973, Carlton faced the Big Red Machine at the Vet. His nemesis, Johnny Bench, caught and hit third for Cincinnati and continued his hitting spree against the defending Cy Young winner in the Reds' 9–7 victory. Bench smacked three homers before Carlton was lifted in the sixth inning. It was the catcher's second three-homer performance against Steve. One year earlier he had three base hits against the tall left-hander and drove in seven runs. "I don't see how a man can cover so much of the plate," Carlton told *The Sporting News*. "I threw Bench six inches inside and six inches outside, but it didn't matter."[16]

When Thomas Boswell of the *Washington Post* asked Bench why he was so successful against Carlton, the Reds catcher said, "I can read him," chuckling. "I can almost tell what's coming," he added. "It's like I'm thinking along with him."[17]

Carlton, one of the most intense competitors in the game, remembered every successful at bat Bench had against him, and it bothered him to no end. Once when Steve was hunting with former Cardinals teammates Tim McCarver and Joe Hoerner, he took aim at a pheasant and missed on the first gunshot. Within seconds Carlton fired off another round and hit the bird straight on. "There," he said with a devilish grin, "that one's for Bench."[18]

Carlton struggled the next few weeks, still unable to locate his fastball. The velocity on his pitches was there, but the pinpoint control that had made him so menacing the previous year was gone. He wasn't losing big games, just two- or three-run contests. After each loss Steve became increasingly distant from the media, leaving his teammates to explain his difficulties. "He can't get into a rhythm," catcher Mike Ryan said. "Maybe he'll come out of it. If he doesn't, we're in trouble."[19] Nor was the Phillies' new manager, Danny Ozark, helping matters.

Ozark's in-game strategy was questionable. He was responsible for at least three of the team's losses when he failed to lift the pitcher for a pinch hitter in the late innings of a game the Phillies could have won. Carlton did not have much respect for Ozark because he believed that the manager didn't understand pitchers. In fact, Steve, as well as his teammates, the beat writers, and the fans, knew little about the forty-eight-year-old former Dodgers coach before he was hired. Those who did didn't consider him a likely candidate for the job. Carlton was hoping that Paul Owens would continue as the manager in 1973.[20] Other players believed that any of the other candidates would have been better suited to manage the team than Ozark. There had been three candidates: (1) Richie Ashburn, who had starred for the Phillies in the 1950s and returned to the organization as a radio broadcaster (and developed a good rapport with many of the players); (2) Jim Bunning, the Phils' ace pitcher during the mid- to late 1960s, a very respected manager in the farm system, and the person who had developed the young talent recently promoted to Philadelphia; and (3) Dave Bristol, who had the most managerial experience in the Majors of all the candidates, having piloted the Cincinnati Reds and Milwaukee Brewers. Any of them would have been a good choice. But Ozark? No one expected the laid-back, beagle-faced Dodgers coach to even apply for the position.[21]

Within the Dodgers organization it was assumed that Ozark, who had been with them for more than two decades as a player, Minor League manager, and Major League coach, would succeed long-time manager Walter Alston when he retired. But Alston had no plans to leave in the near future. Thus, Ozark, with Alston's blessing, applied for the Phillies job. "I knew the Phillies' farm system pretty well," said Ozark in a 2005 interview. "I had managed in the Pacific Coast League and saw a lot of their players at Eugene, Oregon. I liked what I saw in guys like Luzinski, Boone, and Schmidt, and I thought it would be a good fit for me."[22]

Despite his fierce loyalty to Ashburn, owner Bob Carpenter left the final decision to his son, Ruly, respecting his authority as the new president of the club. The younger Carpenter didn't need much convincing to hire Ozark. He was impressed with individuals who had a long-term commitment to an organization, especially when they came from as successful a franchise as the Dodgers. Ruly also felt that Bunning and Bristol would create controversy because of their reputations as disciplinarians. "Danny was more patient than the other candidates," recalled Ruly. "He had a lot more experience with younger kids as a Minor League manager. Danny was like a father figure. Since we had a lot of kids at that time, I felt he would complement our team much better than the others."[23]

When he arrived at spring training, Ozark made it clear that he would emphasize the fundamentals. He intended to bring the "Dodgers style" to the Phillies, explaining the concept as an "expectation of winning, pride in the organization and proper instruction.

"You are going to see a club that is going to show a lot of pride in winning," he told the press. "We'll hit, run, steal and take advantage of a club's weaknesses. They won't know what hit 'em. It'll be beyond their apprehension," Ozark added, foreshadowing the malapropisms that would become a trademark of his press conferences.[24]

The decision to focus on the fundamentals would prove beneficial to a very young team sorely lacking in the basics. But Ozark's strict discipline irked veterans like Carlton, especially when the new manager put the hotel bar off limits to players on road trips. Steve strongly believed that teammates should unwind after a game by getting together over drinks and talking baseball.[25] He had a point, too. Without such gatherings, a clique mentality tends to develop on the ball club, with players going their own separate ways. Matters came to a head when the Phillies made their first trip to the West Coast in the late spring.

On May 30 Carlton lost his seventh game of the season, a 9–4 embarrassment against the Los Angeles Dodgers. Having started the '73 campaign with a 1-6 win-loss record, the Dodgers played their way back into contention during the month of May. They used the Phillies' ace to secure their sixth straight victory and their second consecutive series sweep.[26] Angered that Ozark's policies would not allow him to unwind at the hotel bar with teammates, Carlton, according to Bill Conlin of the *Philadelphia Daily News*, "attempted to oust the manager by getting other players on his side." He organized a meeting in his room at the Hyatt Wilshire Hotel, where they came up with a long list of grievances about the manager. The following day Carlton, along with several other disgruntled teammates, approached general manager Paul Owens and told him that Ozark was "clueless," that he "knew nothing about how to handle pitchers," often "botched in-game strategy," and had "lost control of the clubhouse." They also pleaded with Owens to return to the dugout. Despite his own misgivings about Ozark, Owens resisted and stuck with the manager.[27] But Owens also told Ozark to "improve your communication with the players, or you will be fired."[28] After hearing the ultimatum, Ozark, ever the malapropist, promised Owens that "my repertoire will be better."[29]

Ozark tried to accommodate Carlton by making veteran backup Mike Ryan his personal catcher. When that didn't work, the Phillies' manager went to a five-man rotation to give his ace an additional day of rest. In addition, if Carlton found himself in trouble during the late innings of a game, Ozark lifted him for a reliever, even if the Phillies had a lead.[30] But the manager's actions only made the situation worse. Carlton was convinced that his success the previous year was due to pitching every fourth day. He also didn't appreciate being lifted from a game when he had the lead. He was accustomed to completing his starts and working out of late-inning jams.[31] Nothing seemed to work.

On June 14 Stan Hochman of the *Philadelphia Daily News* but-tonholed pitching coach Ray Rippelmeyer to ask about Carlton's difficulties. Rip admitted that there "could be something physically wrong with [Carlton's] motion," but they had not "been able to pin-point what it was. I'm beginning to believe that the virus he had in spring training is the problem," he added. "Steve must've missed 20 days of not throwing batting practice, the daily workouts, the run-ning. But something is keeping him from getting the rhythm he had last year. His muscles won't let him do the things I know he can do."

Hochman pressed Rippelmeyer, suggesting that Carlton's night-life was the reason for his pitching woes.

"Let me phrase this right," replied Rip, realizing that he was being set up. "Steve Carlton does enjoy a good time. He enjoys living. But that might also be one of the secrets to Carlton's success. It's one of the ways to get the tension out of his system."[32]

The answer was diplomatic. While Rippelmeyer was candid with Hochman, he also protected Carlton's privacy. But the exchange also signaled that Bill Conlin wasn't the only sportswriter who intended to make the Phillies' ace accountable for his failure to win on a con-sistent basis.

Confused and desperate for help, Carlton turned to his old bat-terymate for advice after being knocked out of a June 30 game against the St. Louis Cardinals in the fourth inning. McCarver, who had returned to the Cardinals in 1973 as a backup catcher, immediately identified one of Steve's problems. "You're not getting any pop on your fastball," he told his friend. "It's flat and gliding in across the plate because you're dropping your hand and pushing the ball instead of throwing it."[33] McCarver knew that Carlton's success depended on perfect arm position and delivery. While the catcher's advice helped the Phillies' ace solve the mechanical problems with his fastball, Steve was unable regain his velocity and continued to lose.

Between July 8 and September 3 Carlton started twenty-one games and won just six while dropping ten. On Labor Day he was 11-17 with an inflated 4.03 ERA. With his velocity down, Steve tried to rely on trickery and movement to fool hitters, a gamble that didn't work. Instead, he surrendered more home runs, extra-base hits, and stolen bases than ever before in his career. There was one stretch in late August when he couldn't even last into the fifth inning. Inevitably, Ozark would walk out to the mound and swap out his ace for some rookie reliever who would end his career with just over twenty innings of pitching.[34]

Conlin declared open season on Carlton, routinely excoriating him in the *Philadelphia Daily News.* The beat writer, known for his provocative and acerbic prose, wrote on one occasion that it was an "impostor out there on the mound wearing Carlton's uniform no. 32," quipping that "Steve looks the same, but throws slower."[35] Years later Conlin defended his criticism of the embattled pitcher. "I initially got into trouble with Carlton because I reported that he wasn't taking care of himself," he said. "That wasn't done to titillate, or to blow the whistle on him. It was an attempt to explain how a guy who was one of the most dominating pitchers in the Majors one year—a guy who compiled a 27-10 record for an absolutely wretched team—could come back the next year and lose consistently with a better club."[36] As Carlton's woes continued, Conlin's columns became harsher. He wrote about the pitcher's "nightlife and his drinking, which often led to wild antics like head-butting, sumo wrestling matches and food fights with teammates." Insisting that he "owed his readers . . . the truth," Conlin seemed to take a perverse pleasure in what he called "exposing" the Phillies' ace, who "only had himself to blame for the dismal performance."[37]

To be sure, Steve rarely read the newspapers, but well-meaning teammates fed him quotations from Conlin's columns, often out of context. Conlin claims that there was "no single story" that prompted Carlton's decision to stop speaking with him. Instead, Steve simply began to "walk away from postgame interviews" when the *Daily News* beat writer joined the other scribes around his locker. "Other players told me that Carlton thought I had gotten too personal with his off-field life," explained Conlin in 2005. "I felt that I had not gotten personal enough. As it turned out, he cooperated with the rest of the media for the balance of the '73 season while I was the only name on his 'Leper List,' where I remained in 1974 as well."[38]

By 1974 Carlton had persuaded owner Ruly Carpenter to prohibit writers from flying on the Phillies' charter flights, which had been the custom for more than two decades.[39] Although Carlton did talk to the other sportswriters, he kept his remarks brief and delivered them in an almost trance-like state, staring off into the distance. That idiosyncrasy, along with Carlton's stone-cold silence when asked a question he didn't like, inspired Conlin to give him the nickname "Sphinx of the Schuylkill," after the mythical creature whose most famous rendering is located on the west bank of the Nile River but with the Philadelphia-area river in its stead.[40]

Rookie catcher Bob Boone, who replaced John Bateman as the starting backstop, also took some of the blame for Carlton's reversal of fortune in 1973. Steve criticized Boone instead of admitting that the 346 innings he pitched in 1972 resulted in a tired arm. He didn't like the way the rookie catcher positioned his mitt over the center of the plate and then moved it to receive pitches. Nor did he like Boone's preference to waste pitches when he was ahead in the count. Carlton wanted to go right after the hitter, to strike him out with the fewest pitches possible.[41] "I don't like to keep shaking off a catcher," he complained to Ozark. "It bothers my concentration. I like to get it over with. I only have three pitches and [Boone and I] are always four pitches apart."[42]

Ozark found himself in a bind. He had to tread lightly with Carlton, who was one of the most dominant pitchers in the game when he was throwing well. At the same time, however, Ozark made a commitment to Boone as his regular catcher. Now the Phils' manager realized that the rookie was just as stubborn as his ace pitcher and that there was no way Boone was going to change his style to accommodate Carlton. Nor should he have had to do so when the catcher's style worked well with the other pitchers. "I thought Bob was developing into a fine catcher during his rookie season," said Jim Lonborg, the Phillies' number-two pitcher and a former Cy Young Award winner himself. "We had a great relationship in terms of communicating with each other. Before games we'd talk about hitters and review scouting reports and were able to incorporate those preliminary discussions into a game plan that worked very smoothly for us."[43]

It would've been easy for Ozark to side with Carlton and attribute the problem to Boone's lack of catching experience. After all, Boone was drafted out of Stanford University as a third baseman. He was transitioned to catcher in the Minors and had only one year behind the plate before being promoted to the Phillies in 1973. But Ozark also believed that Carlton was looking for a scapegoat because of his own inability to win games. "I knew Steve had problems with Bobby," he admitted. "He didn't pitch nearly as well in '73 as he had the year before, and I think he blamed Bobby for his poor performance when it had nothing to do with the catcher."[44]

"Steve's failure to win more games in '73 was not Boone's fault," insisted pitching coach Ray Rippelmeyer in a 2019 interview. "He would have had the same problems if Bateman, or McCarver, or any other veteran catcher was behind the plate. The catcher wasn't Steve's problem. His problem was that he wasn't in good shape. He refused to run. He wouldn't do anything I asked him to do, and I wasn't really able to communicate with him." The communication breakdown had become so bad by August that Rip went to Paul Owens and asked the general manager to fine the left-hander.[45]

Boone knew he was being scapegoated by Carlton, but he attributed their difficulties to their "equally huge egos." Boone admitted in 2020 that "both of us wanted to call our own games, so Steve was fighting me all the time." Furthermore, "there were times I didn't know what pitch was coming because we weren't on the same page. But Steve never wanted to sit down and talk about pitch selection either. He was blaming me for a lot of things. The fact of the matter is that I wanted to win just as much as Steve did. If he could win throwing to another catcher, I was fine with that. But the fact remains that Steve just didn't throw well in 1973. He hung more breaking balls, he made a lot of mistakes, and ended up losing twenty games."[46] Boone would have to earn Carlton's respect over the next several years before the two men could work together effectively.

There were some rookies, however, whom Carlton befriended. One of those was twenty-three-year-old third baseman Mike Schmidt, the Phillies' second-round pick in the June 1971 amateur draft. Although Owens and new farm director Dallas Green wanted Schmidt to remain in the Minors for another season, Ozark argued that the young third baseman had already proved he could hit Triple-A pitching. "Mike had great hands, quick reactions, and the ball came off his bat like a rocket," Ozark recalled many years later. "It was all timing and bat speed. He had so much talent, it was only a matter of time before he put it all together. There wasn't much sense in sending him back down."[47] At the same time, Ozark displayed a paternalistic attitude toward Schmidt. He began calling the rookie "Dutch." Ozark used it as a term of endearment for players of German, or "Deutsch," ancestry, though Schmidt was insulted by it.[48]

When the regular season began, Ozark made Schmidt starting third baseman. There were occasions when the rookie lived up to his potential, demonstrating remarkable power, but at other times he looked lost at the plate. On those occasions the fickle fan base showered him with boos. Frustrated, Schmidt tried swinging for the fences every time he was at bat. As the strikeouts mounted, Ozark summoned the third baseman to his office on almost a daily basis to give him advice. Against some of the tougher right-handers, Ozark would bench him, particularly when Schmidt was in a slump.[49] While the manager's intentions were good, his approach was clumsy at best.

Schmidt was also going through the hazing process all rookies experienced in those days. Willie Montanez, who had suffered the same ridicule two seasons earlier, was merciless in his treatment of the young third baseman. Whenever Schmidt walked by him in the batting cage, he would pretend to sneeze as though he had caught a cold from the rookie's swings and the draft they created—an unpleasant reminder of his high strikeout ratio.[50] Larry Bowa, who had had a chip on his shoulder from the very first day the Phillies signed Schmidt, a college All-American shortstop, also rode him endlessly. Bowa felt that he had already earned the right to be the team's starting shortstop, having paid his dues in the Phillies' farm system. He was a fiery, intense competitor who had to work hard at the game, and he thus felt threatened by Schmidt and his more natural abilities. The more threatened he felt, the more he antagonized his younger teammate.[51]

Between Ozark's paternalism, the hazing, and the incessant booing of the hometown fans, Schmidt became depressed. The more he struggled at the plate, the more frustrated and bewildered he became. "All I wanted to do my first season was hit the ball out of sight," he admitted in 2020. "I got into trouble by pulling away from the plate instead of simply swinging the bat to make contact."[52] Schmidt tried to forget about his problems by partying every night. He'd get lost in the nightlife of Philadelphia's dance clubs. "If I do good, I celebrate by partying," he explained. "If I do badly, I forget it by partying. I'm young. I can handle it."[53]

Carlton saw that Schmidt was pressing, and he encouraged his younger teammate to take a more positive mental approach to the game. They spent time together on the golf course and going out to dinner on road trips. "I appreciated Steve's friendship," recalled Schmidt. "He encouraged me to enjoy the game more than I was. We played a lot of golf together. It was a productive way for me to unwind. We also went out to dinner when the team was on the road. Steve seemed to know all the best restaurants in every National League city. He also knew wine. In fact, Steve probably taught me what little I know about enjoying wine and which ones were best suited to a particular meal."[54]

Carlton became even closer to Larry Christenson, the Phillies' number-one pick in the June 1972 amateur draft. Christenson, a right-hander who stood six feet four and weighed 215 pounds, had been an outstanding hurler at Marysville High School near Seattle, Washington, where he posted a 0.28 ERA and struck out 143 batters in seventy-two innings of work.[55] Invited to big league camp the next spring, Christenson, just nineteen years old, pitched better than any of the other starters in the Grapefruit League. No one expected him to make the cut, including Phils pitching coach Ray Rippelmeyer, who believed that National League hitters would "only destroy his confidence and undermine his development."[56] But general manager Paul Owens believed that Christenson had the most potential of all the young pitchers. Owens promoted him to Philadelphia.

After winning his first start on April 13 against the New York Mets, Christenson lost his next four decisions, allowing almost two hits per inning. He was sent down to Eugene in the Pacific Coast

League, where he posted a 7-6 record with an unimpressive 5.13 ERA.[57] "I was mixed up," Christenson admitted in a 2017 interview. "One day I thought I could win by just throwing fastballs. The next day I tried to beat them with junk. Getting banged around like that was a new experience for me. Nobody ever hit me like that in high school."[58] Owens began to question whether the young right-hander could be an effective starter at the big league level.

Like Schmidt, Christenson was also treated terribly by many of the veteran players, who resented the fact that he was a number-one draft pick. "They called me, 'the Kid,' and said it with a sneer," he recalled. "If I had a tough day at the park, they shove a beer in my face and say, 'Here, kid, drink up . . . you'll be going home soon.' They'd borrow money from me and never pay it back. I hated it, but I was afraid to say anything."[59]

Carlton didn't believe in hazing rookies. He treated them with the same respect as any veteran teammate. "Steve was good to me from the very beginning of my career," said Christenson. "He took me under his wing and protected me. He was a wonderful mentor, especially my first year in the majors."[60]

One time Carlton took the boyish-looking Christenson out to dinner with a group of other teammates. When they sat down at the bar for a cocktail, the bartender pointed to Larry and barked, "I can't serve him! He's just a kid!"

Without flinching, Carlton replied, "If you can't serve him, we're all leaving."

After taking a hard look at the group of Major Leaguers standing next to Carlton, the bartender had an immediate change of heart. "Okay, kid, what do you wanna drink?" he asked, eager to receive the hefty tips the ballplayers would leave behind.[61]

When Christenson was called up to Philadelphia for good in 1975, he would become a key cog on Phillies teams that would win three straight National League East titles, from 1976 to 1978. He also lockered next to Carlton, his mentor, and often spoke for Steve when he refused to talk to the sportswriters.

At first glance Carlton appeared to pitch like a mere mortal in 1973, but those statistics can be deceiving. Although his ERA rose to

3.90, it was not far removed from the Major League average of 3.75. Similarly, Steve's 13-20 win-loss record was the worst he had compiled since 1970, when he went 10-19. But he would have posted more victories if he had received better offensive support. In fourteen of Carlton's twenty losses, the Phils were only capable of mustering a total of 12 runs. Despite the drop in statistical totals, Carlton still led the National League in innings pitched (293.1), games started (40), complete games (18), and batters faced (1,262).[62] For Owens those statistics were good enough to issue Carlton another $165,000 contract, saying that he had "too much respect for Steve to even think about giving him a cut in pay."[63]

Carlton also would have liked to play for another manager. But Danny Ozark, who did a commendable job in his first year, wasn't going anywhere. Under his leadership the Phillies showed clear signs of improvement in 1973. With a record of 71-91, the team improved by twelve victories over the previous year and were in a tight pennant race until early September, when they faded to last place. Most of the offensive power was supplied by outfielders Greg Luzinski (.285, 29 HRS, 97 RBIS) and Bill Robinson (.288, 25 HRS, 65 RBIS). Montanez's production dropped off (11 HRS, 65 RBIS), but he still hit a respectable .263 and played well defensively at first base. Schmidt contributed 18 home runs and 52 RBIS in his rookie season, though he also struck out an alarming 136 times in 367 at bats. Del Unser, the new center fielder, hit .289 and played solid defense, and Boone performed admirably behind the plate for a rookie, while also hitting .261 and contributing 61 RBIS. By all indications the Phillies were headed in the right direction. The pitching was solid. Like Carlton, pitchers Lonborg, Brett, and rookie Wayne Twitchell each won thirteen games. Dick Ruthven, a spot starter signed in the January 1973 amateur draft, went 6-9 with 98 strikeouts, demonstrating that he could compete at the big league level.[64]

If Carlton had been able to win half a dozen more games, the Phils might have been in contention for a division title. Still, Ozark expressed pride in his ace, saying that "he really showed me something when he was struggling." Furthermore, "Steve acted like a pro," he explained. "He never gave up or quit on himself. He never missed a turn. If he had any complaints, he kept them to himself."[65] Of course that last remark was a gross exaggeration. Carlton complained about the manager's ineptitude and rarely kept those complaints to himself. But the two men understood that the success of the team and each other's fortunes were inextricably bound.

"We were lucky to have a manager like Danny Ozark," said Christenson. "He let us play the game without constantly interfering, and he took a lot of heat for it, too. But you'd never hear him blast a player in the press. Sure, he'd take the ball from a pitcher who was getting hit hard, and none of us liked it. That's just the emotional makeup of a starting pitcher, though. But Carlton took it to extremes. He didn't listen to anybody at that time. He was his own man. He didn't realize how fortunate he was to have Danny and not some other manager telling him what he needed to do."[66]

Carlton returned to St. Louis in the off-season, determined to improve his performance. He began working out on Nautilus, an innovative fitness system and a welcome alternative to weightlifting. It consisted of a wide range of circuit training equipment, including cardio products such as ellipticals, treadmills, and bikes, as well as variable-resistance cable machines designed to develop endurance and certain muscle groups. For Carlton, Nautilus was especially beneficial for his torso, biceps, triceps, and shoulder.[67] It was also more rigorous than any kind of training he had done before. "I was so stiff and sore after working out on the Nautilus for just a few minutes that I'd stop doing the exercises," recalled Dal Maxvill, a former Cardinals teammate and workout partner. "But Carlton was smart enough and disciplined enough to keep up the routine."[68]

Steve admitted that he'd often become "nauseated" while working out on the machinery but quickly realized the benefits of it. "Just 25 minutes on the Nautilus is at least equal to three or four hours of regular weightlifting," said Carlton. "It's such a tough program because it uses all the muscles in your body and builds stamina in a hurry."[69]

In addition to Nautilus, Steve began doing Shotokan karate, developed from various martial arts by Gichin Funakoshi and his son Gigō in the early twentieth century.[70] Shotokan training techniques are characterized by deep, long stances that provide stability, enable powerful movements, and strengthen the legs. Those who progress in the training develop speed and a much more fluid style that incorporates grappling, throwing, and some standing joint-locking techniques, which are used in fighting. "There's not the same constant motion as you would do in running," explained Carlton. "Instead, it's a range of motion program where you're kicking backwards, you're squatting, you're getting strength and flexibility."[71] Steve was just as fascinated by the philosophy of Shotokan, which emphasized five rules for training: seeking perfection of character, being faithful, endeavoring to excel, respecting others, and refraining from violent behavior. Together with the physical training techniques, these maxims teach humility, respect, compassion, patience, and both an inward and outward calmness.[72]

The off-season conditioning initially appeared to work, as Carlton won his first two decisions of the '74 campaign. They were complete-game victories against St. Louis, 10–3, and Chicago, 7–3. Then the Phils went into an offensive slump, and Steve lost his next three starts. The most disappointing performance came on May 1 against the Giants at San Francisco's Candlestick Park. The Phillies were cruising along with a 6–3 lead entering the fifth inning when things fell apart. Carlton started the inning by punching out pinch hitter Damasco Blanco for his seventh strikeout of the game. Gary Matthews followed with a single, but when Carlton picked him off first, rookie umpire Paul Runge called a balk. Visibly upset, Carlton walked the next batter, utility man Chris Arnold. Garry Maddox and Bobby Bonds followed with back-to-back, ground-rule doubles. When the dust settled, the Giants had scored nine runs in the inning and held a 12–6 lead. Ozark brought in reliever George Culver, who promptly surrendered four walks, forcing in another run. The Phillies lost, 13–8, to end their first West Coast trip that season with a record of 1-7.[73]

"If that balk isn't called, I have two outs, nobody on base, and I get out of that inning," Carlton insisted after the game. "I've committed balks before and that was no balk. I stepped where I always step. There's a mark out there where I step every time I go to first and it's well beyond five degrees in front of the [pitching] rubber."[74]

National League umpire Terry Tata admitted that it was very difficult for the runner—and sometimes the umpire—to determine whether Carlton was going to throw home or to first base because he "had a high leg kick and hesitated when his [stride] foot was up in the air." Furthermore, "umpires assigned to first base were always looking at that [stride] foot to see if it broke the plane of the rubber when he threw to first. But it certainly wasn't easy to pick up," he added.[75] Mike Schmidt believes that Carlton "might have had the greatest move to first base of any left-handed pitcher in history" because he "threw to first while holding his right leg up in the air and perpendicular to the front of the rubber." Carlton "used to pick off ten to fifteen base stealers a year. It shut down the running game completely, which was important when McCarver returned in 1976 to become his personal catcher," explained the Hall of Fame third baseman. "With all due respect, Timmy did many things well as a catcher, but he didn't have the strongest throw to second base."[76]

But there were also occasions when Carlton's unique pick-off move baffled his own first basemen. "When Steve lifted that right leg and paused, he made a last-second decision of throwing to first or going to the plate," recalled utility first baseman Tommy Hutton. "I had to be careful not to leave the bag too early on bunt plays or he'd pick me off!"[77]

Carlton and the Phillies rebounded in May. Steve won nine of his next thirteen decisions, entering the All-Star break with an 11-7 record. The Phillies took over first place in the National League East and remained there through most of August. But in an August 6 game against the Cubs at Chicago's Wrigley Field, the Phillies' ace pulled a hamstring muscle while running to first base. Although Steve won the game, 8–3, he missed his next start and had trouble pushing off the rubber when he returned.[78] Ozark lightened the left-hander's workload by going to a five-man rotation that included thirty-two-year-old veteran Jim Lonborg, a pair of twenty-six-year-olds in Ron Schueler and Wayne Twitchell, and a precocious twenty-three-year-old, Dick Ruthven. When Carlton protested, insisting he was better off working every fourth day, general manager Paul Owens told his twenty-nine-year-old ace that "it's okay for a pitcher who's 25 or 26 years old to work every four days, but when you get up to 29 or 30, it's tough." He also reminded Carlton that his former manager, Red Schoendienst of the Cardinals, "has had a lot of success with the five-man rotation" and that such a schedule "keeps all the pitchers in the rotation sharp."[79]

Between his injured hamstring and the five-man rotation, Carlton went 2-6 in his last twelve starts to finish the season at 16-13 with a 3.22 ERA. What's important to note, however, is that Steve gutted out the remainder of the season, completing seven or more innings of work in ten of those last twelve starts. He also led the National League in strikeouts (240) for the second time in three years and finished among the top ten NL pitchers with a 4.8 WAR.[80]

Although Carlton might've been disappointed in his performance, general manager Paul Owens rewarded him with a new three-year, $500,000 contract.[81] "I don't usually go for multi-year contracts, but I was happy to make an exception in Steve's case," Owens explained. "I just happen to think the extra security is just what he needs. Now that he knows how the club feels about him, I think he'll concentrate strictly on pitching and be as good as he was in 1972."[82]

The multiyear deal meant that the Phillies' ace would make $160,000 a year, which was actually a $5,000 pay cut compared to his previous one-year deals, which were $165,000. "I had to take a decrease," he admitted. "This ball club has always been fair to me, so what's wrong with me trying to be fair to the club?" It was clear that Carlton opted for the longer pact for greater financial security, as well as for the opportunity to play for another contender. "I love living and playing in the Philadelphia area and my family and I look forward to many more years here," he said. "Plus, this ball club is going to win," he added. "It's young and has a lot of talent."[83]

Indeed, the Phillies had become a contender. Not only did the team escape the cellar in 1974 by finishing third, but the Phils also contended for the National League East title for most of the season. The future looked even brighter. Second baseman Dave Cash, who had played for a perennial contender in Pittsburgh, boosted the confidence of his teammates with the motto Yes We Can! It was a constant reminder that the Phils could compete with any team in the league. Cash, a .300 hitter, contributed 206 hits to the cause that season. Although Greg Luzinski (.272, 7 HRS, 48 RBIS, .724 OPS) saw limited action after a June knee injury removed him from the lineup, first baseman Willie Montanez (.304, 7 HRS, 79 RBIS, .753 OPS) and center fielder Del Unser (.264, 11 HRS, 61 RBIS, .736 OPS) picked up the slack, while third baseman Mike Schmidt had a breakout year.[84]

Schmidt smashed a league-leading 36 home runs and became the first Phillie to do so since Hall of Famer Chuck Klein in 1933. "Schmitty" also led the league in slugging average (.546), WAR (9.7), at bats per home run (15.8), and runs created (130) and was among the top five leaders in RBIS (116), extra-base hits (71), OBP (.395), OPS (.941), runs scored (108), total bases (310), and walks (106).[85] Jim Lonborg led the pitching staff with a 17-13 record, followed by Carlton's 16-13, Ron Schueler's 11-16, and Dick Ruthven's 9-13.[86]

Of all their young pitchers, the Phillies expected the most from Ruthven, the club's first-round pick in the January 1973 draft. Nicknamed "Rufus" by teammates, the brash right-hander had jumped directly from Fresno State College into the Phillies rotation a year earlier without the benefit of any Minor League experience. But Ruthven was a thrower who relied on a 90+ mph fastball, not a pitcher who knew how to work the corners and set up hitters. He struggled to make the transition to the Majors during his first two years with the Phillies.[87] If general manager Paul Owens thought Carlton would mentor the young right-hander, he was sorely mistaken. One time Ruthven approached Carlton and asked him how to throw the slider.

"You hold it like this," explained Lefty, gripping the ball with his index and middle fingers tightly together across the U-shaped seam, "and throw the shit out of it."

"Gee, thanks a lot, Steve," Rufus replied sarcastically as he walked away.[88]

When asked about his relationship with Carlton in 2018, Ruthven insisted that the two pitchers "always got along" but that "there wasn't a whole lot I learned from him about pitching. It wasn't until I was traded to the [Atlanta] Braves after the '75 season and became friends with [starting pitcher] Andy Messersmith that I learned how to pitch. Andy was the one who taught me how to change speeds, how to set up hitters, and how to work the corners."[89]

Indeed, when Ruthven returned to the Phillies three years later, he was a completely different pitcher, one who would contribute much to the Phillies' fortunes as they clinched a third straight division title in 1978 and later the club's first World Series championship, in 1980.

After the 1974 campaign Owens still had to address two glaring needs. First, he had to find a reliable closer for the bullpen, which he did on December 2 when he acquired relief pitcher Tug McGraw from the New York Mets, along with outfielders Don Hahn and Dave Schneck, for center fielder Del Unser, reliever Mac Scarce, and catching prospect John Stearns.[90] McGraw, age thirty, was one of the game's premier relievers until arm troubles limited his pitching to a 6-11 record and just three saves in 1974. Still, he was largely credited for the Mets' pennant the previous season, when his twenty-five saves allowed the team to rebound from last place in July to capture the division in the final week of the season.[91] Although New York thought that McGraw's best days were behind him, the Phillies believed that he could revive his career.[92] They were right. During the next five years McGraw would become one of the most effective closers in Phillies history and an instrumental part of the team's first World Series championship, in 1980.

Resolving the Phillies' second need turned out to be more complicated. Owens believed that the team needed another power hitter to take some of the pressure off Schmidt and Luzinski. Throughout the winter he explored the possibility of acquiring veteran slugger Rusty Staub of the Mets and Tony Pérez of the Cincinnati Reds. When those efforts failed, Owens turned his attention to catcher Bill Freehan of the Detroit Tigers. Aware of the ongoing difficulty between Carlton and Bob Boone's pitch calling, Owens tried to resolve two problems with one deal. Accordingly, he traded Boone to Detroit for Freehan and outfielder Jim Northrup and included Christenson in the transaction. Although Freehan's best days were already behind him, he was a power-hitting veteran catcher whose game calling was well respected among the pitchers he caught. The hope was that Carlton would return to his Cy Young form by throwing to a highly experienced backstop.[93]

Owens sealed the deal with a handshake at baseball's winter meetings in New Orleans on December 3. But when Ruly Carpenter learned of the trade the following day, he forced his general manager to cancel it.[94] "Pope [Owens] and I were really close and usually agreed on deals," recalled Carpenter in a 2018 interview. "But I wasn't about to part with Boonie or LC [Larry Christenson]. I told Paul that Boonie was on his way to becoming a damn good Major League catcher and that LC had the potential to be a top-of-the rotation starter, so we weren't going to trade either one. Besides that, we had already committed to building our club on the strength of a very talented farm system."[95]

Owens—and Carlton, for that matter—would have to live with that commitment.

Steve Carlton, pictured here in 1966, was promoted to the St. Louis Cardinals in 1965. (National Baseball Hall of Fame and Museum, Cooperstown, New York)

Tim McCarver, pictured here in 1966, turned down several college football scholarships to sign with the Cardinals in 1959. (National Baseball Hall of Fame and Museum, Cooperstown, New York)

Brewing magnate Augustine "Gussie" Busch Jr. purchased the Cardinals in 1953 and served as president or CEO of the franchise for the next thirty-six years, winning six National League pennants and three World Series titles. (National Baseball Hall of Fame and Museum, Cooperstown, New York)

Bing Devine was a progressive general manager who signed talented Black players, including Bob Gibson, Bill White, and Curt Flood. (National Baseball Hall of Fame and Museum, Cooperstown, New York)

Tim McCarver (*right*) credited pitcher Bob Gibson (*left*) with helping him to overcome "whatever latent prejudices [he] may have had" growing up in Memphis, Tennessee. (Getty Images / Bettmann Archive)

Red Schoendienst managed the St. Louis Cardinals from 1965 through 1976. Under his direction, the Cards won National League pennants in 1967 and 1968 and the 1967 World Series. (National Baseball Hall of Fame and Museum, Cooperstown, New York)

St. Louis Cardinals, 1967 World Series champions. McCarver and Carlton are pictured in middle row, third and fourth from right, respectively. (National Baseball Hall of Fame and Museum, Cooperstown, New York)

Cardinals center fielder Curt Flood challenged baseball's reserve clause in 1969, when he and McCarver were traded to the Phillies. Refusing to report to Philadelphia, Flood took his case to the Supreme Court. Although he lost, Flood's legal action paved the way for free agency. (National Baseball Hall of Fame and Museum, Cooperstown, New York)

Carlton, sporting a full mustache, posted a 27-10 record, a 1.97 earned run average, and a club record 310 strikeouts in 1972, his first season with the Phillies. (Philadelphia Phillies Baseball Club)

On January 16, 1973, Phillies general manager Paul Owens gave Carlton a
$165,000 contract, making him the highest-paid pitcher in Major League
Baseball. (Philadelphia Phillies Baseball Club)

Ruly Carpenter was principal owner and president of the Phillies from 1972 to 1981, one of the most successful eras in the team's history. (National Baseball Hall of Fame and Museum, Cooperstown, New York)

Frank Lucchesi managed the Phillies from 1970 to 1972, the early
years of the team's rebuilding process. (National Baseball Hall of
Fame and Museum, Cooperstown, New York)

Phils pitching coach Ray Rippelmeyer persuaded Carlton to throw his slider, a pitch he had abandoned while he was still with the Cardinals two years earlier. (Philadelphia Phillies Baseball Club)

Shortstop Larry Bowa was infamous for agitating his Phillies teammates, except for Carlton, who intimidated him. (Philadelphia Phillies Baseball Club)

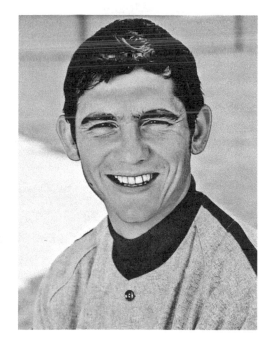

Danny Ozark managed the Phillies to three straight National League East division titles between 1976 and 1978, but his inability to take the team to the World Series cost him his job in 1979. (National Baseball Hall of Fame and Museum, Cooperstown, New York)

Catcher Bob Boone was made a scapegoat by Carlton for his twenty-loss season in 1973. Seven years later, however, the two batterymates would lead the Phillies to their first World Series. (National Baseball Hall of Fame and Museum, Cooperstown, New York)

Third baseman Mike Schmidt provided the offensive power for many of Carlton's victories. The two teammates would be inducted into the Hall of Fame in the mid-1990s. (Philadelphia Phillies Baseball Club)

Larry Christenson was mentored by Carlton and McCarver and became a top-of-the-rotation pitcher in the late 1970s. (National Baseball Hall of Fame and Museum, Cooperstown, New York)

Martial arts guru Gus Hoefling created a strength and conditioning program for Carlton that enabled him to become the best pitcher in baseball between 1976 and 1980. (Philadelphia Phillies Baseball Club)

Tim McCarver returned to the Phillies in 1975, and a year later he became Carlton's personal catcher. (National Baseball Hall of Fame and Museum, Cooperstown, New York)

By 1979 Steve Carlton had established himself as the best left-handed pitcher in baseball and was referred to as "Lefty" by teammates and opponents alike. (National Baseball Hall of Fame and Museum, Cooperstown, New York)

In 1980 Carlton led the Phillies to their first World Series title and won
his third Cy Young Award, going 24-9 with 286 strikeouts and a 2.34 ERA.
(Philadelphia Phillies Baseball Club)

8

McCarver's Pitch

While Carlton was struggling to regain his Cy Young Award–winning form in Philadelphia, McCarver was becoming a baseball vagabond. Tim's time in Montreal was brief, lasting just four months. For the first time in his big league career, McCarver served as a backup catcher and played other positions. In seventy-seven games with the Expos, he appeared behind the plate in fifty-seven of them and played fourteen games as an outfielder and six as a third baseman. Naturally his offensive totals declined; he hit .251, with just 5 homers and 20 RBIS.[1] But McCarver's knowledge of the game, experience, and gregarious personality were assets that would ensure a future in baseball, if only in a limited role.

Reacquired by St. Louis from the Expos for outfielder Jorge Roque, Tim returned to his baseball roots with the Cardinals in 1973 as a utility player. He appeared in 130 games that season—77 of them at first base—and hit a respectable .266 with 49 RBIS.[2] He entered the 1974 campaign as the Cards' top pinch hitter, though he also filled in at catcher and at first base. But as the season unfolded, the thirty-two-year-old veteran struggled, hitting .179 (7-for-39) as a pinch hitter and .217 (23-for-106) overall. On August 29 Bob Kennedy, the Cardinals' player personnel director, informed McCarver he likely would be dealt to the Oakland Athletics. The A's, who were leading the American League West and headed to their third consecutive World Series championship, were seeking a veteran backup to catcher Ray Fosse. With the Cardinals on the road in San Francisco, Tim fully expected to join his new team across the bay.[3]

"I took it very hard," McCarver told Frank Dolson of the *Philadelphia Inquirer*. "People say you have to take it like a man. I don't know how a man takes it, but I'm a very emotional individual and I cried like a baby."[4] Tim called his wife, Anne, for some much needed moral support and asked to her to fly out from Memphis to San Francisco. They had dinner together that Friday night. The next morning he learned that he was heading to Boston instead. "I hadn't the slightest notion the Red Sox had any interest in me," he said.[5] McCarver was not the only one taken by surprise.

The day before, Peter Gammons of *The Sporting News* reportedly asked Red Sox manager Darrell Johnson if Boston was interested in Tim McCarver. "No," Johnson said flat out. But McCarver was picked up the next day. Neal Russo of the *St. Louis Post-Dispatch* was also surprised. "It's usually the custom for a contending team like St. Louis to add a few veterans for a club's final push, but the Cardinals dropped one," he observed.[6]

Tim wasn't much help to Boston, though. He batted only .250, with a single RBI. The Red Sox failed to make the playoffs, finishing third and seven games behind the first-place Baltimore Orioles.[7]

Although McCarver expected to be released after the season ended, Boston held on to him. Starting catcher Carlton Fisk began the season on the disabled list with a fractured wrist, and the Red Sox needed a veteran catcher. "I'm not here to be a fill in," Tim told Clif Keane of the *Boston Globe*. "I have a little pride with the good years I have had behind me."[8] Unfortunately, manager Darrell Johnson decided to use a platoon of two other veteran catchers, Bob Montgomery and Tim Blackwell. But McCarver kept his situation in perspective. At the age of thirty-three, he was content with a utility role. He realized that he couldn't play baseball forever, no matter how much he enjoyed the game. His job now was to wait until he was needed.

On May 18 McCarver, playing first base for an injured Carl Yastrzemski, collected his first hit of the season in the eighth inning—a liner to right, a hard single. "I am now one-for-5½ months," he chuckled. "The last hit I had was on the last day of last season. I was the designated hitter that day because a lot of guys had to leave early to catch airplanes."[9]

Tim appeared in just three more games that May and didn't start until June. Despite a .381 batting average, he was released on June 23 when Fisk was reactivated.[10] The Red Sox would go on to capture the American League pennant and play the Cincinnati Reds in one of the most exciting World Series ever. McCarver went seeking employment elsewhere.

Meanwhile, Carlton's pitching woes continued. The Phillies opened the 1975 season against the Mets at New York's Shea Stadium. It was a pitcher's duel between two aces, Carlton and Tom Seaver. Despite an impressive performance in spring training, Steve struggled with his control during the early innings of the game. In the fourth inning he worked an 0-2 count on slugger Dave Kingman and then tried to get him to chase a slider outside. But the pitch didn't break, instead sailing over the middle of the plate, and Kingman smashed a four-hundred-foot home run to dead center. For the next four innings both pitchers were unhittable, the score deadlocked at 1–1. Carlton lost the game in the ninth, though, when second baseman Félix Millán singled to right, advanced to second on a walk, and scored on Joe Torre's base hit to left.[11]

Carlton's next start came on April 12 against the St. Louis Cardinals. He surrendered 4 earned runs on 5 hits and 5 walks and was lifted after completing the fifth inning. The Phillies went on to lose the game, 7–5. Steve lost his next two starting assignments to begin the season at 0-3. One of those defeats was a 9–3 shellacking by the Cubs in which he gave up 6 earned runs on 7 hits in just two innings of work. Carlton did not record his first victory until April 30. It was a 2–1 gem against the Montreal Expos in which he surrendered just 1 earned run on 6 hits and struck out 7 in nine solid innings of work.[12] Unfortunately, Steve's difficulties continued through the spring due in part to recurring pain in his left elbow. Instead of relying on his fastball and slider like the power pitcher he was, Carlton tried to work the corners of the strike zone with off-speed deliveries. At the end of May he was 3-5 with an uncharacteristic 3.90 ERA and just two complete games.[13]

Steve appeared to rebound in early June, reeling off three consecutive complete-game victories, over the Padres, 5–1; Dodgers, 4–0; and Giants, 4–1. But then he struggled in his next three outings, losing to the Mets, 5–2, and recording no-decisions against the Cubs and Pirates. Although Carlton had lowered his ERA to 3.46 by the end of June, he was lucky to be 6-6.[14] Once again the frustrated hurler began to blame his difficulties on catcher Bob Boone.

Fortunately, Larry Christenson and rookie Tommy Underwood stepped into the starting rotation and pitched masterfully. Christenson would go on to post a record of 11-6 in twenty-six starts that season. It would be the first of four straight double-digit victory seasons between 1975 and 1978, including a brilliant 19-6 season in 1977.[15] Underwood went 14-13 in thirty-five starts with a 4.14 ERA and 123 strikeouts and was named the left-handed pitcher on the Topps All-Star Rookie Team.[16] Together with the power hitting of Schmidt and Luzinski and the bullpen, now anchored by a healthy Tug McGraw, Christenson and Underwood allowed the Phillies to remain in first place in the division during the early months of the season. Owens also made some deals to strengthen the batting order.

On May 4 he traded first baseman Willie Montanez to the San Francisco Giants for center fielder Garry Maddox. Maddox, a Vietnam veteran who wore muttonchop sideburns to hide a skin rash he had acquired due to chemical exposure during his military service, was known for his blazing speed and impeccable defense. He was soon dubbed the "Secretary of Defense" by Phillies radio broadcaster Harry Kalas. Mets broadcaster Ralph Kiner was so impressed with the Phillies' new center fielder, he quipped that "two-thirds of the earth is covered by water, the other third is covered by Garry Maddox." Maddox would go on to win eight Gold Glove awards and post a .983 fielding average during his twelve-year tenure with the Phillies.[17]

"Pope" Owens also acquired first baseman Dick Allen and veteran catcher Johnny Oates from the Atlanta Braves on May 6 for young backstop Jim Essian and outfielder Barry Bonnell.[18] Allen, the Phillies' first African American superstar, had also flourished with the Chicago White Sox during the previous three seasons, winning the American League MVP nod in 1972. But when Chicago traded him to Atlanta, Allen refused to report to the club. Having endured severe racial discrimination as a member of the Triple-A Arkansas Travelers in 1963, the All-Star first baseman insisted that he would not play in the South and retired. When the Phillies convinced their former slugger that he could provide the veteran leadership their young team needed to capture a world championship, he agreed to return to the game and don the red pinstripes again.[19] Allen was the key acquisition. He answered the Phillies' need for a veteran power hitter to protect Schmidt and Luzinski in the batting order. But Owens hoped that Oates would provide the game calling and experience that Carlton required of his catcher.

Boone was understandably angered by the trade. He believed that he had earned the right to be the Phillies' everyday catcher.[20] Apparently, Ozark saw the arrangement as temporary. "I have a gut feeling about Bobby," he told Bill Conlin of the *Philadelphia Daily News*. "I've gone with him for two years and I want him as my catcher."[21] Despite his loyalty to Boone, Ozark began inserting Oates into the lineup when Carlton pitched.

Between May 28 and July 7 the Phillies' ace made ten starts against teams playing .500 or better baseball. Oates was behind the plate for six of those starts, and Carlton went 2-2, with two complete games and a 3.37 ERA. In the four games Boone caught, however, Steve went 3-0, with two complete-game victories, a shutout, and a 3.49 ERA.[22] It really didn't matter who caught Carlton; the catcher wasn't the problem. Ozark said as much on June 28 after his ace lost to the New York Mets by throwing a changeup to slugger Dave Kingman with the bases loaded and two outs in the bottom of the fifth. Kingman just missed a grand slam when the ball ricocheted off the top of the left-field fence, sending two runners home. "I don't blame the catcher [Oates] for that pitch," said the Phils' manager. "[Carlton] has the ball, doesn't he?"[23]

Ozark continued to criticize his ace in the Philadelphia press the following week. *Inquirer* sportswriter Frank Dolson provided the venue this time, further nudging Carlton to adopt a "no-talking" policy. The article was headlined "Super Steve Is Only a Memory" and appeared on July 9, two days after Carlton was crushed by the Big Red Machine, 7–3. "He was so inconsistent from one hitter to the next," said Ozark of his ace. "He'd get two strikes on one guy then go 3-1 to the next. There was no consistency to his fastball. He'd throw one good one, then a couple of mediocre ones. His breaking ball was terrible. He just had no idea of what he was doing."[24]

It was bad enough that Carlton surrendered three base hits and an RBI to his nemesis, Johnny Bench, but then allowed him to steal second—twice—both times on walking leads. The bigger gaffe came in the sixth inning, though. With one out, Merv Rettenmund walked, bringing Pete Rose to the plate. When Reds manager Sparky Anderson called for a hit and run, Oates signaled for a pitch out. Instead, Carlton threw a changeup to Rose, who bounced to third. Rettenmund never stopped running and scored when first baseman Dick Allen's throw to third skipped by for an error, resulting in another unearned run for Cincinnati. After the game an exasperated Ozark shook his head in disbelief as he told Dolson, "[Carlton] didn't pitch out. He knew it was on, but he didn't pitch out. The guy's pitched in the majors ten years now. If he can't get his mind on what he's trying to do, I don't know how we can help him. If he keeps this up, he won't be worth anything on the market. The other clubs see it, too."[25]

If Ozark was hoping that general manager Paul Owens would trade Carlton, he was woefully mistaken. In fact, Owens on July 1 made a transaction he hoped would reverse Steve's fortunes. He reunited the Phillies' ace with his old batterymate, Tim McCarver. When the Boston Red Sox released the veteran catcher in late June, Owens jumped at the opportunity to sign the former Phillie.[26] Although Ozark doubted McCarver's ability to revive Carlton's career, he was excited about the signing. "McCarver is aggressive, a holler guy with playoff experience," explained the Phillies' manager. "He's in the game all the time. He's someone I'd like to have around in September when you need guys who've played for pennant winners."[27] McCarver fit the bill.

For Tim the signing was serendipitous. "I wasn't looking to extend my playing career," he admitted. "I thought my career was over. I was in Philadelphia to audition for a sports broadcasting job with

KYW-TV and I called Bill Giles just to say hello." Giles, the Phillies' executive vice president, told him that the team was interested in signing him. Surprised, McCarver knew he could still hit and still run, so he met with Paul Owens and signed a one-year deal.[28]

Shortly after Tim returned, Phils owner Ruly Carpenter convened a meeting to address Carlton's subpar performance. McCarver, Boone, and Oates were present, as were Ozark and pitching coach Ray Rippelmeyer. Several ideas were discussed, but most of those present agreed that Carlton wasn't locating his fastball. "I'll probably get voted down here," said McCarver, "but I caught Steve in St. Louis when he developed the slider, and I played against him when I returned to the Cardinals in 1973. I heard right-handed hitters like Joe Torre, Lou Brock, Ted Simmons, and Ted Sizemore come into the dugout and say, 'He got me out, but at least he didn't throw me that slider.'

"When you hear comments like that from good right-handed hitters, it makes an impression," Tim added. "They know that slider is devastating. If they don't like to see it, it stands to reason that Carlton should be throwing it more often."[29]

McCarver had made his pitch for the slider, but no one seemed persuaded by it. Then, after the meeting broke up, Rippelmeyer buttonholed Tim. "Maybe you're right," said Rip. "Steve still throws the slider, but maybe he needs to use it more. I know that [Bob] Boone wants to set up hitters with the fastball, but maybe that slider should be used as the setup."[30]

"Well, if I ever catch him," replied Tim, "I'll call for his slider. I'll guarantee you that."[31]

The slider, a combination fastball and curveball, does not have the same velocity as a Major League fastball, though it is faster than a normal curve and breaks more horizontally and less vertically than a curve. The slider is also gripped like a two-seam fastball but slightly off center so that the ball is released off the thumb side of the index finger. One of the reasons the slider is so difficult to hit is because the pitch looks exactly like a fastball as it leaves the pitcher's hand. Specifically, the slider is thrown from the same motion, same arm slot, and same release point as a fastball, but when released the ball veers glove-side from the pitcher. If thrown by a right-hander, the ball will veer left. If thrown by a left-hander, it will veer right. At the same time, great variations of the slider can be found on a continuum between the fastball and curve depending on the pitcher who is throwing it.[32]

In his book *K: A History of Baseball in Ten Pitches*, Tyler Kepner traces the origins of the slider to the turn of the twentieth century, when Cy Young of the Boston Red Sox threw the pitch. Young described the slider as a "narrow curve that broke away from the batter and went by, just like a fastball." Chief Bender of the Philadelphia Athletics also threw a variation of the slider, something he called a "fast curve." Between 1905 and 1914 Bender used the pitch to forge one of the best records in postseason play, which included an impressive 6-4 record with a 2.44 ERA. In the 1920s George Uhle of the Detroit Tigers allegedly gave the slider its name because "the movement was like a car skidding on ice." To him, the slider "was really a fastball that I turned loose with two fingers along the seams," he explained. "But the movement was such that the ball slid sharply across the plate and down." Although there were a few other pitchers who eventually adopted the slider, Bob Feller of the Cleveland Indians popularized the pitch in the 1940s. Feller's slider only broke four to six inches, but the drop was sudden, like a dart. He mixed the pitch so effectively with a devastating 95+ mph fastball that he really did not need to throw a third pitch. According to Ted Williams, the last .400 hitter, "By 1948 all the good pitchers had one [a slider]."[33]

In the 1960s and 1970s the slider became popular with pitchers who possessed a tall, lean body type. Their ability to generate tremendous power from hip rotation allowed the lanky hurlers to drive the ball low and through the strike zone. Carlton, standing six feet four and weighing about 210 pounds, was one of those pitchers. While experimenting with the slider as a Cardinal, Carlton threw a cut fastball as his out pitch. Thus, when he began to throw the slider in games, it was more like a cutter that broke down and away so suddenly from a left-handed hitter that all he could do was flail at the ball in a desperate effort to make contact. The "down-and-in movement" to a right-handed hitter was so severe that Carlton's slider often struck the batter's back foot. But what made his slider so effective was the deceptiveness of the pitch.

"I throw all my pitches over the top," he explained in 1973. "This is important in disguising the slider because it is actually thrown off the same motion as the fast ball with a slight difference: I hold my slider directly along the seam so that I can grip the ball hard and pull hard on the seam when I release the ball. As I release the ball, I turn my wrist or 'cut down through the ball.' I always have the back of my hand on top or to the side, but never under the ball as this can cause stress and possible injury to the elbow. The ball then comes to the plate with the same velocity as a fastball, but [it] breaks suddenly in almost a straight [plane] and can be a difficult pitch to hit because of the deception involved."[34]

According to McCarver, Carlton's slider was so deceptive that most of them "weren't even in the strike zone." Instead, the hitters were "swinging at the *illusion* of a strike or the illusion of a fastball because that's what it looked like when it left Steve's hand."[35] Carlton's slider had such a sharp, sudden—and late—break that the hitter was caught off guard, much like a deer in the headlights. If the batter managed to make contact, the best he could do was foul off the pitch or hit a hard ground ball to third or first base. This was the kind of slider Carlton threw in 1972, when he won his first Cy Young Award. It was the pitch that Willie Stargell described as "drinking coffee with a fork," that became "Super Steve's" out pitch, and that ultimately defined his career. But after 1972 Carlton lost that devastating movement and threw the slider less frequently, opting for the fastball as his out pitch. McCarver would change that.

On July 12 Tim finally got his chance to catch Carlton. It came against the Astros in Houston. Things did not start well. After a lead-off single by Wilbur Howard and a Bob Watson home run, Carlton was down, 2–0. But after that he was overpowering, surrendering just 2 singles and 2 walks. The Phillies exploded for 7 runs in the second, giving their ace all the offense he needed. When the game was over, the Phils had scored 14 runs, largely off the bats of Garry Maddox (4-for-4, 3 RBIS), Jay Johnstone (3-for-6, 3 RBIS), and Greg Luzinski (3-for-4, 2 RBIs). Inspired by the start, McCarver went 1-for-3 with 2 RBIs and 2 runs scored. And Carlton had won his eighth game of the season, 14–2.[36]

"I was a little too strong in the first," Carlton said of his performance. "I was trying to overpower the hitters. But after that I had good rhythm, and a good curve ball as well as a good fastball."[37]

McCarver was behind the plate again for Steve's next start, on July 17 against the Astros at the Vet. The veteran catcher's lead-off homer in the fourth tied the contest at 4–4 and sent Houston starter Doug Konieczny to the showers. Although the Phillies won, 6–5, in extra innings, Carlton did not get the decision. He hurt himself with walks, surrendering six in seven innings of work. Three of the free passes resulted in runs.[38]

On July 22 the Carlton-McCarver battery made its third straight start, this one against Carl Morton of the Atlanta Braves in Philadelphia. Carlton was impressive, allowing just three hits—a game-opening single to Ralph Garr and eighth-inning singles by Larvell Blanks and Roland Office—in the 1–0 victory. He struck out eight and walked just three. The key to his success, according to McCarver, was the slider. "That was the most encouraging thing about tonight," said Tim. "[Carlton's] slider set up his other pitches. He had three great pitches and he hit the spots. He was overpowering early and he was more of a pitcher later. It's by far the best performance I've seen from him since I've been back."[39]

The Phillies won the game in the bottom of the ninth, when Dick Allen and Greg Luzinski drew walks to load the bases with no outs. Mike Schmidt followed, hitting a pop fly to third for the first out. Pinch hitter Johnny Oates grounded to second baseman Marty Perez, who threw home for the second out. But catcher Vic Correll's relay to first hit Oates in the back, and Luzinski slid home before right fielder Clarence Gaston's relay reached Correll.[40]

Oates, the first-string catcher, was encouraged by Carlton's performance. "Steve's the one we need," said Oates. "Let's be realistic. Pitching is a big part of the game. We've got a powerful offense and our defense is no problem. But it's tough to go with just two good starting pitchers like we have in [Larry] Christenson and [Tommy]

Underwood. If Carlton pitches like he did tonight, we'll have three guys who can carry us to the playoffs."[41]

Carlton's success with McCarver behind the plate was no coincidence. Tim tried to dispel any notion that his acquisition by the Phillies was done to rejuvenate his batterymate's career, but it was difficult to agree with his contention that "a pitcher with Steve's stuff can pitch to anybody and be successful." In McCarver's view, "if you diagrammed the way a young pitcher should throw a baseball from the toeing of the rubber, the arm location and the grip on the ball," then "Lefty would be your model. I caught a lot of good pitchers, but Steve from sixty feet, six inches away was the closest to perfection [of] anybody I caught."[42]

Carlton gave credit to McCarver in turn for "knowing the hitters so well that it takes the strain off me for setting those hitters up," he said. "We think the same and work well together," he added. It sounded like an endorsement.[43] Even Ozark, who repeatedly insisted that McCarver was not intended to be Carlton's personal catcher, seemed to have second thoughts. "I just put Timmy in there to see if I could get Carlton straightened out," he said after the game. "But maybe he *is* the remedy."[44]

Inspired by their success, Ozark stayed with the Carlton/McCarver battery on July 26 in St. Louis, and the Phillies won again. It was a one-run game until the seventh. With the Phillies clinging to a slim 3–2 lead, Carlton led off the inning with a catchable fly ball to center that was dropped by outfielder Buddy Bradford. Dave Cash beat out a high bouncer to second, and Bowa followed with a double, scoring Carlton from second. Redbirds starter Harry Rasmussen was lifted for reliever Al Hrabosky, who promptly surrendered another run when Mike Schmidt singled to left center. Greg Luzinski drove in a third run with a sacrifice fly to right field. The Phillies now led 6–2, but the Cards got back two of those runs in the bottom of the frame to cut the Philadelphia lead to 6–4. McCarver led off the eighth with an infield single and scored when Cards left fielder Luis Melendez dropped Carlton's drive to deep left-center. Cash singled Carlton home, and Tommy Hutton, a late-inning defensive replacement for Dick

Allen at first base, doubled in a ninth-inning run in the Phillies' 9–4 win.[45]

Carlton went the distance for his tenth win of the season, but it was not one of his better efforts. He surrendered ten hits, including homers by Ted Simmons, his former St. Louis batterymate, in the fourth and Ken Rudolph in the seventh. After the game McCarver told Allen Lewis of the *Philadelphia Inquirer* that Steve's "only problem was being inconsistent with his breaking ball." The runs all "came on breaking balls, three on sliders," he explained. "The ball Simmons hit for a homer was a curve. It was down, but it was in. Still[,] you can't fault Steve for that because in the process of trying to improve on his slider, he's got to throw the curve."[46]

Carlton's victory on July 26, coupled with the Pirates' afternoon loss to the Expos at Montreal, reduced Pittsburgh's first-place lead over the Phillies to four games in the National League East. The Phils then headed to Pittsburgh for the next three-game series, savoring the opportunity to close the gap even more. Larry Christenson won the first game, 5–2, to improve his record to 6-2. Tommy Underwood followed the next night with a 5–1 victory, thereby boosting his record to 11-7. With that the Phillies had reduced the Pirates' lead to just two games. When Carlton took the mound on Wednesday night, July 30, it looked like the Phils would sweep the series and narrow Pittsburgh's lead to a single game. Instead, the Pirates clobbered Carlton and the Phillies, 8–1. Bucs catcher Manny Sanguillén was a one-man wrecking crew, hammering out five hits, including a two-run, hit-and-run homer in the fourth inning.[47]

After that loss *Philadelphia Daily News* columnist Stan Hochman, who was hoping to get a few quotes, tried to find Carlton in the visitors' clubhouse. But Hochman discovered that the so-called "Sphinx of the Schuylkill" had frozen out the writers. According to McCarver, Carlton "seemed to be on edge" that season. "He wasn't himself," Tim explained. "He didn't appear happy. He said he felt maligned by the subjectivity of the press. He told me that there had been some remarks in print that drinking was affecting his physical condition. Steve reasoned that when he had a good year the press didn't write or speculate about such things. Why did they do it now?"[48]

It was rather naïve of Carlton to think that he would escape the malevolence of the *Daily News* sportswriters, especially by 1975, when he had played in Philadelphia for four seasons. Those sportswriters were a breed of their own, holdovers from the famously irreverent "Chipmunk" writers of the previous decade.[49] Writers like Hochman and Conlin felt entitled to stir controversy when a player wasn't performing to their unreasonable expectations. They deluded themselves into believing that it was their job—*not* the owner's, general manager's, or manager's—to make the players accountable and that nothing—not even the athlete's personal life—was off limits. Hochman, seeking revenge for Carlton's refusal to be interviewed, blasted the left-hander on the pages of the next day's *Daily News* in a column headlined "Carlton Show a Poor Rerun."

Using the metaphor of a feature film, Hochman compared Carlton to a thin-skinned, elitist actor who had turned in yet another bad performance. He also likened Owens, Ozark, Rippelmeyer, and McCarver to a patronizing film crew who excused the inexcusable:

"Steve Carlton won the award for 'Best Performance in a Disaster Movie' last night. The trophy is called Pollyanna. It is made of 24-karat brass and depicts an Oriental with a German Shepherd on a tattered leash. The dog has left his rear leg poised while standing on a field of four-leaf clovers.

"Mr. Carlton was unavailable after the performance. He was off doing the Greta Garbo bit. Some nights, Mr. Carlton does his 'Invisible Man' bit.

"He does not enjoy the media on the grounds that his theories of pitching will be misunderstood since they are on a higher plane. Which is where many of his pitches have been thrown lately . . . on a high plane.

"Mr. Carlton's performance was brief and dramatic: four innings, seven runs, eight hits, two of them back-to-back homers by Manny Sanguillen and Al Oliver. The critics might have hated it, but the people who count savored every raggedy minute of it.

"Paul Owens, the producer: 'I thought he threw pretty good. It was just one of those damn games when you can't do anything right.'

"Sure, and Sandra Dee was great in rehearsals. Mr. Carlton is 39-41 since his brilliant year in 1972, which is not the stuff that Academy awards are made of. Nor Cy Young awards.

"Danny Ozark, the director: 'I'm not unhappy with the way he threw. Who knows what might have happened if it had been 3–1 or 3–2 early. The only thing I'm displeased about is the fact that we lost.'

"Ray Rippelmeyer, acting coach, film editor and choreographer: 'I was totally satisfied with Steve's stuff. To me, he didn't have a chance to get into a groove. You've got to give the hitters credit.'

"Let the credits show that the Pirates are terrific hitters. The same guys muffled by Tommy Underwood the night before and Larry Christenson the night before that.

"Tim McCarver, supporting actor, who has been giving Carlton his cues during a recent winning streak: 'He was throwing the ball real well. In games like that, if you get out of the early innings, it might be a different ballgame.'

"McCarver was a late addition to the cast, replacing a character actor named Bob Boone. They could have got [Yankees Hall of Famer] Bill Dickey for the role of catcher last night and it wouldn't have mattered . . . so few of Carlton's pitches reached the catcher."[50]

Hochman's column was petty, spiteful, and meant to embarrass Carlton, as well as the Phillies. If he believed that he was going to provoke the southpaw into defending himself on the record, he was sorely mistaken. Hochman's malice only strengthened Carlton's eventual decision to ignore the press altogether, and not just the *Daily News* writers, either, but *all* members of the media. Ironically, it was Hochman who on July 4, 1979, conducted the last newspaper interview Carlton granted, at least before the Phillies released him on June 24, 1986.[51]

"I sympathized with Steve Carlton," said owner Ruly Carpenter in a 2018 interview. "When he first came to the Phillies in 1972, I don't think he had problems with Frank Dolson and Allen Lewis of the *Inquirer* or Ray Kelly of the *Bulletin*. Those writers were pretty fair, and when they criticized us, we usually deserved it. The writers who gave Steve difficulty were Bill Conlin and Stan Hochman of the *Daily News*. They expected him to win twenty games every year after 1972, when we had a young team that did not always give him the run support he needed to do that. The *Daily News* writers never really understood that. They refused to leave him alone. In the end Steve had no choice but to stop talking with them. Besides, we weren't paying him to talk with the media. We were paying him to pitch."[52]

Publicity director Larry Shenk tried to serve as a mediator between Carlton and the press. "Steve was the most cooperative player I'd been around in 1972," recalled Shenk. "He did endless interviews and appearances during and after the season." But in 1973, when he did not pitch as well, Carlton was burned routinely by the same writers who had once praised him. He took the criticism personally. Gradually over the course of six years the interviews became less and less frequent. Whenever Shenk approached him during that span, Carlton would find excuses not to talk with the media. "I give my time and they take my words out of context," he complained. Other times he told Shenk that "without my quotes they can be more creative in their writing, so why should I continue to take time for them?" But Steve's most popular excuse was, "I concentrate better without the distraction of speaking to reporters."[53]

McCarver would catch Carlton four more times during the '75 season. On August 3 Steve faced the Expos and their ace, Steve Rogers, at Montreal's Jarry Park. The Phils scratched out a two-run lead for their ace in the first inning on singles by Larry Bowa and Garry Maddox, a walk to Greg Luzinski, Dick Allen's sacrifice fly, and an infield single by Jay Johnstone. But Carlton got into trouble in the third, when he surrendered four unearned runs. Montreal's number-seven hitter, Tim Foli, started off the inning by singling off the left-hander's leg. Mike Schmidt blew a double play ball when he allowed Barry Foote's grounder through his legs and Montreal had runners on first and second. Carlton walked Rogers to load the bases. After Pepe Manuel's sacrifice fly scored one run, he walked Pete Mackanin to load the bases again. Gary Carter struck out, but José Morales doubled to right and Jay Johnstone hesitated throwing home. That was enough time for Mackanin, Foote, and Rogers to race home for a 4–2 lead.

The Phillies added a run in the sixth and tied the game in the eighth on Schmidt's twenty-first homer of the season. Carlton, who pitched scoreless ball after the third, was lifted in the seventh. Tug McGraw came on to pitch two scoreless innings and get the win after reserve first baseman Tommy Hutton singled home Johnny Oates in the top of the tenth for the 5–4 Phillies victory. Gene Garber retired the Expos in the bottom of the frame for the save.[54]

Six days later, on August 9, Carlton improved his record to 11-8, beating the San Francisco Giants at the Vet, 11–4. After a shaky first inning he settled down, surrendering just 2 earned runs on 9 hits in eight innings of work. He also recorded 9 strikeouts, the highest single-game total to that point in the season. Schmidt provided all the offense Carlton needed, igniting a 6-run rally in the fifth with his twenty-fifth home run of the season. The victory moved the second-place Phillies to within two games of the NL East–leading Pirates as Pittsburgh lost its third straight to the Houston Astros, the cellar dwellers of the West division.[55]

But instead of overtaking the Bucs, the Phillies dropped the next four games, including Carlton's next start on August 13 at the Vet against the Los Angeles Dodgers. With the fans calling for Ozark's firing, the Fightins dropped a 5–4 heartbreaker. Carlton lasted only five innings and gave up four Dodger runs before Wayne Twitchell relieved him. When Ozark came out to get him, Carlton heard the boos.[56] The fans weren't the only ones who were disturbed by his dismal performance. This time it wasn't the *Daily News* sportswriters who came down on Carlton, either. *Inquirer* beat writer Allen Lewis, who had a solid reputation for objectivity, pointed out that the Phillies, who had dropped ten of their last fifteen games, relied on Carlton to be their stopper when the losses began to pile up. Instead, the "supposed ace of the Phils' pitching staff" was adding to the misery because "he had won only five of his last 12 starts since mid-June."[57] Dolson, on the other hand, fixed the blame for the Phillies' woes squarely on Ozark. "The best chance this very talented team has to win in '75 is to get a new manager," he wrote in his next day's column. "Now. Before too many games that might have been won are lost. Before the lack of confidence and the lack of respect the great majority of the players feel for Danny Ozark becomes too much to overcome. Without the players' respect and their confidence a man cannot be an effective leader."[58] Considering that the Phillies were just three games out of first place in their division, the criticism did not seem justified.

Perhaps Ozark was not the best communicator with his veteran players, but no one could question his commitment to winning or his record. Under Ozark the team had finished sixth in 1973 and third in '74, and it was contending for most of the '75 season.[59] On the other hand, the Phillies had been a second-division team for the previous decade. The fans and the press had grown desperate for a winner. So had owner Ruly Carpenter. That's why he was paying Carlton $160,000 and why he brought Dick Allen back to Philadelphia for $225,000.[60] That's why Carpenter built up the farm system and waited patiently for prospects like Larry Bowa, Larry Christenson, Greg Luzinski, and Mike Schmidt to get Major League experience. That's why general manager Paul Owens acquired talented veterans like Allen, Dave Cash, Jim Lonborg, Garry Maddox, and Tug McGraw to bolster the lineup. It was time to win the division; nothing else would suffice, at least for the fans and the sportswriters.

The Phillies responded by winning three of the next four games, including Carlton's next start on August 18, against the Atlanta Braves, though he did not get the decision. Steve went four innings, giving up 3 runs on 7 hits before yielding to reliever Tom Hilgendorf, who recorded the 6–3 win. The victory improved the Phils' record to 67–55, allowing them to move into a first-place tie with Pittsburgh in the NL East.[61] Bill Conlin of the *Daily News* still was not satisfied.

The next day Conlin ripped Carlton for "another slovenly performance" in a column headlined "Phillies Find the REAL Imposter." Ozark, who had been criticized for staying too long with Carlton too often, was given faint praise for lifting the "$160,000 imposter" in the fifth. After surrendering an unearned run in the bottom of the first, Allen and Schmidt gave the Phillies a 3–1 lead on two-run and solo homers, respectively. But the Phillies' ace, according to Conlin, "treated the lead like a 200-volt wire" by loading the bases on two walks and a hit batter in the bottom of the third. Then he gave up a two-run double to Atlanta catcher Vic Correll, which tied the game at three runs apiece. "Carlton went 3-2, 3-2, 3-2," wrote Conlin, referring to the deep counts that resulted in the walks and hit batter. "He should be awarded special license plates at the end of the season bearing SC 3-2. Conferred by the state to which he is traded."[62]

However, with McCarver behind the plate in those nine games, Carlton went 4-2 with three no-decisions and a 3.54 ERA. While it was a small body of work, it was enough to convince Tim that the left-hander needed to throw his slider much more often to be successful. "Steve was throwing his fastball as his out pitch and not enough of his slider, which was his best pitch, the one that should have been his out pitch," explained McCarver in a 2019 interview. "His fastball was too light and feathery to be his out pitch. But since he could control his slider, his fastball was an ideal setup pitch for his slider, which sank and slid. It was the pitch that gave him an advantage over batters. He needed to throw it more." Thus, in the nine games he caught, Tim called for "sliders, sliders, and more sliders" and "went to the fastball to set up those sliders."[63] The objective was to build Steve's confidence in throwing the pitch that had earned him a Cy Young Award three years earlier.

McCarver also noted a mechanical problem. Whenever Carlton was hit hard in those nine games, he was "dropping his left hand and pushing his fastball instead of throwing it." As a result, the fastball "flattened out" and was crushed by the hitters. When that happened, Tim called time, trotted out to the mound, and reminded his batterymate to "keep his left hand straight up" and to "keep two fingers on the inside of the ball to prevent his hand from dropping."[64] It was a valuable observation that Tim would store away and use to his advantage in the future.

With the Phillies still in the chase for a division title, Ozark needed more offense from the catching position and decided to keep Johnny Oates behind the plate for Carlton's last nine starts, a span in which Steve went 4-5 with a 3.73 ERA. One of the reasons for the inconsistency was a bone spur in his left elbow. He was pitching with pain for most of the season and didn't want to go on the injured reserve list to have surgery. Besides, the spur was lodged in an area of the elbow where it would be extremely difficult to remove. Instead, Carlton soldiered on, making various mechanical adjustments to relieve the pain—adjustments that adversely affected his pitching.[65]

Carlton's final start came on September 27, and he defeated the New York Mets, 8–1. It was a complete-game, one-hit victory, one of six one-hitters Steve hurled in his career.[66] But the Phillies had been mathematically eliminated five days earlier in Pittsburgh, when the Pirates' Bruce Kison defeated Tommy Underwood, 11–3, to clinch their fifth division title in six years.[67] The Phils completed the '75 campaign with an 86-76 record, finishing a distant second behind the Bucs, six and a half games out.[68]

Carlton, who went 15-14 in 1975, began to hear rumors that he was washed up, that his Cy Young season of 1972 had been a fluke, and that he was an average pitcher at best. There was some validity to the criticism, too. Between 1973 and 1975 Carlton's win-loss records were 13-20, 16-13, and 15-14. Added together, Steve's cumulative record was 58-58 during that three-year span.[69] Thus, while the Phillies had become a contender, they were just a .500 club whenever their ace took the mound. Carlton knew he was capable of much more. So did McCarver.

9

Lefty

Philadelphia captured the national spotlight in 1976 as Americans celebrated the nation's bicentennial. Millions of tourists flocked to the city to visit Independence Hall, where the Second Continental Congress voted for separation from Great Britain and later adopted the Declaration of Independence. Across the street the Liberty Bell beckoned visitors, and images of the iconic symbol could be found throughout the City of Brotherly Love, including one at Veterans Stadium, which was tapped to host Major League Baseball's All-Star Game.

The Phillies were primed to capture the national spotlight, too. After years of mediocrity, the 1976 team boasted the talent to contend for the franchise's first World Series title. The lineup was stocked with exceptional young talent. The offense was powered by third baseman Mike Schmidt, who had captured his second straight home run title the previous season, and left fielder Greg "The Bull" Luzinski, who led the National League with 120 RBIs in '75. The Phils also enjoyed a remarkable defense that was bolstered by shortstop Larry Bowa, second baseman Dave Cash, center fielder Garry Maddox, and right fielder Jay Johnstone. All these players had not even reached their prime, being only in their mid- to late twenties, and they were coming off the best offensive performances of their respective careers. Thirty-three-year-old first baseman Dick Allen was the eldest member of the starting lineup. Although he hit a disappointing .233 with just 12 homers and 62 RBIs in '75, Allen's prodigious history as a power hitter still struck fear in opposing pitchers who realized that he was still a dangerous long-ball threat. Schmidt and Luzinski respected him so much, they turned to him for advice.

The biggest question mark was the starting pitching, which had been shaky at best in '75. At the top of the rotation were two previous Cy Young Award winners who appeared as if their best days were already behind them. Thirty-one-year-old Steve Carlton (15-14, 192 SO, 3.56 ERA) had struggled to recapture his brilliance of 1972, when he had earned the award. Thirty-four-year-old Jim Lonborg (8-6, 4.12 ERA) had been hampered by injuries the previous season and seemed to be even further from a return to the glory of his 1967 Cy Young season with the Boston Red Sox. The Phillies were pinning their hopes on a pair of twenty-two-year-olds—Larry Christenson (11-6, 3.67 ERA) and Tommy Underwood (14-13, 4.14 ERA)—to pick up the slack.[1] But Carlton surprised the naysayers, proving that he was still one of the best pitchers in baseball.

The year 1976 turned out to be the one in which the Phillies' ace resurrected his career. With McCarver catching him, Carlton finally found the right mental balance on the mound and won twenty games for a Phillies team that captured its first of three straight division titles. Tim also gave his batterymate a new nickname, "Lefty," which is baseball parlance reserved for the left-handed ace of the pitching staff. McCarver would make sure that Carlton lived up to the complimentary moniker, too.

The '76 season got off to a rocky start when labor conflict interrupted spring training. Marvin Miller, director of the MLB Players Association, discovered a loophole in the reserve clause preventing free agency, and an independent arbitrator ruled in his favor and against the owners. With the ruling, pitchers Andy Messersmith of the Dodgers and Dave McNally of the Expos suddenly became free agents. Infuriated by the cataclysmic development, the owners locked the players out of spring training camps from March 1 to 17.[2] Unable to use the stadiums, spring training facilities, or Minor League parks, the Phillies held daily workouts at Grant Field in Dunedin, Florida, while labor negotiations continued in St. Petersburg. The workouts were organized by the team's player representative, Bob Boone, as well as Tony Taylor and Tim McCarver, and as many as twenty-two players attended them, including Carlton.[3] But that didn't stop *Daily News* columnist Bill Conlin from resuming his criticism.

This time Conlin used both Carlton and McCarver as examples of greed, to which he attributed the lockout. "Despite their first-class travel and four-star hotel accommodations," he wrote, "the ballplayers are griping about their grim working conditions when they actually stand at the very top of the twentieth century food chain. Take the Phillies, who retreat to Bellaire Beach each day for their informal 'workouts': There you will find Tim McCarver frolicking in the 73-degree Gulf of Mexico after a grueling game of Frisbee Keepaway with a large school of teammates' children. Tim's sidekick, Steve Carlton, [lies] somnolently on a poolside lounge sipping a Bloody Mary. . . .

"McCarver, a former player rep, wiped the tears from his eyes when he learned of the proposed shutdown of the informal workouts. 'Obviously, it's a rebuttal to the owners' closing the camps,' Timmy said. 'It's a negotiating ploy, I guess. It's unpleasant to me. I don't particularly like it. I'm 34. It takes me a little longer to get in shape than when I was 21. Hell, I'll keep working. Lefty and I will run and he can throw to me.'

"Carlton opened one eye. 'Should have done it a long time ago, put more pressure on the owners,' he said before drifting off to sleep."[4]

In fact, for the first time in years Carlton did some jogging that spring, but it was not with McCarver. Despite Lefty's aversion to running, he reluctantly agreed to join Tug McGraw on one of his morning jogs. McGraw, an avid jogger, stayed in a condo at Indian Rocks Beach and occasionally jogged the eight-mile distance to the Phillies' spring training site in Clearwater. Curious as to why the reliever enjoyed running so much, Carlton, who also rented a condo at Indian Rocks Beach, asked McGraw, "What's with all the running?"

"It's a great cardio workout," replied Tug. "You should really try it."

"Well, okay," said Lefty. "I'll give it a shot."

The next morning the two teammates jogged the eight miles to Clearwater's Jack Russell Stadium. When they arrived, McGraw was completely exhausted. Carlton, on the other hand, had barely broken a sweat. "What kind of workout was that?!" he snapped. "I never saw the point in running and that little jog just reinforced my opinion."[5]

When negotiations concluded, the owners and the players' union agreed to the introduction of free agency for the first time. Among the key provisions of the new, three-year collective bargaining agreement were the following: (1) A player was eligible for free agency after six years of service; (2) Any club losing a free agent was entitled to draft-choice compensation from the signing club; (3) A player with at least five years of service could demand that his club trade him; (4) Players with at least two years of service were eligible to submit their salaries for arbitration. If a player was eligible for free agency, his salary dispute could go to arbitration only upon mutual consent by player and club; (5) The minimum salary was increased to $19,000 for 1976 and 1977, and $21,000 for 1978 and 1979 (the increase was made retroactive for the 1976 season); and (6) Owners increased their contribution to the players' pension fund to $8.3 million, an annual increase of $1.85 million.[6]

Meanwhile, the Phillies got off to a dismal 1-3 start. They lost first-string catcher Johnny Oates in the April 10 opener against Pittsburgh when he fractured his collarbone in a collision with Dave Parker at home plate. The Phils also lost the game, 5–4.[7] The second loss came the next day on Carlton's first start of the season, when the Pirates dispatched him in just four and a third innings en route to an 8–3 victory. Lefty was never in the game, giving up 5 earned runs on 5 hits and 3 walks before he was relieved by Tommy Underwood.[8] Carlton's second start came on April 17 against the Cubs at Chicago's Wrigley Field. He was knocked out in the second inning, surrendering 7 earned runs on 7 hits, including a 2-run homer by Rick Monday and a solo shot by Steve Swisher, both coming in the second inning. Seven other pitchers followed in a slugfest that saw the Phillies trailing 12–1 at one point. But the Fightins fought back, paced by Mike Schmidt's 4 home runs, and won the game in the tenth inning, 18–16.[9] The victory ignited the offense, and the Phillies won the next four of five games, including a 10–5 victory over the Braves that put them in first place in the National League East. Although Carlton started that game, he did not get the decision, giving up 4 earned runs on 4 hits in six innings of work.[10]

Boone was behind the plate for all three of Carlton's starts. Frustrated with an 0-1 record and two no-decisions, Lefty asked Ozark if McCarver could catch him in his next start. The Phils' skipper agreed. That assignment came on May 1 in the nightcap of a doubleheader against the Braves in Atlanta. Carlton pitched a complete-game victory, 4–2, giving up just 2 earned runs on 6 hits. He also recorded 7 strikeouts. The only real mistake he made came in the sixth. After walking Jim Wynn, he threw a 3-2 fastball down the middle of the plate to Earl Williams, and the Braves catcher lined it over the left-field fence.[11]

Ozark decided to pair Carlton with McCarver for his next four starts, which came against San Diego, Houston, St. Louis, and New York. Lefty won all four with complete-game victories: 9–1, 12–2, 2–1, and 5–0, respectively. In that four-game span, May 11–26, Carlton's record improved to 5-1 and his earned run average dropped from 7.27 to 3.48.[12] Ozark made McCarver Lefty's personal catcher, a role he would retain through the 1979 season. In fact, Tim became the most famous example of a "personal catcher" in the 1970s.

McCarver said in a 2019 interview that the "personal catcher arrangement" is unique. "You can't depend on it to work all the time," he explained. "With Lefty and me it had to work immediately. There were so many things that had to fall into place. The biggest thing is that Carlton had to win. And I'm not talking about three out of five starts. I'm talking about four out of five. It had to work immediately, otherwise they would've ditched it."[13]

When asked why the arrangement was so successful, McCarver insisted that the "biggest thing [he] did was call for the slider." He did so because "Lefty's slider was that devastating," he explained, "and for whatever reason, Bob Boone tried to set him up with a fastball or a curveball like normal pitchers. With Lefty, everything [was] off the slider."[14] But Carlton insisted that McCarver did much more than that. "Timmy was a very good bridge player," said Lefty. "In cards, you have to remember all the sequences. He applied that to his catching skills. He remembered sequences and strengths and weaknesses of hitters."[15] Carlton also admitted that he and Boone "were never in sync." That was "no knock on Boonie, who became a tremendous catcher," he said. "But in the early '70s, I'd shake him off four or five times before he'd finally ask for the pitch I wanted to throw. With Timmy it was different. We worked real well together. If I shook him off, his next sign was exactly what I wanted."[16]

Ironically, Carlton had forgotten that McCarver, as a young catcher back in the mid-1960s, was just as adamant as Boone about calling pitches. Lefty also seemed to forget that he had often criticized Tim for not calling more breaking balls when they played together in St. Louis. It took time for the two teammates to reach an understanding on how to set up hitters and how to dispatch them. In that sense, Boone was no different than McCarver when he caught for the Cardinals a decade earlier. Both firmly believed that they—not the pitcher—should decide the pitch. Most catchers in the 1960s and 1970s thought that way because they played every day and possessed a more extensive knowledge of the opposing hitters and their vulnerabilities. Many pitchers appreciated that advantage and deferred to their catcher's judgment. There were some pitchers, however, who insisted on calling their own games. Carlton, like his mentor, Bob Gibson, was one of those stubborn hurlers. He believed it was better to throw a pitch of his own choosing with conviction and get hit hard than to allow the catcher to call a pitch he disagreed with but resulted in an out. In other words, part of McCarver's success as Carlton's batterymate was his understanding that "Lefty would rather be 100 percent behind the wrong pitch than 50 percent behind the right pitch."[17] Thus, Tim worked hard to understand Carlton's thinking and to establish a game plan that would complement it. That is why he exploited Lefty's slider in his pitch calling and ultimately why he became Carlton's exclusive batterymate.

On May 31 the Phillies were in first place with second-place Pittsburgh six and a half back and New York in third, nine and a half back. Carlton (6-1), Jim Lonborg (6-0), and Larry Christenson (6-1) had combined for seventeen straight victories. The offense was just as potent. The team hit .285 for the month with shortstop Larry

Bowa, first baseman Dick Allen, center fielder Garry Maddox, and third baseman Mike Schmidt batting .300 or better. In addition, Schmidt's 15 home runs by the end of May were second only to New York Met Dave Kingman's 17. Together with an explosive offense, the lockdown pitching enabled the Phillies to finish the month of May at 22-5, a new club record. When asked to compare the Phillies to the Cincinnati Reds, who were leading the National League West, pitcher Tommy John of the Los Angeles Dodgers replied, "That's like trying to compare the hydrogen bomb and the atom bomb—they both kill."[18]

Between June 5 and July 29 Carlton regained his winning form. Of the twelve games he started during that span, Lefty won six, including three complete-game victories, and lost only two. Although the other four games resulted in no-decisions, the Phillies won three of those contests and Carlton pitched at least seven innings in all four. His season record improved to 11-4 with an earned run average of 3.25.[19]

McCarver also settled into a comfortable routine, catching every five days and on the other days sitting in the dugout and needling the opposition. "I do it to keep my mind from wandering," said Tim. "Besides, it's fun."[20] Not as fun as hitting, though. McCarver, in seventy-one plate appearances, was batting .296 with 21 hits and 14 RBIs.[21] He should have had at least one home run, but the 375-foot grand slam he hit off the Pirates' Larry Demery in the first game of a July 4 doubleheader at Pittsburgh's Three Rivers Stadium was erased when he inadvertently passed Garry Maddox on the base paths. Although Tim was called out for passing the base runner, he did receive credit for a single and 3 RBIs in a game Carlton went on to win, 10–5.[22]

"It was definitely the longest single I've ever hit," McCarver chuckled. "I knew it was gone and I'm into my Cadillac trot, head down, then all of a sudden I notice I'm even with Garry [Maddox]. I tried to backpedal but [first base umpire] Ed Vargo looks at me and says I'm out. I guess the moral is to hit 'em so they get out of the park quicker."[23]

When asked by Bill Lyon of the *Inquirer* if he was angry about the gaffe, McCarver said, "Hey, what could I do except laugh about it? I mean, you screw up right out in front of 30,000 people it's kinda tough to hide. Besides, how can you dig a hole in artificial turf?" His teammates thought the mistake was hilarious. "Anyone else in baseball, and nobody would have said a word," Tommy Hutton noted. "But Tim has such a terrific attitude we couldn't help but laugh." Comedic reliever Tug McGraw labeled McCarver's grand slam/single "The Grand Sob." Even Ozark had to admit that the incident was funny. "At first, I was teed off. But pretty soon my sides were aching from laughing so hard," said the Phils' manager.[24]

Winning tends to minimize mistakes, and the Phillies certainly had a lot to laugh about being nine games in front of the second-place Pirates in the NL East. Although the Phils dropped the next four games, Carlton stopped the losing streak on July 10 in the first game of a doubleheader against the San Diego Padres at the Vet. Lefty was simply brilliant in the 5–0, complete-game shutout. He was never in danger of losing after the Phillies got him three first-inning runs off of San Diego starter Alan Foster. Carlton also received a standing ovation and a thunder of cheers when he fanned Padres slugger Dave Winfield in the ninth to record his two thousandth career strikeout. The Phillies added two more runs in the sixth on a solo homer by Garry Maddox and an RBI single by Carlton himself. Bob Boone was the hero of the nightcap, going 2-for-4, including a 2-run homer and 3 RBIs to give Jim Lonborg a 4–2 victory and the Phillies the sweep.[25]

Boone's impressive hitting performance was just the most recent in a season when he established himself as an All-Star. It hadn't been easy for the six-foot-two, 208-pound Stanford University grad since his promotion to the Phillies in 1973. That season he hit .261 and took the brunt of the blame for Carlton's lackluster performance. The next year he hurt his back in spring training and played through pain that would have put a lesser man into traction. Still, he caught 146 games while Lefty continued to criticize him for his pitch calling. In 1975 Boonie hit .373 in April before the Phillies acquired veteran catcher Johnny Oates from Atlanta to appease Carlton.[26] But in '76 Boone, now free of pain, was finally able to show the Phillies how capable he was behind and at the plate. Through the first half of the season the young catcher was among the top twenty batters in the National League. In 215 at bats he was hitting .307, with 66 hits and 37 RBIs.[27] The performance earned Boone a spot on the National League All-Star team in a year when the Midsummer Classic was being played in Philadelphia.

On July 13 Major League Baseball's greatest stars gathered at Veterans Stadium, and Boone, selected as a reserve catcher, was among them. When Cincinnati's Johnny Bench was announced as the National League's starting catcher, Boonie heard some long-deserved cheers as the hometown faithful erupted with the chant "We want Boone!" Their demand was granted in the fifth inning, when he replaced Bench and caught the rest of the game. Although Boonie popped out to short and flew out to right in his only two at bats, he was thrilled with both his experience as a first-time All-Star and the National League's 7–1 victory over the American League.[28]

Boone's All-Star status reinforced his value to the Phillies even though Carlton didn't want to pitch to him. After Oates was injured, Boone became the primary catcher at least four times a week. In addition, whenever Carlton was relieved, McCarver was also lifted, so Boone would complete the game behind the plate. As a result, Boonie established good working relationships with all the pitchers. He also accepted the fact that Lefty preferred to pitch to McCarver. "I could've pouted, or gone to the press with it," he admitted in a 2020 interview. "But what good would that have done? As long as we were winning, why complain? I couldn't take it personally. Besides, I was catching every day and I probably needed that fifth day off to rest. That gave Lefty the opportunity to watch me catch and eventually see that I was a good receiver."[29]

Carlton was not selected for the National League All-Star team that year, probably because the Phils already had five representatives. In addition to Boone's nod for All-Star status, Greg Luzinski was named the starting left-fielder, and Mike Schmidt, Larry Bowa, and Dave Cash were selected as reserves by NL manager Sparky Anderson of the Cincinnati Reds. In addition, Lefty had been named to five earlier All-Star squads ('68, '69, '71, '72, '74), and there were other pitchers who had better records that season or had never been selected for the Midsummer Classic. Of the eight pitchers chosen by Anderson, starter Randy Jones of the Padres (16-3) and Jon Matlack of the New York Mets (10-2) had tallied more victories than Carlton's nine. Four of the other hurlers were first-time All-Stars (John Montefusco of the San Francisco Giants, Rick Rhoden of the Los Angeles Dodgers, former Phillie Dick Ruthven of the Atlanta Braves, and Ken Forsch of the Houston Astros). The remaining two pitchers were the legendary Tom Seaver, who was one of only two Mets on the squad, and Woodie Fryman, the lone representative of the Montreal Expos.[30] But Carlton probably welcomed the three-day reprieve of the All-Star break. Besides, he would be selected for five future All-Star teams.

Between July 15 and August 24 Carlton pitched like the Cy Young Award winner of four seasons earlier. He started ten games and won seven, including three complete-game victories, and had a single loss. His record improved to 16-4, and he saw his earned run average drop from 3.53 to just 3.09. During that ten-game span, Lefty enjoyed a five-game winning streak that began on August 3 when he defeated the Chicago Cubs, 8–5, at Wrigley Field. The next week he won a nail-biter against Harry Rasmussen and the Cardinals at Busch Stadium. Although Lefty did not have the best control, he relied on cunning to limit the Cards to single runs in the third and seventh innings. Mike Schmidt provided a two-run homer, his thirtieth of the season, in the fourth, and Jerry Martin, a run-scoring sacrifice fly in the ninth, to seal the 3–2 victory.

On August 14 Carlton breezed to his fourteenth win of the season, this one a 13–2 rout of the San Francisco Giants. Bobby Tolan, Garry Maddox, Jay Johnstone, and Larry Bowa led the attack with 3 hits each. Five days later Lefty defeated the Astros, 7–1, in the nightcap of a doubleheader at the Vet. Schmidt, Johnstone, and Boone, who was playing first base, all collected a pair of RBIs each.[31] The fifth and final game of the winning streak came on August 24. Carlton threw another gem, this one against the Braves at Atlanta's Fulton County Stadium. With cable-TV mogul Ted Turner outfitted in an Indian headdress and seated in the owner's box, the Phillies destroyed his Braves, tagging their million-dollar pitcher Andy Messersmith for 8 runs in the three innings he lasted. Bobby Tolan led the 17-hit attack, driving in 5 runs with a pair of singles and his fifth home run of the season. Carlton, who held Atlanta to 3 runs on 7 hits, also joined the offensive explosion, banging out 3 hits, driving in 3 runs, and scoring another in the 14–3 win. The victory improved the Phillies' record to 82-41 and increased their first-place lead over Pittsburgh to fifteen and a half games in the East. New York was in third place, nineteen games out.[32]

There were times during Carlton's five-game winning streak when he was simply unhittable because of a devastating slider. "Lefty threw his slider by cutting through the ball instead of breaking his wrist," explained McCarver. "Because he didn't use the damaging twisting motion of his hand, he rarely made a mistake and he *never* hurt his elbow. He was so strong from his fingertips to his elbow that he didn't have turn his hand. Lefty could put the same spin, only better, on his slider that other pitchers got throwing the cut fastball."[33]

With Carlton's slider the seams of the baseball spun in a horizontal rotation. But the spin was so tight, it appeared like a "little bitty dot" on the ball. "When I threw the slider, I wanted the spin real tight so the ball was blurry like a fastball and you couldn't see the dot," Carlton told Tyler Kepner, the national baseball writer for the *New York Times*, in a 2019 interview. "The intent was to fool the hitter as long as I could, so he had to commit to a fastball to come out and try to get it. But if the dot was as big as a quarter, the spin would be like a circle and the hitter could easily recognize it. That's when they laid off the pitch."[34]

From the hitter's perspective, the spin on the slider made it appear like a "gyroscope," creating an illusory effect. "Lefty's slider had a 'dime spin,' which is a tighter spin than the 'quarter' or 'half-dollar spin,'" explained McCarver. The tighter spin allowed Carlton's slider to move faster and drop with more bite than sliders thrown by other pitchers. Since he was a southpaw, his slider ran in on a right-handed batter and ran away from a left-handed hitter. Just as important, according to McCarver, "the tighter the spin, the more control Lefty had in locating the pitch." In fact, Carlton could place the pitch exactly where he wanted it—inside or outside the strike zone.[35]

The reason Carlton could throw such a devastating slider was due to his extraordinary strength. He was, said McCarver, the "strongest man I ever knew from his fingertips to his elbow."[36] His strength came from an unusual—and grueling—training regimen created by Gus Hoefling, a pioneering strength and conditioning coach.

Hoefling was a martial arts teacher in Southern California. In 1973 he relocated to the East Coast to work for the Eagles in Philadelphia, where he created a series of grueling, year-round workouts rooted in the martial arts. At the same time, Gus was also a strong believer in Nautilus, isometrics, push-ups, sit-ups, and a battery of other physical exercises. Together the mental and physical training not only allowed Hoefling's students to improve their strength, agility, and cardiovascular system but also made him a pioneer in sports psychology.[37]

Intelligent, loquacious, and opinionated, Gus Hoefling quickly gained a following among the city's pro athletes. Bob Boone began training with him in the winter of 1975 and was impressed. When the Eagles dismissed Hoefling in 1976, Phillies owner Ruly Carpenter hired him. Boone, knowing that Carlton hated to run and was already invested in the martial arts, introduced the pitcher to the fitness guru. The three men started training together.[38]

Lefty, a black belt in Shotokan karate, immediately became one of Hoefling's greatest advocates. Gus introduced him to carefully choreographed martial arts exercises that resembled a dance form. These were designed not only to build a strong base and core through range of motion, especially at flex positions, but also to improve endurance and mental focus. Carlton excelled at one of the most demanding of these martial arts forms, one known as "sillum kung-fu," which was only for elite students. "Lefty was superior at this art," said Hoefling in a 2019 interview. "He had an appetite for brutally hard work. He was a 'Work Master,' which is the literal definition of 'Kung' (work) 'Fu' (master). I've always said that whoever put that man together genetically did one hell of a job."[39]

Other exercises were designed strictly to build physical strength.

"Gus taught me how to build strength in areas that most people didn't know how to exploit as trainers," Carlton told Tyler Kepner of the *New York Times*. "We went after weak tissue all the time, which is in the ulnar regions [of the thumb, wrist, and elbow]. We made those areas stronger, more able to take stress."[40] Under Hoefling's guidance, Carlton incorporated a series of rice treatments into his training regimen. One exercise called for the left-hander to push the palm of his hand into a fifty-five-gallon garbage can filled with white rice until he reached the bottom. This was done to strengthen his forearm and wrists. Another exercise had Lefty walk back and forth in a twenty-foot-long box that was filled three feet deep with rice in order to build superior leg and body strength.[41] "The rice provides a form of positive—and negative—resistance at the same time," Hoefling told Mike Sielski of the *Philadelphia Inquirer* in a 2020 interview. "It was different from pumping iron or push-ups. The ancient Chinese used it as early as 520 A.D."[42]

The Phillies' number-two starting pitcher, Jim Lonborg, also gravitated toward the rice workouts. "Early in my career I did a lot of long-distance running to stay in shape," said Lonborg. "All pitchers ran to stay in shape. But Steve, who hated to run, became a great advocate of Gus's techniques, especially the martial arts and rice tubs. I bought into the rice exercises because it strengthened my forearms and the ulna collateral ligament. I never had any problems with my elbow after that."[43]

Hoefling also used other, more traditional conditioning exercises designed to strengthen the stomach muscles, which are essential to the torso rotation a pitcher needs to generate power. These exercises included one-legged push-ups and sit-ups with fifteen-pound weights strapped to the wrists and ankles. Carlton became so proficient at the latter that he was able to do 1,100 sit-ups at a time.[44]

"There were times after I pitched nine innings, I'd work out with Gus the following day," recalled Lefty in a 2013 interview with Stan Hochman of the *Philadelphia Daily News*. "I'd be sore going into the workout and when I came out, all the soreness was gone from my arm. I'd gotten rid of the lactic acid buildup, the kind of thing running couldn't do, by itself. Prior to working with Gus, I'd carry that soreness into the day of my next start. But Gus's training gave me the stamina to pitch in hot, hot weather, without getting tired."[45]

Teammates were astounded by Carlton's stamina. "Lefty and Gus did their workout routine for at least ninety minutes," according to Larry Bowa. "It wasn't a quick twenty-minute routine. Lefty really pushed himself, especially the day after he pitched. He'd drive his hands and forearms into a huge barrel of rice until he reached the bottom. Most guys were lucky to get their hand eight to twelve inches into that same barrel."[46] Pitcher Larry Christenson, who also experimented with the rice tub workouts, called Lefty "an animal" because he was in "such great shape."[47] McCarver, who did not join his batterymate in Gus's grueling workouts, echoed Christenson's admiration. "Steve worked so much harder than any other pitcher," he said. "No one could keep up with him."[48] Although Tim admitted that "Gus influenced a lot of us," the veteran catcher wanted no part of him. Once, before a Carlton start, McCarver's back was tight, and he asked Hoefling to stretch him out. As Gus manipulated his legs into various contortions, the catcher let loose with a barrage of profanities, eliciting an eruption of uncontrollable laughter from his teammates.[49] "Yeah, there was some swearing going on," Hoefling recalled, in a gross understatement. "But it was good for team spirit," he added with a sly grin.[50]

The physical conditioning was only one aspect of the regimen. Hoefling, who believed that "the body is a person's temple," also stressed the importance of positive thinking. The dual emphasis on conditioning the body and the mind has "withstood the antiquities of time, so you know it works," he said.[51] Mental focus was developed through meditation, visualization, and positive thinking. The psychological boost of the mental training allowed Carlton to block out the negative as well as the physical challenges he faced. "The day I pitched was a day off from martial arts," he explained. "It was like a state of euphoria, I didn't have to work out. The game became, psychologically, and from a physical standpoint, like an easy day. It was a big boost. It was like, 'Geez, this is a day off, let's go out and pitch nine innings.'"[52]

The mental training also enabled Carlton to embrace a positive attitude, not just about the game but about his approach to life itself. Everything he did was based on positive thinking and his desire to succeed, whether it was training his mind, conditioning his body, or eventually his decision to stop talking to the media. The mental training also improved Lefty's effort to become devoid of emotion. He believed that "emotion [was] subjective," and Hoefling's training regimen was designed to "remove any form of distraction that could disrupt his concentration on the mound."[53]

Owner Ruly Carpenter went so far as to build Carlton a $15,000 "mood behavior" room next to the clubhouse. Seated in an easy chair in the soundproof sanctuary, Lefty would stare at a painting of ocean waves rushing against the shore and listen to a tape recording repeating, "I am courageous, calm, confident[,] and relaxed. I can control my destiny."[54] The visualization did not stop there, however.

On days Carlton was scheduled to pitch, Larry Christenson would find him in the trainer's room lying on the table as if taking a rest. "Once, I asked Lefty what he was doing," recalled Christenson. "He told me that he was visualizing the pitcher's part of home plate, or the corners, and blocking out the hitter's part of the plate, which is down the middle. The heart of the plate didn't exist for Lefty. Only the corners where he intended to throw his pitches. If the hitter was taking the corners away from him, Lefty would pitch in or brush him back." Another time Carlton, again on the trainer's table with eyes closed, told his younger teammate that he was visualizing the spin on his slider and how he was planning to throw it against the various batters in the opposing team's lineup that night. "No question," said Christenson. "Lefty was a strange bird. But there's no denying that his methods made him one of the most successful pitchers of all time."[55]

For most of the '76 season the Phillies had been playing .600 baseball, and it's difficult for any team, regardless of how talented they are, to keep up that kind of pace over a 162-game grind. The Phils were due for a letdown, and it began on August 27 when the team went into a two-week tailspin. During that time frame the Phillies lost thirteen of their fifteen games, while the second-place Pirates won twelve of their fourteen. On days the Phils had good pitching, nobody hit. On days when the team hit, they didn't get the pitching. All the regulars were mired in terrible hitting slumps. Dave Cash had just 13 hits in 45 at bats. Schmidt was 9-for-55; Bowa, 8-for-52; Luzinski, 7-for-32; Boone, 9-for-33; and Allen, 1-for-25, before he was benched. The team was hitting an anemic .128.[56] The pitching wasn't much better. Even Carlton dropped a pair of games and recorded a no-decision in another losing contest.

Lefty's hard luck began on August 29, when he faced the Big Red Machine in Cincinnati. He surrendered 3 earned runs on 8 hits in just five and two-thirds innings of work in a game the Phillies eventually lost, 6–5.[57] His next start came on September 3 against Tom Seaver and the Mets at Shea Stadium in New York. It was a pitcher's duel, just like the previous seven times the two aces had faced each other since 1970. By September 3 the Phillies had lost their previous six games and were counting on Lefty to stop the skid. Unfortunately, Carlton also lost this one, 1–0, on three straight one-out singles in the fourth inning.[58] Meanwhile, the red-hot Pirates swept a doubleheader against Montreal, thereby reducing the Phillies' first-place lead to seven and a half games in the National League East.[59]

Carlton struggled again on September 8 against the Pirates' Jim Rooker at Three Rivers Stadium. After suffering a pulled back muscle in the second inning, Lefty surrendered five runs before he was lifted in the fourth. When the dust cleared, the Phillies had lost their eleventh out of the last twelve games, 6–1, and were just four and a half games in front of the Pirates in the NL East.[60]

The prolonged losing streak enabled Bill Conlin to resume his negative commentary on the sports pages of the *Daily News*. Evoking the "ghosts of the 1964 Phillies," who were up by six and a half games with a dozen left to play and dropped ten straight to blow the pennant, Conlin provoked the fans with references to the '64 and '76 teams as "choke artists." According to the *Daily News* critic, there was "no questioning the Phillies' offense, depth and pitching." However, he continued, "there are serious doubts building about intangibles like courage, grace under pressure and the ability to turn a losing situation around. It's a nagging question of whether this magnificent array of talent can shrug off a two-week nightmare."[61]

"Hell, we played four of the best months of baseball this town has ever seen," McCarver told Conlin, trying to put the losing streak in perspective. "Let's face it, when you see a 15-game lead down to four games, you're concerned. But [the Pirates] are in a position where they HAVE to win two games, where if we win tomorrow night our position is strengthened. Momentum is a very big thing in our game, much more so than in football where you play one game a week."[62]

Carlton silenced the naysayers, winning his next three starts despite recurring back pain. On September 13 he won his seventeenth game, 7–2, over the Montreal Expos at the Vet with Schmidt hitting his thirty-fourth and thirty-fifth homers of the season.[63] Five days later Lefty fanned eleven Cubs for his eighteenth victory, a 4–1 win over Chicago's Rick Reuschel at Wrigley Field.[64] And on September 23 Carlton breezed to his nineteenth win, 7–3, over the Cardinals at the Vet.[65] Conspicuously absent was any criticism or praise from the *Daily News* sportswriters.

Finally, on September 26 the Phillies clinched the National League East on Jim Lonborg's seventeenth win of the season, a 4-hitter against the Montreal Expos. Greg Luzinski's 3 homers sealed the 4–1 victory. Phils also won the nightcap behind the 6-hit pitching of Ron Reed and Ron Schueler, 2–1.[66]

Carlton pitched the season finale against Craig Swan and the Mets on October 3 at the Vet. He gave up a single run on 3 hits and recorded a season-high 12 strikeouts en route to the 2–1 victory. McCarver ended up driving in the winning run on a fifth-inning single to chase Swan from the game.

"This is the happiest day of my life," Carlton told Bruce Keidan of the *Inquirer*. "I'm happy about winning my twentieth. I'm happy for Mike Schmidt[,] who won another home run title. I'm happy for the club." Lefty also credited his batterymate for calling a "super game." When he overheard the compliment, McCarver joked that he was "going to ask for a multi-year contract for one hundred and fifty thousand [dollars], 175 and 200 over three years."[67]

Having clinched the National League East, finishing nine games in front of the second-place Pittsburgh Pirates, the Phillies would face the Cincinnati Reds, the winners of the NL West, in the league's best-of-three playoff.[68] It wouldn't be a cakewalk. Cincinnati dominated Major League Baseball in the 1970s. Known as the Big Red Machine for its offensive prowess, the team carried itself with a controlled arrogance, realizing just how good it was. Led by catcher Johnny Bench (.234, 16 HRS, 74 RBIs) and third baseman Pete Rose (.323, 10 HRS, 63 RBIs), the Reds had a cadre of other stars as well, including first baseman Tony Pérez (.260, 19 HRS, 91 RBIs), right fielder Ken Griffey (.336, 6 HRS, 74 RBIs), shortstop Dave Concepción (.281, 9 HRS, 69 RBIs), center fielder César Gerónimo (.307, 2 HRS, 49 RBIs), left fielder George Foster (.306, 29 HRS, 121 RBIs), and second baseman Joe Morgan (.320, 27 HRS, 111 RBIs), who had won consecutive National League Most Valuable Player Awards in 1975 and 1976. The pitching staff was not as impressive, but it didn't need to be, what with all the run support it received for the offensive juggernaut. Gary Nolan (15-9, 3.46 ERA) was the ace of the staff. Pat Zachry (14-7, 2.74 ERA), Fred Norman (12-7, 3.10 ERA), Jack Billingham (12-10, 4.43 ERA), and Don Gullett (11-3, 3.00 ERA) rounded out the starting rotation. Rawly Eastwick (11-5, 26 SV, 2.08 ERA) and Will McEnaney (2-6, 7 SV, 4.85 ERA) headed a strong bullpen.[69]

During the 1970s the Reds averaged ninety-five wins a season and were perennial contenders, having captured four pennants and a world championship. Their experience in postseason play gave the Reds a significant advantage over the Phillies. On the other hand, the Phils had won eight of their twelve regular-season contests against Cincinnati and had the kind of team that could dominate a short, three-game series. The Phillies had stronger pitching than the Reds; the Phils' rotation was Carlton (20-7, 3.13 ERA), Lonborg (18-10, 3.08 ERA), Christenson (13-8, 3.67 ERA), Underwood (10-5, 3.52 ERA), and spot starter/middle reliever Jim Kaat (12-14, 3.47 ERA). Tug McGraw (7-6, 11 SV, 2.51 ERA), Ron Reed (8-7, 14 SV, 2.46 ERA), and Gene Garber (9-3, 11 SV, 2.81 ERA) made up the bullpen. The Fightins also had firepower comparable to that of the Reds in Schmidt (.262, 38 HRS, 107 RBIs), Luzinski (.304, 21 HRS, 95 RBIs), Allen (.268, 15 HRS, 49 RBIs), and Maddox (.330, 6 HRS, 68 RBIs).[70]

"I thought we had a team that matched up pretty well with the Reds," said Jim Lonborg in a 2018 interview. "We had finished up the season on a strong note, and that's the kind of thing that enables a team to go into a tough, three-out-of-five-games series with a positive attitude. Statistically, our pitching was better, and, offensively, we had power hitters like Schmidt and Luzinski who were just as good as Pérez, Foster, and Bench."[71] But the Reds' depth and postseason experience proved to be too much for the Phillies.

The National League Championship Series opened in Philadelphia on Saturday, October 9, with Steve Carlton facing Don Gullett. More than 62,640 fans packed Veterans Stadium to watch the Phils' ace in his first postseason start since 1968, when he hurled for the Cardinals. Although Carlton was 0-0 with a 4.32 ERA in three starts against the Reds during the regular season, the Phillies were still favored to win the first game. But it was Gullett who turned out to be the star of the game instead.

Carlton pitched out of a bases-loaded jam in the first inning to hold the Reds scoreless. The Phils gave their starter a 1-0 lead in the bottom of the frame when Dave Cash scored on a sacrifice fly by Mike Schmidt. Gullett proceeded to walk the bases full with two outs but escaped further damage when he got Tim McCarver to fly out to shallow left field. After that he pitched flawless baseball. The Reds tied the game in the third, when Pete Rose led off with a triple and scored on a sacrifice fly by Tony Pérez. The score remained tied at one run apiece until the sixth, when Carlton surrendered a solo homer to George Foster, a double to Dave Concepción, and an RBI single to Gullett, giving the Reds a 3–1 lead.[72]

Terry Tata, one of the umpires, recalled that Carlton pitched aggressively. "He didn't care if it was the Big Red Machine or not," said Tata. "Carlton loved to throw inside, and McCarver knew that and used it to his advantage. They liked keeping the hitters on their toes. I remember Rose crowding the plate that game, and Lefty nearly made him eat dirt. You knew it was coming after Rose hit that triple in the third. The other thing I remember about Carlton was that he never complained, even if he disagreed with [umpire Ed] Sudol, who was behind home plate. He just took the ball back from McCarver and got ready to throw the next pitch."[73]

Carlton lasted until the eighth. His nemesis, Johnny Bench, doubled off the left-field fence to open the inning. Lefty then walked Concepción before Ozark lifted him. Tug McGraw entered the game and struck out César Gerónimo before uncorking a wild pitch that advanced both runners. Gullett knocked a double down the right-field line to score Bench and Concepción and increase the Reds' lead to 5–1. Rose followed with a line-drive double to left to score Gullett with the final Cincinnati run.

Reds manager Sparky Anderson brought in his closer Rawly Eastwick in the ninth to face the heart of the Phillies' order. Maddox led off the inning with a single to right. Luzinski followed with a broken-bat double. Although the two runners scored on singles by Dick Allen and pinch hitter Jay Johnstone, the Reds won the game, 6–3. After the game Pete Rose, who had contributed three extra-base hits, added insult to injury when he told the media, "Steve Carlton is their best. We beat their best, and that's got to make them think a little."[74]

Jim Lonborg faced Pat Zachry in the second playoff game, on Sunday afternoon, October 10. Lonborg held the Reds hitless through five innings. With a 2–0 lead heading into the sixth, the Phillies saw their lead evaporate. An error by Dick Allen and two questionable hits opened the floodgates, and Cincinnati scored four runs. The Reds added another two runs in the seventh, one against McGraw, and the other against Ron Reed, winning the game by a 6–2 margin.[75] The Phillies had their backs to the proverbial wall. Now they would have to sweep the Reds in Cincinnati to reach the World Series.

The series moved to Riverfront Stadium on Tuesday, October 12, for the third contest. Ozark gambled by starting veteran Jim Kaat, who had won only two of his last twelve decisions during the regular season. But he opted for Kaat, believing a veteran with World Series experience would handle the pressure better than either Christenson or Underwood, the youngest pitchers in the rotation. Ozark's hunch proved to be correct. Kaat pitched brilliantly, taking a 3–0 shutout into the seventh inning. Back-to-back doubles by Schmidt and Luzinski gave the Phils a 1–0 lead in the fourth off Reds starter Gary Nolan. Philadelphia increased its lead in the seventh on a walk and doubles by Schmidt and Maddox. But the Reds came back in the bottom of the inning.

After allowing the first two runners to reach base, Kaat was replaced by Ron Reed, who promptly surrendered four earned runs on three hits. Down 4–3, the Phils battled back, scoring twice in the eighth and once in the ninth for a 6–4 lead. Unfortunately, Reed surrendered back-to-back homers by Foster and Bench, and the Reds tied the game. Ozark brought in Gene Garber, who surrendered a single to Concepción. Garber was then lifted for Underwood, who proceeded to load the bases. Ken Griffey knocked in the winning run, and Cincinnati clinched its second straight pennant with a 7–6 victory.[76]

Despite their quick elimination from the playoffs, the '76 Phillies had demonstrated significant improvement. The team compiled a club-record 101 victories and made the postseason for the first time since 1950. In so doing, the Phils made baseball relevant again in the City of Brotherly Love, at least for the 2,480,150 fans (another franchise record) who had come out to watch them at Veterans Stadium that season. Danny Ozark was named Manager of the Year by *The Sporting News* and the National League Manager of the Year by United Press International and the Associated Press. Talented players like Mike Schmidt, who finished third in voting for NL MVP behind Cincinnati's Joe Morgan and George Foster, as well as Greg Luzinski, Larry Bowa, and Bob Boone, were finally recognized outside of Philadelphia after being selected for the National League's All-Star squad. Garry Maddox finished third in the NL batting race with a .330 average.[77]

Of all the improvements, however, Carlton's return to form as one of the most dominant pitchers in the Majors was arguably the most significant for a young team with the potential to be a perennial contender. With a 20-7 record, 195 strikeouts, and 3.13 ERA, Lefty finished fourth in voting for the NL Cy Young Award behind San Diego's Randy Jones (22-14, 93 SO, 2.74 ERA), who won the award; New York's Jerry Koosman (21-10, 200 SO, 2.69 ERA); and Los Angeles's Don Sutton (21-10, 161 SO, 3.06 ERA).[78] In addition, Tim McCarver's role in Carlton's transformation from a .500 pitcher to a Cy Young candidate cannot be overstated.

"When I came back to the Phillies in '75, Lefty needed some help," recalled McCarver. "He was confused by his three subpar years, and his relationship with the press was starting to wear on him. He'd been trying too hard for his own good. I might have helped him relax a little bit by talking with him about his mechanics and by calling for more sliders, but I certainly didn't structure him for victory. Steve did that himself with his physical conditioning and his mental approach to the game."[79] In fact, Tim did much more than he gave himself credit for.

When McCarver became Carlton's personal catcher, he restored the left-hander's confidence in himself and his pitching abilities. He became Lefty's most trusted friend—a soul mate behind the plate. Tim, long before he reached the Majors, had learned from Hall of Fame catcher Bill Dickey that "there is no stronger bond between two players in any sport than the one between the pitcher and catcher," and that lesson stayed with him for the rest of his career. According to McCarver, the pitcher-catcher relationship is a symbiotic one, "almost as if there is a string running from one to the other so that one's motion pulls the other along. The thinking comes before the game to allow for instinct, activity, and animation during the game. More than any other combination in sports, the [pitcher-catcher] tandem relies on a rhythm and cadence to be successful. The two are on the same wavelength, communicating without talking."[80]

Tim saw his role in the pitcher-catcher partnership in football terms, as both the "receiver" who "catches the ball" and the "quarterback" who "makes the calls." But he also knew he was responsible for "smart pitch selection" that "made the best use of the pitcher's good stuff." McCarver understood Carlton's thinking—how he set up hitters, how he dispatched them—so well that his pitch calling conformed to Lefty's instincts. Tim realized that pregame meetings to review the opposing lineup were a "waste of time" because he and Carlton thought alike. At the same time, Tim determined which pitches—fastball, curveball, and/or slider—were most successful for Carlton on a given day, identified the vulnerabilities of opposing hitters in order to determine which pitch to call, and worked the umpire to Lefty's advantage.[81]

"Tim was very professional," recalled umpire Jerry Crawford. "If he disagreed with a call, he'd never embarrass me. He'd never get in my face to show me up. Instead, Tim always kept staring straight ahead and [would] say something like, 'Jerry, we gotta have that pitch.' Then maybe I'd moved closer to the plate to get a better look. If he wanted to know why I called a ball, he'd ask something like, 'Was the pitch inside?' Then I'd tell him if it was or not. That really helped me out, too, since I was one of the younger umpires in the league back then."[82]

Carlton appreciated—and benefited—from McCarver's efforts. "There was a synchronicity between us," Lefty said in 1994. "Timmy was uncanny. He had such a good mind, and he was a great strategist. We might go through the first two or three innings using just one pitch, instead of showing the other team my whole repertoire in the first two innings. And we wouldn't change until somebody told us to change by the way he swung."[83]

Just as important, Tim *never* second-guessed himself. He made rapid decisions and did so with conviction. "Indecision is an awful curse for a pitcher," said McCarver, "but it's worse for a catcher because he can take the pitcher down that uncertain path with him." He learned that lesson from Bob Gibson, who had told him, "The first sign you think of, put it down."[84]

"Sure, you might make a mistake with a quick choice," admitted Tim, "but over the long haul, it's the right approach. If you put down too many tentative signs, you're going to get tentative pitches. That's when your pitcher gets hit and hit hard."[85] In all these ways, the veteran catcher gave his batterymate confidence and laid the groundwork for his success.

"Lefty, in 1976, resumed his stature as a power pitcher, but now he had twelve years of experience to go with it," said McCarver, referring to the transformation of his batterymate. "So, he was first a power pitcher, then a pitcher, then a power pitcher with experience."[86]

No pitcher could be more dominant than that.

10

Closer Than Sixty Feet, Six Inches

When asked to describe his relationship with Carlton, McCarver once quipped, "When we die, Lefty and I will be buried sixty feet, six inches apart," which is the distance between the pitching rubber and home plate.[1] Indeed, Carlton and McCarver were inseparable. Their teammates joked that if Lefty sneezed, Tim would wipe his nose; if Lefty got an itch, Tim scratched; and if Lefty stubbed his toe, Tim hollered, "Ouch!"[2]

"For two years I've been Steve's designated catcher," McCarver told sportswriters when asked about his relationship with Carlton. "Now they call me his designated talker, too. But sometimes it gets a little ridiculous. Once Steve got diarrhea, but nobody asked him how he felt. They swarmed around to ask me! All I could say was, 'Who do you think I am—his designated doctor, too?!'" McCarver constantly joked about the exclusive relationship. "Once I caught a doubleheader," he said, "and Steve came into the clubhouse and said he was going to divorce me. 'OK,' I said, 'but I get the house.'"[3]

Their friendship was not limited to the baseball diamond. Lefty and Tim also spent considerable time together in the off-season. Hunting was one of their favorite pastimes, though Carlton had much more experience with the sport than McCarver, who sometimes questioned the wisdom of following his batterymate's lead. Lefty savored the exhilaration he experienced when hunting. "The kill is not important, although I understand the psychology of that," he said. "For me, it's the challenge, even the danger."[4]

One time Carlton, while hunting elk in Canada with McCarver, decided to save time by sliding down the side of a snow-covered mountain on his rear end. He hit an ice patch and could not stop. In a desperate effort to save himself, Steve tried to grab hold of bushes, logs, or anything to break the slide. Rapidly approaching the edge of a cliff, Lefty saw his life flash before him when suddenly he was saved by a thicket of bushes. "I was so close to death," he recalled. "I guess I was scared. But mostly I felt thrilled."[5]

McCarver must have questioned his friend's sanity after the episode, but it certainly didn't stop him from joining Carlton for future adventures. After the '76 season, for example, the two teammates headed for South Dakota for some pheasant hunting. Lefty had recently purchased a brand-new Chevy Blazer and was proud of its ample storage space. Hoping to fill every inch, Carlton packed anything he could find, including rope, glue, tape, and a caulking gun.

"Why did you pack a caulking gun?" asked Tim, before they left.

"Well, you never know when you're going to need one," replied Steve.

Dumbfounded, Tim sighed, "Lefty, you're strange!"

A few days later the two teammates found themselves near Mitchell, South Dakota, which seemed like the middle of nowhere to them. McCarver was driving the Blazer while Carlton, riding shotgun, was napping. Suddenly a pheasant appeared. Tim swerved but hit the bird head on, instantly killing it. Feathers were flying everywhere. The pheasant was lodged, beak first, in the Blazer's front grille, and a warning light began to blink on the dashboard, indicating that the radiator was leaking antifreeze.

"What are we gonna do now?" asked Tim, surveying the damage.

"Don't worry," exclaimed Steve, with a sly grin. "I got just the thing to fix it!"

Carlton opened the tailgate, found the caulking gun, and, after removing the pheasant's beak, repaired the radiator.

McCarver stood there chuckling. "I take that back, Lefty," he said, after Carlton repaired the radiator. "You're not strange after all. You're brilliant!"

As Tim recalled in 2019, "Lefty sold that Blazer eight years later," and when the sale was made "the caulking was still holding together that radiator!"[6]

Of the four and a half seasons Carlton and McCarver spent together in Philadelphia during the mid- to late 1970s, the '77 campaign was their most successful. Not only did Lefty's twenty-three victories carry the Phillies to a second straight National League East title, but he also won his second Cy Young Award, joining the rarefied company of Sandy Koufax, Tom Seaver, Jim Palmer, Bob Gibson, and Denny McLain as a repeat recipient of the coveted award.[7] Never before had Carlton enjoyed the offensive support or defense the Phillies provided that season. The young nucleus of talented prospects who struggled to score runs for Lefty in 1972 were now entering their prime and ready to make the team a perennial contender.

The 1977 Phillies were arguably the most talented team of the franchise's most successful era, which lasted from 1976 to 1983. Carlton and Larry Christenson, who posted a career-best nineteen victories, were the workhorses of the starting rotation, notching a combined win-loss record of 42-16. Rookie Randy Lerch (10-6) and veterans Jim Kaat (6-11) and Jim Lonborg (11-4) went a combined 69-37. The bullpen was even better. Ozark used his four best relievers interchangeably. As a result, Tug McGraw (7-3, 9 SV), Ron Reed (7-5, 15 SV), Gene Garber (8-6, 19 SV), and Warren Brusstar (7-2, 3 SV) combined for twenty-nine wins and forty-six saves.

The Phils' offensive juggernaut was led by National League MVP candidate Greg Luzinski (.309, 39 HRS, 130 RBIS, .988 OPS) and Mike Schmidt (.274, 38 HRS, 101 RBIS, .967 OPS). Free agent Richie Hebner replaced Dick Allen at first base and batted .285 with 18 homers, and catcher Bob Boone's numbers (.284, 11 HRS, 66 RBIS, .780 OPS) were even better than the previous season, when he was an All-Star. Center fielder Garry Maddox (.292, 14 HRS, 79 RBIS) and the right-field platoon of Bake McBride (.339, 11 HRS, 41 RBIS) and Jay Johnstone (.284, 15 HRS, 59 RBIS) also added significantly to the firepower. No wonder the team led the National League in batting average (.279), runs scored (847), on-base percentage (.346), and slugging (.448). Only the Los Angeles Dodgers hit more than the Phillies' 186 home runs in that '77 season.

There was speed on the base paths, with Larry Bowa stealing a career-best 32 bases, McBride contributing 27 steals to the running game, and Maddox another 22. Even Schmidt, who was hampered by bad knees, swiped 15 bases. Defensively, the Phillies were solid, especially up the middle. Ted Sizemore, who replaced Dave Cash at second, led NL second basemen in double plays (104) and posted a fielding percentage of .986. Boone (.989), Bowa (.983), and Maddox (.978) were just as reliable.[8]

Despite all the talent, the Phillies got off to a slow start, losing their first four games. On Opening Day, April 9, Carlton faced Steve Rogers and the Montreal Expos at the Vet. Lefty coasted through the first five innings, pitching scoreless ball. Luzinski gave him a 3–0 lead in the third when he cleared the bases with a double. The tide turned in the top of the sixth when former Phillie Dave Cash led off with a single to right. An out later Ellis Valentine slammed a 1-0 slider into the lower deck in left field to close the margin at 3–2. Tony Pérez, a free agent who had recently signed with Montreal, and Gary Carter followed with back-to-back solo shots, and suddenly the Expos were on top, 4–3. Journeyman junkballer Jackie Brown, who replaced Rogers, shut down the Phillies' offense for the last four frames to earn the victory.[9]

Carlton was nowhere to be found after the game. Instead, McCarver did his talking for him. "Lefty didn't really lose his rhythm," said Tim. "The Expos just lost three baseballs," he added, in a glib attempt to dismiss the three homers Montreal hit in the sixth.

"He threw Valentine a slider that just laid there," added McCarver. "Then he got behind against Perez, who's a bad guy to get behind on. Steve threw him a fastball down the middle. And then Carter hit a good fastball, a good pitch."[10]

Three more losses followed for the Phillies—another one to the Expos and two to the Chicago Cubs. But Carlton snapped the losing streak on April 15 when the Phils and the Expos played the very first game in Montreal's new Olympic Stadium. Again the Phillies gave Lefty a 3–0 lead, but this time he made it hold up for a 7–2 victory. Maddox and Luzinski were the stars of the game. Maddox killed an Expos rally in the eighth when he made a sensational catch in right-center to take extra bases away from Tony Pérez, and Luzinski hit a 2-run, tape-measure homer in the seventh to seal the victory. Carlton, who surrendered just 2 earned runs while scattering 10 hits, recorded 6 strikeouts and saw his earned run average drop from an unusually high 5.14 to a more respectable 3.18.[11]

McCarver, who helped ignite the Phillies' three-run rally in the third with a double off Montreal starter Don Stanhouse, told Bill Conlin of the *Daily News* that Carlton "stayed stronger much longer than his previous outing." The veteran catcher explained that "Lefty definitely improved the location of his fastball." He went on to add that "it's a matter of not dropping his hand on the pitch. He struck out a couple of hitters with fastballs that tailed onto the black, but I prefer it when he stays on top and throws the rise. That's his most effective fastball. The other one flattens out and he likes to be reminded to stay on top."[12]

McCarver rarely visited the mound, but when he did, Lefty listened. Carlton trusted not only his batterymate's encyclopedic knowledge of opposing hitters but also his genius for identifying a mechanical problem in his delivery and fixing it instantly. For example, when Lefty's fastball was flat, it was clear to Tim that he was not keeping his index and middle fingers on top of the ball but gripping the outside to the left or right of center. When that happened, his fastball was flat and the batter would usually get a hit.

The other mechanical flaw Carlton struggled with was lowering his arm slot from straight over the top, or the "twelve o'clock" position, to a "three-quarters" position. This happened when he relied heavily on his slider. As the game progressed, Steve's left arm gradually dropped to the "three-quarters" slot, taking away the bite on his slider and elevating his fastball. On those occasions McCarver would call for a curve to elevate the left-hander's arm slot and thus return it to the "twelve o'clock" position. Identifying and correcting these mistakes during the game was critical to Carlton's success as a power pitcher.

When his mechanics were flawless, hitters didn't like to face Lefty because of the extension he had in his delivery. It not only ruined their timing but prevented them from getting the barrel of the bat over the plate, where they could do the most damage. Carlton, six feet four and 210 pounds, had long arms, which gave him remarkable extension and enabled him to force hitters to keep the bat back and fight off pitches. Because Lefty kept his front shoulder closed until the last second before he delivered the pitch, the hitter could not identify the ball until he released it. As a result, Steve appeared to release the pitch deep inside the hitting zone, leaving the batter with the impression that he did not have time to get the barrel out in front of home plate.[13] Together with his exceptional strength, Carlton's arm extension allowed him to overpower hitters with either his fastball or his slider.

"When you looked at Carlton out on the mound, he was very imposing," recalled Braves slugger Hank Aaron in a 2017 interview. "Then, when he started his delivery, you couldn't see the ball until it was on top of you. His arm looked like it was coming right at you. He was extremely hard to hit, not only because he had that kind of extension but also because he just had great stuff."[14]

The Phillies played .500 baseball for the next two weeks. Carlton was the bright spot, defeating the Cardinals, 6–3, and Giants, 6–5, to improve his record to 3-1.[15] Still, by late April the Phils were mired in last place. Maddox (.229) and Schmidt (.182) were in slumps. The bench, once a strength, was also faltering as Tommy Hutton (.200), Bobby Tolan (.222), and Jerry Martin (.118) struggled at the plate.[16] Bowa, a world-class agitator, wouldn't let any of them forget about it, either. He was especially hard on the slugging third baseman. Once, after Schmidt had struck out in three straight at bats against the Pittsburgh Pirates, Bowa sat at his locker doing a mock play-by-play of the dismal performance: "Here's Mike Schmidt. . . . He's hit one ball hard in three games. Bottom of the ninth. One run down. Two outs. We'll have the wrap-up in 20 seconds."[17]

Bowa was ultracompetitive. He was a hard-nosed player who absolutely hated to lose and cajoled teammates with negative motivation. He ripped them for a bad game, their choice of clothing, or a quote that found its way onto the pages of the local newspapers. Nothing was off limits. In fact, the insufferable shortstop told Luzinski that he was "as fat as a hog."[18] And the Bull, who was enjoying a career-best year, was his closest friend on the club! The only teammate who was spared from Bowa's vitriol was Carlton.

"Lefty refused to take Bowa's crap," recalled Larry Christenson. "He made that clear to him very early on. Bowa had a lot of fire, and I admired that. But I didn't like his hypercriticism. So when Carlton walked into the clubhouse on the day he was scheduled to pitch, I'd ask Bowa if he had any smartass thing to say to him. Of course he just clammed up. He knew it was 'Win-day' and that Lefty was in the zone. You just didn't bother him on the day he pitched."[19]

The Phillies' fortunes turned on May 10, when Carlton began a streak in which he won eight of his next twelve starts. Luzinski also went on an offensive tear, hitting at a .360 clip, enabling the Phillies to escape the basement by the end of the month. On May 31 the Phils found themselves in fourth place, just three games behind the National League East–leading Chicago Cubs. Then the team suffered another tailspin, losing nine of their next fifteen games. Christenson, who struggled from the start of the season, was 4-5 with a bloated earned run average of 7.55. Ozark wanted to send him down to the Minors, but pitching coach Ray Rippelmeyer discouraged him, insisting that LC would "fight his way out of the slump." Rip went to work with Christenson, teaching him how to become more of a finesse pitcher by working on his breaking ball, changing speeds, and developing a straight changeup to complement his 90+ mph fastball.[20]

Carlton was not much help. The losing stretch included a no decision and two of his three starts: a 2–0 defeat to the Mets on June 4 and a 5–4 loss against the Cincinnati Reds on June 13.[21] After all three starts, Carlton, in what would become standard operating procedure, retreated to the trainer's room, which was off limits to the media. Lefty considered the press to be both "an obstacle that interfered with [his] performance on the field" and "one of the biggest enemies [he had] in Philadelphia."[22] Nevertheless, he reluctantly agreed to do occasional interviews, and even those sessions dwindled once McCarver became his personal catcher. Tim became Carlton's mouthpiece, dissecting his performance for the media after every game and answering their mostly mundane questions.

One time the gregarious catcher did a postgame interview for the whole club. After giving the sportswriters a few quotes as Carlton, he circulated the empty clubhouse, stopping in front of each locker and delivering quotes for his various teammates.[23]

As the Phillies' performance ebbed and flowed, general manager Paul Owens was working the phones, trying to make a deal that could improve the pitching or offense. During the first few weeks of June, Owens tried to add Mets ace Tom Seaver to the starting rotation. Pope Owens proposed a four-for-one deal that would send Christenson, reserve outfielder Jerry Martin, and Minor Leaguers Rick Bosetti and Jim Morrison to New York for Seaver. But the Mets declined the offer and traded their disenchanted ace to the Cincinnati Reds.[24] On June 15 Owens struck gold when he traded pitcher Tommy Underwood and outfielders Dane Iorg and Bosetti to the St. Louis Cardinals for Bake McBride, a speedy right fielder who had been the 1975 NL Rookie of the Year. The Cards believed that McBride's career was over because of chronic knee problems. Instead, the outfielder became a dependable lead-off hitter for the Phils and a serious threat on the base paths. He also proved to be tremendously popular with the fans, who nicknamed him "Shake 'n Bake."[25] McBride joined Luzinski and Maddox to give the Phillies one of the best outfields in baseball and a potent combination of speed, defense, and power at the plate.

On June 19 Carlton defeated the Atlanta Braves, 4–2, for his one hundredth career victory as a Phillie. Lefty retired the first fourteen batters he faced before issuing his only walk of the game. He still hadn't allowed a hit when pinch hitter Tom Paciorek blooped a single into short center field with one out in the sixth. "It was a fastball in his kitchen that jammed him," explained McCarver after the game. "Lefty's slider was his best pitch today. That's the one that got him most of the outs." The victory moved the Phils into second place ahead of St. Louis and five and a half games behind first-place Chicago.[26] Three days later Schmidt led his teammates in a 15–9 assault against the Cincinnati Reds, hitting his seventeenth and eighteenth homers of the season and driving in four runs. Bowa, who went 4-for-4, contributed to the offensive rally in the seventh, hitting his first and only Major League grand slam. The four-bagger set the stage for a major payback. When taking batting practice before the game, Cincinnati third baseman Pete Rose stopped by the cage to tell Bowa that he "hit like a girl." After hitting the grand slam, the fiery little shortstop, who never forgot anyone's slight, pranced slowly across third base and chirped at Rose, "Take a ride on that!"[27]

Schmidt continued his hot streak over the next two weeks, hitting 3 more homers and driving in 16 more runs. Luzinski was also hot, on pace to hit 40 home runs. Both would play in the All-Star Game the next month at Yankee Stadium, with Luzinski contributing a 2-run homer to the National League's 7–5 victory. McBride was also a game changer, starting several offensive rallies, stealing bases, and hitting in the clutch.[28]

Carlton went 4-2 in July and was named to the National League's All-Star squad, though he did not pitch in the Midsummer Classic. All his victories were at the Vet—against the Mets, 12–1; Cardinals, 5–2; Cubs, 4–2; and Giants, 9–3—and the losses came on the road against San Francisco, 6–2; and Los Angeles, 5–1.[29] But he struggled with lower back pain throughout the month. "Lefty's one of those guys who says if you can't pitch with a little pain, you better go home," explained manager Danny Ozark when asked why he continued to send his ace out to the mound every fourth day. "It's not the first time he's gone out there with a backache. Besides, no one's going to stop him from pitching if he wants to go out there."[30]

Carlton's back pain might have been aggravated by his rigorous training program with Gus Hoefling, which the pitcher continued throughout the season. "I very rarely remember Steve Carlton chang[ing] his routine," recalled Garry Maddox. "He worked extremely hard between starts, even when he might be feeling some pain."[31] Pitching coach Ray Rippelmeyer expressed some concern about continuing the martial arts training, but he left the decision up to Carlton.

"Gus worked on strength conditioning and flexibility," explained Rippelmeyer. "If Gus helped Steve stay in shape, all the better for him and the team because he certainly didn't want to run. And to be honest with you, Carlton worked his tail off. Gus made him as strong as an ox. Even when Steve's lower back was hurting, he needed to do some kind of flexibility exercises. Besides, I had already watched Gus's workouts, and I thought they were legitimate. I had no problem with them. In fact, I went so far as to give all the pitchers the choice, either to work with Gus or go running on the field with me. A few tried Gus's program, like Christenson and Lonborg, but most of the pitchers chose to run. They just couldn't keep up with Steve."[32]

Carlton's back problems were the result of an increased workload. With Jim Lonborg on the injured reserved list, Ozark was forced to go with a four-man rotation. What's more, of the seven starts Lefty made in July, the last three were on just three days' rest. Most pitchers would buckle under the pressure, but not Carlton. When McCarver was asked how his batterymate could pitch so well despite a sore back, he compared Lefty to a hitter with a back problem. "It keeps the hitter from overswinging because he stays back on the ball," he explained. "It's the same with a pitcher. You don't overthrow. While Steve didn't have great velocity the last few games, his breaking ball was outstanding because it was slower and dropped into the strike zone later. Because of that, the hitters were giving up on it too soon."[33] More impressive, after ninety games, Carlton boasted a 14–6 record, which was just two games off pace from 1972, when he won his Cy Young Award.

The Phillies finally took over first place on August 5 with an 8–3 win over Los Angeles and never looked back. During the next three weeks the team won sixteen of their seventeen games, sweeping the Dodgers and Expos at Veterans Stadium and then traveling to Chicago, where they swept a four-game series against the Cubs. Carlton's performance was especially impressive during the streak. On August 7 Lefty pitched a complete-game victory against the Dodgers, 3–1, surrendering a single earned run while scattering 7 hits and recording 8 strikeouts. On August 12 he hurled another complete-game victory, this one against the Cubs, 10–3, at Wrigley.[34]

Carlton won his eighteenth game of the season on August 21, when he struck out fourteen Houston Astros en route to a 7–3 win. It was yet another complete-game victory for the tall left-hander and the Phillies' seventeenth win in the last eighteen games they'd played. If not for the Astros' Enos Cabell, Lefty would have had a shutout. The lanky Houston third baseman hit two home runs, then doubled and scored on two infield outs in the ninth.

"Steve had such superb stuff tonight," gushed McCarver, who was batting a team-leading .333 and hit a three-run homer in the fourth that brought the Phillies from behind and put them ahead to stay. "There were some pitches he threw that were simply unhittable. Everything was working and he had an unbelievable slider. If ever there was a time he could've pitched a no-hitter, this was it. Even the homers Cabell hit were off two fine pitches exactly where we wanted them."[35]

On August 31 Carlton won his fourth complete game of the month, this one against Atlanta, 6–1, at Veterans Stadium. The only two defeats he suffered in August came against the Montreal Expos, in a 13–0 rout, and the Cincinnati Reds, in a 4–2 heartbreaker.[36] Despite losing to the Big Red Machine, Lefty and Tim had to laugh when they dined out the following evening at the Maisonette, a French restaurant in Cincinnati. Carlton, a fanatic about conditioning, sometimes carried steel balls to squeeze in order to build strength in his hands and forearms. He had been squeezing the balls during their meal, but he left them on the table and forgot about them. As the two teammates left to hail a cab, the maître d' came running out of the restaurant, shouting, "Monsieur Carlton, you left your balls on ze table!" Steve checked just to make sure, adding to the hilarity of the moment.[37]

One of Carlton's greatest strengths was his exceptional ability to put a loss behind him and give his full attention to the next start. That kind of positive thinking was reinforced by his martial arts training, as well as a rare ability to focus intensely on the task at hand. "One of the biggest obstacles in life is yourself," he explained after he retired. "Whenever I pitched, I got out of my own way and let my talent take over. I became big, mean and aggressive. I didn't have to be that way in my heart, but I knew if I looked that way, the hitter really believed I *was* that way."[38] By removing those two obstacles—himself and the hitter—Carlton was in complete control of the strike zone.

Lefty insisted that he did not pitch to hitters but rather to sectors of the plate. "I never looked at the hitter to see who he was," he said. "My purpose was to get the ball to the catcher. It was part of the weeding out of obstacles process that I went through. I realized that if I made the types of pitches I was capable of, and in the areas I visualized—high and tight, low and away—the hitter would not be a factor. I never changed my thinking, either, even though a particular hitter might have been hot."[39]

It's difficult to believe that Carlton *never* considered which hitters he was facing, especially when Johnny Bench, Rusty Staub, Gary Carter, Dusty Baker, or Steve Garvey was standing at the plate. They were the hitters who gave him the most trouble during his career. Mike Schmidt, who played alongside Carlton for fourteen years, believes that his teammate was simplifying the issue. "Lefty knew where his outs were in the opposing lineup," recalled the Hall of Fame third baseman in 2020. "He was really good at choosing the hitters he could get out. He might even walk someone like Bench to get to a hitter he knew he could get out. Other times, if he had a 3-2 count on someone who hit him well, he might bounce a slider up there. Then he'd try to get a swing rather than challenge that hitter and strike the next guy out, especially if he was a left-handed hitter. Lefty did not like to pitch to really good right-handed hitters like Bench, Carter, and Garvey. Opposing managers would stack right-handed hitters against him, but that slider of his neutralized the lineup."

Schmidt also pointed out that McCarver was "every bit as smart" as Carlton when it came to "pitch selection and pitching to a lineup." The batterymates "were on the same page," he explained. "Timmy knew exactly what Steve was thinking. You rarely saw Lefty shake him off or Tim go to the mound. That's why the two of them were so successful."[40]

McCarver, on the other hand, confirmed Carlton's assertion that he never considered the hitter: "Steve used to say that pitching should be a sophisticated game of catch between the pitcher and catcher. . . . He'd tell me, 'Let's go play some pitch and catch,' and he'd act as if the hitter didn't exist or was just a spectator who had wandered onto the field with his bat. Carlton had unbelievable concentration. He was brilliant at eliminating all obstacles from his mind, including the hitter. He genuinely believed that if he ignored the hitter and threw to the catcher's mitt he would be successful. And he was right.

"If you throw to the catcher, there will be late action in the hitting zone. But if you throw to the hitter, the action of the pitch will stop when it reaches the plate. That's really what a hanger is, a pitch where the action has stopped. A hanger can be high, low, inside, outside—it can be a breaking ball, changeup, fastball, or anything else—and when it hovers over the plate, the hitter will send it hard the other way. That's a danger that can be avoided if you eliminate the hitter from your thinking. That's exactly what Lefty did."[41]

Bob Boone, who caught Carlton from 1973 to 1975 and again in the early 1980s, claimed that McCarver and Schmidt were *both* correct. "On the day he pitched, Lefty went into the trainer's room, lay down on the table, and went through the opposing lineup in his mind," recalled Boone. "[Carlton] would visualize the right-handed hitters and the left-handed hitters. Like Schmitty said, Lefty knew exactly who those hitters were. He would review the pitches and the locations he was going to use to get each of 'em out. What Steve was actually doing was visualizing the inside of the plate, or the outside of the plate, because each hitter was vulnerable to one side or the other.

"But he also made it as simple as possible. That's where McCarver was right. Once he got on the mound, Steve really did play an elevated game of catch with Timmy. As long as they were on the same page in terms of pitch calling, it really didn't matter who the batter was because Carlton had great stuff and great control."[42]

If nothing else, Schmidt and McCarver agreed that when Carlton pitched, the two most important people on the field were the third baseman and the first-base umpire, especially when the opposing lineup was loaded with right-handed hitters. "The first-base umpire was important because of all the checked-swing strikes Lefty would get," explained McCarver. "And the third baseman was important because he had to be able to play the line and play deep. Of course Schmitty could do both of those things, and he had a cannon for an arm, so he got a lot of action down there at third with all those right-handed hitters pulling the ball down the line."[43]

Schmidt recalled that whenever Carlton pitched, shortstop Larry Bowa, who had a better view of McCarver's pitch calling, would yell "Schmitty!" when a slider was coming so the third baseman would be prepared to go to his right for a hard grounder down the line. "McCarver's right about the checked swings, too," said Schmidt. "If Lefty pitched today, he would be getting three hundred strikeouts or more a season because the checked swing is called much more often than it was when we played."[44]

On September 5 Carlton won his twentieth game in an 11–1 rout of the Pirates in the second game of a twin bill at Pittsburgh. After dropping the opener, 3–1, the Phillies turned to their ace to snap their bad luck at Three Rivers Stadium, where they had dropped ten straight games. Lefty responded magnificently. He pitched eight strong innings, giving up a single run on 9 hits. He also smashed a home run and an RBI single and scored 3 runs in the rout. Manager Danny Ozark juggled his rotation, making rookie Randy Lerch the starter in the first game against Pirates ace John Candelaria, a southpaw, instead of Carlton, and moved his own ace to the nightcap to face the Bucs' number-two starter, Bruce Kison, a right-hander. "I was just trying to take advantage of the lefthanded versus righthanded situation with McCarver and Carlton both being lefthanded hitters," Ozark insisted. "If Kison had started the first game, Carlton would have started against him."[45]

But Larry Bowa had another explanation. "If you happen to lose with Carlton in the opener," he said, "the pressure's really going to be on Lerch in the second game. Whereas with Steve, the pressure doesn't really matter."[46]

Carlton notched his twenty-first win—and sixteenth straight home victory—on September 9 against the St. Louis Cardinals, a performance in which he struck out fourteen hitters.[47] Unfortunately, Lefty would lose his consecutive-win streak at the Vet in his next start on September 14 in a 13–0 rout by the Mets. But he bounced back to defeat the Cubs, 4–2, and Expos, 1–0, to complete the regular season with a 23-10 record.[48] It was Larry Christenson, however, who clinched the second straight division title for the Phillies on September 27 with a wild 15–9 victory over the Chicago Cubs at Wrigley Field. LC rebounded from a mediocre spring to post his eighteenth win of the season. Despite a painful blister on the index finger of his pitching hand, the right-hander went seven innings and also crushed a grand slam homer.

When Christenson's turn at bat came up in the seventh with the bases loaded, Ozark tried to pull him. But LC refused to leave the game. Ozark sent pinch hitter Greg Gross out to the on-deck circle to hit and shouted to Christenson to return to the dugout. Instead, the stubborn right-hander stepped into the batter's box to hit. Ozark continued to bark at his pitcher to stand down, and he then ordered Gross to go to the plate. Confused, the umpire halted the game. Now he had two batters at the plate.

Determined to hit, Christenson pointed to Ozark and yelled, "I'm not coming out until I hit!" Then he pointed to pinch hitter Greg Gross and ordered him back to the dugout. Gross, a mild-mattered individual who did not like confrontation, did as he was told. Finally, LC pointed to the home plate umpire and said, "You can call the game now."[49]

Christenson got behind in the count 1-2 to Cubs reliever Dennis Lamp before crushing a fastball deep into the right-field bleachers for his third homer of the season and first career grand slam.[50]

Despite a 12–4 lead, LC allowed Ozark to lift him in the bottom of the eighth. Screwball specialist Tug McGraw entered the game and struck out the first two batters on six pitches. True to form, the Tugger lost control of the strike zone and gave up five hits in a row, cutting the Phillies' lead to just three runs, 12–9. "Tug comes in the dugout after the inning ends and he's laughing," recalled McCarver. "Bowa looked at him and started screaming, 'What the fuck's so funny? We don't have the fuckin' thing clinched yet! We need more fuckin' runs!' I mean he's SCREAMING at the top of his lungs."[51]

The following inning McGraw retired the Cubs in order to seal the division clincher. Afterward, when the Phillies were celebrating the victory, the comedic reliever frolicked around the visitors' clubhouse dousing teammates with champagne and shouting, "You gotta believe!" McCarver, a wine connoisseur, was not as jovial. Tim took a sip of the Chateau Deer Valley champagne provided by the Phillies and complained, "Where was this stuff made? In Wilmington? A monk invented champagne and we get this shit! What else do they make, 'Janitor in a Drum'?"[52]

McCarver might've groused about the champagne, but no one could criticize him for the season he had just completed. In 169 at bats as a pinch hitter and part-time catcher, Tim set personal career highs in batting average (.320), slugging average (.527), on-base percentage (.410), on-base plus slugging percentage (.936), and OPS+ (145). He was just as impressive behind the plate. In the forty-two games (329 innings) Tim caught, he posted a .988 fielding percentage, with 233 put-outs in 250 chances with just 3 errors.[53]

Carlton also credited his batterymate with helping him capture a second Cy Young Award. Lefty completed the regular season with a Major League–leading twenty-three victories. He was also among the top four leaders among National League pitchers in complete games (17), innings pitched (283), strikeouts (198), and earned run average (2.64).[54] With the Carlton/McCarver battery performing so well, it appeared as if Tim would remain Lefty's personal catcher in the foreseeable future. Bob Boone, the Phillies' primary catcher, knew it, too.

"Lefty had confidence in Timmy," Boone recalled in a 2020 interview. "Timmy caught him in St. Louis when he first began his career. He had a way better relationship with Carlton. That didn't bother me at all. I had absolutely no doubt in my ability to catch. In fact, when Timmy caught it gave me a rest every fourth day. If throwing to McCarver is what it took to improve Lefty's pitching, well, I was all for it."

Furthermore, Boone didn't harbor any resentment toward Carlton or McCarver. "If I complained about the situation, maybe all three of us would have been released by the Phillies," he speculated. Instead, Boone remained on good terms with both teammates. He not only introduced Carlton to Gus Hoefling, the martial arts guru, but also trained with the two of them. "Only Lefty and I were able to go through Gus's wall [of rigorous training]," said the catcher. "Other players tried and just couldn't do it." Boone also had a "good relationship" with McCarver. "He was good to me when I first met him at spring training in 1972," he remembered. "When Timmy returned in '75, he was a great addition to our team, being very knowledgeable, very supportive. He might've been older than most of us, but he was still an extremely good catcher."[55]

McCarver understood Boone's difficult position and knew that his younger teammate could have easily developed some animosity toward him when he became Carlton's personal catcher. "It would have been natural," Tim noted. "But Boonie is one of the finest gentlemen ever to suit up on a ball field and he never made a disparaging remark about me to the media. He's a class act, a pro without peers. If I had a son, I wouldn't mind having him be a carbon copy of Bob Boone."[56]

The Phillies faced the Los Angeles Dodgers in the playoffs. The Dodgers finished ten games ahead of the defending World Series champion Cincinnati Reds in the National League West. The key to their success was their starting pitching. Tommy John (20-7, 2.78 ERA) was their ace and Don Sutton (14-8, 3.19 ERA), their number-two starter, with Burt Hooton (12-7, 2.67 ERA), Rick Rhoden (16-10, 3.75 ERA), and Doug Rau (14-8, 3.44 ERA) rounding out the rotation. The Dodgers' bullpen was less reliable. With the exceptions of closer Charlie Hough (22 SV, 3.33 ERA) and setup man Mike Garman (12 SV, 2.71 ERA), the relief corps had neither the depth nor the experience of the Phillies' bullpen.

The Dodgers' infield was not as good defensively as the Phils', but its members did pose a dangerous offensive threat. Catcher Steve Yeager (.256, 16 HRS, 55 RBIS) was solid defensively and capable of hitting the ball out of the park. Shortstop Bill Russell (.278, 4 HRS, 51 RBIS) and second baseman Davey Lopes (.283, 11 HRS, 53 RBIS) were good, steady ballplayers capable of stealing a base as well as hitting home runs. First baseman Steve Garvey (.297, 33 HRS, 115 RBIS) and third baseman Ron Cey (.241, 30 HRS, 110 RBIS) were more dangerous. The outfield also produced runs. Right fielder Reggie Smith (.307, 32 HRS, 87 RBIS) and left fielder Dusty Baker (.291, 30 HRS, 86 RBIS) were young power hitters who could deliver in the clutch. Rick Monday (.230, 15 HRS, 48 RBIS), the center fielder, wasn't much of an offensive threat, but he covered a lot of ground in the outfield.[57]

The Phillies and Dodgers matched up well. The season series between the two teams was even at 6–6, with the Phillies winning four of the six games played at Philadelphia.[58] But the experts believed that if the Phillies could earn a split in Los Angeles, where the National League Championship Series opened, they would be a cinch to win the pennant, having posted a 60-21 regular season record at the Vet. The initial game of the NLCS on October 4 was supposed to be a pitcher's duel between two left-handed aces, Carlton and the Dodgers' Tommy John. Instead, neither starter could contain the opposing lineup, and the game became a contest of bullpens.

The Phillies jumped to a 2–0 lead in the first off Greg Luzinski's two-run homer. They increased their lead in the fifth on reserve first baseman Dave Johnson's two-run single. Carlton singled home McCarver for another run in the seventh for a 5–1 lead. After striking out the first batter in the bottom of the seventh, Lefty suddenly lost control of the strike zone. He walked pinch hitter Jerry Grote and gave up a single to Davey Lopes. Although Carlton got Bill Russell to ground into a force at third for the second out of the inning, he walked Reggie Smith to load the bases. Ron Cey stepped to the plate, worked a full count, and then hit a grand slam into the left-field seats to even the score, 5–5. Ozark went to his bullpen and brought in Gene Garber, who retired the next batter for the final out of the inning.

The Phillies fought back in the ninth with three consecutive singles, by Bake McBride, Larry Bowa, and Mike Schmidt, to break the deadlock. Seconds later Dodgers reliever Elías Sosa gifted another run on a balk, and the Phillies went ahead, 7–5. Tug McGraw blanked the Dodgers in the bottom of the frame for the Phillies' first postseason victory since Hall of Fame pitcher Grover Alexander defeated the Boston Red Sox in 1915.[59]

Since Carlton had as usual retreated to the trainer's room, Mike Schmidt was left to sum up the story of the game for the national sportswriters. "Momentum's a big thing in a series like this," he explained, "and the momentum took a drastic turn on Cey's home run. For us to rise to the occasion and turn the momentum back around—that's a tough thing to do."[60]

The Phillies were confident now, knowing that they would return to the Vet with at least a split in the first two games. That's exactly what they got, too. The next day the Dodgers evened the series at two games a piece with a 7–1 rout. Don Sutton outpitched Jim Lonborg, and Dusty Baker provided all the offense the Dodgers needed with a grand slam homer in the fourth inning to snap a 1–1 tie.[61] Now the pennant race moved to Philadelphia.

The third NLCS game was played on Friday, October 7. Larry Christenson faced Burt Hooton before a sellout crowd of 63,719 at the Vet. LC surrendered two runs in the top of the second, but the Phils rallied in the bottom half. Hooton became wild, to the delight of the Boo Birds. The more they jeered the Dodgers pitcher, the more unnerved he became. He issued four straight walks to force three runs across the plate, and the Phillies held a 3–2 lead.[62] "I don't think I ever heard noise like," remarked Bowa. "They hooted the guy right off the mound."[63] Stan Hochman of the *Daily News* later applauded the fans' boorish behavior, calling it a "clutch performance" worthy of an "MVP—'Most Valuable Patrons'—Award."[64]

The Phillies added another two runs in the eighth on Richie Hebner's double, a single by Garry Maddox, and two separate two-base throwing errors by the Dodgers. With a 5–3 lead entering the ninth inning, the Phils seemed ensured a victory, especially after reliever Gene Garber retired the first two batters. But then the floodgates opened. Garber surrendered an infield single to pinch hitter Vic Davalillo. Manny Mota, another pinch hitter, followed. He hit a deep but catchable fly ball toward the warning track in the left-field corner. Luzinski got his glove on the ball but couldn't hold on to it. When he retrieved the ball, the Bull threw home, attempting to nail Davalillo at the plate. But second baseman Ted Sizemore botched the relay throw, allowing Mota to advance to third. Now the Dodgers had the tying run in scoring position.[65]

"I can't understand why Danny [Ozark] left Bull in the game," Bowa said later. "All year long, he'd take him out for a defensive replacement late in the game. Sure as hell, a fly ball goes out there to Jerry Martin, he'd just suck it up. If he's out there, we'd win the game."[66]

With the Phillies clinging to a one-run lead, Dodgers second baseman Davey Lopes smashed a hard liner to third. The ball struck Schmidt's left leg and deflected to an alert Bowa, who threw to first in a last-ditch effort to get the final out. It was a bang-bang play, but umpire Bruce Froemming ruled Lopes safe as the tying run crossed the plate. Bowa, incredulous, went after Froemming, screaming that he had blown the call. First baseman Richie Hebner beat him to it, and Ozark was forced to restrain both of them.[67] "Lopes was out," insisted Hebner in a 2017 interview, still reeling at the memory. "That was a big ass play in the game, and it really broke our backs. But what are you going to do? It didn't go our way."[68] More chaos followed. An errant pick-off attempt by Garber and a single by Dodgers shortstop Bill Russell scored Lopes, giving Los Angeles a 6–5 lead, which they preserved in the bottom of the inning for the victory.

During the postgame interview Ozark was asked to explain why he didn't replace Luzinski with Jerry Martin in the ninth inning, an obvious defensive move he had made throughout the season when the Phillies had a lead. "In this kind of a series, you don't know what's going to happen," insisted the Phils' manager. "If the Dodgers tie or go ahead in the ninth, I still have Bull coming to bat in the bottom of the inning."[69]

The press homed in for the kill. Bruce Keidan of the *Inquirer* referred to the 6–5 loss as "giveaway day at the Vet."[70] His colleague, Frank Dolson, called Ozark's reasoning "astounding." He wrote that "instead of managing to protect a two-run lead in the top of the ninth," the Phillies' manager "was concerned with having his top RBI man available to bat in the bottom of the ninth in the event that the Dodgers scored two or three runs. It was negative thinking carried to the extreme."[71] Dolson had made a valid point.

Ozark should have quit while he was ahead. Instead, he made the situation worse by trying to defend Luzinski's miscue. "Bull broke in on the ball a little bit," he explained. "If he went back right away, he'd have caught it very easily. If I knew the same ball was going to be hit, I'd have put Martin in there. But Mota's a guy who doesn't pull the ball."[72] Realizing that he was getting nowhere, Ozark changed the subject. He diverted blame for the loss to Froemming's controversial call at first base. "He was stunned by Bowa's throw," insisted the Phils' skipper. "He just anticipated that Bowa couldn't make the throw. He didn't know what the fuck to call it, so he called it safe."[73] The writers didn't care about Froemming's call, though. The following day Ozark was excoriated in the newspapers for having blown the game by leaving Luzinski in left field.

Regardless of who was to blame, the game was the most heartbreaking loss for a Phillies team that was perhaps the best ever in the history of the franchise. It would go down in the annals of Philadelphia sports history as "Black Friday," an eternal reminder that if anything can go wrong in the postseason, it will for the Phillies.[74]

Down two games to one in the best-of-three-games series, the Phils turned to their ace for the fourth contest, a rain-soaked rematch between Carlton and Dodgers ace Tommy John. Los Angeles scored first when Dusty Baker hit a two-run homer off Carlton in the second. The Phils blew a scoring opportunity in the bottom of the frame with two on and one out, but John escaped with a 2–0 lead still intact. Rich Hebner cut the Dodgers' lead in half in the fourth when he doubled home Luzinski, but that's all the offense the Phillies could muster.

Carlton imploded in the fifth when he issued a lead-off walk to Dusty Baker, who advanced to second on Steve Yeager's single to left-center field. Lefty retired Tommy John on three pitches, bringing Davey Lopes to the plate. After working a 2-1 count on the Dodgers second baseman, Carlton unleashed a wild pitch that got past McCarver, ricocheted off the backstop, and ended up in the Phillies' dugout. While the veteran catcher was retrieving the ball, Baker scored from second and Yeager advanced to third.[75]

"I've always considered luck a matter of design," McCarver told *Daily News* columnist Stan Hochman after the game. "I don't believe in luck. But it was a weird bounce. That wild pitch took a hop that hadn't happened all year in this ballpark."[76]

Carlton was still not out of trouble. With two outs and a runner on third, he faced shortstop Bill Russell, who laid down a bunt between the pitcher's mound and the third base line. It was too close to the home plate cutout for Schmidt to make a play, so Lefty went after the ball and slipped on the wet surface, enabling Russell to reach first base safely and Yeager to score the Dodgers' fourth and final run of the game.[77]

The 4–1 loss was yet another heartbreaker, especially since the Phillies believed that they should have won the third game. It was difficult not to blame Froemming's controversial call for the Phils' reversal of fortunes, just as it was hard not to blame the poor weather conditions in the subsequent game for the team's agonizing exit from the postseason. "I hope there are no unprofessional remarks that hit the papers," said McCarver after the Phils were eliminated. "We're too dedicated and too professional to make excuses about the [weather] conditions tonight, or the umpires' decisions last night. Remember, the Dodgers were playing in the same conditions. The luster of their winning shouldn't be defaced by our making remarks to the contrary."[78]

Beyond the nagging feeling that the Phillies had had the pennant stolen from them, there were growing doubts among the sportswriters and fans about Carlton's ability to win in the postseason. A year ago the veteran southpaw had surrendered 8 hits, 5 walks, and 5 runs in the seven innings he pitched in the first game of the NLCS against the Cincinnati Reds. Now, in the two games he started against the Dodgers, he had given up 13 hits, 8 walks, and 9 earned runs in eleven and two-thirds innings with a bloated ERA of 6.94.[79] The Phillies' ace, for the second straight year, was not able to rise to the occasion in the really big games the way that Sandy Koufax and Bob Gibson had. If Carlton could not do that, the Phillies had little hope of ever winning a pennant, let alone a World Series.

11

Mastery and Mystery

By 1978 Steve Carlton was in the process of transforming a once-fading pitching career into a first-ballot Hall of Fame induction. But for all his mastery on the mound, Lefty remained a mystery off it, refusing to share anything about himself with the public. Because the media constituted the fans' primary link to Carlton, he cut himself off from both groups when he stopped giving interviews. His contempt for the sportswriters was understandable because they invaded his privacy and distracted him from his work. As a result, Carlton made a conscious effort to intimidate the writers so they would leave him alone.[1]

Once, when Lefty found sportswriter Stan Hochman of the *Daily News* peeking into his locker, he drew up his frame to his full, towering height and lectured the scribe. "You have no right to look in my locker," he snapped, his voice quivering with barely controlled emotion. Picking up a baseball bat and placing it on his shoulder, Carlton stared menacingly into the eyes of the offending sportswriter and said, "You've made a big mistake," before walking away. The next day Lefty had his nameplate and uniform number removed from the locker.[2] After that, Hochman was more careful.

Instead of approaching the veteran southpaw directly, the *Daily News* scribe would go to Larry Christenson, who lockered next to Lefty, and ask, "LC, do you think Steve will answer a few questions?"

Christenson would then turn to Carlton and ask, "Steve, Stan would like to speak with you. Will you answer a few questions for him?"

"No!" barked the Phillies' ace as he continued to dress.[3]

Interestingly, the longer Carlton refused to speak with Hochman, the more obsessed the sportswriter became with him. At the beginning of the 1978 season the *Daily News* scribe's frustration boiled over into a column titled "Why, Oh Why, Won't Super Steve Carlton Talk Shop with Us?" In the column Hochman compares the sportswriter to a "hunter who has bagged the big-horn sheep and the mountain lion, and must now pursue the elk or the unicorn, or whatever-the-hell he needs for the hunter's hat trick." In his view, "Steve Carlton should understand that." Hochman wrote that the hurler was "a hunter. We know that much about him. But the rest he wants to keep to himself. . . . Carlton says he does not intend to grant any interviews this year because he 'has nothing to say.' That isn't the reason, though. He knows it. I know it. You know it. He has plenty to say. He just doesn't want to say it. Why? For the same reason someone into Transcendental Meditation doesn't tell anyone his personal mantra, for fear it will shatter his magic.

"Does he think he owes the public only a skillful performance on game nights and nothing else? Does he see his contract with the ballclub calling for pitching only, and not even a smattering of public relations?"[4]

Hochman also suggested that catcher Tim McCarver was nothing more than a lackey for his batterymate. "McCarver answers questions when Carlton won't," he charged. "Someone else might feel bitter, belittled, talking ABOUT Carlton all the time, even on days when he's gone 2-for-4 with three RBIS."[5]

But McCarver refused to take the bait. "I don't mind talking about Steve," he replied. "I am a loquacious individual. Let's face it, the primary reason I'm here is to catch Lefty. So I don't get tired of the questions. I don't think my dignity has been shattered or lessened." Then the veteran catcher went on to explain his theory about Carlton's silence:

"In fairness to Lefty, you couldn't have found a more accommodating athlete than him in '72 when he was going well. He would talk about anything, including private things, his theories on life.

And then it was used against him in '73 and '74 when he was struggling. So, he cut off the sportswriters.

"Lefty's man enough to stand by that. The thing is, he's not the type of person who goes halfway. He either gives of himself or he ignores you. I guess indifference is worse than hate, though."[6]

A few years later, however, McCarver admitted that he "never wanted to be a designated spokesman" for Carlton. Since Tim "wanted to preserve the dignity of [their] relationship," he only "tried to talk about the game Steve pitched," not about Carlton's beliefs or feelings. And the only reason McCarver did that was because he realized that Carlton's inaccessibility "made it difficult for people in the media who covered the team regularly."[7]

Phillies owner Ruly Carpenter believed that there were "times [when] Lefty should give an interview" but that he "was not going to make a major issue of it." He reminded the sportswriter that, "after all, there were things written about him that went into his personal life after that '72 season." As Carpenter pointed out, "Steve was resentful of that. He's basically a shy guy."[8]

While Carlton's contempt for the sportswriters was understandable, it was more difficult to accept his alienation of the fans. But the left-hander genuinely believed that he owed the fans nothing more than his best effort whenever he took the mound.[9] That is why he refused to do endorsements, autograph signings, and photo ops. In fact, each season when the Phillies held Camera Night, an event in which fans could go onto the field to take photos of their favorite players, Carlton avoided the event by hiding in a concession stand, restroom, or a broom closet. "It's not that I don't respect the fans," he explained. "I just feel silly parading around out there like I'm in a petting zoo. It's a very dehumanizing and painful thing for me."[10]

Even in the Phillies' yearbooks Lefty consciously isolated himself from the fan base. Among the many photos of players with their families, there were, after 1973, none of Carlton with his wife, Beverly, and their two sons. When the Phillies' ace did reveal something about himself, it was so esoteric that the fans were unable to relate to him. For example, in a survey of player interests, all twenty-four of Carlton's teammates sought the "regular guy" image by listing favorite rock musicians like Elton John, Boz Skaggs, or the groups Chicago and Earth, Wind and Fire. But Carlton listed Jascha Heifetz, a classical violinist, and Jean-Pierre Rampal, a French flautist who specialized in music of the baroque era. Similarly, in a survey of the people they'd most like to meet, Carlton's teammates mentioned pro sports figures, but he listed Socrates, Albert Einstein, Thomas Jefferson, Napoleon, and Jesus Christ.[11] Such responses only served to underscore his abstruse personality.

Indeed, Lefty was an enigma, even to his teammates. Not many ballplayers are wine connoisseurs who spend off days traveling to vineyards. Fewer still can be found at a bookstore purchasing volumes on subjects such as yoga, wine, Buddhism, and Pennsylvania's covered bridges. But these were two of Carlton's favorite pastimes. These preferences were also consistent with his introverted nature, which concealed tremendous intensity. Constantly in search of peace and tranquility to offset a hair-trigger temper, Lefty was obsessive about the study of martial arts and Eastern philosophies. Determined to maximize his body's potential on the mound, he engaged daily and rigorously in kung fu. The idiosyncratic combination of these practices enabled Carlton to reach deep and marshal his physical and mental resources so he could eliminate all factors that might prevent him from winning whenever he pitched. Eye contact with hitters was purposely avoided. Bad calls by the umpire were ignored. Fielding errors elicited a brief shake of the head and then were forgotten. The cheers or boos of the fans went unacknowledged. Carlton even plugged his ears with cotton to block out the noise.[12]

However, Lefty had another side to his personality that made him exceptionally popular among teammates—he behaved crazily off the playing field. One of the finest examples came in February 1978, just before pitchers and catchers were to report to Clearwater, Florida, for spring training. Carlton participated in a bike-a-thon for the Muscular Dystrophy Association, along with teammates Larry Christenson, Tug McGraw, and Randy Lerch, as well as former Eagles quarterback Roman Gabriel. They began their trek in Seattle, Washington, intending to complete the journey in San Diego. A Greyhound bus followed to support the group, especially in case of an emergency. It also carried everything the group needed, including replacement tires, tubes, mobile phones, water, and energy bars.

When riding through northern Oregon, Carlton became so bored that he challenged Lerch and Gabriel to see just how fast their ten-speed bikes could go. Cycling side by side, the three men pulled in directly behind the bus so they could catch the draft. Carlton kept waving to the driver to go faster and faster. Suddenly, they heard a siren and an Oregon state trooper on a loudspeaker ordering them to pull over.

"What's wrong, Officer?" Lefty asked innocently, standing on the shoulder of the road.

"What in the hell do you think you're doing?" screamed the trooper. "I clocked you idiots going well over the 60 mph speed limit!"

The commotion awakened McGraw, who was napping inside the bus, and he came outside to see what was happening.

"Gee, Officer, I'm sorry about my friends," Tug began. "See, we play for the Philadelphia Phillies and are doing a bike-a-thon for muscular dystrophy. But we're behind schedule, so we're trying to make up time. We have to be down in Clearwater, Florida, in just a few days for spring training."

Shaking his head in amazement, the trooper smiled and asked for their autographs. "You guys be careful," he warned before leaving, "and don't pull anything like that again!"[13]

The Phillies were expected to repeat as the National League East champions in 1978, and for good reason. Their eight starters were returning, giving the Phils a potent offense and a strong defense. Schmidt, Luzinski, and Hebner would provide the power, while Bowa, Sizemore, McBride, and Maddox stabilized the defense and led the running attack. The pitching staff was every bit as good. Carlton, the ace, had returned to his Cy Young form. Larry Christenson, who had won nineteen games the previous season, was coming off the best year of his career. General manager Paul Owens, who had tried to trade LC on two occasions in the past, was now talking about the right-hander as a "superstar" who "could be our ace for the next seven or eight years."[14] Randy Lerch, coming off a rookie season in which he won ten games in twenty-eight starts, would compete with Dick Ruthven for the third slot in the starting rotation. Ruthven, reacquired from the Braves, won twenty-three games during his two years in Atlanta and was a much more refined pitcher than when he left the Phillies. And Ron Reed was expected to split closing duties with Tug McGraw in the bullpen.

Despite their considerable talent, the '78 Phillies got off to a slow start. For the fourth straight year they dropped their season opener, this time to the St. Louis Cardinals by a score of 5–1 at Veterans Stadium. Instead of greeting the defending NL East champions with cheers, the 47,791 fans who attended the game booed their lungs out almost from the start. The Phils were never really in the game. They fell behind early due to Carlton's failure on two occasions to cover first base on a ground ball and errors by shortstop Larry Bowa and second baseman Ted Sizemore. Lefty lasted only four innings, surrendering 4 runs on 10 hits while striking out just 3 batters. Not until the eighth inning did the Phils mount a serious challenge when, trailing 5–0, they loaded the bases with one out and the heart of the order coming to bat. Still, Mike Schmidt, Greg Luzinski, and Rich Hebner could do no more than manage a single run, and that came on a walk.[15]

Carlton's next start, on April 14 against the Cardinals, was not much better. The Phillies stranded fifteen runners, twelve of them in the first six innings, while Lefty gave up 3 runs on 10 hits over eight innings. But the inning that mattered most was the bottom of the eighth, with the score tied, 3–3. With one out, Redbirds catcher Ted Simmons singled and first baseman Keith Hernandez lined a shot past Bake McBride into the right-field corner. McBride raced to the wall, picked up the ball off the carom, and fired to second baseman Davey Johnson, who nailed Simmons at the plate. With two outs, Carlton walked Ken Reitz, which brought Tony Scott to the plate. Scott hit a screaming line drive down the third base line, but Mike Schmidt speared it for the third out. The Phils picked up another run in the ninth and shut down the Cards in the bottom of the frame to win, 4–3.[16] Still, Carlton and the Phillies continued to struggle in April, closing out the month with a ten-game losing streak. Two of those losses were credited to Lefty: a 7–3 defeat by Montreal and a 4–2 loss against the Cubs.[17] But the team's—and Carlton's—fortunes changed as the spring unfolded.

On May 1 Lefty snapped the Phils' losing streak by beating Tom Seaver of the Reds, 12–1. Carlton was masterful, hurling a five-hitter and surrendering just one run, a solo homer by his nemesis Johnny Bench in the seventh. On May 11 Lefty defeated Seaver again, 4–1, as the Phillies won their ninth in the last eleven games. Carlton won again on Memorial Day, this one against the Pirates, 6–1.[18] In addition, McCarver was proving that he was just as effective at the plate as he was behind it.

Tim sported a .406 batting average through mid-May, with 13 hits in 32 at bats.[19] In fact, McCarver's bat was so hot that Ozark decided in April to keep him in games at first base after Carlton was relieved. On April 22, for example, in the first game of a doubleheader against the Expos at Olympic Stadium, McCarver started behind plate and moved to first in the seventh inning after Carlton was lifted. Although the Phillies lost the game, 7–3, Tim went 2-for-3 and scored 2 of the runs. Again on April 26, against the Cubs at the Vet, McCarver started behind the plate and moved to first in the seventh after Carlton was lifted. The Phillies lost, 2–0, but Tim went 2-for-3 and scored a run. On May 20, against the Mets at Shea Stadium, McCarver started the game as catcher and moved to first base when Carlton was lifted in the seventh. Tim went 4-for-6 with 2 doubles and an RBI. The Phillies won, 9–4.[20] Ozark would leave McCarver in those games he started behind the plate whenever the veteran catcher was hitting well. Not only was the move effective roster management, but it allowed Tim the opportunity to contribute even more to the club's fortunes in the twilight of his playing career.

Carlton struggled again during the summer. Between June 5 and August 1 he made thirteen starts and won only four while dropping six. Most of the games Lefty lost were decided by a single run, and he was still averaging five strikeouts a game. He just came out on the losing end. Carlton's frustration boiled over after he pitched a complete game against Cincinnati on July 28 and lost, 2–1.[21] Lefty, still reeling from the loss, kicked out a few windows of the Martz Trailways bus the Phillies were taking back to their hotel. Carlton had been known to indulge in such wild behavior before, but this time teammates noticed an unusual fulmination to his destructive act.[22]

On a more positive note, two of the thirteen starts Carlton made during the two-month span marked major milestones in his pitching career. On July 19 Lefty fanned Ken Griffey of the Cincinnati Reds and moved into sixteenth place on the all-time strikeout list, just ahead of Sandy Koufax. Although he lost the game, 7–2, Carlton would become a serious contender for the all-time strikeout record over the next decade.[23] Three days later, on July 23, Lefty won his two hundredth Major League game with a 13–2 romp over the Houston Astros. Feeling unusually generous after the game, he agreed to a mass interview with the sportswriters after the game.

Stan Hochman, of the *Daily News*, began by asking the Phillies' ace why it "took seven starts to get his 200th career win."

"During the last seven starts, I was getting behind with the curve," explained Carlton. "Fall behind 2-and-0, 3-and-1 and that gives the percentage to the hitter. A .300 hitter becomes a .400 hitter in 2-and-0, 3-and-1 situations. But if you get ahead of 'em consistently, the .300 hitter becomes a .220 hitter. You go up against a big, powerful team like Cincy, you've got to throw a high percentage of strikes. So Timmy [McCarver] and I decided not to throw a curve until the sixth inning. I went with the slider instead."[24]

Hochman's follow-up question began with the words, "Danny Ozark has a theory. . . ." "This oughtta be good," chuckled Lefty, who had little respect for his manager's knowledge of the game. The very next day Hochman reported Carlton's chuckle in the *Daily News*, and other newspapers reprinted it. Angered by the incident, Carlton refused to speak with the press for the rest of the season.[25] At the same time, Lefty's spirits were buoyed by his recent milestone victory. During the next few days his behavior became crazier than usual.

At one point the Phillies were working out at the Vet. Coach John Vukovich, who was in the outfield shagging fly balls, noticed that Carlton was at shortstop "bouncing all over the place, taking grounders and throwing to first." He could not help but marvel at Lefty's endurance, especially since Carlton had recently completed one of his rigorous training sessions with Gus Hoefling. McCarver, who had just finished hitting, walked out to right field to visit with Vukovich, who pointed out the six-foot, four-inch pitcher making a spectacle of himself at short. "The only thing I can figure is that there are two Leftys," said McCarver. "One of them is at home right now sleeping, and when we go home he gets up and comes here and this one goes home to sleep."[26]

In early August the Phillies went on the road to Pittsburgh for a four-game series against the Pirates. The team arrived on Thursday night for the weekend series and checked into their hotel. About midnight Greg Luzinski and Larry Christenson heard a strange noise in the hallway and opened the door to find Carlton hitting golf balls with a three-wood. The balls would get caught in the door wells and rattle around, waking up his teammates.

"Hey Lefty, what are you trying to do?" asked Luzinski.

"See that door at the end of the hallway?" Carlton replied. "I'm trying to hit it with these balls without any of them touching the floor or the ceiling."

Satisfied with the answer, and knowing how crazy Carlton was, LC and Bull retreated to their rooms and tried to go back to sleep. "But all you could hear was 'BANG, BANG, BANG,'" recalled Christenson. "Then, after sixteen or seventeen shots, Lefty yelled, 'I did it!'"

When the Phillies arrived at Three Rivers Stadium the next day, Eddie Ferenz, the traveling secretary, called a team meeting. Unsure of which player had inflicted all the damage in the hotel's hallway, Ferenz addressed all the players, saying, "The green fees on the thirteenth floor are $1,600.00. I'll take either cash or a check." Of course, they all knew who the culprit was and could not contain their laughter.[27]

Three days later, on August 6, the Phillies played a Sunday afternoon twin bill against the Pirates. Ruthven started the opener and won, 3–2. Carlton pitched the second game. For once the Phillies gave him an early lead, scoring three runs in the second. Lefty himself singled home the first run. McCarver scored on a wild pitch, and Bake McBride drove Carlton home with a double. Lefty no-hit the Bucs until Bill Robinson hit a one-out single in the fifth. Carlton would only give up two more hits, pitching a complete-game victory, 5–0, for his thirty-seventh career shutout and tenth win of the season.[28] Five days later Carlton faced the Bucs again, this time at the Vet. Lefty, who drove in three runs in the 15–4 rout, evened his record at 11-11. He missed his next start due to bursitis in his left shoulder, but he returned to the rotation on August 19 and shut out the San Francisco Giants, 3–0, for his twelfth win of the season.[29]

The Phillies entered September in first place in the NL East with a record of 71-59. It was a three-team race at that point, with second-place Pittsburgh five games back and third-place Chicago five and a half games out.[30] Carlton, who struggled to stay at .500 for most of the season, suddenly got hot. After losing to the Giants, 4–3, on September 1 in San Francisco, Lefty went on a four-game winning streak. He hurled complete-game victories against the Cubs, 8–1; Pirates, 10–3; and Mets, 2–1, striking out at least nine batters in each game. On September 24 Carlton defeated the Mets again, 8–2, for his sixteenth and final victory of the season.[31]

McCarver also got hot in the final month of the season, contributing to his batterymate's success behind the plate and at bat. On September 1 against the Giants, Tim went 1-for-3 with a triple off Jim Barr and one run scored. Five days later, against the Cubs at Wrigley, McCarver doubled off Paul Reuschel in the ninth inning of an 8–1 Phillies victory. On September 24 at New York the Phils' veteran catcher went 1-for-2 with a two-run homer in the sixth off Mets starter Nino Espinosa and knocked in another run in the eighth to help Carlton gain his sixteenth victory, 8–2.[32]

Heading into the last weekend of the season, the Phillies were 20-9 for September. But the Pirates kept pace, cutting the Phils' NL East lead to three and a half games with four left to play, and the division came down to a season-ending series in Pittsburgh. The Pirates swept the Phillies in a Friday night doubleheader, beating Carlton and Ron Reed.[33] With his team having just a one-and-a-half-game lead, Ozark sent Randy Lerch to the mound the next day. Willie Stargell hit a mammoth grand slam home run in the first inning to give the Bucs a 4–1 lead. But Lerch calmed down and led the comeback with two homers of his own. Luzinski's three-run shot and a three-run double by Hebner put the Phils on top, 10–4. Although the Pirates rallied for four runs in the ninth, Ron Reed struck out Stargell and forced Phil Gardner to ground out, sealing the division-clinching victory.[34]

Once again the Phillies' playoff opponents were the Los Angeles Dodgers, and again the Dodgers won. Larry Christenson faced Burt Hooton in the opener and was knocked out of the game early, surrendering 7 runs, 6 of them earned, on 7 hits in just four and a third innings. Steve Garvey's 3-run homer proved to be the decisive blow in the Dodgers' 9–5 victory.[35] Dick Ruthven pitched the second playoff contest against Tommy John. Ruthven pitched perfect ball through the first three innings before surrendering a solo home run in the fourth to Davey Lopes. It was all the support John needed. Capitalizing on his sinker, the Dodgers' veteran threw 18 ground ball outs, and Los Angeles won, 4–0, as the Phillies' bats fell silent.[36] Carlton started the third playoff game and went the distance in the 9–4 win. He also hit a homer and drove in 4 runs to earn his first postseason victory as a Phillie, but it wasn't enough.[37] The Phils dropped the fourth playoff contest, 4–3, in extra innings as the Dodgers clinched their second straight pennant.[38]

The Phillies had run out of excuses. Despite having talent that was equal to or superior to that of the teams that had defeated them, they had lost three straight playoffs. Fans and sportswriters accused them of "choking" and a "lack of mental toughness."[39] Owner Ruly Carpenter wondered whether he should keep the team together or break it up and rebuild.[40] Even some of the players questioned whether the team could win it all. "You go so long and you don't win, you begin to wonder," said Larry Bowa, recalling the disappointment more than forty years later. "Then you fall short in the playoffs three years in a row. You go from saying, 'We're just glad to be here,' to saying, 'This group can't win.' The more you read about it in the newspapers, you start thinking maybe we can't win or aren't good enough to win."[41]

If the Phillies of the mid- to late 1970s were a failed dynasty, no one felt it more than Steve Carlton. Three times Lefty pitched the team into the postseason, only to lose. In four playoff starts, he was

1-2 with a 5.79 ERA, his regular season brilliance failing him when it mattered most.[42] Heading into the 1979 season, the Phillies, on paper, appeared to be the favorites in the National League East.

Desperate to reach the World Series, the Phillies dipped into their National League–leading $4.9 million payroll to sign thirty-seven-year-old free agent Pete Rose to a four-year contract worth $3.2 million, making him the highest-paid player in the game.[43] Rose, an indispensable cog in the success of Cincinnati's Big Red Machine, was the one player many believed could deliver a world championship to Philadelphia. He was a throwback who did not have much natural ability but took advantage of the exceptional hand-eye coordination he did possess to transform himself into one of the finest hitters in the history of the game. Slotted to lead off and play first base, Rose's sheer presence on the team made the Phillies favorites to win the National League pennant.[44]

With Rose on board, the Phillies looked unbeatable through the spring of '79, but Carlton struggled in his first six starts, going 2-4. Ozark blamed McCarver. The Phillies' manager criticized Tim for calling too many breaking pitches, many of which resulted in costly walks for Carlton. Dodgers catcher Steve Yeager had said the same thing after Los Angeles beat the Phillies' ace, 5–2, in his previous start on May 3. "You never used to be able to sit on his breaking ball," said Yeager, "because he'd bury you with his fastball. Now he's throwing a lot more breaking stuff."[45] Ozark also cited McCarver's inability to throw out runners and his .167 batting average, which wasn't helping Lefty when he wasn't getting much run support as it was.[46]

While Tim did not disagree, he insisted that "throughout my career I've had to establish certain standards and re-establish standards and it's obvious that I have to re-establish those standards again."[47]

Nevertheless, Ozark benched McCarver and went with Boone for Carlton's next start on May 7. Boone opened the game by calling for seven straight fastballs—a clear deviation from McCarver's pitch calling. In fact, Lefty only threw one breaking pitch in the first inning, and by the third he was starting to strike out hitters with his slider. In six innings of work Carlton surrendered 1 earned run on 5 hits and 3 walks while striking out 6 to defeat the hapless San Diego Padres, 11–6. The victory was number 16 for the Phillies in their last 20 games. It also made Carlton the winningest left-hander in club history, with 133 victories.[48]

McCarver's benching broke an uninterrupted streak of 107 games catching Carlton, which amounted to nearly three full seasons dating to May 1, 1976. "I gave Lefty the best three years of my life," chuckled Tim, trying to retain his sense of humor on a night that must have been heartbreaking for him. What made matters worse was the clumsy way Ozark handled the change. Although he had told Boone the day before that he would be catching Carlton, Lefty and Tim only got the word just before the game, and from new pitching coach Herm Starrette. "Certainly, I was hurt," admitted McCarver. "I had no notice of it until 5 o'clock. I was surprised and disappointed, but I ain't eulogizing myself. I'm not dead in this game yet."[49]

Boone caught Carlton again in his next start, on May 11, but this time Lefty lost a 2–1 heartbreaker. McCarver would be behind the plate for the left-hander's next start five days later and remain there for the rest of May and the entire month of June before he was benched again. During that span Carlton made ten starts and went 5-3. Although he did not get the decision in two other games the Phillies won, against the Cincinnati Reds, 4–3, and St. Louis Cardinals, 6–4, Lefty pitched more than five innings in both those outings.[50]

While Carlton said he felt comfortable with either Boone or McCarver behind the plate, the inconsistency bothered him.[51] He was a creature of habit; routines were extremely important to him. That Ozark was disrupting his routine only made matters between them worse. Carlton also did not appreciate his manager's tendency to relieve him, something that had become more frequent that season. "Lefty was pretty frustrated with Danny that season," recalled pitcher Randy Lerch in a 2019 interview. Ozark had the bullpen ready to go and went out to the mound to get him, but Lefty refused to leave the game. "He'd tell Ozark, 'This is my game. You're not going to the bullpen.'"[52]

On June 30 Carlton, who was 8-8, started against the St. Louis Cardinals in a Saturday night game. Lefty took a one-run lead into the sixth, but then things fell apart. Keith Hernandez led off with a double, and George Hendrick tied the game at 1–1 by stroking a single up the middle. Carlton then got Tony Scott to pop up, intentionally walked Ken Reitz, and, after wild-pitching the runners to second and third, fanned Steve Swisher. Then he walked Mike Tyson to get to pitcher John Fulgham, who had had no big league hits. Lefty threw a fastball for a strike and snapped a curve for strike two. With an 0-2 count, Carlton, according to proper pitching etiquette, should have either gotten Fulgham to chase a pitch outside the zone or throw him a fastball for strike three. Instead, McCarver called for a curveball, and Lefty threw a hanging curve to Fulgham, who bounced the ball up the middle to make the score 2–1 in favor of St. Louis.[53] McCarver defended the call in a postgame interview, explaining that "Fulgham hadn't come close to hitting a curve all night and we thought it was the best pitch to call."[54] After Carlton allowed a two-run double by Garry Templeton, increasing the Cards' lead to 4–1, Ozark came out to the mound to relieve him. As the Phillies' manager reached for the baseball, Carlton petulantly spiked it at Ozark's feet and stomped off in disgust. When McCarver bent over to pick up the ball, Ozark snapped, "Don't you dare pick that ball up. Just let it sit there!"[55]

The Phils' manager called Tug McGraw in from the bullpen, and when the comedic reliever reached the mound, he simply picked the ball up, took a few more warm-up tosses, and proceeded to retire the side. Fortunately, the Phillies rallied in the tenth to win the game, 6–4.[56] But Carlton's belligerence was not forgotten, or forgiven, at least by one teammate.

Larry Bowa made matters worse by telling Frank Dolson of the *Inquirer* that Lefty "has never had discipline." Carlton "played for Red Schoendienst [in St. Louis] and Frank Lucchesi when he first came here," explained the shortstop. "And now he's playing for Ozark. None of those managers are disciplinarians. The young guys—Randy Lerch and Larry Christenson—socialize with Lefty and all they hear is what an idiot Ozark is. They listen. They believe him." Bowa's proposed solution to the problem was to make all the pitchers run, including Carlton, who was allowed to train with Gus Hoefling instead.

"You start at the top," he said, meaning team owner Ruly Carpenter. "Ruly has to tell [pitching coach] Herm Starrette that they *all* run, *all* the pitchers. Somebody's got to do it. Danny's never done it."[57]

The negative remark reflected not only Bowa's frustration with the Phillies, who were in second place in the NL East, six and a half games behind the division-leading Expos and slipping fast, but also a personal grudge against Carlton, who refused to tolerate the shortstop's constant criticism of teammates. Ozark was also angered by Lefty's stunt, though he initially dismissed it, telling the sportswriters that his pitcher was "just expressing anger at the bad 0-2 pitch he made." But one writer circled back to Ozark's office after the gaggle of reporters left and asked the manager, "Who do you think you're kidding?"

"I know," replied the Phils' skipper. "The guy tried to show me up out there and I'm damned upset about it," he admitted.[58] Not only did Ozark slap Carlton with a hefty fine, but he benched McCarver for calling the curveball and substituted Boone for Lefty's next four scheduled starts.[59]

Carlton realized that he had gone too far. He came closest to apologizing to Ozark four days later, after he defeated the New York Mets, 1–0. Ironically, Lefty, who despised sportswriters, chose to issue the apology in the newspapers. Sending word to Stan Hochman that he wanted to speak with him, Carlton made the *Daily News* scribe wait around the clubhouse until midnight, after all the other writers had gone.[60] Then he emerged from the trainer's room, sat down in front of his locker, and began his act of contrition, admitting that spiking the ball instead of handing it to his manager "was wrong" and that "it wasn't directed at Danny." He said that he was "extremely angry" at himself because he "felt good," was "throwing well" against the Cardinals, but still could "not maximize his effort" to get the win. Lefty also called the incident "the low point of my career."[61]

Carlton must have been feeling very humble that night because he also chose the interview to mend whatever differences he had with Bob Boone, who had caught the 1–0 victory against the Mets. "Bob called a helluva game," Lefty told Hochman. "He did the other two times I pitched to him, too. He's come a long way in his thinking. He's made some great gains as far as setting up hitters."[62] It was the last newspaper interview that Carlton would grant until June 1986, when the Phillies released him.[63]

Lefty would not have to worry about Ozark much longer. On August 31, while the Phillies were in Atlanta, general manager Paul Owens fired the embattled manager. Mired in fifth place in the NL East with a 65-67 record, the Phillies were out of contention. Ozark was not totally to blame, however. Injuries and prolonged losing streaks due to poor pitching and/or hitting contributed to his downfall.[64] If Ozark was responsible for his firing, it was due to an inability to communicate effectively with his pitchers, especially Carlton. He had relied heavily on his former pitching coach Ray Rippelmeyer to mediate any problems he had with the pitching staff, and when Rip retired at the end of the '78 season, Ozark was at a loss. "During my seven years with the Phillies, I had my run-ins with Steve," he admitted years later. "But we always seemed to straighten things out. Of course, the worst of it came in 1979, when I went out to the mound to relieve him against St. Louis and he threw the ball on the ground. But Steve is a competitor, and I'm sure he was more frustrated with the four runs he'd just given up than with me."[65] The diplomatic remark was characteristic of Ozark, who often defended his players in spite of their sometimes boorish behavior.

"If Danny had a fault, it was that he was too damn nice," said owner Ruly Carpenter of Ozark. "He was tremendously loyal to his players. There were just times when he should have been a hell of a lot tougher on them. On the other hand, Danny was a real tough person to put up with all the crap he took from the players, the sportswriters, and the fans."[66]

Carpenter had very mixed emotions about the firing. After all, Ozark had accomplished the goal that the ownership had set for him seven years earlier: to develop a nucleus of talented young players into a perennial contender. In the process, Ozark posted a 594-510-1 win-loss-tie record and three division titles.[67]

Farm director Dallas Green was hired as interim manager and given the task of "finding out who want[ed] to play and who [didn't] want to play for the Phillies." He explained, "I'm honest enough to tell the players how I feel" but added that "if I don't get a complete effort, I'm going to tell 'em. Right now, these guys can't hold their heads up, and they are too good not to win."[68]

Three decades later Green admitted that he was not popular among the players. "When I came on board in '79, I battled with the players on a daily basis," he said in 2015. "Guys like Schmidt, Luzinski, Bowa, Maddox, and Boone viewed me with outright hostility. I told 'em that if they were upset that Danny Ozark was fired, it was their own damn fault because they did not play up to their potential. It helped that I had Pete Rose, Tug McGraw, and Steve Carlton on my side. Carlton was real happy because he didn't think that Ozark was capable of delivering a World Series championship."[69]

Predictably, Green did not tamper with Carlton's routine. McCarver continued to be Lefty's primary catcher, while Boone caught him a total of eight times that season. In those eight contests Carlton posted a 6-2 record with a 3.70 ERA.[70] But McCarver was still Carlton's catcher, and if the manager didn't bench him, it would take a serious injury to dislodge Tim from that role. Such an accident occurred in mid-August when the Phillies were playing the Reds in Cincinnati. Lefty faced Bill Bonham in a pitcher's duel. The game was deadlocked, 1–1, in the tenth, and Paul Blair was at bat. With a 2-2 count, McCarver called for a slider low and inside and literally slapped his mitt on the ground to reinforce the point. Lefty threw the pitch, but Blair laid off it and the ball ricocheted off the ground and caught Tim in the Adam's apple. He spent the next two days in the hospital with a blood clot on his vocal cord. After that, McCarver had a steel attachment welded into his mask for protection, a precursor of the throat guard catchers wear today. Although Lefty threw a 12-strikeout, 4-hit complete game, the Phils lost a heartbreaker, 2–1.[71]

Carlton's loyalty to McCarver was just as strong; he promoted his batterymate as a backstop for the other starters.[72] "Tim had an uncanny way with pitchers," said Carlton. "Not just me. Dick Ruthven liked pitching to him. So did LC [Larry Christenson]. A lot of catchers are just putting down fingers. Not Tim. He was always thinking. He remembered the sequences of pitches we used to get a hitter out. He had great instincts."[73]

Christenson threw mostly to Boone during his eleven-year Major League career. But he did have the opportunity to pitch to McCarver on a few occasions and offered a good comparison of the two catchers and their respective styles:

"Boonie caught most of my starts. He used a smaller catcher's mitt and held his target low and knee-high in the strike zone, just off the inside or outside of the plate, depending on the hitter. When we got ahead in the count, Boonie would either move his glove off the plate or high in the strike zone to see if we could get the hitter to chase a high fastball. We were also in sync with each other most of the time, especially when we were working quickly. But there were other times when we disagreed on a pitch.

"While my best pitch was a fastball, my second-best pitch was the slider, and third, a changeup. But there were times I wanted to throw the curve and he wanted the fastball. I'd shake him off. He would put that one finger down again, insisting on the fastball. But I was stubborn and I'd shake him off again. So he'd call time and come running out to the mound to state his case. I would usually get my way, but before he'd leave Boonie would ask, 'Are you sure you want to throw your fourth-best pitch?' I'd say, 'Yes.' Of course, it never worked out well after all that second-guessing, and I usually got hit, but I also took full responsibility for it, too.

"I think catchers need to know their pitchers and make them go with their best stuff, which can change from game to game. Boonie did that and he did it well.

"McCarver was different. He would not tolerate a pitcher shaking him off. If you did that to Tim, he'd come out to the mound and demand that you throw the pitch he was calling and in the location where he wanted it. He'd say, 'Don't even think of shaking me off.' Of course he didn't do that to Carlton, but he did when he caught me and Ruthven.

"Tim was also emphatic with his body language behind the plate. I remember watching him catch Lefty. He'd call for a slider in the dirt and literally place his glove on the ground so that pitch would bounce in the dirt. McCarver also made you throw inside, probably because the umpires back in the 1970s gave us more latitude with a brushback pitch. Some umps would give you a lot of latitude on the outside corner, too. I think a catcher who makes his pitcher pitch and sets up with a great target and moves it off the plate—never down the middle—is the best kind of catcher a pitcher can have. McCarver did that.

"Looking back, I was fortunate to have Boonie and Tim as teammates. They were two of the greatest catchers in the history of the game."[74]

It was a Sunday afternoon, September 30, 1979, when the Carlton/McCarver battery made its final appearance. The game was against the Montreal Expos at Olympic Stadium. Relying on a 90 mph fastball and a devastating slider, Lefty eliminated the Expos from a National League playoff berth with a brilliant three-hit, 2–0 shutout for his eighteenth and final victory of the season.[75]

After the game Tim pointed out that Lefty had pitched "so much better" than his final record of 18-11 indicated. In fact, McCarver rated the season "second only" to Carlton's 27-10 Cy Young Award–winning season of 1972. "Lefty was 8-1 after August 14," he explained. "He passed 200 strikeouts for the first time since 1974, and took no-hitters into the sixth inning five different times."[76]

Despite the Phillies' fourth-place finish in 1979, Lefty had a good year, posting an 18-11 record. More important, the Carlton/McCarver battery had been a mutually advantageous partnership for the previous four seasons. While Tim's encyclopedic knowledge of National League hitters, his pitch calling, and the emotional support he offered enabled Lefty to regain his Cy Young Award–winning form, Lefty allowed Tim to extend his Major League tenure and to enhance his career statistics. McCarver, a lifetime .271 hitter, performed much better at the plate when he was catching Carlton. Between 1976 and 1979 the veteran catcher hit just .213 with 4 homers in 357 at bats in games he played when Carlton was not pitching. But when he caught Lefty, Tim batted .306, with 10 homers and 66 RBIs.[77]

At the same time, McCarver felt the sadness that comes with all endings. Tim, who had begun his Major League career in 1959, retired after the game. "I realize, and always have, that my baseball career wasn't going to last forever," he told Jayson Stark of the *Inquirer*. But he did entertain the possibility of returning to the playing field the following September to become the first catcher ever to play in four decades—an idea promoted by owner Ruly Carpenter and general manager Paul Owens.[78]

12

Cooperstown Bound

Between 1976 and 1979 Steve Carlton and Tim McCarver composed the best battery in Major League Baseball in terms of starting assignments and victories. Carlton made 140 starts during that span, and McCarver was behind the plate for 128 (91 percent) of them. That is a pairing that exceeds any other combination of batterymates in the Majors in terms of longevity and durability during those four years. The Carlton/McCarver tandem also won more games than any other battery in Major League Baseball during that span, compiling a 72-38 win-loss record and a winning percentage of .655 (see appendix A). Their success was not even limited to those four years.

Carlton and McCarver were also one of the best batteries in the history of the national pastime. Lefty made a total of 709 starts in his twenty-four-year Major League career, and McCarver caught 228 (32 percent) of them, first with the St. Louis Cardinals between 1965 and 1969 and then with the Philadelphia Phillies between 1972 and 1979. Those 228 starts rank twentieth of all time among those batteries who started 200 or more games. More impressive, the Carlton/McCarver battery ranks sixteenth of all time, with 120 wins. If an additional 24 team victories are included when Lefty started the game but did not earn the decision, the tandem ranks tenth in terms of team wins and ninth in winning percentage (.632). Those rankings place the Carlton/McCarver tandem ahead of some of the most prominent batteries in baseball history, including Whitey Ford and Yogi Berra of the perennial champion New York Yankees of

1950–63, Don Newcombe and Roy Campanella of the great Brooklyn Dodgers teams of the 1950s, and Lew Burdette and Del Crandall of the 1953–63 Milwaukee Braves (see appendix A).

Yet for all the success Carlton had experienced by 1979, the best years of his Major League career were still ahead. Between 1980 and 1983 he would win two more Cy Young Awards and would return to the postseason on three occasions, posting a 5-2 record and a 2.36 ERA. In the process, Lefty helped the Phillies win their first World Series title in 1980 and another pennant in 1983. He would also compete with Nolan Ryan for the all-time career strikeout record.

Of all those seasons, however, Carlton's banner year came 1980, when he finally established himself as one of the greatest pitchers in the game. He led National League hurlers with twenty-four wins and topped all Major League pitchers in strikeouts (286) and WAR, or wins above replacement (10.2).[1] Without Carlton, the Phillies would not have even made the postseason that year. The starting pitching was questionable at best entering the season. Dick Ruthven was returning from injury, and his earned run average coming out of spring training was a whopping 7.36. Larry Christenson, who was suffering from a tender elbow, had pitched just five and two-thirds innings in the Grapefruit League. When the regular season began, LC went 3-3 in six starts before undergoing elbow surgery in late May, and he didn't see the mound again until August 15. Nino Espinosa started the season on the disabled list with a severely strained rotator cuff. Although Randy Lerch was healthy, he began the season with an 0-6 record.[2] Dallas Green, who was promoted to manager from the previous year's interim status, made matters worse.

Green was a disciplinarian who refused to cater to the high-salaried superstars on his club. At the beginning of the season he posted a list of team rules on every locker door in the Phillies' clubhouse. Among the rules were a mandatory curfew and dress code, as well as a policy against drinking on team flights without the manager's permission. While most of the players fumed, Carlton didn't even bother to read the list.[3] Although Green genuinely believed that his ace pitcher was "on my side," some teammates believed that Lefty simply tolerated him.[4] Green ingratiated himself with Carlton by excusing the southpaw from training runs with the other pitchers and signed off on Gus Hoefling's program. If Carlton lost a close game, Green would scream at the hitters for not providing more offense. After one of those defeats, a 3–0 loss to the Mets on April 21 at the Vet in which Lefty struck out seven and gave up a single earned run, Green read the team the riot act. "You sons of bitches can't even play for a future Hall of Famer!" he exploded. "You forget where you are! You forget what you're doing. We're supposed to have pride and character, but you don't show it! Well, if you can't show it for the best pitcher in the game, who the hell are you going to show it for?"[5]

For the first six months of the season, Green screamed at his players or ripped them in the sports pages to get them to perform. But the negative motivation didn't work. The Phillies would win three or four games and then lose just as many. At the All-Star break the Phils were in second place at 41-35, a game behind the division-leading Expos. Few of the players were performing up to their potential, with the exception of Carlton, who was 14-4 and largely responsible for the keeping the Phillies competitive in the NL East.[6]

"Lefty did three of the most amazing things I ever saw a pitcher do in my career," recalled Bob Boone, who had become Carlton's primary catcher. "During the first half of the season he made no mistakes. In other words, if we were going to throw a pitch inside, it was either right there on the corner or inside. It was *never* over the plate. If we threw away, he either hit the spot or it would be away. It never came back over the plate, which is where the home runs occur. And in the second half of the season he might've made one or two mistake pitches. It was definitely the most amazing thing I ever saw a pitcher do in my catching career.

"The second thing Lefty did unbelievably well that season was throwing the slider. When he threw the slider down and into a right-handed hitter, it would bury him in the dirt if he swung at it. If, on the other hand, the batter laid off the pitch, it would stay right there for a strike."[7]

To be sure, Carlton did not have his best stuff every time he took the mound that season. But according to Phillies reliever Sparky

Lyle, who had been one of baseball's best closers with the New York Yankees in the 1970s, Lefty "adjusted by the second or third inning and all his pitches were firmly in the [strike] zone." Making those kinds of in-game adjustments was why "he was so successful," said Lyle. "He had the best stuff of any starting pitcher I'd ever seen. And his consistency came because he was so disciplined."[8]

Among Carlton's regular-season highlights were a complete-game, 1-hit shutout, 7–0, against his former team, the St. Louis Cardinals, in his fourth start of the season.[9] In June, Lefty, in two consecutive starts against the San Diego Padres, struck out 22 in sixteen innings to earn his eleventh and twelfth victories of the season.[10] But Carlton's best game came on October 1, when the Phillies were a half game out of first and badly needing a win to stay in the division race against the Montreal Expos. Lefty delivered by hurling a complete-game, 2-hit shutout over the Chicago Cubs, 5–0. He also achieved another milestone in the game when he passed the three-hundred-innings-pitched mark for a single season.[11] The victory set the stage for a showdown against the Expos in Montreal, where the Phillies clinched the division title on October 4.[12]

Carlton was just as impressive in the postseason, when he went 3-0 with a 2.30 ERA. He won the opening game of the best-of-five-games National League Championship Series (NLCS) against the Houston Astros, 3–1. Although the Phils dropped the next two games, Carlton pitched five strong innings in the fourth game before turning the contest over to the bullpen, who won it, 5–3. The victory gave the Phillies the confidence they needed to clinch the pennant the following day.[13]

Since the NLCS against Houston went to five games and all but the first contest went into extra innings, Green was forced to use his starting pitchers as relievers in multiple games. As a result, the Phillies' pitching staff was depleted entering the World Series against the Kansas City Royals. Green could have opted to send Carlton to the mound on two days' rest for Game One of the Fall Classic at Veterans Stadium, but the risk was too great. Lefty had pitched more than three hundred innings during the regular season, more than any pitcher in the Majors. Besides, Carlton over the course of his pitching career had proven to be most effective on four days' rest. Instead, Green gave the ball to rookie Bob Walk, one of the few pitchers who did not appear in the NLCS.[14] Walk delivered, winning the Series opener, 7–6, and setting the stage for Carlton.[15]

Lefty went to the mound for the all-important Game Two of the World Series. With the next three games in Kansas City, the Phillies did not want to go on the road having to win a game to stay alive. Carlton faced Royals starter Larry Gura in a pitcher's duel. The game was scoreless into the fifth inning, when the Phillies scored first with a sacrifice fly by Manny Trillo and an RBI single by Larry Bowa. Carlton gave up an unearned run in the sixth and 3 in the seventh, giving Kansas City a 4–2 lead. But the Phillies rallied, scoring four times in the eighth off reliever Dan Quisenberry to go ahead, 6–4. Ron Reed pitched a scoreless ninth, saving it for Carlton, who struck out 10 over eight innings, allowing 3 earned runs.[16]

Lefty was much more focused in Game Six. He pitched seven innings of scoreless ball, striking out 7 and walking 3. The Phillies gave their ace a 4-run lead, with Schmidt knocking in 2 of the 4 over six innings. But in the eighth Carlton allowed the first two Royals to reach base. McGraw remembered entering the game and getting the ball from the Phillies' ace. "It was a little scary to relieve Carlton," admitted Tug years later. "When I first came to the Phillies, I'd come in to relieve him and say, 'I got this one for you, Lefty. Don't worry about it.' And he'd look at me like he was about to tear off my head. He was intense and never wanted to leave the game. But by 1980 things had changed. I remember going into Game Six and we just made eye contact. We understood each other, and I think he had the confidence to know I'd save the game for him."[17]

Although the Royals scored a run on a sacrifice fly before McGraw retired the side in the eighth, the Tugger provided a little drama in the ninth by loading the bases with two outs before striking out the Royals' Willie Wilson to end the game. Carlton earned the win, 4–1, and McGraw, the save, to clinch the Phillies' first World Series title.[18]

While the city of Philadelphia erupted in celebration and the Phillies retired to their Veterans Stadium clubhouse to shower each other with champagne, Carlton retreated to the trainer's room, just as he had after every other game. There, he sat quietly on the table, sipping champagne from a plastic cup.[19] Tim McCarver, now a member of the Phillies' Prism TV broadcast crew, knew better than to disturb his friend. Lefty had granted him two postgame interviews earlier in the fall, but afterward he had told Tim that he "felt uncomfortable" because it "wasn't fair . . . to do interviews with a friend, and turn others [in the media] down." McCarver understood and accepted his decision and remained in the clubhouse interviewing other former teammates.[20] Still, a steady stream of Phillies pitchers entered the trainer's room to congratulate their ace. Each teammate seemed to respect Lefty's privacy, staying long enough to give him a congratulatory hug. Only reliever Dickie Noles broke protocol by barging in and dousing Carlton with champagne. Lefty, momentarily stunned, backed off, smiled, then firmly but gently shook his head. Noles grinned, shrugged, and settled for a hug before returning to the raucous party that was taking place in the clubhouse.[21]

Carlton appeared to be in a wonderful daze. For as wild and wacky as he could be with his teammates on road trips and in the clubhouse, he didn't quite know how to handle the greatest achievement in his career: starting and earning the victory in a World Series clincher in front of the hometown fans. The following day more than a million Philadelphians turned out for the victory parade. Phillies players parked their cars at the Vet and were bused to Eighteenth and JFK Boulevard, where there were eleven flatbed trucks waiting to carry them down Broad Street. At 11:17 a.m. Carlton, dressed in a three-piece suit, stepped off the bus and was bowled over by the sight of cheering fans jamming the streets and the surrounding rooftops.[22] Lefty would later call the parade his "fondest memory." He recalled being "amazed at the outpouring of emotion," concluding, "I guess it was a combination of joy and relief that after all those years, the Phillies had finally won it all!"[23]

"You'll never know how much winning the championship meant to him," echoed his wife, Beverly. "After the season ended, he would sit up in bed in the middle of the night and nearly shout, 'We're world champions!'"[24]

Carlton's performance in both the regular and postseason was so exceptional that the Baseball Writers' Association of America voted him the winner of the 1980 NL Cy Young Award by an overwhelming margin. Lefty also finished fifth in the NL MVP voting behind teammate Mike Schmidt.[25] It seemed as if only one thing was missing, and that was McCarver, who had been so instrumental in his success over the years. Although Tim made six plate appearances in September, thus enjoying the distinction of being one of the very few Major Leaguers to play in four decades, he had officially retired at the end of the '79 season.[26] Thus, McCarver was unable to experience the same exhilaration of winning the World Series he would have had he still been Lefty's personal catcher.

Ironically, Bob Boone, who as a young catcher had been the target of Carlton's criticism and even refusal to pitch to him, was his Series batterymate. Boone had come to realize that it was his responsibility to be on the same wavelength as Lefty and not the other way around. That was his mistake as a young catcher. "Steve was going to do what he wanted, and there was absolutely no question about that," said Boone, who went on to play another nine seasons after leaving the Phillies and later to manage the Kansas City Royals and Cincinnati Reds. "When I talk to young catchers these days, I tell them not to fight with the pitcher, that as a catcher you have to build trust with your pitchers. I didn't do that in my early years with Steve. It came later when he accepted that I knew what I was doing."[27]

Like all of the Phillies, Carlton and Boone were ready to repeat as world champions in 1981. There was also another personal milestone on the horizon for Lefty. Entering the '81 season, he was just 31 strikeouts shy of 3,000 for his career, and it didn't take long at all for him to reach the milestone.

On April 29, 1981, the Phillies hosted the Montreal Expos at Veterans Stadium in a battle between Carlton and Montreal ace Steve Rogers. Both teams were off to an excellent start, the Expos at 12-3 and the Phillies at 11-6. Only 3 strikeouts shy of 3,000, Lefty struck out the side in the top of the first inning. Lead-off hitters Tim Raines and Jerry Manuel went down looking. Tim Wallach, the number-three hitter, flailed and missed on a 2-strike slider for the third out, and Carlton achieved the rare pitching milestone. In reaching 3,000 strikeouts, Lefty became the first southpaw and the sixth pitcher in Major League history to reach it. He went on to pitch a complete game, improving to 4–0 while striking out 9 in the 6–2 victory.[28]

Carlton was having one of the best seasons of his career before it was cut short by a players' strike protesting the owners' demand for a compensation system to accommodate teams that lost a free agent. Essentially, the owners wanted to reclaim some of the ground they had lost with the advent of free agency in 1975, but the players believed that it was an attempt to break the union.

Baseball had suffered work stoppages in 1972, '73, '76, and '80, three of them confined to spring training. But those strikes lasted just eight to seventeen days. In 1981 the stoppage lasted fifty-nine days, from June 12 to August 9.[29] In the end the new Basic Agreement stipulated that, beginning with the 1981 reentry draft, clubs that lost quality free agents were to receive a Major Leaguer or top Minor Leaguer in return. But the players never made up the missed games.[30] As a result, Carlton, in the strike-shortened season, finished 13-4 with a 2.42 ERA, 179 strikeouts, and ten complete games in just twenty-four starts. He finished third in the Cy Young Award voting behind Dodgers rookie left-hander Fernando Valenzuela.[31]

Since the regular season was split into two halves—one before the strike, the other after—the postseason structure was altered from the standard league championship series between the winners of the East and West divisions of each league to a new divisional series pitting the first- and second-half winners from each division against one another. Winners of the divisional series would move on to the standard league championship series.[32] Intended to kick-start fan interest by virtually giving every team a fresh start, the split-season idea doomed the Phillies' chances to repeat as world champions.

The Phils were one of four divisional winners of the first half, the others being the Dodgers, Yankees, and A's. But they found themselves playing lame-duck teams through the second half, with nothing to gain or lose. As expected, none of the teams that won the first half played to the level of intensity or success they had exhibited before the strike. The Phillies, who played sub-.500 baseball

in the second half, played the Montreal Expos—second-half winners who were making their first-ever postseason appearance.[33]
The divisional series opened in Montreal, where Carlton faced the
Expos' ace, Steve Rogers. Montreal's hitters took as many pitches
as possible, realizing that if they avoided the slider, the pitch would
more times than not land outside of the strike zone. The strategy
worked, too. Lefty had his toughest outing of the season, walking
5 and running deep counts all game. He lasted six innings, giving
up 3 earned runs on 7 hits as the Expos went on to capture the first
playoff game, 3–1.[34] Dick Ruthven lost the next night by the same
score on a Gary Carter home run, and the Phillies were down two
games to none in the best-of-five playoff.[35]

When the series shifted to Philadelphia for the third contest, Larry
Christenson gave the Phils six strong innings, surrendering a single run on four hits. Sparky Lyle and Ron Reed combined to limit
Montreal to one other run as the Phils defeated the Expos, 6–2.[36]
Dickie Noles started the next night but surrendered two runs on
four hits in the five innings he pitched. Home runs by Mike Schmidt
and Gary Matthews kept the Phillies in the game, though. With the
score deadlocked at 5–5, in the bottom of the tenth reserve outfielder
George Vukovich slammed a home run into the left-field bullpen to
keep the Phillies' hopes alive for another division championship.[37]

The momentum now appeared to be in the Phillies' favor. Lefty
was on the mound for the decisive fifth game, which would also be
played at the Vet. "We knew we had our backs to the wall," admitted Gary Carter, the Expos' catcher. "Carlton was the best overall
southpaw I ever faced. He never gave anything away. With home
field advantage and their ace on the mound, the Phillies had everything in their favor."[38] Carlton faced Steve Rogers in a repeat of the
series' first matchup. Not only did Rogers blank the Phillies, scattering six hits over nine innings, but he got the key hit—a two-run
single—in the 3–0 victory.[39] Montreal advanced to the National
League Championship Series, where they would lose to the Los
Angeles Dodgers, who went on to defeat the New York Yankees in
the 1981 World Series.

For the Phillies there would be no return trip to the Fall Classic, no back-to-back world championships, no dynasty. The split season had broken their momentum and initiated the dismantling of the team. On October 29, 1981, Carpenter sold the Phillies to a group of investors headed by executive vice president Bill Giles.[40] Before the next season manager Dallas Green would be gone, as would catcher Bob Boone, shortstop Larry Bowa, reliever Dickie Noles, and outfielders Bake McBride and Lonnie Smith.[41] Still, the Phillies retained a talented but aging nucleus that included Mike Schmidt, who won his second MVP, as well as Pete Rose, Manny Trillo, Gary Matthews, and Garry Maddox. Carlton was still the undisputed ace of the team and headed a starting rotation that still included Larry Christenson and Dick Ruthven, as well as a bullpen that retained its two best performers in Tug McGraw and Ron Reed.

Despite all his success, Lefty remained essentially the same person. Those who knew him in his early years with the Phillies insisted that Carlton was exactly the same guy he was in his last years with the team—a very intense competitor, but a genuine person with a great sense of humor.[42] "Everyone liked Lefty because he was such a great teammate," Sparky Lyle commented. "If you were a pitcher and asked for his advice, he'd give you as much as you wanted," he explained. "If you were a hitter and the opposing pitcher threw at you, Lefty protected you when he went out to the mound the next inning" by throwing at one of their hitters.[43]

Carlton also continued to mentor his younger teammates. If he was not pitching, Lefty spent his time in the video room adjoining the Phillies' clubhouse watching the game on television, often with a half dozen younger pitchers. They crowded around to soak up his extensive knowledge about the game, the hitters, pitching mechanics, or any other observations he cared to share with them. "Video Dan" Stephenson, the team videographer, admitted that he "learned a lot of baseball" during those sessions. "Steve never carried himself as if he was better than other people," said Stephenson. "It didn't matter if you were a player, coach, or employee. He included everybody. If he liked you, you were his friend. If he disagreed with you, he never made an issue of it. He didn't hold grudges. That is why he was loved by his teammates and the people who worked for the Phillies."[44]

Darren Daulton, a promising young catcher who was promoted to the Phillies in 1983, credited Carlton as "a great role model," saying, "By the time I came up to Philadelphia, Lefty was near the end of his career." Daulton recalled that despite Carlton's veteran status "he was in better physical condition than guys my age. He was an expert in martial arts, which gave him unbelievable strength and flexibility and the power to concentrate on the mound. Lefty showed me how to prepare myself mentally and how to stay in top physical shape."[45] Daulton would go on to lead a colorful band of veteran Phillies to the National League pennant a decade later, in 1993.

Carlton did not limit his mentoring to the finer points of pitching or physical conditioning. "I tried to teach the younger guys about the art of living," he recalled in 1986 after he was released by the Phillies, "that there are other parts of life that should be enjoyed while you are playing because a Major League career is so short. It was the same thing Timmy [McCarver] did for me when I was a young player with the Cardinals. So, when the team was on the road I'd take the younger guys out to a good restaurant, buy them a meal, and explain how the quality of the food they ate and the wine they drank was important to a healthy body."[46]

Of course, Carlton never missed an opportunity to mix pleasure with some good old-fashioned rowdyism. One night when the Phillies were out in San Francisco to play the Giants, Lefty took Daulton and a few of the other young players out to dinner at a nice restaurant in a small Bay Area town. It happened to be the mayor's birthday, and the restaurant presented him with a huge cake that was cut into slices and shared with the patrons. "We had already polished off a few bottles of wine and were feeling pretty good," recalled Daulton. "When Lefty got his piece of cake, he started a food fight. Let me tell you, we just tore the place apart. It finally ended when Lefty head-butted the mayor's wife. We were lucky we weren't thrown in jail that night."[47]

Carlton's sense of humor certainly wasn't as highbrow as his taste in music or wine, and his lowbrow hijinks constituted still another quality that made him extremely popular with teammates. Pitchers Larry Christenson and Don Carman could attest to his penchant for head-butting, having been frequent victims of the sophomoric prank. "Lefty loved head-butting so much that I avoided him for nearly two years," admitted Carman.[48] He also loved movies like *Animal House*, *Caddyshack*, *Monty Python's Holy Grail*, and *Monty Python's Life of Brian* and could be heard quoting lines from them on the spur of the moment. "Steve was very funny," said Stephenson. "He was extremely entertaining to be around. I think some of the sportswriters dismissed his quirkiness to being left-handed. But I don't know how much truth there is to that. What's so interesting—and this flies in the face of their theory—is that Steve actually signed his autographs with his right hand and did it with perfect penmanship!"[49]

Another thing that didn't change was Carlton's refusal to talk to the media. By the 1980s the sportswriters had apparently accepted that fact, and some even joked about it. In 1981, for example, when the Mexican left-hander Fernando Valenzuela of the Los Angeles Dodgers took the Majors by storm, winning both the Cy Young and Rookie of the Year Awards, one writer quipped, "The two best pitchers in the National League don't speak English—Fernando Valenzuela and Steve Carlton!"[50]

Other writers attempted to trick Carlton into speaking with them. Ralph Bernstein of the Associated Press, for example, approached Lefty during one spring training and said, "My notebook is closed, my tape recorder is off, my pen is in my pocket. Can we talk off the record for a few minutes?" Carlton paused for a moment, considered the request and then, before walking away, placed his hand on Bernstein's right shoulder and replied, "Sorry, Ralph, policy is policy."[51]

Larry Shenk, the Phils' public relations director, also did not fault Carlton. "Lefty opted not to talk to the writers, and he stuck with that policy," said Shenk. "I think the media accepted and respected his consistency. If nothing else, Lefty's no-talking policy made my life easier because the writers stopped hounding me to get them interviews with him."[52]

Although the Phillies finished second in the NL East in 1982, three games behind the St. Louis Cardinals, Carlton enjoyed another banner year. The Phils' thirty-seven-year-old ace became the first pitcher to win a fourth Cy Young Award.[53] Lefty led all Major League pitchers in victories (23) and strikeouts (286). He also tossed six shutouts and completed nineteen games.[54] Carlton was now being acknowledged as the best pitcher in the Majors. "He's setting the standards that pitchers will be chasing years from now," said Jim Palmer, a three-time Cy Young Award winner with the Baltimore Orioles. Dodgers manager Tommy Lasorda was just as effusive in his praise: "Carlton's physical condition and performance for his age is truly remarkable. What he's done for the pitching profession will be long remembered."[55]

On March 3, 1983, the Phillies rewarded their ace with a four-year, $4.15 million contract, making him the highest-paid pitcher in MLB history at the time. While most salaries were backloaded, Carlton requested that his be frontloaded with $1.15 million in the first year.[56] Team president Bill Giles agreed to do this because the Dodgers had increased Fernando Valenzuela's contract to $1 million for the 1983 season, and the Phillies' president wanted Carlton "to be the highest paid player in the game for once in his life."[57]

The 1983 season was Lefty's last memorable campaign, and he made his final appearance in the Fall Classic with a heavily veteran-laden team. During the off-season the Phils had acquired Joe Morgan (age thirty-nine) and Tony Pérez (forty) to complement Pete Rose (forty-one) and reunite three of the biggest stars of the Big Red Machine championship dynasty. Since the roster also included Ron Reed (forty), Bill Robinson (thirty-nine), Steve Carlton (thirty-eight), and Tug McGraw (thirty-eight), the addition of Morgan and Pérez increased the average age of the team to nearly thirty-three.[58] *Philadelphia Daily News* sportswriter Stan Hochman nicknamed the team the "Wheeze Kids," a sarcastic reference to the 1950 pennant-winning Phillies, who had been called the "Whiz Kids" due to a roster of very talented twenty-year-olds.[59] During the first half of the season, the Phils played like a bunch of "has-beens," too. Fortunately for them, so did the rest of the NL East, with no single team taking command.

One of the more memorable events to occur that spring came on May 4, when Carlton faced off against the Reds at the Vet. His long-time nemesis Johnny Bench, now a corner infielder who would retire at the end of the season, was just one hit shy of his 2,000th career hit. Carlton buzzed through the first three innings without surrendering a hit. After striking out the first two batters in the fourth, Lefty surrendered a base hit to Reds shortstop Dave Concepción. Bench came to the plate next. Lefty quickly jumped out ahead 0-2 in the count. Then Bench fouled off the next eleven pitches before ripping a double to left-center for his 1,999th career hit.

Bench came to bat again in the seventh and, after working a 3-2 count, lashed a line drive single to left field for his 2,000th career hit. As the future Hall of Fame catcher stood at first base, the PhanaVision board in right field informed the 22,619 fans of the milestone, and they responded with a rousing standing ovation. Even Carlton turned toward first, pointed at Bench, and tipped his cap to the one batter who always seemed to hit him hardest.[60]

Bench's lifetime batting average against Carlton was .305 (39-for-128). The twelve home runs he belted against Lefty were the most he hit in his career against any left-hander.[61] After the game, when Bill Lyon of the *Philadelphia Inquirer* asked Bench why he had been so successful against the Phillies' ace, the Reds star explained:

"I've always been able to read Lefty. I know how he thinks. Lefty's got three great pitches and he has command of every one of them, and he stays ahead of the hitters. He's a master at mixing up those three pitches. But hitting is mostly a matter of adjusting. And that's what it takes to hit against Lefty. I know most hitters hate to go against him because they never feel comfortable. But I seem to concentrate better against him than a lot of other pitchers. Maybe because I was a catcher for so long, it's like I'm wired into his selection process.

"Tonight, Lefty kept throwing strikes. He wasn't about to give in. And neither was I. I guess it was like a couple of heavyweights trading their best punches. We really went at each other. It was one of those confrontations you live for. I'll replay that one in my mind for the rest of my life."[62]

While Carlton went on to win the game, recording nine strikeouts en route to the 9–4 victory, the pitcher-hitter duel with Bench was, indeed, one of the great moments in baseball history.[63]

Paul Owens replaced manager Pat Corrales at midseason and

brought some much-needed discipline to the team. The Phillies responded magnificently, winning eleven in a row, as well as fourteen of their last sixteen, to clinch the division on September 28.[64] Five days earlier, on September 23, Carlton won his three hundredth career victory against the St. Louis Cardinals. Lefty struck out 2 in a scoreless first and got the Phillies on the board in the second with a two-out single, scoring Gary "Sarge" Matthews. The Phillies went ahead, 2–0, on an RBI single by Greg Gross. After a scoreless third, the Cardinals tied the game with a 2-run home run by David Green in the fourth. The Phillies immediately responded with 3 runs in the fifth on an RBI single by Matthews and a 2-run single by catcher Bo Díaz. The Phils added another run on a Mike Schmidt double in the sixth, and Carlton took over from there. He struck out 12 while allowing 2 runs and just 1 walk in eight innings. Closer Al Holland pitched a scoreless ninth, and Carlton earned his three hundredth win, a 6–2 victory.[65]

It even appeared as if Lefty would do his first media interview in five years. A week earlier Carlton had agreed that he would speak to reporters after winning his three hundredth game. Publicity director Larry Shenk informed the media in advance of the event, and on the morning of September 23 the *Philadelphia Inquirer* ran a five-column story headlined "Lefty to Talk after 300th Win." When Carlton saw the headline, he went to find Shenk. "Did you see the paper?" he asked incredulously. "They are making a big deal out of me speaking when we're trying to win a pennant. That's more important than an individual record. Let's forget the interview!"[66]

Throughout the 1983 season Lefty competed with Nolan Ryan of the Houston Astros for the top spot on the all-time strikeout list. Their goal was to beat Walter Johnson's mark of 3,509 career strikeouts, a record that stood for more than sixty years.[67] It was a seesaw battle with Ryan, who was in his midthirties, leading the race one month and Carlton, in his late thirties, going ahead in the race the next. Ryan, then with the Houston Astros, tied Johnson's record on April 27, 1983, against the Montreal Expos.[68] Carlton surpassed Ryan on June 7, 1983, with his 3,526th strikeout in a 2–1 loss against the St. Louis Cardinals at Veterans Stadium. Lefty's feat was immediately displayed on the huge PhanaVision screen in right field, and the hometown fans responded with a standing ovation. Carlton stepped off the mound and acknowledged them with a tip of his cap. After he retired the side, the Phils' ace, oblivious to his achievement, went into the dugout and asked a teammate, "Why did they give me that standing ovation?"[69]

Although Carlton was ahead in the race at the end of the 1983 season with 3,709 strikeouts compared to Ryan's 3,677, the Astros' fireballer would take command in the later years of the decade and claim the all-time strikeout crown with 5,714. Lefty, who finished his career with a total of 4,136 strikeouts, would hold the record for southpaws until he was passed by Randy Johnson, who in 2009 completed his career with 4,875 strikeouts.[70]

Carlton completed the 1983 campaign with a record of 15-16 but was replaced by Cy Young Award–winner John Denny as the Phils' ace. Still, Lefty had a solid 3.11 ERA and led the National League with 283⅔ innings pitched and 275 strikeouts.[71] On Friday, October 14, in what would be his final World Series appearance, Carlton struck out 7 in 6⅔ solid innings of work, but the Phillies lost Game Three, 3–2, to the Baltimore Orioles, who would clinch the championship two days later.[72] The Phillies' glory era was over. A team that was supposed to dominate the 1980s would not see the postseason again until 1993 and would finish above fourth place only twice in the intervening period. Carlton also experienced a noticeable decline.[73]

In 1984 Lefty compiled a 13-7 record, the last season he would post double-digit wins. In 1985 he started just sixteen games, going 1-8 before he found himself on the disabled list for the first time in his career, with a strain in his rotator cuff.[74] Carlton started another sixteen games in the spring of 1986, going 4-8 with a 6.18 ERA. In late May team president Bill Giles visited Lefty at his Rittenhouse Square apartment to persuade him to retire. "He was just brutal to watch out there," Giles recalled in a 2017 interview. "I told him how difficult it was for me and all Phillies fans to watch him struggle, that I wanted to see him go out on top and be remembered for his greatness, not as a 'hanger-on.' I even offered to pay him for the remainder of the year and honor him with a 'Steve Carlton Night' where we would retire his number 32." Lefty was grateful for Giles's offer but insisted that he intended "to pitch until the age of fifty."[75]

For Carlton, who had spent his entire life preparing to win, both physically and mentally, retirement was unthinkable. He could not perceive, or at least admit to himself, the reality of his situation—specifically, that he was forty-one years old, his shoulder was always ailing, and he no longer possessed the ability to get hitters out. McCarver saw it, but he also understood that his batterymate "always had an irascible contempt for being human," just like any other great pitcher who believed he was superhuman. "There was absolutely no way that Steve would've entertained the idea of retirement," added McCarver. "They were going to have to tear the uniform off his back."[76]

On June 25 an emotional Bill Giles called a press conference to announce Carlton's release. "The Steve Carlton era has ended in Philadelphia," he began. "The greatest lefthanded pitcher in Phillies history, and one of the greatest lefthanded pitchers of all time, will no longer be pitching in Philadelphia."[77] During his fifteen seasons with the Phillies, Lefty was 241-161 with a 3.09 ERA. He started 499 games with 185 complete games, 39 shutouts, and 3,031 strikeouts against 1,252 walks in 3,697 innings. He was also a seven-time All-Star with the Phillies and won the NL Cy Young Award four times: in 1972, 1977, 1980, and 1982.[78]

Lefty signed with the San Francisco Giants ten days after his release by the Phillies. He would achieve another milestone as a Giant when on August 5 he became the second pitcher to record 4,000 strikeouts by fanning Eric Davis of the Cincinnati Reds. Still, Carlton did not pitch well during his brief tenure in San Francisco and was released a few days later. He finished the 1986 season with the Chicago White Sox, going 4-3 with a 3.69 ERA. When the White Sox did not offer him a contract for the '87 season, Carlton signed with the Cleveland Indians, who dealt him to the Minnesota Twins at the July trading deadline. On August 8, 1987, Lefty posted his 329th and final victory as the Twins defeated the Oakland A's, 9–2. Carlton pitched his final Major League game against Cleveland on April

23, 1988. He allowed 8 earned runs in five innings of work and was the losing pitcher. He was released by the Twins on April 28 after four games, with an 0-1 record and a 16.76 ERA. Although Carlton wanted to pitch in 1989, no club would sign him—even for the $100,000 Major League minimum salary. Out of options, he retired at the age of forty-four.[79]

When the Phillies retired his jersey number (32) on July 29, 1989, Carlton was showered with gifts from the organization and words of praise from former teammates and coaches. Perhaps the biggest tribute was the 47,277 fans who showed up for what was an otherwise meaningless game between the sixth-place Phillies and the fifth-place Pittsburgh Pirates. "Baseball is indeed a field of dreams," Carlton told the crowd. "And it really was heaven down here when I played." Of course, Lefty would have been remiss to leave out the media, who had alternately praised and criticized him during his fifteen seasons in the City of Brotherly Love. "I must take time to say something about the sportswriters," he began with a chuckle. "So there will now be 10 minutes of silence." After a pregnant pause to allow the laughter to subside, Carlton continued. "In all seriousness," he said, "I want to thank the writers for the way they treated me. I know we had our differences, but I feel they did a better job without my quotes. They were much more creative and, in the process, did a much better job. And in the future, I think there should be fewer quotes in all athletic endeavors. I know the athletes would appreciate it."[80]

With his sons, Steven and Scott, grown and living in different states, Carlton and his wife, Bev, relocated from their St. Louis home to a four-hundred-acre farm in Durango, Colorado, in 1989. "It was difficult to find something to replace baseball," he admitted at the time. "But to dwell on the game would not be beneficial to my spiritual, intellectual and physical well-being."[81] Instead, the future Hall of Famer chose to lead a very private life. He raised livestock, mostly turkeys, pheasants, and horses; cultivated a substantial orchard, which comprised more than 160 fruit trees; and tended to a variety of plants and flowers in a large greenhouse. He also took up skiing and riding motorcycles and dirt bikes—activities that had been prohibited by his MLB contracts—and became an avid reader of books on Eastern philosophy.[82] But the spotlight would come calling again.

On January 12, 1994, Carlton, in his first year of eligibility, was selected by the Baseball Writers' Association of America for induction to the National Baseball Hall of Fame with 95.6 percent of the vote.[83] At the time of his induction, Lefty, one of the all-time great pitchers, ranked second among all left-handed starters in career wins with 329. He was fifth all-time among left-handed pitchers in career WAR with 84.1. He had struck out 4,136 batters, good enough for fourth place on the all-time list, and he was the Major League record holder for pick-offs with 144.[84] Other accolades would follow. In 1998 Carlton was ranked number thirty by *The Sporting News* on its list of the one hundred greatest baseball players.[85] In 2004 the Phillies honored their greatest pitcher with a statue outside their brand-new Citizens Bank Park.[86]

McCarver, however, would have to wait for his Hall of Fame induction. When it finally came, it was for his skills at broadcasting, not behind the plate. When asked by sportswriter Kevin Kerrane in 1989 if he harbored any resentment over not being appreciated for his catching ability, Tim replied, "Any resentment I might have felt was always balanced out by the pitchers who knew what I was doing back there. Some of them didn't appreciate me until the time came when they had to pitch to somebody else."[87]

The Phillies enabled McCarver to make a seamless transition to the broadcast booth in 1980. They paired him with play-by-play announcer Harry Kalas and Rich Ashburn, the beloved former Phillies center fielder, who did color commentary. While Kalas and Ashburn switched between WPHL-TV and radio broadcasts between games, Tim was primarily on television. "I couldn't have gone into a better situation," he recalled in a recent interview. "Just by watching Harry and Rich I learned a lot, and they couldn't have treated me any better."[88]

In 1983 McCarver moved to the New York Mets broadcast booth, where he joined Ralph Kiner and Gary Thorne to do play-by-play. He began to receive national recognition as an insightful analyst in 1985, when just days before the World Series ABC fired Howard

Cosell and then invited Tim to share the booth with Al Michaels and Jim Palmer.[89] He was an instant hit on the national stage, but he was also humbled by the experience. "No question about it," he said. "Broadcasting a World Series is much, much tougher than playing in it. When you're playing in it, you allow your ability to come through. But when you're broadcasting it, a lot of the things you say are before the fact. You really have to know what you are talking about. The timing is very, very important."[90]

In 2003 McCarver set a record by broadcasting his thirteenth World Series on national television (surpassing Curt Gowdy). In all, Tim called twenty-four Fall Classics for ABC, CBS, and Fox. In addition, McCarver called regular-season baseball for all four major U.S. television networks. His work at NBC was followed by stints with ABC, where he teamed with Don Drysdale on backup *Monday Night Baseball* broadcasts in 1984 and with Al Michaels and Jim Palmer from 1985 to 1989. Tim returned to ABC in 1994 to 1995 under the "Baseball Network" umbrella. Prior to that, McCarver teamed with Jack Buck on CBS from 1990 to 1991 and Sean McDonough from 1992 to 1993. Both networks were so impressed with Tim's work that ABC invited him to serve as a correspondent and play-by-play announcer for freestyle skiing at the 1988 Winter Olympics in Calgary, and CBS asked him to cohost prime-time coverage of the 1992 Winter Olympics with Paula Zahn for CBS.[91]

Opinionated, studious, and witty, McCarver survived in the booth for more than thirty-five years.[92] He broadcast the Mets from 1983 to 1998, the Yankees from 1999 to 2001, the San Francisco Giants in 2002, and the St. Louis Cardinals from 2013 to 2015. But fans across the nation knew him best for his work with Joe Buck on the Fox network's MLB telecasts, a role he held from 1996 to 2013. He later hosted a weekly syndicated television interview that drew more than 90 million viewers.[93]

McCarver won three Emmy Awards for Sports Event Analyst. His impressive work was recognized in 2012 when the National Baseball Hall of Fame named him their Ford C. Frick Award winner for excellence in broadcasting. "Tim McCarver has been the face and voice of baseball's biggest moments on national television,"

Hall of Fame president Jeff Idelson said at the time. "His wit and intuition, combined with his passion for the game and his down-home style, delivers a trusted insight for viewers."[94] But Tim took just as much pride in having caught Steve Carlton. "I was fortunate to catch Lefty in hundreds of games," he said modestly when the Phillies retired his batterymate's uniform number in 1989. "He was a friend I advised, took advice from, cussed out, was cussed out by, joked with, cajoled, fought for, fought with and learned to appreciate as one of the finest pitchers of any era. It was an honor to catch the big left-hander. I relish those memories as I do his friendship.

"I once said kiddingly that when Steve and I die, we're going to be buried sixty feet six inches apart. Maybe not. But I'll see that slider of his in my mind forever."[95]

APPENDIX A

Baseball's Best Battery

Between 1976 and 1979 Steve Carlton and Tim McCarver constituted the best battery in Major League Baseball, as well as one of the
best in the history of the national pastime. Their metrics establish
the pair as the best pitcher-catcher duo during that four-year span
in terms of starts, victories, and winning percentage.

In terms of starting assignments, Carlton made 140 starts between
1976 and 1979, and McCarver was behind the plate for 128 (91 percent) of them. That pairing exceeds any other combination of batterymates in the Majors in terms of longevity and durability during
those four years. One hundred starts for the same battery over a
four-year period, or 25 starts per season, is the standard of excellence. By that measure only three other batteries reached that mark
between 1976 and 1979: Goltz/Wynegar (119 starts), Rogers/Car-
ter (108), and Bob Forsch/Simmons (107). What's more, of the 140
starts Carlton made during that four-year span, 118 of them were
quality starts in which he pitched at least six innings and allowed
three or fewer earned runs, and McCarver caught him in 106 of
those quality starts.

Most starts by MLB pitchers/batteries, 1976–79

Pitcher	Team	League	Total starts	Catcher	Starts with catcher
Steve Carlton	**Phillies**	NL	**140**	**Tim McCarver**	**128**
Dave Goltz	Twins	AL	138	Butch Wynegar	119

Steve Rogers	Expos	NL	138	Gary Carter	108
Bob Forsch	Cardinals	NL	133	Ted Simmons	107
Dennis Leonard	Royals	AL	109	Darrell Porter	98
Mike Flanagan	Orioles	AL	121	Rick Dempsey	94
Ed Figueroa	Yankees	AL	117	Thurman Munson	94
Larry Christenson	Phillies	NL	113	Bob Boone	93
John Denny	Cardinals	NL	120	Ted Simmons	93
Jim Palmer	Orioles	AL	139	Rick Dempsey	92
Luis Tiant	Red Sox	AL	101	Carlton Fisk	92
Fred Norman	Reds	NL	120	Johnny Bench	85
Paul Splittorff	Royals	AL	110	Darrell Porter	83
Geoff Zahn	Twins	AL	91	Butch Wynegar	82
Randy Lerch	Phillies	NL	91	Bob Boone	81
Don Sutton	Dodgers	NL	133	Steve Yeager	77
Tom Seaver	Mets	NL	88	Johnny Bench	72
Jim Lonborg	Phillies	NL	79	Bob Boone	72
Doug Rau	Dodgers	NL	105	Steve Yeager	71
Burt Hooton	Dodgers	NL	125	Steve Yeager	70
Mike Caldwell	Brewers	AL	76	Charlie Moore	66
Ron Guidry	Yankees	AL	90	Thurman Munson	65
Tommy John	Dodgers	NL	92	Steve Yeager	59

Source: Data from the author and Julian McCracken.

Julian McCracken, a statistician formerly with the Phillies and later with Fleer Trading Cards, researched the Major League batteries that made at least 25 starts in each season between 1976 and 1979. Using the defensive lineup data at the Baseball Reference website, McCracken found that the Carlton/McCarver tandem started more games than any other National League battery in 1976 (31), 1977 (36), and 1978 (34) and was the top battery, with 36 starts, in all of Major League Baseball in 1977, when Lefty won his second Cy Young Award.[1]

Most starts by season by MLB pitchers/batteries, 1976–79

1976

Pitcher	Team	League	Total starts	Catcher	Starts with catcher
Goltz	Twins	AL	35	Wynegar	32
Carlton	**Phillies**	NL	**35**	**McCarver**	**31**
Tiant	Red Sox	AL	38	Fisk	31
Figueroa	Yankees	AL	34	Munson	27
Sutton	Dodgers	NL	34	Yeager	27
Lonborg	Phillies	NL	32	Boone	26

1977

Pitcher	Team	League	Total starts	Catcher	Starts with catcher
Carlton	**Phillies**	NL	**36**	**McCarver**	**36**
Rogers	Expos	NL	40	Carter	35
Goltz	Twins	AL	39	Wynegar	34
Leonard	Royals	AL	37	Porter	33
B. Forsch	Cardinals	NL	35	Simmons	33
Tiant	Red Sox	AL	32	Fisk	31
Christenson	Phillies	NL	34	Boone	30
Zahn	Twins	AL	32	Wynegar	28
Lerch	Phillies	NL	28	Boone	27
Figueroa	Yankees	AL	32	Munson	27
Rau	Dodgers	NL	32	Yeager	27
John	Dodgers	NL	31	Yeager	25

1978

Pitcher	Team	League	Total starts	Catcher	Starts with catcher
Palmer	Orioles	AL	38	Dempsey	37
Flanagan	Orioles	AL	40	Dempsey	36
Leonard	Royals	AL	40	Porter	36
Splittorff	Royals	AL	38	Porter	35

Carlton	Phillies	NL	34	McCarver	34
Zahn	Twins	AL	35	Wynegar	31
Tiant	Red Sox	AL	31	Fisk	30
Caldwell	Brewers	AL	34	Moore	28
Guidry	Yankees	AL	35	Munson	28
Rogers	Expos	NL	29	Carter	28
Lerch	Phillies	NL	28	Boone	28
Denny	Cardinals	NL	33	Simmons	27
Christenson	Phillies	NL	33	Boone	27
Seaver	Reds	NL	36	Bench	26
B. Forsch	Cardinals	NL	34	Simmons	25

1979

Pitcher	Team	League	Total starts	Catcher	Starts with catcher
Flanagan	Orioles	AL	38	Dempsey	35
Rogers	Expos	NL	37	Carter	33
Goltz	Twins	AL	35	Wynegar	29
Leonard	Royals	AL	32	Porter	29
Seaver	Reds	NL	32	Bench	29
Caldwell	Brewers	AL	30	Moore	29
Splittorff	Royals	AL	35	Porter	28
Carlton	**Phillies**	NL	**35**	**McCarver**	27
Lerch	Phillies	NL	35	Boone	26
Norman	Reds	NL	31	Bench	26
B. Forsch	Cardinals	NL	32	Simmons	25

Source: Data from the author and Julian McCracken.

The 128 starts made by the Carlton/McCarver battery over the four-year time frame of 1976–79 is a good barometer not only of endurance from season to season but also of longevity. That factor can be attributed to the physical condition of both teammates. While Lefty was in excellent physical condition because of his daily martial arts routines, Tim was also in exceptional condition for a veteran catcher who had averaged one hundred games per season behind the plate from 1963 to 1969. But number of starts is just one indication of a battery's performance.

Winning defines greatness. By that measure the Carlton/Mc-Carver battery was the best in Major League Baseball between 1976 and 1979. During that four-year span, Carlton won 72 games, lost 38, and recorded a winning percentage of .655 when McCarver was behind the plate. The Minnesota Twins' battery of Dave Goltz and Butch Wynegar was a distant second with 51 victories and a .537 winning percentage. In addition, the Carlton/McCarver duo was far superior to any other National League battery, with the St. Louis Cardinals' Bob Forsch and Ted Simmons being ranked seventh, with 45 victories. The Carlton/McCarver battery's winning percentage of .655 is tied for third with Mike Caldwell and Charlie Moore of the Milwaukee Brewers and behind the New York Yankees' duo of Ron Guidry and Thurman Munson (.717) and Cincinnati's Tom Seaver and Johnny Bench (.667). However, all three of those batteries made considerably fewer starts and recorded many fewer wins. Thus, Carlton/McCarver's .655 winning percentage is substantially better than any of the others.

Most wins by starting MLB batteries from 1976 through 1979

Battery	Team	League	Wins	Losses	Starts	Winning %
Carlton/ McCarver	**Phillies**	NL	72	38	128	.655
Goltz/Wynegar	Twins	AL	51	44	119	.537
Leonard/Porter	Royals	AL	49	37	98	.570
Flanagan/ Dempsey	Orioles	AL	48	30	94	.615
Palmer/ Dempsey	Orioles	AL	48	28	92	.632
Figueroa/ Munson	Yankees	AL	46	28	94	.622
B. Forsch/ Simmons	Cardinals	NL	45	34	107	.570

Rogers/Carter	Expos	NL	42	36	108	.538
Tiant/Fisk	Red Sox	AL	42	24	92	.636
Christenson/ Boone	Phillies	NL	41	31	93	.569
Guidry/Munson	Yankees	AL	38	15	65	.717
Splittorff/Porter	Royals	AL	36	28	83	.563
Seaver/Bench	Reds	NL	36	18	72	.667
Caldwell/Moore	Brewers	AL	36	19	66	.655
Sutton/Yeager	Dodgers	NL	35	29	77	.547
Lonborg/Boone	Phillies	NL	35	20	72	.636
Norman/Bench	Reds	NL	34	28	85	.548
Zahn/Wynegar	Twins	AL	34	30	82	.531
Rau/Yeager	Dodgers	NL	33	21	71	.611
John/Yeager	Dodgers	NL	32	17	59	.653
Hooton/Yeager	Dodgers	NL	31	25	72	.554
Denny/ Simmons	Cardinals	NL	29	32	93	.475
Lerch/Boone	Phillies	NL	29	22	81	.569

Source: Data from the author and Julian McCracken.

McCracken's research on individual seasons between 1976 and 1979 indicates that Carlton and McCarver formed the winningest pitcher/catcher duo in Major League Baseball in 1976 (20 wins) and 1977 (23 wins) among those batteries with 25 or more starts. While the Carlton/McCarver tandem also had the highest winning percentage (.769) in 1976, their .697 winning percentage in 1977 was ranked fourth, behind Bob Forsch/Ted Simmons of the Cardinals (.800), teammates Larry Christenson/Bob Boone of the Phillies (.727), and Tommy John/Steve Yeager of the Dodgers (.714). Among National League batteries with 25 or more starts, the Carlton/McCarver tandem won more games than any other battery in 1976, 1977, and 1978 (16) and was tied for wins with the Seaver/ Bench battery in 1979 (13).[2]

Most wins by MLB batteries by season, 1976–79

1976

Battery	Team	League	Wins	Losses	Starts	Winning %
Carlton/ McCarver	**Phillies**	NL	**20**	**6**	**31**	**.769**
Tiant/Fisk	Red Sox	AL	19	8	31	.704
Lonborg/Boone	Phillies	NL	16	7	26	.696
Figueroa/ Munson	Yankees	AL	15	8	27	.652
Sutton/Yeager	Dodgers	NL	14	10	27	.583
Goltz/Wynegar	Twins	AL	12	13	32	.480

1977

Battery	Team	League	Wins	Losses	Starts	Winning %
Carlton/ McCarver	**Phillies**	NL	**23**	**10**	**36**	**.697**
B. Forsch/ Simmons	Cardinals	NL	20	5	33	.800
Goltz/Wynegar	Twins	AL	18	10	34	.643
Leonard/Porter	Royals	AL	17	11	33	.607
Christenson/ Boone	Phillies	NL	16	6	30	.727
John/Yeager	Dodgers	NL	15	6	25	.714
Rogers/Carter	Expos	NL	15	14	35	.517

1978

Battery	Team	League	Wins	Losses	Starts	Winning %
Guidry/Munson	Yankees	AL	21	3	29	.875
Palmer/ Dempsey	Orioles	AL	21	11	37	.656
Leonard/ Porter	Royals	AL	19	16	36	.543
Caldwell/Moore	Brewers	AL	18	7	28	.720

Flanagan/Dempsey	Orioles	AL	18	13	36	.581
Splittorff/Porter	Royals	AL	18	11	28	.462
Carlton/McCarver	**Phillies**	**NL**	**16**	**13**	**34**	**.552**
Rogers/Carter	Expos	NL	13	9	28	.591
Zahn/Wynegar	Twins	AL	13	12	31	.520
Tiant/Fisk	Red Sox	AL	11	8	30	.579
Lerch/Boone	Phillies	NL	11	8	28	.579
Seaver/Bench	Reds	NL	11	9	26	.550
Christenson/Boone	Phillies	NL	11	11	27	.500
Denny/Simmons	Cardinals	NL	10	10	27	.500
B. Forsch/Simmons	Cardinals	NL	9	14	25	.391

1979

Battery	Team	League	Wins	Losses	Starts	Winning %
Flanagan/Dempsey	Orioles	AL	20	9	35	.690
Caldwell/Moore	Brewers	AL	15	6	29	.714
Seaver/Bench	Reds	NL	13	6	29	.684
Carlton/McCarver	**Phillies**	**NL**	**13**	**9**	**27**	**.591**
Leonard/Porter	Royals	AL	13	10	29	.565
Rogers/Carter	Expos	NL	12	9	33	.571
Splittorff/Porter	Royals	AL	12	14	28	.462
Goltz/Wynegar	Twins	AL	10	12	29	.455
Lerch/Boone	Phillies	NL	9	8	26	.529
B. Forsch/Simmons	Cardinals	NL	9	8	25	.529
Norman/Bench	Reds	NL	9	11	26	.450

Source: Data from the author and Julian McCracken.

Steve Carlton and Tim McCarver were the best battery in Major League Baseball in terms of starts and wins between 1976 and 1979. But they are also one of baseball's top batteries of all time based on those same categories. Carlton made a total of 709 starts in his twenty-four-year Major League career, and McCarver caught 228 (32 percent) of them. Such a high percentage of games caught is notable since the two were batterymates for just ten of Carlton's twenty-four seasons. Regardless, the 228 starts made by the Carlton/McCarver tandem make them one of the very best batteries in the history of the national pastime.

According to Doug Niblock of High Heat Stats, the most durable batteries in baseball history "started 200 games or more," considering that "starting pitchers rarely made more than 40 starts in a season." Using the game-log data available on the Retrosheet website for the seasons from 1901 to 2020, Niblock identified 309 batteries with 100 or more starts. Thirty-five of those batteries started 200 or more games. The percentages shown "represent the indicated game starts by the pitcher in the seasons in which the battery was active."[3] On this basis, the Carlton/McCarver battery, which was active with the St. Louis Cardinals between 1965 and 1969 and again with the Philadelphia Phillies between 1972 and 1979, is ranked the twentieth most durable in MLB history.

200-game batteries, 1901–2020

Number of games	Percentage	Batterymates	Years	Teams
324	70.6	Mickey Lolich/ Bill Freehan	1963–75	Tigers
316	70.1	Warren Spahn/ Del Crandall	1949–63	Braves
306	85.5	Red Faber/ Ray Schalk	1914–26	White Sox
283	69.0	Don Drysdale/ John Roseboro	1957–67	Dodgers
282	74.2	Red Ruffing/ Bill Dickey	1930–46	Yankees

274	84.0	Adam Wainwright/ Yadier Molina	2007–20	Cardinals
270	81.6	Steve Rogers/ Gary Carter	1975–84	Expos
264	75.6	Bob Lemon/ Jim Hegan	1946–57	Indians
252	66.8	Pete Alexander/ Bill Killefer	1911–17, 1918–21	Phillies, Cubs
250	85.9	Early Wynn/ Jim Hegan	1949–57	Indians
248	83.5	Tom Glavine/ Javy Lopez	1994–2002	Braves
247	78.9	Lefty Gomez/ Bill Dickey	1931–42	Yankees
246	89.5	Dazzy Vance/ Hank DeBerry	1922–30	Robins
240	70.6	Bob Feller/ Jim Hegan	1941–56	Indians
239	74.7	Fernando Valenzuela/ Mike Scioscia	1981–90	Dodgers
237	87.1	Stan Coveleski/ Steve O'Neill	1916–23	Indians
237	65.7	Tom Seaver/ Jerry Grote	1967–77	Mets
230	71.7	Lew Burdette/ Del Crandall	1953–63	Braves
229	77.1	Cy Young/ Lou Criger	1901–8	Americans/ Red Sox
228	**71.0**	**Steve Carlton/Tim McCarver**	**1965–69, 1972–79**	**Cards, Phillies**
226	79.0	Madison Bumgarner/ Buster Posey	2009–19	Giants
224	83.9	Lefty Grove/Mickey Cochrane	1925–33	Athletics
221	74.9	Paul Derringer/ Ernie Lombardi	1933–41	Reds
212	60.6	Whitey Ford/ Yogi Berra	1950–63	Yankees

211	81.8	Eddie Cicotte/ Ray Schalk	1912–20	White Sox
209	63.0	Walter Johnson/ Eddie Ainsmith	1910–18	Senators
208	69.6	Sandy Koufax/ John Roseboro	1957–66	Dodgers
208	67.1	Mike Flanagan/ Rick Dempsey	1976–86	Orioles
207	75.5	Jack Morris/ Lance Parrish	1978–86	Tigers
207	70.4	Cole Hamels/ Carlos Ruiz	2006–15	Phillies
206	65.6	Eddie Plank/ Doc Powers	1901–9	Athletics
203	79.9	Rube Walberg/ Mickey Cochrane	1925–33	Athletics
203	65.9	Billy Pierce/ Sherm Lollar	1952–61	White Sox
202	61.0	Dave Stieb/ Ernie Whitt	1980–89	Blue Jays
200	68.3	Doc White/ Billy Sullivan	1903–12	White Sox

Source: Doug Niblock.

The graph below ranks the thirty-five batteries according to the percentages shown above. The percentages indicate the battery game starts as a percentage of all pitcher starts in the seasons in which the battery was active. Higher numbers indicate a large majority of his team's games caught by the catcher and/or a preference by the pitcher for that catcher. Smaller numbers indicate some combination of catchers who also played other positions, or who regularly shared the catching workload with teammates, or who lost considerable playing time due to injuries.[4] McCarver fits both roles.

Battery percentage of pitcher starts, 1901–2020

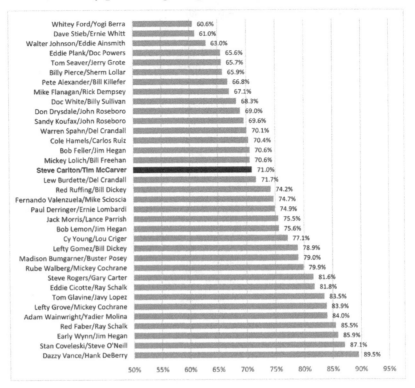

Whitey Ford/Yogi Berra	60.6%
Dave Stieb/Ernie Whitt	61.0%
Walter Johnson/Eddie Ainsmith	63.0%
Eddie Plank/Doc Powers	65.6%
Tom Seaver/Jerry Grote	65.7%
Billy Pierce/Sherm Lollar	65.9%
Pete Alexander/Bill Killefer	66.8%
Mike Flanagan/Rick Dempsey	67.1%
Doc White/Billy Sullivan	68.3%
Don Drysdale/John Roseboro	69.0%
Sandy Koufax/John Roseboro	69.6%
Warren Spahn/Del Crandall	70.1%
Cole Hamels/Carlos Ruiz	70.4%
Bob Feller/Jim Hegan	70.6%
Mickey Lolich/Bill Freehan	70.6%
Steve Carlton/Tim McCarver	**71.0%**
Lew Burdette/Del Crandall	71.7%
Red Ruffing/Bill Dickey	74.2%
Fernando Valenzuela/Mike Scioscia	74.7%
Paul Derringer/Ernie Lombardi	74.9%
Jack Morris/Lance Parrish	75.5%
Bob Lemon/Jim Hegan	75.6%
Cy Young/Lou Criger	77.1%
Lefty Gomez/Bill Dickey	78.9%
Madison Bumgarner/Buster Posey	79.0%
Rube Walberg/Mickey Cochrane	79.9%
Steve Rogers/Gary Carter	81.6%
Eddie Cicotte/Ray Schalk	81.8%
Tom Glavine/Javy Lopez	83.5%
Lefty Grove/Mickey Cochrane	83.9%
Adam Wainwright/Yadier Molina	84.0%
Red Faber/Ray Schalk	85.5%
Early Wynn/Jim Hegan	85.9%
Stan Coveleski/Steve O'Neill	87.1%
Dazzy Vance/Hank DeBerry	89.5%

Source: Doug Niblock.

Between 1965 and 1969 McCarver caught a large majority of the games played by the St. Louis Cardinals since he was the team's starting catcher. Carlton debuted with the Redbirds in 1965, the third straight season McCarver caught at least one hundred games. During the battery's three years together in St. Louis, Carlton posted three seasons with an earned run average under 3.00. McCarver was also the Phillies' starting catcher when Carlton arrived in Philadelphia in 1972, but he was traded to the Expos midway through that season. When McCarver returned to the Phillies in 1975, he became Carlton's personal catcher until 1979. The interruption in their team status, shown in the graph below, resulted in the Carlton/McCarver battery percentage of pitcher starts at 71 percent.[5]

Starts for Carlton/McCarver battery, 1965–79

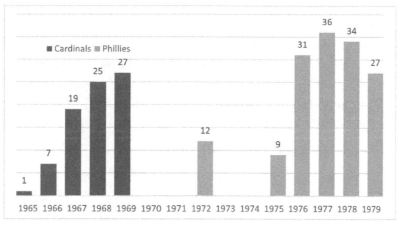

Note: 228 games (71.0%), Steve Carlton/Tim McCarver, 1965–69 Cardinals, 1972–79 Phillies.
Source: Doug Niblock.

While the above tables indicate the durability and longevity of a battery, they also suggest that the thirty-five pitcher/catcher combinations were successful in terms of victories. According to Niblock, "a long-standing battery is a hallmark of better teams," or those who earn a postseason berth.[6] In fact, of the top thirty-five batteries identified by Niblock, only Dazzy Vance and Hank DeBerry of the 1922–30 Brooklyn Robins and Walter Johnson and Eddie Ainsmith of the 1910–18 Washington Senators failed to make the postseason, while two other batteries—Steve Rogers/Gary Carter of the 1975–84 Montreal Expos and Dave Stieb/Ernie Whitt of the 1980–89 Toronto Blue Jays—failed to reach the World Series. The Carlton/McCarver battery, on the other hand, led the Phillies to the National League Championship Series in 1976, 1977, and 1978 and was also a tandem for the 1967 and 1968 St. Louis Cardinals, which went to the World Series.

Niblock also calculated and ranked the all-time batteries based on wins and team value (see the following table). The Carlton/McCarver battery, which competed for the Cardinals and Phillies in parts of eleven seasons during the 1965–79 period, ranks sixteenth all-time best, with 120 wins. Their teams also won an additional 24 games in which Carlton did not earn the decision. Thus, the Carlton/McCarver battery ranks tenth in terms of team wins and ninth in winning percentage (.632) whenever they started.[7] Those rankings place the Carlton/McCarver tandem ahead of some of the most prominent batteries in baseball history, including Whitey Ford and Yogi Berra of the perennial champion 1950–63 New York Yankees, Don Newcombe and Roy Campanella of the great Brooklyn Dodgers teams of the 1950s, and Lew Burdette and Del Crandall of the 1953–63 Milwaukee Braves.

All-time battery wins and team winning percentage with battery

Battery	Seasons/ teams	Pitcher wins	Team wins	Team win % with battery
Warren Spahn/ Del Crandall	1949–50, 1953–63 Braves	184	202	.639
Red Faber/ Ray Schalk	1914–26 White Sox	163	186	.608
Pete Alexander/ Bill Killefer	1911–17 Phillies, 1918–21 Cubs	157	165	.655
Red Ruffing/ Bill Dickey	1930–42, 1946 Yankees	156	169	.599
Cy Young/ Lou Criger	1901–8 Americans/ Red Sox	147	148	.646
Bob Lemon/ Jim Hegan	1946–57 Indians	146	163	.617
Lefty Grove/ Mickey Cochrane	1925–33 Athletics	145	163	.728
Dazzy Vance/ Hank DeBerry	1922–30 Robins	145	156	.634
Early Wynn/ Jim Hegan	1949–57 Indians	144	159	.636
Mickey Lolich/ Bill Freehan	1963–76 Tigers	143	174	.537

Lefty Gomez/ Bill Dickey	1930–42 Yankees	143	164	.664
Adam Wainwright/Yadier Molina	2007–10, 2012–20 Cardinals	142	179	.653
Walter Johnson/ Eddie Ainsmith	1910–18 Senators	139	141	.675
Stan Coveleski/ Steve O'Neill	1916–23 Indians	133	142	.599
Bob Feller/ Jim Hegan	1941, 1946–56 Indians	127	144	.600
Christy Mathewson/ Chief Meyers	1909–15 Giants	123	127	.683
Eddie Plank/ Doc Powers	1901–9 Athletics	122	128	.621
Steve Carlton/ Tim McCarver	**1965–69 Cardinals, 1972, 1975–79 Phillies**	**120**	**144**	**.632**
Sandy Koufax/ John Roseboro	1957–66 Dodgers	120	148	.712
Tom Seaver/ Jerry Grote	1967–77 Mets	120	134	.565
Don Drysdale/ John Roseboro	1957–67 Dodgers	120	154	.544
Tom Glavine/ Javy Lopez	1994–2002 Braves	119	152	.613
Eddie Cicotte/ Ray Schalk	1912–20 White Sox	119	132	.626
Whitey Ford/ Yogi Berra	1950, 1953–63 Yankees	118	149	.703
Steve Rogers/ Gary Carter	1975–84 Expos	113	139	.515
Bob Gibson/ Tim McCarver	1959–61, 1963–69, 1973–74 Cardinals	112	127	.645

Rube Waddell/ Osee Schrecongost	1902–7 Athletics	111	123	.624
Paul Derringer/ Ernie Lombardi	1933–41 Reds	110	119	.538
Lew Burdette/ Del Crandall	1953–63 Braves	107	135	.587
Don Newcombe/ Roy Campanella	1949–51, 1954–57 Dodgers	104	128	.699
Fernando Valenzuela/ Mike Scioscia	1981–90 Dodgers	104	126	.527
Doc White/ Billy Sullivan	1903–12 White Sox	104	119	.595
Jack Morris/ Lance Parrish	1978–86 Tigers	101	115	.556
Roy Oswalt/ Brad Ausmus	2001–8 Astros	100	122	.632
Andy Pettitte/ Jorge Posada	1997–2003, 2007–10 Yankees	100	126	.660

Source: Doug Niblock.

Statistically, Steve Carlton and Tim McCarver constituted not only the best battery in the Major Leagues between 1976 and 1979 but also one of the best batteries in the history of the national pastime.

APPENDIX B

Steve Carlton's Career Pitching Statistics

STEVEN NORMAN CARLTON
Height: 6'4"
Weight: 210
Threw: Left
Batted: Left
Born: December 22, 1944, Miami FL
MLB debut: April 12, 1965
Final game: April 23, 1988

Year	Team	League	W	L	ERA	G	GS	CG	SHO	IP	H	HRS	R	ER	BB	SO	HBP
1965	STL	NL	0	0	2.52	15	2	0	0	25	27	3	7	7	8	21	1
1966	STL	NL	3	3	3.12	9	9	2	1	52	56	2	22	18	18	25	0
1967	STL	NL	14	9	2.98	30	28	11	2	193	173	10	71	64	62	168	2
1968	STL	NL	13	11	2.99	34	33	10	5	232	214	11	87	77	61	162	3
1969	STL	NL	17	11	2.17	31	31	12	2	236.1	185	15	66	57	93	210	4
1970	STL	NL	10	19	3.73	34	33	13	2	253.2	239	25	123	105	109	193	2
1971	STL	NL	20	9	3.56	37	36	18	4	273.1	275	23	120	108	98	172	5
1972	PHI	NL	27	10	1.97	41	41	30	8	346.1	257	17	84	76	87	310	1
1973	PHI	NL	13	20	3.90	40	40	18	3	293.1	293	29	146	127	113	223	3
1974	PHI	NL	16	13	3.22	39	39	17	1	291	249	21	118	104	136	240	5
1975	PHI	NL	15	14	3.56	37	37	14	3	255.1	217	24	116	101	104	192	2
1976	PHI	NL	20	7	3.13	35	35	13	2	252.2	224	19	94	88	72	195	1
1977	PHI	NL	23	10	2.64	36	36	17	2	283	229	25	99	83	89	198	4
1978	PHI	NL	16	13	2.84	34	34	12	3	247.1	228	30	91	78	63	161	3
1979	PHI	NL	18	11	3.62	35	35	13	4	251	202	25	112	101	89	213	5
1980	PHI	NL	24	9	2.34	38	38	13	3	304	243	15	87	79	90	286	2
1981	PHI	NL	13	4	2.42	24	24	10	1	190	152	9	59	51	62	179	1
1982	PHI	NL	23	11	3.10	38	38	19	6	295.2	253	17	114	102	86	286	1
1983	PHI	NL	15	16	3.11	37	37	8	3	283.2	277	20	117	98	84	275	3

1984	PHI	NL	13	7	3.58	33	33	1	0	229	214	14	104	91	79	163	0
1985	PHI	NL	1	8	3.33	16	16	0	0	92	84	6	43	34	53	48	0
1986	PHI	NL	4	8	6.18	16	16	0	0	83	102	15	70	57	45	62	0
1986	SF	NL	1	3	5.10	6	6	0	0	30	36	4	20	17	16	18	1
1986	CHI	AL	4	3	3.69	10	10	0	0	63.1	58	6	30	26	25	40	0
1986	TOT*	NL/AL	9	14	5.10	32	32	0	0	176.1	196	25	120	100	86	120	1
1987	CLE	AL	5	9	5.37	23	14	3	0	109	111	17	76	65	63	1	2
1987	MIN	AL	1	5	6.70	9	7	0	0	43	54	7	35	32	23	20	2
1987	TOT*	AL	6	14	5.74	32	21	3	0	152	165	24	111	97	86	91	4
1988	MIN	AL	0	1	16.76	4	1	0	0	9.2	20	5	19	18	5	5	0
Total NL (22 years)			319	226	3.11	695	677	251	55	4992.2	4429	379	1970	1723	1717	4000	49
Total AL (3 years)			10	18	5.64	46	32	3	0	225	243	35	160	141	116	136	4
Total (24 years)			329	244	3.22	741	709	254	55	5217.2	4672	414	2130	1864	1833	4136	53

* Two other teams.

Source: Baseball Reference, https://www.baseball-reference.com/players/c/carlst01.shtml.

APPENDIX C

Tim McCarver's Career Batting Statistics

JAMES TIMOTHY MCCARVER
Height: 6'0"
Weight: 183
Batted: Left
Threw: Right
Born: October 16, 1941, Memphis TN
MLB debut: September 10, 1959
Final game: October 5, 1980

Year	Team	League	G	AB	R	H	2B	3B	HRS	RBIS	BB	IBB	K	AVG	OBP	SLG
1959	STL	NL	8	24	3	4	1	0	0	0	2	0	1	.167	.231	.208
1960	STL	NL	10	10	3	2	0	0	0	0	0	0	2	.200	.200	.200
1961	STL	NL	22	67	5	16	2	1	1	6	0	0	5	.239	.239	.343
1963	STL	NL	127	405	39	117	12	7	4	51	27	5	43	.289	.333	.383
1964	STL	NL	143	465	53	134	19	3	9	52	40	15	44	.288	.343	.400
1965	STL	NL	113	409	48	113	17	2	11	48	31	11	26	.276	.327	.408
1966	STL	NL	150	543	50	149	19	13	12	68	36	10	38	.274	.319	.424
1967	STL	NL	138	471	68	139	26	3	14	69	54	19	32	.295	.369	.452
1968	STL	NL	128	434	35	110	15	6	5	48	26	8	31	.253	.295	.350
1969	STL	NL	138	515	46	134	27	3	7	51	49	9	26	.260	.323	.365
1970	PHI	NL	44	164	16	47	11	1	4	14	14	4	10	.287	.346	.439
1971	PHI	NL	134	474	51	132	20	5	8	46	43	7	26	.278	.337	.392
1972	PHI	NL	45	152	14	36	8	0	2	14	17	2	15	.237	.318	.329
1972	MON	NL	77	239	19	60	5	1	5	20	19	3	14	.251	.309	.343
1972	TOT*	NL	122	391	33	96	13	1	7	34	36	5	29	.246	.313	.338
1973	STL	NL	130	331	30	88	16	4	3	49	38	6	31	.266	.339	.366
1974	STL	NL	74	106	13	23	0	1	0	11	22	0	6	.217	.353	.236
1974	BOS	AL	11	28	3	7	1	0	0	1	4	2	1	.250	.344	.286
1974	TOT*	NL/AL	85	134	16	30	1	1	0	12	26	2	7	.224	.351	.246

1975	BOS	AL	12	21	1	8	2	1	0	3	1	1	3	.381	.409	.571
1975	PHI	NL	47	59	6	15	2	0	1	7	14	3	7	.254	.397	.339
1975	TOT*	AL/NL	59	80	7	23	4	1	1	10	15	4	10	.288	.400	.400
1976	PHI	NL	90	155	26	43	11	2	3	29	35	2	14	.277	.409	.432
1977	PHI	NL	93	169	28	54	13	2	6	30	28	1	11	.320	.410	.527
1978	PHI	NL	90	146	18	36	9	1	1	14	28	6	24	.247	.367	.342
1979	PHI	NL	79	127	13	33	5	1	1	12	19	5	12	.241	.333	.314
1980	PHI	NL	6	5	2	1	1	0	0	2	1	0	0	.200	.333	.400
Total NL			1886	5450	586	1486	239	56	97	641	543	116	418	.271	.337	.388
Total AL			23	49	4	15	3	1	0	4	5	3	4	.306	.370	.408
Total (21 years)			1909	5529	590	1501	242	57	97	645	548	119	422	.271	.337	.388

* Two other teams.

Source: Baseball Reference, https://www.baseball-reference.com/players/m/mccarti0.shtml.

NOTES

Introduction

1. Steve Carlton's Career Pitching Statistics, Baseball Reference, accessed June 6, 2019, https://www.baseball-reference.com/players/c/carltst01.shtml.

2. Steve Carlton's Career Pitching Statistics.

3. Boone quoted in Larry Keith, "Odd Couple, but Winning Combination," *Sports Illustrated*, August 29, 1977, 16.

4. Westcott and Bilovsky, *Phillies Encyclopedia*, 218, 580.

5. Keith, "Odd Couple, but Winning Combination," 16; Stan Grosshandler, "Pitcher's Choice," SABR Research Archives, accessed September 10, 2018, http://research .sabr.org/journals/pitchers-choice.

6. McCarver quoted in Brian Costello, "The All-Important, Ever-Changing Dynamic between Pitcher and Catcher," *New York Post*, July 5, 2009.

7. "Philadelphia Phillies 4, Atlanta Braves 2, May 1, 1976, Box Score," Baseball Almanac, accessed June 11, 2019, https://www.baseball-almanac.com/box-scores /boxscore.php?boxid=197605011ATL; Allen Lewis, "Phillies Defeat Braves Twice," *Philadelphia Inquirer*, May 2, 1976.

8. Costello, "All-Important, Ever-Changing Dynamic."

9. Westcott and Bilovsky, *Phillies Encyclopedia*, 89.

10. Westcott and Bilovsky, *Phillies Encyclopedia*, 146–48.

11. Walt Wilson, "Steve Carlton's Battery Mates," Society of American Baseball Research, accessed August 14, 2018, http://members.tripod.com/bb_catchers/catchers /battery-hof05.htm.

12. Michael Mavrogiannis, "Personal Catchers," Retrosheet, accessed August 11, 2018, https://members.tripod.com/bb_catchers/catchers/perscatch.htm/.

13. Larry Shenk, "Carlton, McCarver a Pair for the Ages," MLB.com, August 24, 2017, https://www.mlb.com/news/steve-carlton-tim-mccarver-a-historic-pair/c-250338748.

14. McCarver quoted in Shenk, "Carlton, McCarver a Pair for the Ages."

15. See B. Snyder, *Well-Paid Slave*. On October 7, 1969, the Cardinals traded Flood, catcher Tim McCarver, outfielder Byron Browne, and pitcher Joe Hoerner to the Philadelphia Phillies for Dick Allen, infielder Cookie Rojas, and pitcher Jerry Johnson.

16. McCarver quotes are from *Sports Illustrated Baseball*, 55–58.

17. Originally, catchers did not receive any credit for their influence on a pitcher's performance. In fact, the term "battery," first used by Henry Chadwick in the 1860s, applied strictly to the pitcher. Chadwick, called the "Father of Baseball" for his early reporting on and contributions to the development of the game, came up with the term in a nod to the "firepower" of Civil War artillery. By the 1880s managers, players, and sportswriters were using the term to refer to both the pitcher and catcher. Between 1875 and 1910 the strategic influence of the catcher grew increasingly as catchers like Roger Bresnahan, Deacon White, Buck Ewing, and Wilbert Robinson excelled at the position, earning greater respect among pitchers, teammates, and fans. See Kerrane, *Hurlers*, 147.

18. The two books are Bucci and Brown, *Drinking Coffee with a Fork*; and Morgan, *Steve Carlton and the 1972 Phillies*.

19. McCarver with Robinson, *OH, BABY, I LOVE IT!* Other books by McCarver include McCarver with Peary, *Tim McCarver's Baseball for Brain Surgeons and Other Fans*; McCarver with Peary, *Perfect Season*; McCarver with Pepe, *Few and Chosen*; and McCarver with Moskovitz and Peary, *Tim McCarver's Diamond Gems*.

20. Voigt, "History of Major League Baseball."

21. For hitting and pitching statistics of the 1960s and 1970s, see Palmer and Gillette, *ESPN Baseball Encyclopedia*, 1524–63.

22. Ward and Burns, *Baseball*.

1. Always a Catcher

1. Mike Lupica, "Wild about Cards, not Stan Who Ran," *Sports on Earth*, September 21, 2016 (accessed online July 1, 2019; no longer available).

2. See "MLB World Series Winners," ESPN, accessed July 2, 2019, https://www.espn.com/mlb/worldseries/history/winners.

3. Eisenbath, *Cardinals Encyclopedia*, 1. Although St. Louis was home to previous baseball teams, the Cardinals trace their roots to the Brown Stockings of the American Association, which survived for only ten seasons in the late 1800s due to the turbulent and ever-changing nature of the professional game.

4. Lowenfish, *Branch Rickey*, 61–87, 109–54; Eisenbath, *Cardinals Encyclopedia*, 399–401. Rickey also pioneered the use of batting cages, pitching machines, and batting helmets and foreshadowed the modern-day sabermetric movement by hiring a full-time statistical analyst.

5. Eisenbath, *Cardinals Encyclopedia*, 465–70; Broeg and Vickery, *St. Louis Cardinals Encyclopedia*, 28–36. The name "Gashouse Gang" originally applied to a section of the Lower East Side of Manhattan that once housed several large gas tanks. The neighborhood was home to vagrants from New York City, including Brooklyn, and New Jersey. See Burrows and Wallace, *Gotham*, 826.

6. Eisenbath, *Cardinals Encyclopedia*, 3, 250–51, 471–92.

7. McCarver with Pepe, *Few and Chosen*, xvii. Caray was nicknamed the "Mayor of Rush Street" in the 1980s when he began doing play-by-play for the Chicago Cubs.

The pseudonym is a reference to Chicago's famous tavern-dominated neighborhood and Caray's well-known taste for Budweiser.

8. McCarver with Pepe, *Few and Chosen*, xix.

9. McCarver with Robinson, *OH, BABY, I LOVE IT!*, 5.

10. McCarver with Robinson, *OH, BABY, I LOVE IT!*, 6.

11. McCarver with Robinson, *OH, BABY, I LOVE IT!*, 6–7.

12. Tim McCarver, interview by author, Fort Lauderdale FL, May 3, 2018.

13. McCarver with Pepe, *Few and Chosen*, xviii.

14. Tim McCarver, interview by author, Fort Lauderdale FL, November 9, 2019.

15. McCarver with Pepe, *Few and Chosen*, xviii.

16. McCarver with Robinson, *OH, BABY, I LOVE IT!*, 9.

17. McCarver with Pepe, *Few and Chosen*, xix.

18. Mark Tomasik, "How Tim McCarver Became a Cardinal at 17," *RetroSimba*, July 16, 2012, https://retrosimba.com/2012/07/16/how-tim-mccarver-became-a-cardinal-at-17/.

19. McCarver interview, May 3, 2018.

20. Dickey quoted in Tomasik, "How Tim McCarver Became a Cardinal."

21. Dickey and McCarver quoted in Costello, "All-Important, Ever-Changing Dynamic."

22. Dickey quoted in Tomasik, "How McCarver Became a Cardinal"; McCarver interview, November 9, 2019.

23. Lewis quoted in Tomasik, "How McCarver Became a Cardinal."

24. McCarver with Robinson, *OH, BABY, I LOVE IT!*, 11.

25. McCarver quoted in Tomasik, "How McCarver Became a Cardinal."

26. McCarver interview, November 9, 2019.

27. McCarver interview, November 9, 2019.

28. McCarver with Robinson, *OH, BABY, I LOVE IT!*, 13–14.

29. McCarver interview, November 9, 2019.

30. McCarver with Robinson, *OH, BABY, I LOVE IT!*, 4.

31. McCarver with Robinson, *OH, BABY, I LOVE IT!*, 4.

32. *The Sporting News*, September 16, 1959.

33. St. Louis Cardinals vs Chicago Cubs, September 13, 1959, Box Score, Baseball Almanac, accessed July 17, 2019, http://www.baseball almanac.com/box-scores/boxscore.php?boxid=195909130CHN.

34. Florio and Shapiro, *One Nation under Baseball*, 8.

35. Bill White, interview by author, Upper Black Eddy PA, February 22, 2020.

36. White with Dillow, *Uppity*, 68.

37. Halberstam, *October 1964*, 56–57.

38. Robert McG. Thomas Jr., "August A. Busch, Jr. Dies at 90; Built Largest Brewing Company," *New York Times*, September 30, 1989.

39. The Browns played their last game at Sportsman's Park on September 27, 1953, before a crowd of just 3,174. True to form, the Browns lost, this time to the Chicago White Sox by a score of 2–1 in eleven innings. Two days after the 1953 season ended,

Browns owner Bill Veeck sold the franchise to a group of Baltimore businessmen. Ritter, *Lost Ballparks*, 191–92.

40. Ritter, *Lost Ballparks*, 191.

41. Quotes from Halberstam, *October 1964*, 58.

42. Knoedelseder, *Bitter Brew*, 57–66. Lane's two signings were Memo Luna, who was from Mexico and ended up pitching a total of one inning for the Cardinals; he surrendered 2 walks and 2 hits. Shortly thereafter, he retired from baseball with an earned run average of 27.00. Tom Alston, from North Carolina, made a better impression. He was a first baseman with good hands but a weak bat. Promoted to the Majors in 1954, Alston hit .246 with just 4 home runs—not the kind of numbers expected from a corner infielder. Alston remained with the Cards for the next three years as a utility player before being released. See Derrick Goold, "Tom Alston: Seven Years after Jackie, 53 Years Ago Today," *St. Louis Post-Dispatch*, April 13, 2007; and Halberstam, *October 1964*, 58.

43. Armour, "Bing Devine," 271–72; Eisenbath, *Cardinals Encyclopedia*, 411.

44. Florio and Shapiro, *One Nation under Baseball*, 138.

45. Eisenbath, *Cardinals Encyclopedia*, 189; J. Snyder, *Cardinals Journal*, 437.

46. Florio and Shapiro, *One Nation under Baseball*, 138.

47. Gibson with Wheeler, *Stranger to the Game*, 53.

48. Gibson with Wheeler, *Stranger to the Game*, 63.

49. Gibson with Wheeler, *Stranger to the Game*, 59.

50. Gibson with Wheeler, *Stranger to the Game*, 59–60. McCarver had a slightly different recollection of the story. In his 1987 book *OH, BABY, I LOVE IT!*, he wrote that he was drinking a "bottle of cold orange pop," not eating an ice cream cone. McCarver with Robinson, *OH, BABY, I LOVE IT!*, 61.

51. Gibson with Wheeler, *Stranger to the Game*, 59–60; McCarver interview, November 9, 2019.

52. Williams, "Tim McCarver," 138–39.

53. Eisenbath, *Cardinals Encyclopedia*, 76–80.

54. Halberstam, *October 1964*, 17–18.

55. J. Snyder, *Cardinals Journal*, 459, 471.

56. Eisenbath, *Cardinals Encyclopedia*, 411, 566. Devine sent pitchers Willard Schmidt, Marty Kutyna, and Ted Wieand to the Cincinnati Reds for outfielders Curt Flood and Joe Taylor.

57. Eisenbath, *Cardinals Encyclopedia*, 566. Devine traded pitchers Sam Jones and Don Choate to San Francisco for outfielder–first baseman Bill White and third baseman Ray Jablonski.

58. Eisenbath, *Cardinals Encyclopedia*, 411, 567.

59. J. Snyder, *Cardinals Journal*, 459, 471.

60. Halberstam, *October 1964*, 34–36.

61. Eisenbath, *Cardinals Encyclopedia*, 202, 385.

62. Halberstam, *October 1964*, 25.

63. Eisenbath, *Cardinals Encyclopedia*, 385.

64. Eisenbath, *Cardinals Encyclopedia*, 78.

65. Eisenbath, *Cardinals Encyclopedia*, 386.

66. Eisenbath, *Cardinals Encyclopedia*, 138–39.

67. McCarver interview, November 9, 2019.

68. McCarver interview, November 9, 2019.

69. White interview.

70. McCarver with Robinson, *OH, BABY, I LOVE IT!*, 17.

71. Gibson with Wheeler, *Stranger to the Game*, 87; Williams, "Tim McCarver," 139.

72. Gibson with Wheeler, *Stranger to the Game*, 82, 92.

73. Eisenbath, *Cardinals Encyclopedia*, 80–81.

74. Rickey quoted in Lowenfish, *Branch Rickey*, 588.

75. McCarver interview, May 3, 2018.

76. Eisenbath, *Cardinals Encyclopedia*, 567.

77. J. Snyder, *Cardinals Journal*, 462–63.

78. J. Snyder, *Cardinals Journal*, 463.

79. J. Snyder, *Cardinals Journal*, 464.

80. J. Snyder, *Cardinals Journal*, 464–65; Eisenbath, *Cardinals Encyclopedia*, 80.

81. Williams, "Tim McCarver," 139; Eisenbath, *Cardinals Encyclopedia*, 81.

82. Schang quoted in *The Sporting News*, July 22, 1967.

83. Rickey quoted in *The Sporting News*, July 22, 1967. Rickey's biographer Lee Lowenfish explains that Branch, to a fault, found room for improvement in every player. He believed that all criticism, no matter how harsh, could only lead to improvement. As a result, players either despised or admired Rickey. McCarver belonged to the former group. See Lowenfish, *Branch Rickey*, 588–89.

84. Halberstam, *October 1964*, 132–33; Armour, "Bing Devine," 273; J. Snyder, *Cardinals Journal*, 469.

85. J. Snyder, *Cardinals Journal*, 469. It should be noted that Ernie Broglio, in three seasons with the Chicago Cubs, posted a 7-19 record with a 5.40 ERA.

86. J. Snyder, *Cardinals Journal*, 471.

87. Lake, "Three-Way Tie for the Pennant?"; Halberstam, *October 1964*, 309–14; J. Snyder, *Cardinals Journal*, 473–74; Eisenbath, *Cardinals Encyclopedia*, 82–83.

88. Stahl, "1964 World Series"; Halberstam, *October 1964*, 317–50; J. Snyder, *Cardinals Journal*, 475–77; Eisenbath, *Cardinals Encyclopedia*, 493–99.

89. Mark Tomasik, "Tim McCarver Challenged Bob Gibson for World Series MVP," *RetroSimba*, May 23, 2014, https://retrosimba.com/2014/05/23/tim-mccarver-challenged-bob-gibson-for-world-series-mvp/. In 1964, when McCarver hit .478 in the Fall Classic, there were only six other catchers to hit .400 or better (with a minimum of ten at bats) in a single World Series: Hank Gowdy, 1914 Boston Braves (.545); Larry McLean, 1913 New York Giants (.500); Elston Howard, 1960 New York Yankees (.462); Bill Dickey, 1932 New York Yankees (.438); Yogi Berra, 1953 New York Yankees (.429); Yogi Berra, 1955 New York Yankees, (.417); Mickey Cochrane, 1929 Philadelphia Athletics (.400); and Bill Dickey, 1938 New York Yankees (.400).

Since 1964 there have been six additional catchers to accomplish the feat: Johnny Bench, 1976 Cincinnati Reds (.533); Thurman Munson, 1976 New York Yankees (.529); Pat Borders, 1992 Toronto Blue Jays (.450); Bob Boone, 1980 Philadelphia Phillies (.412); Yadier Molina, 2006 St. Louis Cardinals (.412); and Tony Pena, 1987 St. Louis Cardinals (.409). *Encyclopedia of Baseball Catchers*, accessed July 4, 2019, http://bb _catchers.tripod.com/catchers/list.htm.

Prior to 1964, only two catchers had ever hit a double, a triple, and a home run in a single World Series: Hank Gowdy of the 1914 Boston Braves and Elston Howard of the 1960 New York Yankees. McCarver was the third catcher to accomplish the feat. He was followed in 1976 by Johnny Bench of the Cincinnati Reds. *Encyclopedia of Baseball Catchers*, accessed July 4, 2019, http://bb_catchers.tripod.com /catchers/list.htm.

90. Tomasik, "Tim McCarver Challenged Bob Gibson for World Series MVP." McCarver turned twenty-three the day after the Series ended. He capped the year by marrying his high school sweetheart, Anne McDaniel, on December 29, 1964. The couple would eventually have two daughters, Kelly and Kathy.

91. Musial quoted in *The Sporting News*, October 16, 1964.

2. Odd Couple

1. McCarver with Robinson, *OH, BABY, I LOVE IT!*, 51–52.

2. Dickey quoted by McCarver in Costello, "All-Important, Ever Changing Dynamic."

3. McCarver with Robinson, *OH, BABY, I LOVE IT!*, 52. Many years later McCarver would admit that he was wrong to demand a particular pitch and that a pitcher has every right to determine what his best pitch is in a given situation. McCarver interview, May 3, 2018.

4. Dal Maxvill, interview by author, Wildwood MO, August 8, 2020.

5. Bob Broeg, "Even Bubble-Gum Cards Can't Keep Up with Carlton," *The Sporting News*, March 23, 1968.

6. Keith, "Odd Couple, but Winning Combination."

7. Mark Kram, "Cold Shoulder Steve Carlton's Parents and Family Bewildered by Hall of Famer's Mysterious Silent Treatment," *St. Louis Post-Dispatch*, July 31, 1994.

8. Hannum quoted in Tommy West, "Steve Carlton: Folks in Florida Still Say Hello," *Philadelphia Inquirer*, August 27, 1979.

9. Hannum quoted in West, "Steve Carlton: Folks in Florida Still Say Hello."

10. Ron Fimrite, "Steve Carlton: Eliminator of the Variables," *Sports Illustrated*, April 9, 1973, 82.

11. Hannum quoted in West, "Steve Carlton: Folks in Florida Still Say Hello."

12. Carlton quoted in Eisenbath, *Cardinals Encyclopedia*, 148.

13. Fimrite, "Steve Carlton: Eliminator of the Variables," 82.

14. Fimrite, "Steve Carlton: Eliminator of the Variables," 82.

15. Cosme Vivanco, "Steve Carlton," SABR Biographies, accessed June 3, 2018, https://sabr.org/bioproj/person/e438064d.

16. Cave quoted in West, "Steve Carlton: Folks in Florida Still Say Hello."

17. Hyrne quoted in West, "Steve Carlton: Folks in Florida Still Say Hello."

18. West, "Steve Carlton: Folks in Florida Still Say Hello."

19. Gordon Edes, "Fame and Fate," *Miami Sun Sentinel*, July 31, 1994.

20. Kram, "Cold Shoulder Steve Carlton's Parents."

21. Clark quoted in Edes, "Fame and Fate."

22. Duncan quoted in West, "Steve Carlton: Folks in Florida Still Say Hello."

23. Mainieri, *Mainieri Factor*, 41.

24. Bob Broeg, "Growing-Boy Carlton Eyes Growing Win Total," *St. Louis Post-Dispatch*, March 14, 1967.

25. Bowen quoted in Neal Russo, "Redbirds Salute Skinny Steve," *The Sporting News*, May 13, 1967.

26. Carlton quoted in Russo, "Redbirds Salute Skinny Steve."

27. Chase Riddle was a Cardinals Minor League manager from 1955 to 1962. He then became a scout, with responsibilities primarily for the Caribbean region and southeastern United States. In 1978 Riddle left the Cardinals to become manager of the Troy University baseball team in Alabama. His Troy teams won NCAA Division II national titles in 1986 and 1987. Riddle remained Troy's manager until 1990, compiling more than 430 wins. He died on June 12, 2011, in Troy, Alabama, at the age of eighty-five. See Mark Tomasik, "How Chase Riddle got Steve Carlton for the Cardinals," *RetroSimba*, June 14, 2011, https://www.retrosimba.com/2011/06/14/how-chase-riddle-got-steve-carlton-for-cardinals/.

28. Mainieri, *Mainieri Factor*, 41.

29. Mainieri, *Mainieri Factor*, 41.

30. Pollet quoted in Russo, "Redbirds Salute Skinny Steve." Pollet offered Carlton the $5,000 bonus in 1963, three years before the MLB amateur draft was established, so the future Cardinal was allowed to accept the money.

31. Maxvill interview.

32. Mainieri, *Mainieri Factor*, 41–42.

33. Mainieri, *Mainieri Factor*, 139.

34. Mainieri quoted in Walter Villa, "Miami-Dade College Baseball Coach from 1964 Championship Season Is Honored," *Miami Herald*, July 31, 2014.

35. Kevin Glew, "Carlton the Most Famous Winnipeg Goldeye," *Cooperstown in Canada* (blog), August 17, 2010, https://.cooperstownersincanada.com/2010/08/17/steve-carlton-is-the-most-famous-winnipeg-goldeye/.

36. Steve Carlton's 1965 Pitching Log, Baseball Reference, accessed June 12, 2019, https://www.baseball-reference.com/players/gl.fcgi?id=carltst01&t=p&year=1965.

37. Steve Carlton's 1965 Pitching Log.

38. Carlton quoted in Broeg, "Growing-Boy Carlton Eyes Growing Win Total."

39. Steve Carlton's 1965 Pitching Log.

40. Dave Williams, "Tim McCarver," SABR Biographies, accessed March 10, 2019, https://sabr.org/bioproj/person/tim-mccarver/.

41. Eisenbath, *Cardinals Encyclopedia*, 83.

42. J. Snyder, *Cardinals Journal*, 486.

43. Palmer and Gillette, ESPN *Baseball Encyclopedia*, 1534, 1536.

44. J. Snyder, *Cardinals Journal*, 486–87.

45. "1966 All-Star Game," Baseball Almanac, accessed June 30, 2019, http://www.baseball-almanac.com/asgbox/yr1966as.shtml.

46. Carlton went 9-5, with an ERA of 3.59, at Triple-A Tulsa.

47. Steve Carlton's 1965 Pitching Log; Jim Brosnan, "Steve Carlton: One Pitch Better Than Koufax," *Boys' Life*, July 1974, 24.

48. Carlton quoted in Mark Tomasik, "How Steve Carlton Got His First Win for [the] Cardinals," *RetroSimba*, August 2, 2016, https://retrosimba.com/?s=How+Steve+Carlton+got+his+first+win.

49. Carlton quoted in Russo, "Redbirds Salute Skinny Steve."

50. Eisenbath, *Cardinals Encyclopedia*, 84–85.

51. Larry Jaster, interview by author, West Palm Beach FL, February 10, 2020. In 1966 Jaster, in defeating the Los Angeles Dodgers four times, tied Grover Alexander of the Phillies for most shutouts against one team in a single season. Alexander had accomplished the feat against the Cincinnati Reds in 1916.

52. Steve Carlton's 1965 Pitching Log.

53. Jaster interview.

54. Tim McCarver's Hitting Statistics, Baseball Reference, accessed June 30, 2019, https://www.baseball-reference.com/players/m/mccarti01.shtml. McCarver's thirteen triples tied him with Johnny Kling (1903) for the post-1900 record for three-baggers by a catcher.

55. On standard contracts, see Helyar, *Lords of the Realm*. See Steve Carlton's 1967 Game Log, Baseball Reference, accessed August 7, 2019, https://www.baseball-reference.com/players/gl.fcgi?id=carltst01&t=p&year=1967.

56. Carlton quoted in Broeg, "Growing-Boy Carlton Eyes Growing Win Total."

57. Steve Carlton's 1966 Pitching Log, Baseball Reference, accessed August 6, 2019, https://www.baseball-reference.com/players/gl.fcgi?id=carltst01&t=p&year=1966.

58. Steve Carlton's 1966 Pitching Log.

59. Steve Carlton's 1966 Pitching Log.

60. Eisenbath, *Cardinals Encyclopedia*, 86; J. Snyder, *Cardinals Journal*, 495. Gibson's injury was not the only adversity the Cardinals faced. Pitcher Ray Washburn and center fielder Curt Flood also spent time on the disabled list. Third baseman Mike Shannon was out for more than a month with injuries. Closer Joe Hoerner broke a toe and did not pitch very well until midseason, when it had healed.

61. Steve Carlton's 1967 Game Log; and J. Snyder, *Cardinals Journal*, 496.

62. Lock quoted in Neal Russo, "16 Strikeouts for Loser Carlton," *The Sporting News*, October 7, 1967.

63. Carlton quoted in Russo, "16 Strikeouts."

64. "Carlton in Exclusive Club with 16-Whiff Job on Phils," Associated Press, October 14, 1967; Career Leaders and Records for Strikeouts, Baseball Reference, accessed December 1, 2010, https://www.baseball-reference.com/leaders/SO_career

.shtml. Charlie Sweeney set the single-game strikeout record of 19 on June 7, 1884, in a 2–1 victory over the Boston Beaneaters. The following month Hugh Daily of the Chicago Browns tied Sweeney's record in a 10–4 win over the Boston Reds. Carlton would go on to tie the 19-strikeouts single-game record on September 15, 1969, in a 4–3 loss against the New York Mets.

On April 29, 1986, Roger Clemens of the Boston Red Sox set a new record of 20 strikeouts in a 3–1 victory over the Seattle Mariners. Clemens repeated the feat on September 18, 1996, against the Detroit Tigers, winning the game, 4–0. Since then, two other pitchers have tied the record: Kerry Wood of the Chicago Cubs on May 6, 1998, in a 2–0 win over the Houston Astros, and Max Scherzer of the Washington Nationals on May 11, 2016, in a 3–2 victory over the Detroit Tigers.

65. Carlton quoted in Russo, "16 Strikeouts."

66. Russo, "16 Strikeouts."

67. Eisenbath, *Cardinals Encyclopedia*, 87; Steve Carlton's 1967 Game Log.

68. Eisenbath, *Cardinals Encyclopedia*, 86–87.

69. J. Snyder, *Cardinals Journal*, 496.

70. Schoendienst quoted in Eisenbath, *Cardinals Encyclopedia*, 236.

71. J. Snyder, *Cardinals Journal*, 496.

72. Palmer and Gillette, ESPN *Baseball Encyclopedia*, 1539.

73. Flood quoted in William Leggett, "El Birds Fly High," *Sports Illustrated*, October 16, 1967, 23–24. For more details on the 1967 American League pennant race, see Bright, *1967 American League Pennant Race*; and Nowlin and Desrochers, *1967 Impossible Dream Red Sox*.

74. Gibson quoted in Leggett, "El Birds Fly High," 24.

75. Maris quoted in Leggett, "El Birds Fly High," 24.

76. Eisenbath, *Cardinals Encyclopedia*, 500–501; J. Snyder, *Cardinals Journal*, 496–97.

77. Eisenbath, *Cardinals Encyclopedia*, 501–2; J. Snyder, *Cardinals Journal*, 497.

78. Maris quoted in Leggett, "El Birds Fly High," 29.

79. Eisenbath, *Cardinals Encyclopedia*, 501–2; J. Snyder, *Cardinals Journal*, 497.

80. Carlton quoted in Brosnan, "Steve Carlton: One Pitch Better Than Koufax," 24.

81. Schoendienst quoted in Leggett, "El Birds Fly High," 24.

82. Eisenbath, *Cardinals Encyclopedia*, 502.

83. Yastrzemski and McCarver quoted in Eisenbath, *Cardinals Encyclopedia*, 503.

84. Eisenbath, *Cardinals Encyclopedia*, 503–5; J. Snyder, *Cardinals Journal*, 497.

85. McCarver quoted in Eisenbath, *Cardinals Encyclopedia*, 505.

3. Learning Curve

1. Mead, *Explosive Sixties*, 46.

2. Vaccaro, "Origins of the Pitching Rotation"; Pitching Rotation, Baseball Reference, accessed January 2, 2020, https://www.baseball-reference.com/bullpen/Pitching _rotation; Rany Jazayerli, "A Brief History of Pitcher Usage," Baseball Prospectus, March 2, 2004, https://www.baseballprospectus.com/news/article/2627/baseball -prospectus-basics-a-brief-history-of-pitcher-usage. The Los Angeles Dodgers were

the first team to return to a five-man starting rotation in the early 1970s. The pitchers were Tommy John, Don Sutton, Burt Hooton, Rick Rhoden, and Doug Rau. Shortly thereafter, all other MLB teams returned to the five-man rotation.

3. Steve Carlton's Pitching Game Logs, 1965, 1966.

4. Jaster interview.

5. Steve Carlton's 1965 Pitching Game Log.

6. Ward and Burns, *Baseball*, 377. In 1950 the strike zone was deliberately narrowed from the batter's armpits to the top of the knees. This was done to favor the hitters and to attract more fans, who loved to see the home run. But in the early 1960s, Commissioner Ford C. Frick persuaded the Playing Rules Committee to return to the strike zone that had existed between 1887 to 1949, when anything thrown between the hitter's shoulders and knees was a strike.

7. Kinlaw, "Whitey Ford," 348–49.

8. Wolpin, "Mickey Lolich," 630; Lolich with Gage, *Joy in Tigertown*.

9. Cantor, *Tigers of '68*, 225; McLain and Zaret, *I Told You I Wasn't Perfect*.

10. Kinlaw, "Sam McDowell," 706–7.

11. Holtje, "Luis Tiant, Jr.," 1088–89; Tiant with Wisnia, *Son of Havana*.

12. Langford, "Sandy Koufax," 584–85; J. Levy, *Sandy Koufax*, xvii, 114–20.

13. Gallagher, "Don Drysdale," 294–95; Drysdale with Verdi, *Once a Bum, Always a Dodger*.

14. Clifton, "Juan Marichal," 667–68; Marichal with Freedman, *Juan Marichal*, 259–60.

15. Lewis, "Jim Bunning," 132–33; Dolson, *Jim Bunning*.

16. Eisenbath, *Cardinals Encyclopedia*, 189–90.

17. Gibson with Wheeler, *Stranger to the Game*, 129.

18. Carlton quoted in Russo, "Redbirds Salute Skinny Steve."

19. Carlton quoted in Stephenson, *Lefty*.

20. Gibson with Wheeler, *Stranger to the Game*, 153.

21. Allen quoted in White with Dillow, *Uppity*, 69.

22. McCarver with Peary, *Tim McCarver's Baseball for Brain Surgeons and Other Fans*, 116.

23. Tim McCarver, interview by author, New York NY, December 21, 1999.

24. McCarver interview, May 3, 2018.

25. Carlton quoted in Stephenson, *Lefty*.

26. Carlton quoted in Rotfeld, *Steve Carlton*. In a May 20, 2018, interview Carlton called Gibson a "teacher by his presentation on the field." He also admitted that he tried to model himself after the Cardinals' ace in terms of his intensity and pace of delivery. Carlton quoted in "Steve Carlton on Bob Gibson," Fox Midwest, May 20, 2018, https://foxsports.com/midwest/video/1237336643544.

27. Quoted in Mead, *Explosive Sixties*, 51–52.

28. McCarver with Pepe, *Few and Chosen*, 139; McCarver quoted in "Steve Carlton," ESPN *Sportscentury Classic*, aired March 1, 2004, https://www.youtube.com/watch?v=jq7fSzT3yHM.

29. McCarver interview, November 9, 2019.

30. Gibson, *Stranger to the Game*, 168–69.

31. Florio and Shapiro, *One Nation under Baseball*, 138.

32. McCarver interview, December 21, 1999. See also McCarver quoted in Mike Lupica, "A Baseball Friendship to Celebrate," *Sports on Earth*, January 15, 2018, http://www.sportsonearth.com/article/264712788/bob-gibson-tim-mccarver-cardinals-friendship.

33. McCarver interview, November 9, 2019.

34. Shannon quoted in Stephenson, *Lefty*.

35. McCarver quoted in Brosnan, "Steve Carlton: One Pitch Better Than Koufax," 24.

36. Carlton quoted in Bob Broeg, "Even Bubble-Gum Cards Can't Keep Up with Carlton," *The Sporting News*, March 23, 1968. Carlton's weight-lifting program consisted of lifting fifty-pound weights ten to twelve times a day. It was suggested by Cardinals trainer Bob Bauman, who told Carlton that it would strengthen his hands and his forearm, shoulder, and back muscles.

37. Carlton quoted in Broeg, "Even Bubble-Gum Cards Can't Keep Up with Carlton."

38. Kepner, *K*, 12.

39. Carlton quoting Gibson in Kepner, *K*, 12.

40. McDermott, *Off Speed*, xii.

41. Eisenbath, *Cardinals Encyclopedia*, 88.

42. Conversation recalled in Gibson, *Stranger to the Game*, 185–86.

43. J. Snyder, *Cardinals Journal*, 500.

44. Gibson quoted in Eisenbath, *Cardinals Encyclopedia*, 88.

45. J. Snyder, *Cardinals Journal*, 500–504.

46. J. Snyder, *Cardinals Journal*, 503. Gibson's shutouts were recorded on June 6, 11, 15, 20, and 26.

47. Eisenbath, *Cardinals Encyclopedia*, 189–90. For the most complete account of the 1968 season, see Pappu, *Year of the Pitcher*.

48. Eisenbath, *Cardinals Encyclopedia*, 507–13. For the most complete account of the 1968 World Series, see Donley, *October to Remember*. Gibson's 17 strikeouts in Game One of the 1968 World Series bested Dodger Sandy Koufax's 1963 record by two; as of 2020 it was still the World Series record.

49. Eisenbath, *Cardinals Encyclopedia*, 514.

50. Eisenbath, *Cardinals Encyclopedia*, 236, 509–10, 514.

51. Mark Tomasik, "Why Cardinals Were Offended by Talk from Gussie Busch," *RetroSimba*, March 15, 2019, https://retrosimba.com/2019/03/15/why-cardinals-were-offended-by-talk-from-gussie-busch/.

52. Tomasik, "Why Cardinals Were Offended by Talk from Gussie Busch"; Gibson, *Stranger to the Game*, 209–10. The Cardinals became a "morose and touchy team," according to center fielder Curt Flood. "Our concentration suffered," he said. "So did the remarkable spirit of fraternity that had helped us dominate the league for two years in succession." Flood with Carter, *Way It Is*, 108.

53. Carlton quoted in Kepner, *K*, 12.

54. Carlton quoted in Steve Wulf, "Steve Carlton," *Sports Illustrated*, January 24, 1994, 48; Carlton quoted in Kepner, *K*, 12.

55. "How Steve Carlton Learned to Throw Slider," *RetroSimba*, July 9, 2014, https://retrosimba.com/2014/07/09/how-steve-carlton-models-the-way-for-adam -wainwright/.

56. J. Snyder, *Cardinals Journal*, 511–12. Although Carlton surrendered solo home runs to Frank Howard and Bill Freehan in his three innings of work, he earned the victory for the NL in the 1969 All-Star Game.

57. Eisenbath, *Cardinals Encyclopedia*, 90.

58. Eisenbath, *Cardinals Encyclopedia*, 90.

59. Mike Bryson, "Carlton Sets Record, Fans 19 Mets," Associated Press, September 15, 1969.

60. Carlton and Swoboda quoted in Bryson, "Carlton Sets Record, Fans 19 Mets."

61. Carlton quoted in Bryson, "Carlton Sets Record, Fans 19 Mets."

62. Neal Russo, "A Record 19 KS Cure Ailing Carlton," *The Sporting News*, September 27, 1969. Russo cites statistics from Charley Galati, who charted pitches regularly for the St. Louis Cardinals in the 1960s.

63. McCarver with Peary, *McCarver's Baseball for Brain Surgeons*, 44.

64. McCarver quoted in Lauber, *Big 50*, 35.

65. Carlton quoted in Bryson, "Carlton Sets Record, Fans 19 Mets."

66. Carlton's 19-strikeout performance also tied the all-time record of 19 set by Charlie Sweeney of Providence in 1884, when it took 6 balls to draw a walk. See J. Snyder, *Cardinals Journal*, 514.

67. J. Snyder, *Cardinals Journal*, 514.

68. J. Snyder, *Cardinals Journal*, 514.

69. Eisenbath, *Cardinals Encyclopedia*, 90, 147.

70. Brosnan, "Steve Carlton: One Pitch Better Than Koufax," 24–27.

4. Moneyball

1. McCarver quoted in "Cards Trade Flood, McCarver to Phillies in 7-Player Deal," *St. Louis Post-Dispatch*, October 8, 1969.

2. McCarver quoted in "Cards Trade Flood, McCarver to Phillies in 7-Player Deal."

3. McCarver quoted in "Cards Trade Flood, McCarver to Phillies in 7-Player Deal."

4. Maxvill interview.

5. McCarver with Robinson, *OH, BABY, I LOVE IT!*, 148.

6. Gibson, *Stranger to the Game*, 217.

7. Curt Flood to MLB Commissioner Bowie Kuhn, December 24, 1969, quoted in Ward and Burns, *Baseball*, 411.

8. Bowie Kuhn, quoted in Ward and Burns, *Baseball*, 411.

9. Flood with Carter, *Way It Is*, 188. Years later Flood's wife insisted that her husband had "no special animus toward Philadelphia," suggesting instead that he rejected the deal because it "violated his dignity as a man; he objected to being treated as

chattel." Judy Pace-Flood quoted in "He Opened the Floodgates," *Philadelphia Daily News*, August 30, 2001.

10. McCarver interview, December 21, 1999.

11. See Flood v. Kuhn, U.S. District Court of New York (1970); Curt Flood, "Why I Challenged Baseball," *Sport Magazine*, March 1970, 10–13; Edmunds and Manz, *Baseball and Antitrust*; and William Gildea, "Curt Flood: Baseball's Angry Rebel," *Baseball Digest*, February 1971, 55–61.

12. See Steve Carlton's Career Pitching Statistics, Baseball Reference, accessed May 31, 2020, https://www.baseball-reference.com/players/c/carltst01.shtml.

13. "1969 MLB Pitching Leaders," Baseball Reference, accessed May 31, 2020, https://www.baseball-reference.com/leagues/MLB/1969-pitching-leaders.shtml.

14. "1970 St. Louis Cardinal Salaries," Baseball Almanac, accessed May 30, 2020, https://www.baseball-almanac.com/teamstats/roster.php?y=1970&t=SLN.

15. Busch quoted in Dick Young, "Allen and Carlton Draw More Fire from Gussie," *New York Daily News*, March 13, 1970. Carlton wasn't the only Cardinals holdout. Dick Allen, recently acquired from the Phillies, refused to report to spring training until Busch offered a $90,000 salary. "If Allen doesn't take our offer," the St. Louis owner told the *Daily News*, "he won't ever play for the Cardinals." Hours later Allen showed up at spring training.

16. Tomasik, "Why Cardinals Were Offended by Talk from Gussie Busch." The players' union called off the proposed spring training boycott in March 1969 after reaching a compromise on the percentage of television revenue shared with players, the amount owners would contribute to the pension fund, and the number of playing years needed to qualify for a pension.

17. Busch quoted in Tomasik, "Why Cardinals Were Offended by Talk from Gussie Busch."

18. Bob Broeg, "Birds Toss Book at Richie and Steve," *The Sporting News*, March 21, 1970. The New York Yankees had invoked the renewal clause a few years earlier when Jim Bouton refused to report to spring training. The threatened fine was $100 a day.

19. Busch quoted in Young, "Allen and Carlton Draw More Fire."

20. "Carlton Accepts Two-Year Contract," *New York Times*, March 18, 1970.

21. Steve Carlton's 1970 Pitching Game Log, Baseball Reference, accessed May 31, 2020, https://www.baseball-reference.com/players/gl.fcgi?id=carltst01&t=p&year=1970.

22. Steve Carlton's 1970 Pitching Game Log.

23. "Johnny Bench Was Nemesis of Steve Carlton," *RetroSimba*, July 26, 2018, https://retrosimba.com/2011/08/05/johnny-bench-was-nemesis-of-steve-carlton/.

24. Sparky Anderson and Red Schoendienst quoted in "Johnny Bench Was Nemesis of Steve Carlton."

25. St. Louis Cardinals [5] vs Cincinnati Reds [12], July 26, 1970, Box Score, Riverfront Stadium, Baseball Almanac, accessed June 3, 2020, https://www.baseball-almanac.com/box-scores/boxscore.php?boxid=197007260CN5.

26. Torre, *Chasing the Dream*, 105.

27. Steve Carlton's 1970 Pitching Game Log. See also box scores for Cardinals versus Reds games of April 25, May 5, July 21, and July 26, Baseball Almanac, https://www.baseball-almanac.com. Bench went on to lead the National League in home runs (45) and RBIs (148) in 1970, winning the Most Valuable Player Award and powering the Reds to the pennant.

28. Carlton quoted in *Philadelphia Phillies Yearbook* (1975), 59.

29. Steve Carlton's 1970 Pitching Game Log.

30. Kepner, *K*, 13; Vivanco, "Steve Carlton."

31. Steve Carlton's 1970 Pitching Game Log.

32. St. Louis Cardinals [12] vs San Francisco Giants [1], June 2, 1970, Box Score, Busch Stadium, Baseball Almanac, accessed June 20, 2020, https://www.baseball-almanac.com/box-scores/boxscore.php?boxid=197006020SLN.

33. Carlton quoted in Fimrite, "Steve Carlton: Eliminator of the Variables," 84; and in Brosnan, "Steve Carlton: One Pitch Better Than Koufax," 26.

34. Fimrite, "Steve Carlton: Eliminator of the Variables," 87; Vivanco, "Steve Carlton."

35. Bob Broeg, "Steve Ditches 'Made in Japan' Slider," *The Sporting News*, May 15, 1971; Brosnan, "Steve Carlton: One Pitch Better Than Koufax," 26.

36. Eisenbath, *Cardinals Encyclopedia*, 92

37. J. Snyder, *Cardinals Journal*, 527–28.

38. See Steve Carlton's 1971 Pitching Game Log, Baseball Reference, accessed June 20, 2020, https://www.baseball-reference.com/players/gl.fcgi?id=carltst01&t=p&year=1971; and "Ted Simmons Flexed Muscles vs. Hall of Fame Hurlers," *RetroSimba*, January 1, 2020, https://www.retrosimba.com/2020/01/01/ted-simmons-flexed-muscles-vs-hall-of-fame-hurlers/.

39. Carlton, who was dealt to the Phillies in February 1972, finished his MLB career with 329 wins (eleventh all-time best), 4,136 strikeouts (fourth best), and four Cy Young Awards. Ryan, dealt to the California Angels in December 1971, finished with 324 wins (fourteenth best), 5,714 strikeouts (all-time best), and 7 no-hitters (all-time best).

40. "Steve Carlton vs. Nolan Ryan: Fateful '71 Finale of Aces," *RetroSimba*, March 12, 2012, https://www.retrosimba.com/2012/03/15/steve-carlton-vs-nolan-ryan-fateful-71-finale-of-aces/.

41. Steve Carlton's 1970 Pitching Game Log.

42. McCarver quoted in "Cards Trade Flood, McCarver to Phillies in 7-Player Deal."

43. McCarver quoted in *Philadelphia Phillies Yearbook* (1971), 35.

44. *Philadelphia Phillies Yearbook* (1971), 35.

45. Westcott and Bilovsky, *Phillies Encyclopedia*, 84.

46. Williams, "Tim McCarver."

47. Quoted in Westcott and Bilovsky, *Phillies Encyclopedia*, 452–53.

48. Maxvill interview.

49. Maxvill interview. See also McCarver with Robinson, OH, BABY, I LOVE IT!, 55.

50. McCarver interview, May 3, 2018.

51. McCarver interview, May 3, 2018.

52. Larry Fox, "Carlton-Wise Trade: Strictly Business," *New York Daily News*, February 26, 1972.

53. Joseph Durso, "Cards Trade Carlton to Phillies for Wise in Pitcher Exchange," *New York Times*, February 26, 1972. Durso wrote that in 1971 Wise's salary was $32,500 and Carlton's was $50,000. Others, such as Tim McCarver, report that both pitchers were making $55,000 in 1971 and were asking for an additional $10,000 for 1972. See McCarver with Pepe, *Few and Chosen*, 140–41. But my account is based on the salary figures disclosed by BaseballAlmanac.com, which identifies Wise's 1971 salary as $45,000 and Carlton's as $40,000.

54. Helyar, *Lords of the Realm*, 36–37, 79.

55. Helyar, *Lords of the Realm*, 37–38.

56. Helyar, *Lords of the Realm*, 110.

57. Helyar, *Lords of the Realm*, 110.

58. Helyar, *Lords of the Realm*, 111.

59. McCarver with Pepe, *Few and Chosen*, 140–41.

60. Wise quoted in Durso, "Cards Trade Carlton to Phillies for Wise."

61. Rick Wise, interview by author, Beaverton OR, October 15, 2015.

62. Maxvill interview. After Dal Maxvill was hired as general manager of the Cardinals in 1984, he had lunch with former GM Bing Devine and told him about Carlton's decision to sign for $57,500. Stunned by the revelation, Devine lost his appetite. "Just think how the history of the St. Louis Cardinals would've changed if Devine had re-signed Carlton for $57,500," speculated Maxvill in 2020. "We'd probably have won two or three more pennants. As it turned out, we didn't get back to the postseason until the 1980s."

63. Carlton quoted in Rotfeld, *Steve Carlton*; Dolson, "Steve Carlton," 4.

64. Devine quoted in Fox, "Carlton-Wise Trade."

65. Devine with Wheatley, *Memoirs of Bing Devine*, 83.

66. Carlton quoted in Fox, "Carlton-Wise Trade."

67. Miller quoted in Dick Young, "The Wise-Carlton Trade," *New York Daily News*, March 1, 1972.

68. Busch quoted in Helyar, *Lords of the Realm*, 113.

69. "No April Fools—Players Go on Strike," *The Sporting News*, April 3, 1972.

70. Helyar, *Lords of the Realm*, 120–22.

71. Helyar, *Lords of the Realm*, 127.

72. Belth, *Stepping Up*. Belth argues that Flood knew he would not win his Supreme Court case against Major League Baseball but was still willing to sacrifice his career and whatever income he would have made just so that the system's wrongs could be made public.

73. Ervin quoted in Ward and Burns, *Baseball*, 423–24.

74. Ward and Burns, *Baseball*, 424.

75. Carlton quoted in Dolson, "Steve Carlton," 4.

76. Quinn quoted in Fox, "Carlton-Wise Trade."

77. Ruly Carpenter, interview by author, Montchanin DE, June 29, 2018.

78. Frank Lucchesi, interview by author, Colleyville TX, January 6, 2016.

79. Fox, "Carlton-Wise Trade."

80. McCarver interview, May 3, 2018. McCarver, who had caught for Carlton in St. Louis and for Wise in Philadelphia, described the trade at the time as "a real good one for a real good one." He felt Carlton had more raw talent, but Wise had better command on the mound. McCarver quoted in *The Sporting News*, March 11, 1972. The statistics of each pitcher appear to confirm McCarver's observation. Up to that point, Wise had a career total of seventy-five wins and Carlton had seventy-seven. While Carlton averaged more career strikeouts per nine innings (5) at the time, Wise allowed fewer walks per game (1.5) and actually had the better strikeout-to-walk ratio (3:1) through the 1971 season.

81. Eisenbath, *Cardinals Encyclopedia*, 86–92.

82. Westcott and Bilovsky, *Phillies Encyclopedia*, 81–85, 595–97.

83. Jere Longman, "Milestone Marks That Phillies Fans Already Knew," *New York Times*, June 12, 2007.

84. See Kashatus, *September Swoon*.

85. Kashatus, *September Swoon*, 147–78.

86. Kashatus, *Almost a Dynasty*, 29–33.

87. Kashatus, *Almost a Dynasty*, 35–49.

88. Lucchesi quoted in Westcott and Bilovsky, *Phillies Encyclopedia*, 352–53.

89. Westcott and Bilovsky, *Phillies Encyclopedia*, 83–85.

90. Westcott, *Veterans Stadium*, 13.

91. Westcott, *Veterans Stadium*, 16–18.

92. Westcott, *Veterans Stadium*, 16–18.

93. Westcott, *Veterans Stadium*, 16–18.

94. Giles with Myers, *Pouring Six Beers at a Time*, 91–98.

5. Reunited

1. Bernstein, "Steve Carlton," 16–18.

2. Bucci and Brown, *Drinking Coffee with a Fork*, xii.

3. Ray Rippelmeyer, interview by author, Waterloo IL, November 14, 2019.

4. Kepner, *K*, 5; Rippelmeyer interview.

5. Rippelmeyer interview.

6. Rippelmeyer interview.

7. "Scouting Report: National League East," *Sports Illustrated*, April 10, 1972, 61.

8. Larry Bowa, interview by author, Conshohocken PA, April 6, 2020.

9. Westcott and Bilovsky, *Phillies Encyclopedia*, 86; Bucci and Brown, *Drinking Coffee with a Fork*, 29.

10. Don Money, interview by author, Vineland NJ, August 7, 2020; Bowa interview.

11. Larry Shenk, interview by author, Philadelphia PA, September 10, 2015.

12. Carlton quoted in Bernstein, "Steve Carlton," 16.

13. Neal Russo, "Steve Charts Road Back Via 'Nautilus,'" *The Sporting News*, March 2, 1974.

14. Carlton quoted in Bernstein, "Steve Carlton," 17–18.

15. McCarver interview, May 3, 2018.

16. Bruce Keidan, "Carlton Strong as Phils Win Opener, 4–2," *Philadelphia Inquirer*, April 16, 1972.

17. Ferguson Jenkins, interview by author, Phoenix AZ, December 19, 2019.

18. Frank Dolson, "And Now, Baseball Like Always Before," *Philadelphia Inquirer*, April 16, 1972.

19. Hoerner quoted in Morgan, *Steve Carlton and the 1972 Phillies*, 31.

20. Although Gibson lost the game, he did eclipse Bob Feller and Warren Spahn for fourth place on the all-time strikeout record when he fanned Greg Luzinski in the fourth inning to register his 2,584th career strikeout. See Ray Kelly, "Carlton Defeats Gibson, Cards, 1–0," *Philadelphia Evening Bulletin*, April 20, 1972.

21. Money interview.

22. Carlton quoted in Kelly, "Carlton Defeats Gibson, Cards, 1–0."

23. Greg Luzinski, interview by author, Philadelphia PA, August 3, 2015.

24. McCarver quoted in Kepner, *K*, 14.

25. Allen Lewis, "Carlton Retrieves Discarded Slider and Zooms," *The Sporting News*, May 20, 1972.

26. Carlton quoted in Bill Conlin, "Strike Out! Carltooo-ooo-ooo-n!" *Philadelphia Daily News*, April 26, 1972.

27. McCarver quoted in Conlin, "Strike Out!"

28. Rippelmeyer quoted in Conlin, "Strike Out!"

29. Lewis, "Carlton Retrieves Discarded Slider."

30. Bruce Keidan, "Phillies Fall to Arlin, 4–0," *Philadelphia Inquirer*, April 30, 1972.

31. Morgan, *Steve Carlton and 1972 Phillies*, 44–45.

32. Morgan, *Steve Carlton and 1972 Phillies*, 44.

33. Frank Dolson, "Season Still Young—but So What?" *Philadelphia Inquirer*, May 8, 1972.

34. See Bucci and Brown, *Drinking Coffee with a Fork*, 62–74; Morgan, *Steve Carlton and 1972 Phillies*, 49, 62–66.

35. Morgan, *Steve Carlton and 1972 Phillies*, 72.

36. Carlton quoted in Brosnan, "Steve Carlton: One Pitch Better Than Koufax," 27.

37. Quinn quoted in Frank Dolson, "The Same Man Steps Down Gracefully," *Philadelphia Inquirer*, June 4, 1972.

38. Bruce Keidan, "Meanwhile, Phillies Fall Again, 6–5," *Philadelphia Inquirer*, June 4, 1972; Westcott and Bilovsky, *Phillies Encyclopedia*, 385–86.

39. Owens quoted in Frank Dolson, "Honesty of Owens Turns Rainfall into Deluge of Rumors," *Philadelphia Inquirer*, June 21, 1972. On June 14 the *Atlanta Journal-Constitution* reported the rumor that Owens was on the verge of trading Carlton to the Braves for slugger Rico Carty and right-hander Jim Nash. See Wayne

Minshew, "Rico, Nash to Phils for Phils' Carlton?" *Atlanta Journal-Constitution*, June 14, 1972.

40. Bill Conlin, "Brandon: Player of Months," *Philadelphia Daily News*, June 8, 1972.

41. Tom Cushman, "? Plus ? Plus 2 Caps = Phils Trade Soon," *Philadelphia Inquirer*, June 12, 1972.

42. Steve Carlton, interview by Roy Firestone, ESPN Studios, Los Angeles CA, August 7, 1993, YouTube, posted April 10, 2019, https://www.youtube.com/watch?v=VdvarKJhgwA.

43. Dolson, "Honesty of Owens Turns Rainfall into Deluge of Rumors."

44. Morgan, *Steve Carlton and 1972 Phillies*, 83.

45. McCarver interview, November 9, 2019.

46. Bucci and Brown, *Drinking Coffee with a Fork*, 78.

47. Bill Conlin, "Mauch Tips Off Blunder," *Philadelphia Daily News*, June 15, 1972.

48. Conlin, "Mauch Tips Off Blunder."

49. Lucchesi interview.

50. See Tim McCarver's Career Hitting and Fielding Statistics, Baseball Reference, accessed September 4, 2020, https://www.baseball-reference.com/players/m/mccarti01.shtml; and John Bateman's Career Hitting and Fielding Statistics, Baseball Reference, accessed September 4, 2020, https://www.baseball-reference.com/players/b/batemjo01.shtml.

51. Conlin, "Mauch Tips Off Blunder."

52. McCarver with Robinson, OH, BABY, I LOVE IT!, 148–50 (also quoted in Conlin, "Mauch Tips Off Blunder").

53. Lucchesi interview.

54. McCarver quoted in Conlin, "Mauch Tips Off Blunder."

55. McCarver interview, November 9, 2019.

56. Carpenter quoted in Fitzpatrick, *You Can't Lose 'Em All*, 42.

57. Fitzpatrick, *You Can't Lose 'Em All*, 42–43.

58. Tim McCarver's Career Hitting and Fielding Statistics.

59. Bruce Keidan, "Astros Beat Phils on HR in 11th, 1–0," *Philadelphia Inquirer*, June 17, 1972. The other two extra-inning games were on July 19, when Carlton defeated the San Diego Padres, 3–2, in San Diego, and August 21, when he lost to Phil Niekro and the Atlanta Braves, snapping his fifteen-game winning streak.

60. Bruce Keidan, "Phils Snap Losing Streak at 6," *Philadelphia Inquirer*, June 22, 1972.

61. Carlton quoted in Bruce Keidan, "The Winnah: Roger, Joe, Jim, Pete, Don," *Philadelphia Inquirer*, June 26, 1972.

62. Carlton quoted in Keidan, "The Winnah."

63. Mauch quoted in Keidan, "The Winnah"; Bowa interview.

64. Money interview.

65. Carlton quoted in Bruce Keidan, "Carlton Fans 13 as Phillies Beat Mets," *Philadelphia Inquirer*, June 30, 1972.

66. Bowa interview.

67. Conversation recollected in Luzinski interview.

68. Carlton interview by Firestone.

69. Bowa interview.

70. Bruce Keidan, "Phils Get 4 in 1st, Top Giants," *Philadelphia Inquirer*, July 4, 1972.

71. Allen Lewis, "Phillies Split Twin Bill with Padres," *Philadelphia Inquirer*, July 8, 1972.

72. Bruce Keidan, "Skipper's End: A Few Questions and Some Answers," *Philadelphia Inquirer*, July 11, 1972.

73. Lucchesi quoted in Westcott and Bilovsky, *Phillies Encyclopedia*, 352.

74. Lucchesi interview.

75. Frank Dolson, "Lucchesi Deserved Better," *Philadelphia Inquirer*, July 11, 1972.

76. See T. R. Sullivan, "Beloved Ex-Rangers Skipper Lucchesi Dies," MLB.com, June 9, 2019, https://www.mlb.com/rangers/news/frank-lucchesi-former-rangers-phillies-manager-obituary.

77. Owens quoted in Fitzpatrick, *Can't Lose 'Em All*, 44.

78. According to third baseman Don Money, the players also knew Owens was on a "fact-finding mission." They knew "he came down to find out who really wanted to play and who he needed to get rid of," added Money. Money interview.

6. Drinking Coffee with a Fork

1. Ruly Carpenter interview.

2. Owens quoted in Chris Wheeler, "Paul Owens: I've Got a Feeling," in *Philadelphia Phillies Yearbook* (1976), 8.

3. For the Phillies' lineup, see box scores for April–June 1972 at "1972 Philadelphia Phillies Schedule," Baseball Almanac, accessed September 10, 2020, https://www.baseball-almanac.com/teamstats/schedule.php?y=1972&t=PHI.

4. For the Phillies' lineup, see box scores for July–October 1972 at "1972 Philadelphia Phillies Schedule," Baseball Almanac, accessed September 10, 2020, https://www.baseball-almanac.com/teamstats/schedule.php?y=1972&t=PHI.

5. Owens quoted in Bruce Keidan, "Phils Score 11 Runs in One Inning, Beat Giants," *Philadelphia Inquirer*, July 16, 1972.

6. Bonds quoted in Keidan, "Phils Score 11 Runs in One Inning, Beat Giants."

7. Carlton quoted in Bill Conlin, "Bonds, Maddox Fall Guys for Giant Flip Wilson Act," *Philadelphia Daily News*, July 17, 1972.

8. "Carlton Named All-Star Hurler," *Philadelphia Inquirer*, July 19, 1972.

9. Bruce Keidan, "Carlton Wins No. 13, Beats Padres, 3–2," *Philadelphia Inquirer*, July 20, 1972.

10. Bruce Keidan, "Luzinski's First Season: From Wonders of Spring to Heat of July," *Philadelphia Inquirer*, July 24, 1972.

11. Bruce Keidan, "Carlton Blacks Cubs for 10th in Row," *Philadelphia Inquirer*, July 29, 1972.

12. Rippelmeyer interview.

13. Bruce Keidan, "Carlton Captures 11 in a Row," *Philadelphia Inquirer*, August 2, 1972.

14. Bruce Keidan, "Carlton Blanks Cards as Phils Win 5 in Row," *Philadelphia Inquirer*, August 6, 1972.

15. McCarver with Pepe, *Few and Chosen*, 150.

16. Owens quoted in Keidan, "Carlton Blanks Cards as Phils Win 5 in Row."

17. Stargell quoted in Tom Cushman, "Stargell on Carlton: 'Trying to Hit Him Was Like Drinking Coffee with a Fork,'" *Philadelphia Daily News*, August 10, 1972. See also Stargell quoted in *The Sporting News*, August 26, 1972, 6.

18. Carlton quoted in Bruce Keidan, "Carlton Raps HR, Pitches 3-Hitter," *Philadelphia Inquirer*, August 10, 1972.

19. Keidan, "Carlton Raps HR, Pitches 3-Hitter."

20. Carlton quoted in Keidan, "Carlton Raps HR, Pitches 3-Hitter."

21. Bruce Keidan, "Steve Wins 14th in Row, Gives Expos Three Hits," *Philadelphia Inquirer*, August 14, 1972.

22. Gary Sarnoff, "August 13, 1972: The Great Wallenda and Steve Carlton," SABR, accessed August 1, 2020, https://sabr.org/gamesproj/game/august-13-1972-the-great-wallenda-and-steve-carlton/.

23. Giles quoted in Westcott, *Veterans Stadium*, 86–87.

24. Wallenda quoted in Kathy Begley, "Walk Here 'Toughest Ever Made,' Wallenda Says," *Philadelphia Inquirer*, August 14, 1972. Karl Wallenda was right to be scared. Since 1962 the Flying Wallendas stunt team had suffered three failures resulting in the deaths of four family members and leaving another paralyzed. Less than two weeks before his performance at the Vet, Wallenda's son-in-law, Richard Guzman, fell fifty feet to his death in Wheeling, West Virginia, while bringing Karl his balancing pole at midwire and brushing against an electrical cable. See Sarnoff, "August 13, 1972."

25. Keidan, "Steve Wins 14th in Row."

26. Carlton quoted in Bruce Keidan, "Homers Help Southpaw Rout Reds' Jinx, 9–4," *Philadelphia Inquirer*, August 18, 1972.

27. Keidan, "Homers Help Southpaw Rout Reds' Jinx, 9–4."

28. Owens, Bateman, and Carlton quoted in Bill Conlin, "Bat Splinters Super Steve," *Philadelphia Daily News*, August 22, 1972. The *Daily News* did not actually print Bateman's f-bombs, but Larry Bowa, who was within earshot of Bateman at the time, confirmed that he actually said "fuckin'" and "fucked." Bowa interview.

29. Bucci and Brown, *Drinking Coffee with Fork*, 168–69.

30. Rippelmeyer and Bateman quotes recalled in Bowa interview.

31. Bob Hertzel, "Carlton Scarce-ly Wins 21st," *Cincinnati Enquirer*, August 27, 1972.

32. Bill Conlin, "'Little Things' Tip the Franchise," *Philadelphia Daily News*, August 31, 1972.

33. Frank Dolson, "Carlton Notches 22nd Win, Phillies Bombard Braves, 8–0," *Philadelphia Inquirer*, September 4, 1972.

34. Bill Conlin, "30-Carlton's Super Goal," *Philadelphia Daily News*, September 8, 1972.

35. Conlin, "30-Carlton's Super Goal."

36. Dyer and Carlton quoted in Bruce Keidan, "Carlton's Bid for 24th Comes to a Dyer Ending," *Philadelphia Inquirer*, September 12, 1972.

37. Carlton and Douglas quotes from Bill Conlin, "This Was Your Night, Super Steve," *Philadelphia Daily News*, September 16, 1972.

38. Conlin, "This Was Your Night, Super Steve."

39. Conlin, "This Was Your Night, Super Steve."

40. Associated Press, "Get Picture from Rick?" *Philadelphia Inquirer*, September 21, 1972.

41. Neal Russo, "Carlton's 25th Spoils Reds' 25th," *St. Louis Post Dispatch*, September 21, 1972.

42. Wise quoted in Bill Conlin, "25th Gives Carlton No Extra Surge of Feeling," *Philadelphia Daily News*, September 21, 1972.

43. Wise interview.

44. Rick Wise's 1972 Pitching Log, Baseball Reference, accessed September 15, 2020, https://www.baseball-reference.com/players/gl.fcgi?id=wiseri01&t=p&year=197.

45. Schoendienst quoted in Russo, "Carlton's 25th Spoils Reds' 25th."

46. Carlton quoted in Bruce Keidan, "Carlton Outpitches Wise, Notches 25th as Phils Win," *Philadelphia Inquirer*, September 21, 1972.

47. Frank Dolson, "Mets Spoil Carlton's Bid for 26th," *Philadelphia Inquirer*, September 25, 1972.

48. Bruce Keidan, "Carlton Records 26th as Phils Nip Bucs, 2–1," *Philadelphia Inquirer*, September 29, 1972.

49. Morgan, *Steve Carlton and the 1972 Phillies*, 151.

50. Giles with Myers, *Pouring Six Beers at a Time*, 123.

51. Carlton quoted in Associated Press, "Phils Turn Tiger for Steve[,] Rap Six Homers in 11–1 Win," *Philadelphia Inquirer*, October 4, 1972.

52. Associated Press, "Phils Turn Tiger for Steve."

53. Morgan, *Steve Carlton and the 1972 Phillies*, 59–60.

54. Steve Carlton's 1972 Pitching Log, Baseball Reference, accessed September 15, 2020, https://www.baseball-reference.com/players/gl.fcgi?id=carltst01&t=p&year=1972; McCarver with Pepe, *Few and Chosen*, 148. Carlton set a record for most wins for a last-place team, breaking Frank "Noodles" Hahn's previous mark of twenty-two for the 1901 Cincinnati Reds. The Phillies' ace also set a record for percentage of team's games won, breaking Jack Chesbro's 44.6 percent for the 1904 New York Yankees.

55. Associated Press, "It's Unanimous! Super Steve's Best," *Philadelphia Daily News*, November 2, 1972.

56. "Steve Carlton's Cy Young Season," in *Philadelphia Phillies Yearbook* (1973), 11.

57. Carlton quoted in Associated Press, "It's Unanimous!"

58. Carlton quoted in Stephenson, *Lefty*.

59. Morgan, *Steve Carlton and 1972 Phillies*, 178–79; Bucci and Brown, *Drinking Coffee with a Fork*, 172–73.

60. Morgan, *Steve Carlton and 1972 Phillies*, 181.

61. Bucci and Brown, *Drinking Coffee with a Fork*, 168.

62. Steve Carlton's Standard Batting, Baseball Reference, accessed September 17, 2020, https://www.baseball-reference.com/players/c/carltst01.shtml.

7. Sphinx of the Schuylkill

1. Gene Courtney, "Carlton Signs Record $165,000 Contract," *Philadelphia Inquirer*, January 17, 1973.

2. Carpenter and Owens quoted in Courtney, "Carlton Signs Record $165,000 Contract."

3. Carlton conversation with sportswriters quoted in Courtney, "Carlton Signs Record $165,000 Contract."

4. Carlton quoted in Courtney, "Carlton Signs Record $165,000 Contract."

5. Fimrite, "Steve Carlton: Eliminator of the Variables," 84; Maury Levy, "Would You Buy a Can of Shaving Cream from This Man? The Selling of Steve Carlton," *Philadelphia Magazine*, April 1973, 174.

6. M. Levy, "Would You Buy a Can of Shaving Cream from This Man?," 89.

7. Carlton quoted in M. Levy, "Would You Buy a Can of Shaving Cream from This Man?," 89.

8. Carlton quoted in *Philadelphia Phillies Yearbook* (1973), 12.

9. Carlton quoted in M. Levy, "Would You Buy a Can of Shaving Cream from This Man?," 89–90.

10. Bill Conlin, "Prescription for the Franchise," *Philadelphia Daily News*, March 23, 1973.

11. Bruce Keidan, "Cleon Has Best Day—Phils Front Office Doesn't," *Philadelphia Inquirer*, April 7, 1973; Bruce Keidan, "Phils Chill Expos, 7–5," *Philadelphia Inquirer*, April 11, 1973; Bruce Keidan, "Carlton, Phils Top Mets, 7–3," *Philadelphia Inquirer*, April 15, 1973.

12. Bruce Keidan, "Renko Hurls 4-Hitter to Beat Phils," *Philadelphia Inquirer*, April 19, 1973.

13. Steve Carlton's 1973 Pitching Log, Baseball Reference, accessed November 9, 2020, https://www.baseball-reference.com/players/gl.fcgi?id=carltst01&t=p&year=1973.

14. Steve Carlton's 1973 Pitching Log.

15. Bruce Keidan, "Another Carlton Loss Worries Ozark," *Philadelphia Inquirer*, May 6, 1973.

16. Carlton comment to *The Sporting News* quoted in "Johnny Bench Was Nemesis of Steve Carlton," *RetroSimba*, updated July 26, 2018, https://retrosimba.com/?s=Johnny+Bench+was+nemesis.

17. Bench quoted in Thomas Boswell, "Steve Carlton: Defiant, Single-Minded Struggle to Peak of Perfection," *Washington Post*, July 14, 1980.

18. Carlton quoted in Boswell, "Steve Carlton: Defiant."

19. Bruce Keidan, "Ozark Fumes at Phils' 'Complete Letdown,'" *Philadelphia Inquirer*, May 14, 1973.

20. Fitzpatrick, *You Can't Lose 'Em All*, 44–45.

21. Dolson, *Philadelphia Story*, 182–84.

22. Danny Ozark, interview by author, Vero Beach FL, August 8, 2005.

23. Carpenter interview.

24. Ozark quoted in Bill Conlin, "Ozark, the Fundamentalist," *Philadelphia Daily News*, March 16, 1974.

25. Bill Conlin, "The Sphinx of the Schuylkill," *Philadelphia Daily News*, August 1, 1994.

26. Bruce Keidan, "Pitching OK, Phillies Manager Insists," *Philadelphia Inquirer*, June 1, 1973.

27. Conlin, "Sphinx of the Schuylkill." See also Fitzpatrick, *You Can't Lose 'Em All*, 44–45. Conlin also reported that at the meeting Carlton injured his back when he engaged in a sumo-style wrestling contest against another pitcher, "bull-strong Billy Wilson," and was forced to miss his next start.

28. Owens quoted in Dolson, *Philadelphia Story*, 186.

29. Ozark quoted in Dolson, *Philadelphia Story*, 215.

30. Ozark interview.

31. Carpenter interview.

32. Rippelmeyer quoted in Stan Hochman, "Slick Baseballs Got Carlton's Goat," *Philadelphia Daily News*, June 15, 1973.

33. McCarver with Robinson, *OH, BABY, I LOVE IT!*, 83.

34. Steve Carlton's 1973 Pitching Log. See also Bill Conlin, "Mauch Says Carlton Has Head Problems," *Philadelphia Daily News*, June 23, 1973; Bruce Keidan, "Cards Shell Carlton, Nudge Phils," *Philadelphia Inquirer*, July 1, 1973; Bruce Keidan, "Reds Shell Carlton for 5 in 6th, Beat Phils, 7–3; Robinson HRs," *Philadelphia Inquirer*, July 19, 1973; Bill Conlin, "Thomas Makes a Speedy Exit," *Philadelphia Daily News*, July 27, 1973; Bruce Keidan, "Pirates' Rookie Beats Phillies, 3–1," *Philadelphia Inquirer*, August 4, 1973; Bill Conlin, "Phils Overwhelmed by Grief as Homer Beats Carlton, 3–0," *Philadelphia Daily News*, August 9, 1973; Bruce Keidan, "Carlton Loses 14th as Dodgers Trip Phils in 9th, 2–1; Luzinski Homers," *Philadelphia Inquirer*, August 13, 1973; Bruce Keidan, "Phils, Carlton Lose 8–3, as Kendall Kindles Padres," *Philadelphia Inquirer*, August 23, 1973; and Bruce Keidan, "'Tense' Phils Bow to Dodgers Again," *Philadelphia Inquirer*, August 27, 1973.

35. Conlin, "Mauch Says Carlton Has Head Problems."

36. Bill Conlin, interview by author, Turnersville NJ, June 16, 2005.

37. Conlin interview.

38. Conlin interview.

39. Giles with Myers, *Pouring Six Beers at a Time*, 252.

40. Conlin, "It Wasn't My Fault He Wouldn't Speak," *Philadelphia Daily News*, Supplement, August 1, 1994; Conlin, "Sphinx of the Schuylkill."

41. Fitzpatrick, *You Can't Lose 'Em All*, 80–81.

42. Carlton quoted in McCarver with Robinson, OH, BABY, I LOVE IT!, 56.

43. Jim Lonborg, interview by author, Scituate MA, August 11, 2018.

44. Ozark interview.

45. Rippelmeyer interview.

46. Bob Boone, interview by author, San Marcos CA, May 19, 2020.

47. Ozark quoted in Ray Didinger, "He Remained in Schmidt's 'Hot Corner,'" *Philadelphia Daily News*, special feature, July 26, 1995.

48. Mike Schmidt, interview by author, Jupiter FL, April 16, 2020.

49. Ray Kelly, "Schmidt's 'Strikes' Putting Crimp in Ozark's Schedule," *The Sporting News*, August 18, 1973.

50. Hochman, *Mike Schmidt*, 39.

51. "Michael Jack City," *The Fan*, May 1995, 29; Bowa with Bloom, *Bleep!*, 161–63.

52. Schmidt interview.

53. Schmidt quoted in Hochman, *Mike Schmidt*, 40.

54. Schmidt interview.

55. Ray Didinger, "The Kid Is Now the Key," *Philadelphia Bulletin's Discover Magazine*, April 2, 1978, 20–21.

56. Rippelmeyer interview.

57. Didinger, "Kid Is Now the Key," 21.

58. Larry Christenson, interview by author, Wayne PA, September 29, 2017.

59. Christenson interview.

60. Christenson interview.

61. Conversation recollected in Christenson interview.

62. Steve Carlton's 1973 Pitching Log; Westcott and Bilovsky, *Phillies Encyclopedia*, 87.

63. Owens quoted in Ray Kelley, "Ozark Prouder of Carlton as 'LP' Than as 'WP,'" *The Sporting News*, March 2, 1974.

64. Westcott and Bilovsky, *Phillies Encyclopedia*, 86–87, 354.

65. Ozark quoted in Kelley, "Ozark Prouder of Carlton as 'LP' Than as 'WP.'"

66. Christenson interview.

67. Neal Russo, "Steve Charts Road Back via Nautilus," *The Sporting News*, March 2, 1974.

68. Maxvill interview.

69. Carlton quoted in Russo, "Steve Charts Road Back via Nautilus."

70. Morgan, *Steve Carlton and 1972 Phillies*, 126.

71. Carlton quoted in Stephenson, *Lefty*.

72. Funakoshi, *Karate-Do Kyohan*.

73. Bill Conlin, "Carlton Balks at Danny Blowing Him Off Mound," *Philadelphia Daily News*, May 2, 1974.

74. Carlton quoted in Conlin, "Carlton Balks at Danny Blowing Him Off Mound."

75. Terry Tata, interview by author, Cheshire CT, May 15, 2020.

76. Schmidt interview.

77. Tommy Hutton, interview by author, Palm Beach Gardens FL, August 12, 2015.

78. Ray Kelly, "Three-Year Pact to Revive Super Steve, Phillies Claim," *The Sporting News*, March 1, 1975.

79. Owens quoted in Kelly, "Three-Year Pact to Revive Super Steve, Phillies Claim."

80. Steve Carlton's 1974 Pitching Log, Baseball Reference, accessed December 1, 2020, https://www.baseball-reference.com/players/gl.fcgi?id=carltst01&t=p&year=1974.

81. Bill Lyon, "Phils Sign Carlton to $500,000 Pact," *Philadelphia Inquirer*, February 11, 1975.

82. Owens quoted in Kelly, "Three-Year Pact to Revive Super Steve, Phillies Claim."

83. Carlton quoted in Kelly, "Three-Year Pact to Revive Super Steve, Phillies Claim."

84. Westcott and Bilovsky, *Phillies Encyclopedia*, 88.

85. For Schmidt's 1974 offensive statistics, see "1974 National League Batting Leaders," Baseball Reference, accessed December 2, 2020, https://www.baseball-reference.com/leagues/NL/1974-batting-leaders.shtml.

86. Westcott and Bilovsky, *Phillies Encyclopedia*, 88.

87. Westcott and Bilovsky, *Phillies Encyclopedia*, 246.

88. Carlton and Ruthven quoted in McCarver with Peary, *McCarver's Baseball for Brain Surgeons*, 50.

89. Dick Ruthven, interview by author, Alpharetta GA, April 11, 2018.

90. "Phils Get Tug McGraw from Mets," *Philadelphia Daily News*, December 3, 1974.

91. Red Foley, "Mets Believe! Give Tug 90G," *New York Daily News*, February 15, 1974.

92. McGraw with Yeager, *Ya Gotta Believe!*, 136.

93. Bill Conlin, "Tug No Boone to Tiger Trade," *Philadelphia Daily News*, December 4, 1974.

94. Dolson, *Philadelphia Story*, 188.

95. Carpenter interview.

8. McCarver's Pitch

1. Tim McCarver's 1972 Batting Statistics, Baseball Reference, accessed November 24, 2020, https://www.baseball-reference.com/players/m/mccarti01.shtml.

2. Tim McCarver's 1973 Batting Statistics, Baseball Reference, accessed November 24, 2020, https://www.baseball-reference.com/players/m/mccarti01.shtml.

3. Mike Tomasik, "Leaving the Cardinals Was Twice as Hard for Tim McCarver," *RetroSimba*, August 27, 2014, https://retrosimba.com/2014/08/27/leaving-the-cardinals-was-twice-as-hard-for-tim-mccarver/.

4. McCarver quoted in Frank Dolson, "Like Old Times for McCarver," *Philadelphia Inquirer*, July 2, 1975.

5. McCarver with Robinson, *OH, BABY, I LOVE IT!*, 151.

6. Johnson and Russo quoted in Tomasik, "Leaving the Cardinals Twice as Hard for McCarver."

7. Tim McCarver's 1974 Batting Statistics, Baseball Reference, accessed November 24, 2020, https://www.baseball-reference.com/players/m/mccarti01.shtml.

8. McCarver quoted in Clif Keane, "Fisk's 3 Fill-Ins Say They're Ready and Able," *Boston Globe*, March 15, 1975.

9. McCarver quoted in Leigh Montville, "Timothy McCarver Rises Above," *Boston Globe*, May 19, 1975.

10. Larry Whiteside, "Fisk in, McCarver Out," *Boston Globe*, June 24, 1975.

11. Ray Kelly, "Phils Kick Up Their Heels after Steve Stubs His Toe," *The Sporting News*, April 26, 1975.

12. Steve Carlton's 1975 Pitching Log, Baseball Reference, accessed December 3, 2020, https://www.baseball-reference.com/players/gl.fcgi?id=carltst01&t=p&year=1975.

13. Steve Carlton's 1975 Pitching Log.

14. Steve Carlton's 1975 Pitching Log.

15. Westcott and Bilovsky, *Phillies Encyclopedia*, 88, 151.

16. Westcott and Bilovsky, *Phillies Encyclopedia*, 88; Bruce Markusen, "#Card-Corner: 1981 Topps Tom Underwood," National Baseball Hall of Fame, accessed December 28, 2020, https://baseballhall.org/discover-more/stories/card-corner/1981-tom-underwood-topps-card.

17. Kiner quote found in Allen Lewis, "Montanez Traded to Giants for Maddox," *Philadelphia Inquirer*, May 5, 1975; Westcott, *Phillies Encyclopedia*, 212; and Epstein, *Stars and Strikes*, 28.

18. "Phils Sign Allen, Give Up Essian," *Philadelphia Daily News*, May 7, 1975.

19. See Kashatus, *September Swoon*, 44–47, 204–5. See also Wayne Minshew, "Braves Obtain Allen—but Will He Play?" *The Sporting News*, December 21, 1974; Frank Hyland, "Braves Jump Out of the Frying Pan and into the Fire," *Atlanta Journal*, December 5, 1974; and "Philadelphia Negotiating for Allen," *Philadelphia Inquirer*, February 17, 1975.

20. Dolson, *Philadelphia Story*, 271.

21. Ozark quoted in Dolson, *Philadelphia Story*, 194.

22. Steve Carlton's 1975 Pitching Log.

23. Ozark quoted in Bill Fleischman, "Starters Give Phils the Twitch," *Philadelphia Daily News*, July 2, 1975.

24. Ozark quoted in Frank Dolson, "Super Steve Is Only a Memory," *Philadelphia Inquirer*, July 9, 1975.

25. Ozark quoted in Dolson, "Super Steve Is Only a Memory."

26. Allen Lewis, "Phils Go with Carlton, but Reds Romp, 7–3," *Philadelphia Inquirer*, July 8, 1975.

27. Ozark quoted in Dolson, "Super Steve Is Only a Memory."

28. McCarver interview, May 3, 2018; Frank Dolson, "Like Old Times for McCarver," *Philadelphia Inquirer*, July 2, 1975.

29. McCarver interview, November 9, 2019.

30. Rippelmeyer interview; McCarver with Robinson, OH, BABY, I LOVE IT!, 142.

31. McCarver interview, November 9, 2019.

32. McDermott, *Off Speed*, xi, 135–36. A "fast curve" is how Yale physicist Robert Adair has described the slider. "Thrown at a higher velocity than the standard

curve ball," writes Adair, "the break of the slider is smaller than the deflection of the curve ball and the spin axis is such that the deflection is more nearly left-right than the curve—which, at best, is more of a pure drop." Adair, *Physics of Baseball*, 29.

33. Kepner, *K*, 3 (Young, Bender, and Uhle quotes), 4 (Williams quote), 134–35.

34. Steve Carlton, "The Mechanics of the Slider," in *Philadelphia Phillies Yearbook* (1974), 11.

35. McCarver interview, November 9, 2019.

36. Allen Lewis, "Carlton, Luzinski Bully Astros, 14–2," *Philadelphia Inquirer*, July 13, 1975.

37. Carlton quoted in Lewis, "Carlton, Luzinski Bully Astros, 14–2."

38. Don McKee, "Bowa Steals 6–5 Victory for Phils," *Philadelphia Inquirer*, July 18, 1975.

39. McCarver quoted in Ray Finocchiaro, "Carlton-McCarver Battery Clicks Again for 3-Hitter," *News Journal* (Wilmington DE), July 23, 1975.

40. Finocchiaro, "Carlton-McCarver Battery Clicks Again for 3-Hitter."

41. Oates quoted in Finocchiaro, "Carlton-McCarver Battery Clicks Again for 3-Hitter."

42. McCarver interview, November 9, 2019.

43. Carlton quoted in Finocchiaro, "Carlton-McCarver Battery Clicks Again for 3-Hitter."

44. Ozark quoted in Finocchiaro, "Carlton-McCarver Battery Clicks Again for 3-Hitter."

45. Allen Lewis, "Cards' Outfield Errors Help Phillies Win, 9–4," *Philadelphia Inquirer*, July 27, 1975.

46. McCarver quoted in Lewis, "Cards' Outfield Errors Help Phillies Win, 9–4."

47. Bill Conlin, "Sanguillen Plants the Phils Early," *Philadelphia Daily News*, July 31, 1975.

48. McCarver with Robinson, OH, BABY, I LOVE IT!, 53–54.

49. Marty Appel, "National Pastime Museum: The Chipmunks," Appel PR, accessed September 14, 2021, http://www.appelpr.com/?page_id=3087.

50. Stan Hochman, "Carlton Show a Poor Rerun," *Philadelphia Daily News*, July 31, 1975.

51. Rich Ashburn, "Only Lefty Knows the Answer, and He Isn't Talking," *Philadelphia Daily News*, July 8, 1986.

52. Carpenter interview.

53. Carlton quoted in Shenk, *If These Walls Could Talk*, 33.

54. Allen Lewis, "Hutton's Hit Nips Expos, 5–4, in 10," *Philadelphia Inquirer*, August 4, 1975.

55. Allen Lewis, "Phils Move within Two of Pirates," *Philadelphia Inquirer*, August 10, 1975.

56. Allen Lewis, "Phils Lose Again, 5–4," *Philadelphia Inquirer*, August 14, 1975.

57. Lewis, "Phils Lose Again, 5–4."

58. Frank Dolson, "It's Time to Replacer Danny Ozark," *Philadelphia Inquirer*, August 14, 1975.

59. Westcott and Bilovsky, *Phillies Encyclopedia*, 85–88.

60. "1975 Philadelphia Phillies Roster: 1975 Philadelphia Phillies Salaries," Baseball Almanac, accessed January 3, 2021, https://www.baseball-almanac.com/teamstats/roster.php?y=1975&t=PHI.

61. Allen Lewis, "Phils Beat Braves, Tie Pirates for First," *Philadelphia Inquirer*, August 19, 1975.

62. Bill Conlin, "Phillies Find the REAL Imposter," *Philadelphia Daily News*, August 19, 1975.

63. McCarver interview, November 9, 2019.

64. McCarver with Peary, *McCarver's Baseball for Brain Surgeons*, 44.

65. "Steve Carlton," in *Philadelphia Phillies Yearbook* (1976), 38.

66. Allen Lewis, "For Carlton a One-Hitter, for Taylor 2,000," *Philadelphia Inquirer*, September 27, 1975.

67. Allen Lewis, "Pirates Win Fifth Division Title," *Philadelphia Inquirer*, September 23, 1975.

68. Westcott and Bilovsky, *Phillies Encyclopedia*, 88.

69. Steve Carlton's Pitching Logs, 1973–75, Baseball Reference, accessed January 4, 2021, https://www.baseball-reference.com/players/c/carltst01.shtml.

9. Lefty

1. Epstein, *Stars and Strikes*, 27–30.

2. Helyar, *Lords of the Realm*, 214–15.

3. Bill Conlin, "Is Phillies Camp Suddenly All Wet?" *Philadelphia Daily News*, March 13, 1976.

4. Conlin, "Is Phillies Camp Suddenly All Wet?"

5. Conversation recalled by Tug McGraw, in interview by author, West Chester PA, August 11, 2000.

6. Helyar, *Lords of the Realm*, 214–15; "Collective Bargaining History," Cot's Baseball Contracts, accessed January 5, 2021, https://legacy.baseballprospectus.com/compensation/cots/league-info/cba-history/.

7. Allen Lewis, "Phils Lose Oates and Opener, 5–4," *Philadelphia Inquirer*, April 11, 1976.

8. Allen Lewis, "Gambling Phils Fall to Bucs Again; Schmidt Homers," *Philadelphia Inquirer*, April 12, 1976.

9. Allen Lewis, "Schmidt Hits 4 HRs as Cubs Bow, 18–16," *Philadelphia Inquirer*, April 18, 1976.

10. Allen Lewis, "Phillies Slug Way into First," *Philadelphia Inquirer*, April 25, 1976.

11. Allen Lewis, "Phillies Beat Braves Twice," *Philadelphia Inquirer*, May 2, 1976.

12. Steve Carlton's 1976 Pitching Game Log, Baseball Reference, accessed January 6, 2021, https://www.baseball-reference.com/players/gl.fcgi?id=carltst01&t=p&year=1976.

13. McCarver interview, November 9, 2019.

14. McCarver quoted in Steven Marcus, "Bob and Aaron Boone Have Faced Personal Catcher Situations," *Newsday*, May 5, 2018, https://www.newsday.com/sports/baseball/mlb-personal-catchers-sonny-gray-austin-romine-1.18408639; McCarver quoted in Costello, "All-Important, Ever-Changing Dynamic."

15. Carlton quoted in Marcus, "Bob and Aaron Boone Have Faced Personal Catcher Situations."

16. Carlton quoted in McCarver with Pepe, *Few and Chosen*, 2–3.

17. McCarver quoted in Marcus, "Bob and Aaron Boone Have Faced Personal Catcher Situations."

18. John quoted in "Phillies 1976 Season," in *Philadelphia Phillies Yearbook* (1977), 4.

19. Steve Carlton's 1976 Pitching Game Log.

20. Stan Hochman, "The Phils Get Jolly with Rogers," *Philadelphia Daily News*, June 29, 1976.

21. "Phillies Batting Averages," *Philadelphia Daily News*, July 29, 1976.

22. Bruce Keidan, "Phils Split with Bucs," *Philadelphia Inquirer*, July 5, 1976.

23. McCarver quoted in Bill Lyon, "Tim Enrolled on Trivia List," *Philadelphia Inquirer*, July 5, 1976.

24. McCarver, Hutton, McGraw, and Ozark quoted in Lyon, "Tim Enrolled on Trivia List."

25. Bruce Keidan, "Phillies Sweep Padres, 5–0, 4–2," *Philadelphia Inquirer*, July 11, 1976.

26. Bill Livingston, "Phillies Album: Bob Boone," *Philadelphia Inquirer*, August 25, 1976.

27. "Major League Baseball Averages," *Philadelphia Inquirer*, July 11, 1976.

28. Frank Dolson, "Reds Get a Philadelphia Boo but Get a Cincinnati Show," *Philadelphia Inquirer*, July 14, 1976; "5 Phillie Stars Play but Have 1-for-8 Night," *Philadelphia Inquirer*, July 14, 1976.

29. Boone interview.

30. "National League All Star Squad," *Philadelphia Inquirer*, July 13, 1976.

31. Steve Carlton's 1976 Pitching Game Log.

32. Bruce Keidan, "Phils Romp as Carlton Wins 16th," *Philadelphia Inquirer*, August 25, 1976.

33. McCarver interview, November 9, 2019.

34. Carlton quoted in Kepner, *K*, 2.

35. McCarver with Peary, *Baseball for Brain Surgeons*, 50, 124.

36. McCarver interview, November 9, 2019.

37. Gary Blockus, "Hoefling: The Man behind the Golden Arm," *Morning Call* (Allentown PA), July 5, 1984.

38. Boone interview.

39. Gus Hoefling, interview by author, Lynnville TN, July 6, 2019.

40. Carlton quoted in Kepner, *K*, 15.

41. Hoefling and Bowa interviews; Blockus, "Hoefling"; Westcott, *Tales from the Phillies Dugout*, 150; Giles with Myers, *Pouring Six Beers at a Time*, 252.

42. Hoefling quoted in Mike Sielski, "The Sensei and the Lawsuit," *Philadelphia Inquirer*, July 22, 2020.

43. Lonborg interview.

44. Westcott, *Tales from the Phillies Dugout*, 150; Giles with Myers, *Pouring Six Beers at a Time*, 252.

45. Carlton quoted in Stan Hochman, "The Time Steve Carlton Talked," *Philadelphia Daily News*, May 6, 2013.

46. Bowa interview.

47. Christenson interview.

48. McCarver interview, November 9, 2019.

49. Christenson interview.

50. Hoefling interview.

51. Hoefling quoted in Blockus, "Hoefling."

52. Carlton quoted in Hochman, "Time Steve Carlton Talked."

53. Carlton quoted in Hochman, "Time Steve Carlton Talked."

54. Pat Jordan, "Thin Mountain Air," *Philadelphia Magazine*, April 1994, 91.

55. Christenson interview.

56. Bill Conlin, "Anatomy of a Slump," *Philadelphia Daily News*, September 13, 1976.

57. Allen Lewis, "Reds Stop Phillies, 6–5, in 15 Innings," *Philadelphia Inquirer*, August 30, 1976.

58. Bruce Keidan, "Mets' Ace Outduels Carlton, 1–0," *Philadelphia Inquirer*, September 4, 1976.

59. "Bucs Win 2, Trail Phils by 7½," *Philadelphia Inquirer*, September 4, 1976.

60. Bruce Keidan, "Pirates Stagger Phils, 6–1," *Philadelphia Inquirer*, September 9, 1976.

61. Bill Conlin, "Phils Feeling Their Oates Again," *Philadelphia Daily News*, September 13, 1976; Bill Conlin, "Bucs Keep Bugging the Phillies," *Philadelphia Daily News*, September 16, 1976.

62. McCarver quoted in Conlin, "Bucs Keep Bugging the Phillies."

63. Bill Conlin, "Schmidt Is Going All Out," *Philadelphia Daily News*, September 14, 1976.

64. Bruce Keidan, "Phillies Plug Rain Drain, Defeat Cubs, 4–1," *Philadelphia Inquirer*, September 19, 1976.

65. Bruce Keidan, "Phils Win the Real Debate, 7–3," *Philadelphia Inquirer*, September 24, 1976.

66. Bill Conlin, "Lonborg Revels in Another Clinching," *Philadelphia Daily News*, September 27, 1976.

67. Bruce Keidan, "Carlton Wins 20th as Phillies Get 101st," *Philadelphia Inquirer*, October 4, 1976.

68. Westcott and Bilovsky, *Phillies Encyclopedia*, 89.

69. Wolff, *Baseball Encyclopedia*, 457. See also Walker, *Cincinnati and the Big Red Machine*.

70. For complete 1976 Phillies statistics, see Westcott and Bilovsky, *Phillies Encyclopedia*, 89.

71. Lonborg interview.

72. Bruce Keidan, "Gullett Does It All for Reds; Ninth-Inning Rally Falls Short for Phils as Reds Win, 6–3," *Philadelphia Inquirer*, October 10, 1976.

73. Tata interview.

74. Rose quoted in Keidan, "Gullett Does It All for Reds."

75. Bruce Keidan, "Phils' Backs to Big Red Wall," *Philadelphia Inquirer*, October 11, 1976.

76. Bruce Keidan, "Two Homers in 9th Lead to 7–6 Reds Win and NL Pennant," *Philadelphia Inquirer*, October 13, 1976.

77. Westcott and Bilovsky, *Phillies Encyclopedia*, 89, 354; Chris Wheeler, "Garry Maddox . . . No One Did It Better," in *Philadelphia Phillies Yearbook* (1987), 65; and Dolson, *Philadelphia Story*, 194–96.

78. "1976 NL Cy Young Voting," Baseball Reference, accessed January 15, 2021, https://www.baseball-reference.com/awards/awards_1976.shtml#all_NL_CYA_voting.

79. McCarver interview, December 21, 1999.

80. McCarver with Peary, *Baseball for Brain Surgeons*, 75.

81. McCarver with Peary, *Baseball for Brain Surgeons*, 34, 74–75.

82. Jerry Crawford, interview by author, St. Petersburg FL, May 18, 2020.

83. Carlton quoted in Stephenson, *Lefty*. Carlton also thought pregame meetings were "negative assessments of a pitcher's stuff" because they were predicated on the assumption that the "hitter has the edge, not the pitcher." He explained that "the only thing that anyone tells me in a pregame meeting is what I can't do, not what I can do." Carlton quoted in McCarver with Peary, *Baseball for Brain Surgeons*, 34.

84. Gibson quote recollected in McCarver with Peary, *Baseball for Brain Surgeons*, 75–76.

85. McCarver with Peary, *Baseball for Brain Surgeons*, 75–76

86. McCarver quoted in Fitzpatrick, *You Can't Lose 'Em All*, 89.

10. Closer Than Sixty Feet, Six Inches

1. McCarver with Pepe, *Few and Chosen*, 143.

2. Associated Press, "Baseball's Odd Couple a Boon for Phillies," *Miami Herald*, September 12, 1977.

3. McCarver quoted in Associated Press, "Baseball's Odd Couple."

4. Carlton quoted in Fimrite, "Steve Carlton: Eliminator of the Variables."

5. Carlton quoted in Fimrite, "Steve Carlton: Eliminator of the Variables."

6. McCarver interview, November 9, 2019.

7. Jack Lang, "Carlton Runaway Winner of Cy Young Award in NL," *New York Daily News*, November 12, 1977. Named for the famed right-hander Cy Young, who won 511 games in the Majors, or almost 100 more than any other pitcher in history,

the Cy Young Award was established by MLB commissioner Ford Frick in 1956. Originally, the award was presented to the single best pitcher in the Majors, and the first recipient was Don Newcombe of the Brooklyn Dodgers. In 1967, after Frick retired, the award was given to one pitcher in each league. Ten years later, in 1957, Warren Spahn became the first left-handed pitcher to win the award. In 1963 Sandy Koufax became the first pitcher to win the award in a unanimous vote. Two years later Koufax won his second Cy Young and became the first multiple winner of the award, eventually earning three (1963, 1965–66). Other repeat recipients followed, including Tom Seaver (1969, 1973, 1975), Jim Palmer (1973, 1975–76), Bob Gibson (1968, 1970), and Denny McLain (1968–69). Carlton would become the first pitcher to win the Cy Young Award four times (1972, 1977, 1980, 1982). Since 1982 Carlton has been surpassed by Randy Johnson, a five-time Cy Young Award winner (1995, 1999–2002) and Roger Clemens, who won the award seven times (1986–87, 1991, 1997–98, 2001, 2004). See "Cy Young," National Baseball Hall of Fame, accessed January 15, 2021, https://baseballhall.org/hall-of-famers/young-cy; and "Multiple Cy Young Award Winners, 1965–2004," Baseball Reference, accessed January 19, 2021, https://www.baseball-reference.com/awards/cya.shtml.

8. For the team's complete offensive and defensive statistics in the season, see "1977 Philadelphia Phillies Statistics," Baseball Reference, September 15, 2021, https://www.baseball-reference.com/teams/PHI/1977.shtml. For the most complete account of the 1977 Phillies, see Nathanson, *Fall of the 1977 Phillies*.

9. Bruce Keidan, "Expos Blast by Phillies, 4–3; 3-HR 6th Tops Carlton," *Philadelphia Inquirer*, April 10, 1977.

10. McCarver quoted in Keidan, "Expos Blast by Phillies, 4–3."

11. Bill Conlin, "Phillies Win First on 3,800-Inch Blast," *Philadelphia Daily News*, April 16, 1977.

12. McCarver quoted in Conlin, "Phillies Win First on 3,800-Inch Blast."

13. McCarver with Peary, *Baseball for Brain Surgeons*, 64.

14. Hank Aaron, interview by author, Atlanta GA, November 2, 2017.

15. See "1977 Philadelphia Phillies Schedule," Baseball Almanac, accessed January 20, 2021, https://www.baseball-almanac.com/teamstats/schedule.php?y=1977&t=PHI; and Steve Carlton's 1977 Pitching Game Log, Baseball Reference, accessed January 20, 2021, https://www.baseball-reference.com/players/gl.fcgi?id=carltst01&t=p&year=1977.

16. "Phillies Averages," *Philadelphia Inquirer*, May 1, 1977.

17. Bowa quoted in Frank Fitzpatrick, "The Best That Never Won: 1977 Phillies," *Philadelphia Inquirer*, June 30, 2019.

18. Bowa quote recalled in Christenson interview.

19. Christenson interview.

20. Ray Didinger, "The Kid Is Now the Key," *Philadelphia Bulletin's Discover Magazine*, April 2, 1978, 21.

21. Allen Lewis, "Phillies Blanked by Mets," *Philadelphia Inquirer*, June 5, 1977; Allen Lewis, "Phils Lose Another One in 9th, 5–4," *Philadelphia Inquirer*, June 5, 1977.

22. Carlton quoted in Fitzpatrick, *You Can't Lose 'Em All*, 89; Carlton quoted in Stephenson, *Lefty*.

23. Westcott, *Tales from the Phillies Dugout*, 126; Cook, *Ten Innings at Wrigley*, 98; Larry Steward, "Now It Comes Out, Carlton Is Really Pretty Good Talker," *Los Angeles Times*, September 1, 1989.

24. Bill Conlin, "Reds Best Bet to Get Seaver," *Philadelphia Daily News*, June 14, 1977.

25. Westcott and Bilovsky, *Phillies Encyclopedia*, 217–18.

26. McCarver quoted in Allen Lewis, "Carlton's 9th Victory His 100th as a Phillie," *Philadelphia Inquirer*, June 20, 1977.

27. Bowa quoted in Bruce Keidan, "Bowa's Slam Rocks Reds, 15–9," *Philadelphia Inquirer*, June 23, 1977.

28. "Phillies Averages," *Philadelphia Inquirer*, June 26, 1977.

29. Steve Carlton's 1977 Pitching Game Log.

30. Ozark quoted in Allen Lewis, "Carlton Pitched Past Pain," *Philadelphia Inquirer*, July 18, 1977.

31. Garry Maddox quoted in Stephenson, *Lefty*.

32. Rippelmeyer interview.

33. McCarver quoted in Lewis, "Carlton Pitched Past Pain."

34. Steve Carlton's 1977 Pitching Game Log.

35. McCarver quoted in Allen Lewis, "Phillies Slam Astros by 7–3," *Philadelphia Inquirer*, August 22, 1977.

36. Steve Carlton's 1977 Pitching Game Log.

37. McCarver with Robinson, *OH, BABY, I LOVE IT!*, 53.

38. Carlton quoted in Stephenson, *Lefty*.

39. Carlton quoted in Rotfeld, *Steve Carlton*.

40. Schmidt interview.

41. McCarver interview, November 9, 2019.

42. Boone interview.

43. McCarver interview, November 9, 2019.

44. Schmidt interview.

45. Ozark quoted in Bruce Keidan, "Carlton 1st to Reach 20th, 11–1," *Philadelphia Inquirer*, September 6, 1977.

46. Bowa quoted in Keidan, "Carlton 1st to Reach 20th, 11–1."

47. Bruce Keidan, "Carlton Beats Cards, Whiffs 14," *Philadelphia Inquirer*, September 10, 1977.

48. Steve Carlton's 1977 Pitching Game Log.

49. Christenson interview.

50. Allen Lewis, "Phillies Win East Title on Christenson's Slam," *Philadelphia Inquirer*, September 28, 1977.

51. Frank Dolson, "That Was No Party . . . This Was a Volcano," *Philadelphia Inquirer*, September 28, 1977; McCarver interview, December 21, 1999.

52. McCarver quoted in Fitzpatrick, "Best That Never Won." Janitor in a Drum was a frequently advertised cleaning product.

53. Tim McCarver's Career Statistics, Baseball Reference, accessed February 2, 2021, https://www.baseball-reference.com/players/m/mccarti01.shtml. OPS+, or adjusted on-base percentage plus slugging percentage, measures a player's overall offensive production by calculating the ability of a player to get on base and to hit for power. The metric also adjusts the player's OPS score to reflect such variables as the dimensions of the park, run-scoring environment, or league in which he plays.

54. Jack Lang, "Carlton Runaway Winner of Cy Young Award in NL," *New York Daily News*, November 12, 1977.

55. Boone interview.

56. McCarver with Robinson, *OH, BABY, I LOVE IT!*, 55–56.

57. "Los Angeles Dodgers Team Statistics, 1977," in *Phillies vs. Dodgers: 1977 National League Championship Series Souvenir Program* (Philadelphia: Phillies, 1977), 31.

58. "Phillies vs. Dodgers—1977," in *Phillies vs. Dodgers* (souvenir program), 40–41.

59. Bruce Keidan, "Phils Win Wild One in West; Dodgers Waste Cey Slam," *Philadelphia Inquirer*, October 5, 1977.

60. Schmidt quoted in Frank Dolson, "The Grand Slam's Bang Didn't Scare the Phils," *Philadelphia Inquirer*, October 5, 1977.

61. Bruce Keidan, "Sutton Cools Off Phils, 7–1," *Philadelphia Inquirer*, October 6, 1977; Bill Conlin, "Don Sutton Revives Dodgers," *Philadelphia Daily News*, October 6, 1977.

62. Bruce Keidan, "It Was Giveaway Day at the Vet; Dodgers Score 3 in 9th for 6–5 Win," *Philadelphia Inquirer*, October 8, 1977.

63. Bowa quoted in Keidan, "It Was Giveaway Day at the Vet."

64. Stan Hochman, "Bad Bounces Tell the Tale," *Philadelphia Daily News*, October 10, 1977.

65. Keidan, "It Was Giveaway Day at the Vet."

66. Bowa quoted in Bloom, *Larry Bowa*, 31.

67. Keidan, "It Was Giveaway Day at the Vet."

68. Rich Hebner, interview by author, Norwood MA, October 15, 2017.

69. Ozark quoted in Bill Conlin, "Phillies Can't Dodge Disaster," *Philadelphia Daily News*, October 8, 1977. Years later, in 2005, Ozark would stick with the same reasoning—that he "wanted to keep Luzinski's bat in the lineup if we fell behind." Ozark interview.

70. Keidan, "It Was Giveaway Day at the Vet."

71. Frank Dolson, "For Phils, 'Tomorrow Is Another Day,'" *Philadelphia Inquirer*, October 8, 1977.

72. Ozark quoted in Dolson, "For Phils, 'Tomorrow Is Another Day.'"

73. Ozark quoted in Conlin, "Phillies Can't Dodge Disaster"; and Fitzpatrick, *You Can't Lose 'Em All*, 52.

74. Dolson, *Philadelphia Story*, 207.

75. Bill Conlin, "Phils Couldn't Win Big One—Again," *Philadelphia Daily News*, October 10, 1977; Bruce Keidan, "There Is No Joy in Mudville, John Drowns Phillies' Hopes," *Philadelphia Inquirer*, October 9, 1977.

76. McCarver quoted in Stan Hochman, "Rain, Bad Bounces: A Phillies Autopsy," *Philadelphia Daily News*, October 10, 1977.

77. Keidan, "There Is No Joy in Mudville, John Drowns Phillies' Hopes."

78. McCarver quoted in Frank Dolson, "Phils' Dreams Washed Away," *Philadelphia Inquirer*, October 9, 1977.

79. Frank Dolson, "They Lost as a Team," *Philadelphia Inquirer*, October 10, 1977.

11. Mastery and Mystery

1. George Vecsey, "Strong and Silent," *New York Times*, June 6, 1983; Boswell, "Steve Carlton: Defiant"; Stephenson, *Lefty*.

2. Carlton quoted in Boswell, "Steve Carlton: Defiant."

3. Conversation recollected in Christenson interview.

4. Stan Hochman, "Why, Oh Why, Won't Super Steve Carlton Talk Shop with Us?" *Phillies '78 Baseball Guide, Philadelphia Daily News*, April 6, 1978.

5. Hochman, "Why, Oh Why, Won't Super Steve Carlton Talk Shop with Us?"

6. McCarver quoted in Hochman, "Why, Oh Why, Won't Super Steve Carlton Talk Shop with Us?"

7. McCarver quoted in Red Smith, "Sports of The Times: Again the Cy Young Award," *New York Times*, November 5, 1980.

8. Ruly Carpenter quoted in Hochman, "Why, Oh Why, Won't Super Steve Carlton Talk Shop with Us?"

9. Stephenson, *Lefty*.

10. Carlton quoted in Giles with Myers, *Pouring Six Beers at a Time*, 252.

11. Boswell, "Steve Carlton: Defiant"; Vecsey, "Strong and Silent."

12. Boswell, "Steve Carlton: Defiant"; Vecsey, "Strong and Silent."

13. Conversation recalled by Randy Lerch in interview by author, Shingle Springs CA, September 9, 2019.

14. Owens quoted in Didinger, "Kid Is Now the Key," 23.

15. Larry Eichel, "Carlton Rocked in 5–1 Loss," *Philadelphia Inquirer*, April 8, 1978; Frank Dolson, "Phillies Justify Fans' Lukewarm Greeting," *Philadelphia Inquirer*, April 8, 1978.

16. Larry Eichel, "Phillies Win in 9th, 4–3," *Philadelphia Inquirer*, April 15, 1978.

17. Steve Carlton's 1978 Pitching Game Log, Baseball Reference, accessed February 22, 2021, https://www.baseball-reference.com/players/gl.fcgi?id=carltst01&t=p&year=1978.

18. Steve Carlton's 1978 Pitching Game Log.

19. "Phillies Averages," *Philadelphia Inquirer*, May 21, 1978.

20. For McCarver's hitting performances, see "Phillies 1978 Game Schedule," Baseball Almanac, accessed February 22, 2021, https://www.baseball-almanac.com/teamstats/schedule.php?y=1978&t=PHI.

21. Steve Carlton's 1978 Pitching Game Log.

22. Christenson quoted in Stephenson, *Lefty*.

23. Larry Eichel, "Carlton a Loser by 7–2," *Philadelphia Inquirer*, July 20, 1978.

24. Carlton quoted in Stan Hochman, "Carlton Gets 200th Victory," *Philadelphia Daily News*, July 24, 1978.

25. McCarver with Robinson, *OH, BABY, I LOVE IT!*, 54.

26. Vukovich and McCarver quoted in Stephenson, *Lefty*.

27. Quotes recalled by Greg Luzinski in interview by author, Philadelphia PA, August 3, 2015; and Christenson interview.

28. Bill Conlin, "Phils Show Where Bucs Stop," *Philadelphia Daily News*, August 7, 1978.

29. Steve Carlton's 1978 Pitching Game Log.

30. "National League Standings," *Philadelphia Inquirer*, September 1, 1978. The Montreal Expos, St. Louis Cardinals, and New York Mets were just playing out the schedule, being twelve games or more behind in the National League East standings.

31. Steve Carlton's 1978 Pitching Game Log.

32. Tim McCarver's 1978 Batting Game Log, Baseball Reference, accessed February 28, 2021, https://www.baseball-reference.com/players/gl.fcgi?id=mccarti01&year=1978.

33. Larry Eichel, "Pirates Sweep Phillies on a Balk," *Philadelphia Inquirer*, September 30, 1978.

34. Larry Eichel, "Phillies Win 3rd Straight East title," *Philadelphia Inquirer*, October 1, 1978.

35. Larry Eichel, "Garvey's 2 Homers Lead the Way," *Philadelphia Inquirer*, October 5, 1978.

36. Larry Eichel, "John Silences Phillies Bats; LA Wins, 4–0," *Philadelphia Inquirer*, October 6, 1978.

37. Bill Conlin, "Lefty Gives Phils a Lift," *Philadelphia Daily News*, October 7, 1978; Larry Eichel, "Phils Bounce Back Smartly, 9–4," *Philadelphia Inquirer*, October 7, 1978.

38. Frank Dolson, "Maddox to Be Remembered for What He Can't Forget," *Philadelphia Inquirer*, October 8, 1978.

39. Larry McMullen, "Fans Disappointed Once Again," *Philadelphia Daily News*, October 9, 1978.

40. Carpenter interview.

41. Bowa interview.

42. For Carlton's postseason statistics, see Wolff, *Baseball Encyclopedia*, 1426.

43. Joseph Durso, "Rose Signs with Phillies," *New York Times*, December 6, 1978.

44. Cook, *Ten Innings at Wrigley*, 3.

45. Yeager quoted in Bill Conlin, "Timmy Caught by Surprise; Boone Works Carlton in Phillies' Win," *Philadelphia Daily News*, May 8, 1979.

46. Jayson Stark, "Carlton Pitches, McCarver Sits," *Philadelphia Inquirer*, May 8, 1979.

47. McCarver quoted in Stark, "Carlton Pitches, McCarver Sits."

48. Conlin, "Timmy Caught by Surprise."

49. McCarver quoted in Conlin, "Timmy Caught by Surprise."

50. Steve Carlton's 1979 Pitching Game Log, Baseball Reference, accessed March 2, 2021, https://www.baseball-reference.com/players/gl.fcgi?id=carltst01&t=p&year=1979. Between May 16 and June 30, when McCarver was catching, Carlton defeated the Cubs twice, 13–0 and 6–4; the Cardinals, 5–3; the Astros, 8–0; and the Braves, 10–4. He lost to the Reds, 4–2; the Braves, 10–3; and the Cubs, 8–2. Although Carlton started against the Reds on June 16 and the Cards on June 30, he did not get the decision in either victory.

51. Conlin, "Timmy Caught by Surprise."

52. Lerch interview.

53. Jayson Stark, "Phils Nail Cards in 10th," *Philadelphia Inquirer*, July 1, 1979.

54. McCarver quoted in Bill Conlin, "Lefty's Big 0–2 Mistake," *Philadelphia Daily News*, July 2, 1979.

55. Quote recalled in Ozark interview.

56. Stark, "Phils Nail Cards in 10th."

57. Bowa quoted in Frank Dolson, "Is Ozark Mean Enough to Discipline Phils?" *Philadelphia Inquirer*, July 1, 1979.

58. Ozark quoted in Conlin, "Lefty's Big 0–2 Mistake."

59. Fitzpatrick, *You Can't Lose 'Em All!*, 60.

60. Hochman quoted in Rich Ashburn, "Only Lefty Knows the Answer and He Isn't Talking," *Philadelphia Daily News*, July 9, 1986.

61. Carlton quoted in Stan Hochman, "Carlton: Winning on His Mind," *Philadelphia Daily News*, July 5, 1979.

62. Carlton quoted in Hochman, "Carlton: Winning on His Mind."

63. Ashburn, "Only Lefty Knows the Answer and He Isn't Talking."

64. Bill Conlin, "Ozark Out, Green In," *Philadelphia Daily News*, September 1, 1979.

65. Ozark interview.

66. Carpenter interview.

67. Westcott and Bilovsky, *Phillies Encyclopedia*, 354–55.

68. Dallas Green quoted in Bill Conlin, "Green Starts an Inspection," *Philadelphia Daily News*, September 1, 1979.

69. Dallas Green, interview by author, West Chester PA, October 13, 2015. See also Green with Maimon, *Mouth That Roared*.

70. Steve Carlton's 1979 Pitching Game Log. With Boone behind the plate, Carlton defeated the San Diego Padres, 11–6, on May 7; the New York Mets, 1–0, on July 5; the San Francisco Giants, 5–3, on July 8; the Padres, 4–3, on July 12; the Houston Astros, 3–2, on August 19; and the Chicago Cubs, 9–8, on September 8. He lost to the Giants, 2–1, on May 11, and again, 4–1, on July 21.

71. Jayson Stark, "Phils Wilt before Reds by 2–1 in 10," *Philadelphia Inquirer*, August 15, 1979.

72. Conlin, "Timmy Caught by Surprise."

73. Carlton quoted in Stephenson, *Lefty*.

74. Christenson interview.

75. Jayson Stark, "Carlton Throws the Expos into Winter," *Philadelphia Inquirer*, October 1, 1979.

76. McCarver quoted in Stark, "Carlton Throws the Expos into Winter."

77. Sam Carchidi, "A Pitching Great Is Remembered as Being Strange, Shy, Aloof and the Best," *Philadelphia Inquirer*, July 31, 1994.

78. McCarver quoted in Jayson Stark, "McCarver Retires a Bit Reluctantly," *Philadelphia Inquirer*, September 30, 1979.

12. Cooperstown Bound

1. Murray Chass, "Phillies' Carlton, at 35, Wins Cy Young Award a Third Time," *New York Times*, November 5, 1980.

2. Green, *Mouth That Roared*, 107–8; Larry Christenson's 1980 Pitching Game Log, Baseball Reference, accessed March 18, 2021, https://www.baseball-reference.com/players/gl.fcgi?id=chrisla01&t=p&year=1980; Randy Lerch's 1980 Pitching Game Log, Baseball Reference, accessed March 18, 2021, https://www.baseball-reference.com/players/gl.fcgi?id=lerchra01&t=p&year=1980.

3. Fitzpatrick, *You Can't Lose 'Em All*, 111.

4. Green interview; Green, *Mouth That Roared*, 106. For Carlton's toleration of Green, see Christenson, Boone, Lerch, and Ruthven interviews. See also Cook, *Ten Innings at Wrigley*, 163; and Fitzpatrick, *You Can't Lose 'Em All*, 102.

5. Green, *Mouth That Roared*, 108.

6. Fitzpatrick, *You Can't Lose 'Em All*, 138–40.

7. Boone interview.

8. Sparky Lyle, interview by author, Voorhees NJ, August 10, 2005.

9. Danny Robbins, "Carlton One-Hits Cards," *Philadelphia Inquirer*, April 27, 1980.

10. Lewis Freedman, "Carlton Defeats San Diego, 3–1, Strikes Out 13," *Philadelphia Inquirer*, June 15, 1980; Jayson Stark, "Carlton Wins 12, Phils Trim Padres," *Philadelphia Inquirer*, June 19, 1980.

11. Jayson Stark, "Phils Down Cubs on Carlton's 2-Hitter," *Philadelphia Inquirer*, October 2, 1980.

12. Steve Wulf, "Dilly of a Win for Philly," *Sports Illustrated*, October 13, 1980, 92, 94.

13. Ron Fimrite, "Wow, What a Playoff," *Sports Illustrated*, October 20, 1980, 20–22.

14. Green, *Mouth That Roared*, 139.

15. Jayson Stark, "Rally Beats Royals as McBride Homers, McGraw Saves Walk," *Philadelphia Inquirer*, October 15, 1980.

16. Ron Fimrite, "One Heart Stopper after Another," *Sports Illustrated*, October 27, 1980, 27.

17. McGraw interview.

18. Ron Fimrite, "A Tugger at the Heartstrings," *Sports Illustrated*, November 3, 1980, 24–25; Jayson Stark, "Phillies Do It! Carlton, Tug KO Royals," *Philadelphia Inquirer*, October 22, 1980.

19. Bill Lyon, "And Then There Was Steve Carlton . . . ," *Philadelphia Inquirer*, October 22, 1980.

20. Carlton to McCarver, quoted in Red Smith, "Sports of The Times: Again the Cy Young Award."

21. Lyon, "And Then There Was Steve Carlton . . ."

22. Fitzpatrick, *You Can't Lose 'Em All*, 228.

23. Carlton quoted in Shenk, *If These Walls Could Talk*, 185.

24. Beverly Carlton quoted in McGraw with Kashatus, *Was It as Good for You?*, 49.

25. Chass, "Phillies' Carlton, at 35, Wins Cy Young Award a Third Time."

26. McCarver, whose MLB career spanned the time period 1959 to 1980, was one of only seven catchers to play in parts of four decades. The others are Deacon McGuire (1884–1912), Jack O'Connor (1887–1912), Jack Ryan (1889–1913), Choji Murata (1968–90), Rick Dempsey (1969–92), and Carlton Fisk (1969–93). Those catchers belong to an elite group of just thirty-two MLB players who accomplished the rare feat. See Andrew Simon and David Adler, "These Players' Careers Spanned 4 Decades," MLB.com, April 14, 2020, https://www.mlb.com/news/four-decade-players-c300996490.

27. Boone interview.

28. Jayson Stark, "Carlton Fans 3,000th as Phils Beat Expos, 6–2," *Philadelphia Inquirer*, April 30, 1981.

29. Associated Press, "Chronology of the Baseball Strike," *New York Times*, August 1, 1981. For the most complete account of the split season of 1981, see Katz, *Split Season*.

30. Helyar, *Lords of the Realm*, 286.

31. Steve Carlton's Career Pitching Statistics, Baseball Reference, accessed March 23, 2021, https://www.baseball-reference.com/players/c/carltst01.shtml.

32. Voigt, *American Baseball*, 351–52.

33. Jason Foster, "MLB Playoffs: Remembering the Expos' Semi-forgotten 1981 NLDS win," *The Sporting News*, October 12, 2017.

34. Jayson Stark, "Carlton Struggles in 3–1 Loss," *Philadelphia Inquirer*, October 8, 1981.

35. Westcott and Bilovsky, *Phillies Encyclopedia*, 496–97.

36. Jayson Stark, "Phils Out-Hit Expos to Stay Alive," *Philadelphia Inquirer*, October 10, 1981.

37. Jayson Stark, "Phils Win on Vukovich's 10th Inning Homer," *Philadelphia Inquirer*, October 11, 1981.

38. Gary Carter, interview by author, West Palm Beach FL, July 20, 2005.

39. Jayson Stark, "Expos Win NL East behind Rogers, 3–0," *Philadelphia Inquirer*, October 12, 1981.

40. Chuck Newman, "Bidding Ended Early for Some; Persistence Helped Giles Win the Battle," *Philadelphia Inquirer*, October 30, 1981.

41. Kashatus, *Almost a Dynasty*, 247–49.

42. See Christenson, Schmidt, and Ruly Carpenter interviews; and Bill Giles, interview by author, Philadelphia PA, November 18, 2017.

43. Lyle interview.

44. Dan Stephenson, interview by author, Woodbine NJ, August 10, 2019.

45. Darren Daulton, interview by author, Jenkintown PA, June 3, 2013.

46. Carlton quoted in Stephenson, *Lefty*.

47. Daulton interview.

48. Carman quoted in Stephenson, *Lefty*; Christenson interview.

49. Stephenson interview.

50. Anonymous quote in McCarver with Pepe, *Few and Chosen*, 151.

51. Conversation recalled in Kerrane, *"Batting Cleanup, Bill Conlin,"* 66.

52. Shenk interview.

53. Since 1982, when Carlton won his fourth and final Cy Young Award, his record has been surpassed by Roger Clemens (seven Cy Youngs), Randy Johnson (five), and matched by Greg Maddux (four).

54. "1982 MLB Pitching Leaders," Baseball Reference, accessed April 1, 2021, https://www.baseball-reference.com/leagues/MLB/1982-pitching-leaders.shtml.

55. Palmer and Lasorda quoted in "Steve Carlton: Setting the Standards," in *Philadelphia Phillies Yearbook* (1983), 40.

56. "Steve Carlton of the Philadelphia Phillies Monday Agreed to $4.15 Million Contract," *Philadelphia Inquirer*, March 4, 1983.

57. Giles interview.

58. Westcott and Bilovsky, *Phillies Encyclopedia*, 95–96.

59. Stan Hochman, "One Nickname for Phillies' Aces Rises to the Top," *Philadelphia Daily News*, December 21, 2010.

60. Bill Lyon, "Bench Steals Show with His 2,000th Hit," *Philadelphia Inquirer*, May 5, 1983.

61. "Johnny Bench Was Nemesis of Steve Carlton," *RetroSimba*, updated July 26, 2018, https://retrosimba.com/2011/08/05/johnny-bench-was-nemesis-of-steve-carlton/.

62. Bench quoted in Lyon, "Bench Steals Show with His 2,000th Hit."

63. Peter Pascarelli, "Reds Fall; Carlton Wins 4th," *Philadelphia Inquirer*, May 5, 1983.

64. Westcott and Bilovsky, *Phillies Encyclopedia*, 95–96.

65. Jayson Stark, "Carlton Wins 300th," *Philadelphia Inquirer*, September 24, 1983.

66. Carlton quoted in Shenk, *If These Walls Could Talk*, 34.

67. Kepner, *K*, 15.

68. Kevin Stiner, "Nolan Ryan Eclipses Walter Johnson's Strikeout Record," *Inside Pitch*, National Baseball Hall of Fame, accessed April 1, 2021, https://baseballhall.org/discover-more/stories/inside-pitch/nolan-ryan-eclipses-walter-johnsons-strikeout-record.

69. Carlton quoted in Shenk, *If These Walls Could Talk*, 33.

70. Craig Muder, "Carlton Becomes Lefty Strikeout King," *Inside Pitch*, National Baseball Hall of Fame, accessed April 3, 2021, https://baseballhall.org/discover/inside-pitch/steve-carlton-becomes-lefty-strikeout-king. Ironically, Nolan Ryan never expected to win the career strikeout crown. Since he relied on his fastball and, by his own admission, "always pitched with maximum effort," Ryan believed that Carlton, who relied on his slider and was in excellent physical condition, would pitch much longer. See Kepner, *K*, 45.

71. Westcott and Bilovsky, *Phillies Encyclopedia*, 148.

72. Westcott and Bilovsky, *Phillies Encyclopedia*, 503.

73. Westcott and Bilovsky, *Phillies Encyclopedia*, 96–105. Between 1984 and 1993 the Phillies finished higher than fourth place in the NL East just two times: 1986, when they finished a distant twenty-one and a half games behind the world champion New York Mets, and 1991, when they finished third, twenty games behind the Pittsburgh Pirates.

74. Westcott and Bilovsky, *Phillies Encyclopedia*, 148.

75. Giles interview.

76. McCarver interview, November 9, 2019.

77. Giles quoted in Peter Pascarelli, "The Phillies Release Steve Carlton," *Philadelphia Inquirer*, June 26, 1986.

78. Westcott and Bilovsky, *Phillies Encyclopedia*, 148.

79. Vivanco, "Steve Carlton." When the Twins won the World Series that year, the team made the customary visit to the White House to receive congratulations from the president. In the official photo of the team with President Reagan, all of Carlton's teammates were listed by name, but he was listed as an unidentified Secret Service agent. See Steve Wulf, "Scorecard," *Sports Illustrated*, November 9, 1987, 13.

80. Carlton quoted in Peter Pascarelli, "Night of Guests, Gifts and Gratitude," *Philadelphia Inquirer*, July 30, 1989.

81. Carlton quoted in Stephenson, *Lefty*.

82. Jordan, "Thin Mountain Air," 89–90. Jordan, a former Minor League pitcher, visited Carlton's farm on the eve of his induction into the National Baseball Hall of Fame. In his essay, he implied that the former Phillies pitcher was not only fanatical in his political and economic opinions but also antisemitic.

After *Philadelphia Magazine* published the piece, McCarver rushed to Carlton's defense, insisting that his friend was not a bigot or an anti-Semite. "Steve is a very complicated person," McCarver told Murray Chass of the *New York Times*. "If he's guilty of anything, it's believing some of the material he reads. Does he become confused about reading radical things? Yes, I've told him that. Does that translate into him being anti-Semitic? No." McCarver quoted in Murray Chass, "Was Silence Better for Steve Carlton?" *New York Times*, April 14, 1994.

Ironically, even Bill Conlin of the *Philadelphia Daily News*, who was largely responsible for Carlton's refusal to talk to the press during his MLB career, came to the pitcher's defense. "Pat Jordan is either naïve or mean-spirited," wrote Conlin in his August 1, 1994, column. "Lefty, cursed by an informal education that selectively rejects many of life's unpleasant truths, probably could not supply a working definition of 'anti-Semitism.' Carlton is an elitist, pure and simple. He has contempt for the middle class that spawned him, not for any particular race, color or creed." Conlin, "Sphinx of the Schuylkill."

83. Jayson Stark, "Lefty Nearly Pitches Shutout; with 95.8% of the Votes, Carlton Sweeps into the Hall of Fame," *Philadelphia Inquirer*, January 13, 1994.

84. "Steve Carlton: Appearances on Leaderboards, Awards, and Honors," Baseball Reference, accessed April 5, 2021, https://www.baseball-reference.com/players/c/carltst01.shtml.

85. See Ron Smith, *"The Sporting News" Selects Baseball's Greatest Players*, 70–71.

86. Sam Carchidi, "Four Legends Honored with Statues," *Philadelphia Inquirer*, April 13, 2004.

87. McCarver quoted in Kerrane, *Hurlers*, 144.

88. McCarver interview, May 3, 2018.

89. Cosell had been removed from ABC television broadcasts altogether after excerpts from his controversial book *I Never Played the Game*, which was critical of Cosell's coworkers at ABC Sports, appeared in *TV Guide*.

90. McCarver interview, May 3, 2018.

91. "Tim McCarver Retirement: Joe Buck's Send-Off for Broadcasting Partner Was Classy," *Los Angeles Times*, October 31, 2013.

92. McCarver was occasionally taken to task for being overly analytical and critical of individual players and management. For example, during the 1992 National League Championship Series, he criticized Braves outfielder Deion Sanders, who also had become an NFL star, for playing both sports on the same day. Angered by the remark, Sanders dumped a bucket of water on McCarver three times while he was covering the National League pennant–winning Atlanta Braves' clubhouse celebration for CBS. After being doused with the water, McCarver shouted at Sanders, "You are a real man, Deion. I'll say that." See Pete McEntegart, *The 10 Spot* (blog), January 14, 2007, accessed September 3, 2019 (no longer available).

Again, in October 2008, just before the 2008 NLCS, McCarver made public his feelings about Dodger Manny Ramirez, calling him "despicable." He also criticized Ramirez for his perceived sloppy, lazy play in Boston and how he had suddenly turned it around in Los Angeles. Ramirez declined comment. See Anthony McCarron, "Tim McCarver Calls Dodgers Slugger Manny Ramirez 'Despicable,'" *New York Daily News*, October 8, 2008.

In 2010 McCarver compared the New York Yankees' treatment of former manager Joe Torre to the treatment that Nazi Germany and the Stalinist Soviet state meted out to generals who fell out of favor with their leaders. After receiving negative comments on his position, McCarver apologized. "McCarver Calls Comments Inappropriate," ESPN, July 20, 2010, https://www.espn.com/new-york/mlb/news/story?id=5394349.

93. "'I Am by No Means Retiring': Tim McCarver to Leave Broadcast Booth after Season," CBS *News New York*, March 27, 2013, https://newyork.cbslocal.com/2013/03/27/mlb-analyst-tim-mccarver-to-step-down-from-weekly-mlb-broadcast-after-season/; Jenifer Langosch, "Cards Set to Add Tim McCarver to Broadcast Team," MLB.com, December 8, 2013, https://www.mlb.com/cardinals/news/st-louis-cardinals-set-to-add-tim-mccarver-to-broadcast-team/c-64492348.

94. Associated Press, "Tim McCarver Wins Frick Award," ESPN, December 7, 2011, https://www.espn.com/mlb/hof11/story/_/id/7326715/tim-mccarver-wins-hall-fame-ford-c-frick-award.

95. McCarver quoted in "Steve Carlton Night at the Phillies: July 29, 1989," *Philadelphia Phillies Souvenir Program* (1989), 1.

Appendix A

1. Julian McCracken, email to author, April 3, 2021.

2. McCracken email.

3. Doug Niblock, "200 Game Batteries," High Heat Stats, updated March 20, 2021, http://www.highheatstats.com/2016/01/200-game-batteries/. Between 1901 and 2020, there were a total of 90 batteries that made 150+ starts together, 309 batteries with 100+ starts together, and 1,385 batteries with 50+ starts together.

4. Niblock, "200 Game Batteries."

5. Niblock, "200 Game Batteries."

6. Niblock, "200 Game Batteries."

7. Doug Niblock, email to author, April 25, 2021.

BIBLIOGRAPHY

Adair, Robert. *The Physics of Baseball*. New York: Harper & Row, 1990.

Armour, Mark. "Bing Devine." In Stahl and Nowlin, *Drama and Pride in the Gateway City*, 271–75.

Belth, Alex. *Stepping Up: The Story of Curt Flood and His Fight for Baseball Players' Rights*. New York: Persea, 2006.

Bernstein, Ralph. "Steve Carlton." In *Philadelphia Phillies Yearbook*. Philadelphia: Phillies, 1972.

Bloom, Barry M. *Larry Bowa: "I Still Hate to Lose."* Champaign IL: Sports Publishing, 2004.

Borst, Bill. *Still Last in the American League: The St. Louis Browns Revisited*. West Bloomfield MI: Altwerger & Mandel, 1992.

Bowa, Larry, with Barry Bloom. *Bleep! Larry Bowa Manages*. Chicago: Bonus Books, 1988.

Bright, Cameron. *The 1967 American League Pennant Race: Four Teams, Six Weeks, One Winner*. Jefferson NC: McFarland, 2018.

Broeg, Bob, and Jerry Vickery. *The St. Louis Cardinals Encyclopedia*. Chicago: Masters Press, 1998.

Bucci, Steve, and Dave Brown. *Drinking Coffee with a Fork: The Story of Steve Carlton and the '72 Phillies*. Philadelphia: Camino Books, 2011.

Burrows, Edwin G., and Mike Wallace. *Gotham: A History of New York City to 1898*. New York: Oxford University Press, 1999.

Cantor, George. *The Tigers of '68: Baseball's Last Real Champions*. Lanham MD: Taylor Trade, 1997.

Clifton, Merritt. "Juan Marichal." In Shatzkin, *The Ballplayers*, 667–68.

Cook, Kevin. *Ten Innings at Wrigley*. New York: Henry Holt, 2019.

Devine, Bing, with Tom Wheatley. *The Memoirs of Bing Devine: Stealing Lou Brock and Other Brilliant Moves by a Master G.M.* [Champaign IL]: Sports Publishing, 2004.

Dolson, Frank. *Jim Bunning: Baseball and Beyond*. Philadelphia: Temple University Press, 1998.

———. *The Philadelphia Story: City of Winners*. South Bend IN: Icarus Press, 1981.

———. "Steve Carlton." In *Annual Baseball Hall of Fame Program*. Cooperstown NY: National Baseball Hall of Fame and The Sporting News, 1994.

Donley, Brendan. *An October to Remember 1968: The Tigers-Cardinals World Series as Told by the Men Who Played in It*. New York: Skyhorse, 2018.

Drysdale, Don, with Bob Verdi. *Once a Bum, Always a Dodger: My Life in Baseball from Brooklyn to Los Angeles*. New York: St. Martin's Press, 1990.

Edmunds, Edmund P., and William H. Manz, eds. *Baseball and Antitrust: The Legislative History of the Curt Flood Act of 1998, Public Law No., 105–297, 112 Stat. 2824*. Buffalo NY: William S. Hein, 2001.

Eisenbath, Mike. *The Cardinals Encyclopedia*. Philadelphia: Temple University, Press, 1999.

Epstein, Dan. *Big Hair and Plastic Grass: A Funky Ride through Baseball and America in the Swinging '70s*. New York: St. Martin's Griffin, 2014.

———. *Stars and Strikes: Baseball and America in the Bicentennial Summer of '76*. New York: Thomas Dunne Books, 2014.

Fitzpatrick, Frank. *You Can't Lose 'Em All: The Year the Phillies Finally Won the World Series*. Dallas TX: Taylor Trade, 2001.

Flood, Curt, with Richard Carter. *The Way It Is*. New York: Trident Press, 1971.

Florio, John, and Ouisie Shapiro. *One Nation under Baseball: How the 1960s Collided with the National Pastime*. Lincoln: University of Nebraska Press, 2017.

Funakoshi, Gichin. *Karate-Do Kyohan: The Master Text*. New York: Penguin Random House/Kodansha USA, 2013.

Gallagher, Tom. "Don Drysdale." In Shatzkin, *The Ballplayers*, 294–95.

Gibson, Bob, with Lonnie Wheeler. *Stranger to the Game: The Autobiography of Bob Gibson*. New York: Viking, 1994.

Giles, Bill, with Doug Myers. *Pouring Six Beers at a Time and Other Stories from a Lifetime in Baseball*. Chicago: Triumph Books, 2007.

Green, Dallas, with Alan Maimon. *The Mouth That Roared: My Six Outspoken Decades in Baseball*. Chicago: Triumph Books, 2013.

Halberstam, David. *October 1964*. New York: Villard Books, 1994.

Helyar, John. *Lords of the Realm: The Real History of Baseball*. New York: Villard, 1994.

Hochman, Stan. *Mike Schmidt: Baseball's King of Swing*. New York: Random House, 1983.

Holtje, Stephen. "Luis Tiant, Jr." In Shatzkin, *The Ballplayers*, 1088–89.

Honig, Donald. *The Philadelphia Phillies: An Illustrated History*. New York: Simon & Schuster, 1992.

Jordan, David M. *The Athletics of Philadelphia: Connie Mack's White Elephants, 1901–1954*. Jefferson NC: McFarland, 1999.

———. *Occasional Glory: A History of the Philadelphia Phillies*. Jefferson NC: McFarland, 2002.

Kashatus, William C. *Almost a Dynasty: The Rise and Fall of the 1980 Phillies*. Philadelphia: University of Pennsylvania Press, 2008.

———. *Connie Mack's '29 Triumph: The Rise and Fall of the Philadelphia Athletics Dynasty.* Jefferson NC: McFarland, 1999.

———. *Jackie and Campy: The Untold Story of Their Rocky Relationship and the Breaking of Baseball's Color Line.* Lincoln: University of Nebraska Press, 2014.

———. *Money Pitcher: Chief Bender and the Tragedy of Indian Assimilation.* University Park: Penn State University Press, 2006.

———. *September Swoon: Richie Allen, the 1964 Phillies and Racial Integration.* University Park: Penn State University Press, 2004.

Katz, Jeff. *Split Season: 1981; Fernandomania, the Bronx Zoo, and the Strike That Saved Baseball.* New York: Thomas Dunne Books, 2015.

Kepner, Tyler. *K: A History of Baseball in Ten Pitches.* New York: Random House, 2019.

Kerrane, Kevin, ed. *"Batting Cleanup, Bill Conlin."* Philadelphia: Temple University Press, 1997.

———. *The Hurlers: Pitching Power and Precision.* Alexandria VA: Redefinition, 1989.

Kinlaw, Francis H. "Sam McDowell." In Shatzkin, *The Ballplayers*, 706–7.

———. "Whitey Ford." In Shatzkin, *The Ballplayers*, 348–49.

Knoedelseder, William. *Bitter Brew: The Rise and Fall of Anheuser-Busch and America's Kings of Beer.* New York: HarperCollins, 2012.

Lake, Russell. "A Three-Way Tie for the Pennant?" In Stahl and Nowlin, *Drama and Pride in the Gateway City*, 317–20.

Langford, Jim. "Sandy Koufax." In Shatzkin, *The Ballplayers*, 584–85.

Lauber, Scott. *The Big 50: The Men and Moments That Made the Philadelphia Phillies.* Chicago: Triumph Books, 2020.

Levy, Jean. *Sandy Koufax: A Lefty's Legacy.* New York: Harper Collins, 2002.

Lewis, Allen. "Jim Bunning." In Shatzkin, *The Ballplayers*, 132–33.

———. *The Philadelphia Phillies: A Pictorial History.* Virginia Beach VA: JCP, 1981.

Lolich, Mickey, with Tom Gage. *Joy in Tigertown: A Determined Team, a Resilient City, and Our Magical Run to the 1968 World Series.* Chicago: Triumph Books, 2018.

Lowenfish, Lee. *Branch Rickey: Baseball's Ferocious Gentleman.* Lincoln: University of Nebraska Press, 2009.

Mainieri, Demie. *The Mainieri Factor: Promoting Baseball with a Passion from Miami Dade to Notre Dame, LSU and the Chicago Cubs.* Bloomington IN: Author House, 2007.

Marichal, Juan, with Lew Freedman. *Juan Marichal: My Journey from the Dominican Republic to Cooperstown.* Minneapolis: MVP Books, 2011.

McCarver, Tim, with Dan Peary. *The Perfect Season: Why 1998 Was Baseball's Greatest Year.* New York: Villard, 1999.

———. *Tim McCarver's Baseball for Brain Surgeons and Other Fans.* New York: Villard, 1999.

McCarver, Tim, with Jim Moskovitz and Dan Peary. *Tim McCarver's Diamond Gems: Favorite Baseball Stories from the Legends of the Game.* New York: McGraw-Hill, 2008.

McCarver, Tim, with Phil Pepe. *Few and Chosen: Defining Cardinal Greatness across the Eras*. Chicago: Triumph Books, 2003.

McCarver, Tim, with Ray Robinson. *OH, BABY, I LOVE IT!* Baseball Summers, Hot Pennant Races, Grand Salamis, Jellylegs, El Swervos, Dingers and Dunkers, etc etc etc*. New York: Villard Books, 1987.

McDermott, Terry. *Off Speed: Baseball, Pitching, and the Art of Deception*. New York: Pantheon Books, 2017.

McGraw, Tug, with Don Yeager. *Ya Gotta Believe! My Roller Coaster Life as a Screwball Pitcher and Part-Time Father, and My Hope-Filled Fight against Brain Cancer*. New York: New American Library, 2004.

McGraw, Tug, with William Kashatus. *Was It as Good for You? Tug McGraw and Friends Recall the 1980 World Series*. Media PA: McGraw & Company, 2000.

McLain, Denny, and Eli Zaret. *I Told You I Wasn't Perfect*. Chicago: Triumph Books, 2007.

Mead, William B. *The Explosive Sixties: Baseball's Decade of Expansion*. Alexandria VA: Redefinition, 1989.

Morgan, Bruce. *Steve Carlton and the 1972 Phillies*. Jefferson NC: McFarland, 2012.

Nathanson, Mitchell. *The Fall of the 1977 Phillies: How a Baseball Team's Collapse Sank the Spirit of a City*. Jefferson NC: McFarland, 2007.

Nowlin, Bill, and Dan Desrochers, eds. *The 1967 Impossible Dream Red Sox: Pandemonium on the Field*. Cleveland OH: Society of American Baseball Research, 2017.

Palmer, Pete, and Gary Gillette. *The ESPN Baseball Encyclopedia*. New York: Sterling, 2005.

Pappu, Sridhar. *The Year of the Pitcher: Bob Gibson, Denny McLain and the End of Baseball's Golden Age*. Boston: Houghton Mifflin Harcourt, 2017.

Philadelphia Phillies Yearbook. Philadelphia: Phillies, 1971–77, 1983, 1987.

Ritter, Lawrence. *Lost Ballparks: A Celebration of Baseball's Legendary Fields*. New York: Viking, 1992.

Rotfeld, Berl, producer. *Steve Carlton: Greatest Sports Legends*. Bala Cynwyd PA: Rotfeld Video, 1990.

Seymour, Harold. *Baseball: The Early Years*. New York: Oxford University Press, 1960.

Shatzkin, Mike, ed. *The Ballplayers: Baseball's Ultimate Biographical Reference*. New York: William Morrow, 1990.

Shenk, Larry. *If These Walls Could Talk: Stories from the Philadelphia Phillies Dugout, Locker Room and Press Box*. Chicago: Triumph Books, 2014.

Smith, Ron. *"The Sporting News" Selects Baseball's Greatest Players: A Celebration of the 20th Century's Best*. St. Louis: The Sporting News, 1998.

Snyder, Brad. *A Well-Paid Slave: Curt Flood's Fight for Free Agency in Professional Sports*. New York: Viking, 2006.

Snyder, John. *Cardinals Journal: Year by Year and Day by Day with the St. Louis Cardinals since 1882*. Cincinnati: Clerisy Press, 2010.

Sports Illustrated Baseball. Philadelphia: J. B. Lippincott, 1966.

Stahl, John Harry. "The 1964 World Series." In Stahl and Nowlin, *Drama and Pride in the Gateway City*, 321–28.

Stahl, John Harry, and Bill Nowlin, eds. *Drama and Pride in the Gateway City: The 1964 St. Louis Cardinals*. Lincoln: University of Nebraska Press and Society of American Baseball Research, 2013.

Stephenson, Dan, producer. *Lefty: The Life and Times of Steve Carlton*. Philadelphia: Phillies & Orion Home Video, 1994.

Tiant, Luis, with Saul Wisnia. *Son of Havana: A Baseball Journey from Cuba to the Big Leagues and Back*. New York: Diversion, 2019.

Torre, Joe. *Chasing the Dream: My Lifelong Journey to the World Series*. New York: Bantam, 1997.

Vaccaro, Frank. "Origins of the Pitching Rotation." *Baseball Research Journal* 40, no. 2 (2011): 27–35.

Voigt, David Q. "The History of Major League Baseball." In *Total Baseball*, edited by John Thorn and Pete Palmer, 33–45. New York: Warner Books, 1989.

Voigt, David Quentin. *American Baseball: Volume 3, From Postwar Expansion to the Electronic Age*. University Park: Pennsylvania State University Press, 1983.

Walker, Robert H. *Cincinnati and the Big Red Machine*. Bloomington: Indiana University Press, 1988.

Ward, Geoffrey C., and Ken Burns. *Baseball: An Illustrated History*. New York: Knopf, 1994.

Westcott, Rich. *Philadelphia's Old Ballparks*. Philadelphia: Temple University Press, 1996.

———. *Tales from the Phillies Dugout*. New York: Sports Publishing, 2003.

———. *Veterans Stadium: Field of Memories*. Philadelphia: Temple University Press, 2016.

Westcott, Rich, and Frank Bilovsky. *The Phillies Encyclopedia*. 3rd ed. Philadelphia: Temple University Press, 2004.

White, Bill, with Gordon Dillow. *Uppity: My Untold Story about the Games People Play*. New York: Grand Central, 2012.

Williams, Dave. "Tim McCarver." In Stahl and Nowlin, *Drama and Pride in the Gateway City*, 138–43.

Wolff, Rick, ed. *The Baseball Encyclopedia*. 8th ed. New York: Macmillan, 1990.

Wolpin, Stewart. "Mickey Lolich." In Shatzkin, *The Ballplayers*, 630.

INDEX

Aaron, Hank, 15, 41, 200

Allen, Richie (Dick), 3, 56, 172–73; reacquired by Phillies, 156–57; salary of, 73, 169; traded to Cardinals, 70, 295n15

Ashburn, Richie, 135–36, 255

Bateman, John, 120, 121, 141; and catching Carlton, 107, 118–19, 124; traded to Phillies, 103, 104–6, 110

batteries, 259–74, 284n17

Bench, Johnny, 74–75, 128, 134–35, 158, 180, 189, 190–91, 223, 249–50

Bonds, Bobby, 114, 147

Boone, Bob, 88, 228–29; as All-Star selection, 179–80; on Carlton's pitching, 207, 239–40; catching ability of, 233–35; hitting performance of, 179–80, 197; as player representative, 173–74; relationship of, with Carlton, 1, 140–41, 176, 183, 210–11, 243; relationship of, with McCarver, 210–11; traded to Tigers, 151–52

Boston Red Sox, 46–50, 154–55

Bowa, Larry, 88, 94–95, 102; as agitator, 109–10, 200–201; as All-Star selection, 180; on Carlton's pitching, 109, 208; criticism of Carlton by, 230–31; intimidated by Carlton, 109–10; and NLCS, 212–14, 227; on Phillies fans, 95; relationship of, with Mike Schmidt, 142, 200; and trade rumors, 103

Boyer, Ken, 23, 25, 30, 40

Brandon, Darrell, 95, 96, 12

Bristol, Dave, 135–36

Brock, Lou, 44, 51, 66, 79; acquired by Cardinals, 27; salary of, 73; and World Series (1967), 48–49

Brown, Dave, 103–4, 129

Bucci, Steve, 103–4, 129

Bunning, Jim, 54–55, 128, 135

Busch, August Anheuser, Jr. (Gussie): integration of Cardinals by, 18; and labor conflict, 43, 64, 80–84; purchase of Cardinals by, 17–18, 21; and salary conflict with Carlton, 72–74, 82–83, 99

Busch Stadium, 17, 40–41, 89

Carlton, Steve: as All-Star selection, 63, 65, 76, 114, 180–81, 203; boyhood of, 33–34; career statistics of, 3–4, 275–77, 296n39; in college, 36–37; compared to Rick Wise, 86, 124; compared to Sandy Koufax, 117; and competition with Nolan Ryan, 251–52; and Cy Young Awards, 127–30, 132, 210, 238, 243, 248–49, 253, 313n7, 322n53; elbow pain of, 155, 170–71; elected to Hall of Fame, 255; and endorsements, 132–33; and family, 123, 133, 219, 254; and fans, 217, 219–20, 242, 254; and fastball, 135, 138, 170, 199; in high school, 35–36; hitting performance of, 129–30; and hunting, 34, 79–80, 195–97, 218; idiosyncratic behavior of, 3, 36, 185–86, 219–21, 223–25, 247–48, 323n82; intimidation of, 107–8, 109–10, 114, 190, 217; as journeyman pitcher, 253–54, 323n79; leadership of, 95–96, 109–10; martial arts training of, 76, 146–47, 185–86, 220; Minor League career of, 32, 37–38, 41;

Carlton, Steve (*cont.*)
nicknames of, 119, 140, 173; and NLCS, 190–91, 212–13, 215–16, 227–28, 240; off-season training of, 61, 76, 132, 146–47, 174–75, 183–85, 293n36; physical appearance of, 33, 61, 96, 200; and pick-off move to first, 146–48; pitching philosophy of, 205–6, 313n83; and positive mental approach, 76, 102–3, 185–86, 205, 220, 253; record-setting performances of, 44–45, 66–68, 102, 115, 120–22, 127–30, 179, 192, 224, 228, 240, 244, 249–50, 253; relationship of, with Bob Boone, 140–41, 176, 183, 231–32; relationship of, with Bob Gibson, 55–58, 62, 98–99, 292n26; relationship of, with Dallas Green, 238–39; relationship of, with Danny Ozark, 134–37, 145–46, 229–32; relationship of, with John Bateman, 107, 118–19, 124; relationship of, with Larry Christenson, xi–xii, 143–44; relationship of, with McCarver, 2–4, 32–33, 61, 97, 103, 138, 163, 176–77, 193–94, 195–97, 210–11, 242; relationship of, with Mike Schmidt, 142–43; released by Phillies, 253; retirement of, 254; salary of, 72–74, 80, 82–83, 99, 117, 131, 149, 249, 297n53; season of (1972), 1, 93, 97–100, 101, 127–30, 300n59, 303n54; shoulder pain of, 252–53; signed by Cardinals, 37–38, 289n30; and slider, 61–62, 64–67, 69, 75–76, 92–94, 99, 116, 160–61, 170, 182–83, 199; and sportswriters, 58, 62, 133, 139–40, 164–67, 169–70, 198, 201, 217–19, 224–25, 248, 254; statistics of, with McCarver catching, 4, 42, 45, 69, 226, 228, 237–38, 259–74, 319n50; strength of, 185–86; stubbornness of, 61, 83; as teammate, xi–xii, 142–44, 246–48; traded to Phillies, 83–84, 128–29, 298n80; and trade rumors, 299n39; and World Series (1967), 48; and World Series (1968), 64; and World Series (1980), 238, 240–41; and World Series (1983), 252
Carpenter, Bob, 80, 88–91 101, 106–7
Carpenter, Ruly, 88, 101, 131, 152; on Carlton's relationship with sportswriters, 219; on Paul Owens, 112; on Philadelphia sportswriters, 166–67; on Phillies acquiring Carlton, 85; and rebuilding Phillies, 88; relationship of, with Danny Ozark, 135–36, 232; sale of Phillies by, 246
Cash, Dave, 149–50, 180
Champion, Billy, 95, 100, 127–28
Christenson, Larry, xi–xii, 162–63, 173, 197, 225, 238, 260–66; on Carlton's intensity, 186; as Carlton's spokesman, 217–18; in NLCS, 213, 227; in NLDS, 245; pitching performances of, 156, 164; relationship of, with Bob Boone, 233–35; relationship of, with Carlton, xi–xii, 144, 217–18; relationship of, with Danny Ozark, 146, 201, 209; relationship of, with McCarver, xi–xii, 233–35; rookie year of, 143–44; traded to Tigers, 151–52
Cincinnati Reds, 3, 134, 188–92, 249–50
Clemente, Roberto, xi, 41, 44
Conlin, Bill, 105, 120, 122, 166–67, 187; criticism of Carlton by, 133, 139–40, 169–70, 174; defense of Carlton by, 323n82
Connie Mack Stadium, 89, 90
curveball, 93–94

Daulton, Darren, 246, 247
Devine, Bing: fired by Cardinals, 28; integration of Cardinals by, 18, 21–22; and trades, 21–22, 27, 66, 70–71, 83, 286nn56–57, 297n62
Dickey, Bill, 13–14, 33, 193
Dolson, Frank, 111, 157–58, 166, 168–69
Doyle, Denny, 95, 102, 118
Drinking Coffee with a Fork (Bucci and Brown), 129
Drysdale, Don, 54, 256, 267, 270, 273

fastball, 62, 67, 93–94, 160–61, 182
Flood, Curt, 25, 51, 66, 290n60, 293n52; and racial discrimination, 22, 71; and reserve clause, 5, 71–72, 84–85, 297n72; traded to Phillies, 70–71, 283n15, 294n9; and World Series (1967), 46–48
Freehan, Bill, 151–52
Fryman, Woodie, 95, 100, 128

Gibson, Bob: boyhood of, 18–19; as Harlem Globetrotter, 19; influence of, on Carlton, 55–58; injuries of, 44; intimidation of, 56–

59; leadership of, 60–61; pitching records of, 55, 63, 129–30, 273, 299n20; on race, 59–60; relationship of, with Carlton, 62–63, 98–99; relationship of, with McCarver, 19–20, 58–61, 194; salary of, 73; season of (1968), 55, 62–63; and sportswriters, 58; and World Series(1964), 29–31; and World Series (1967), 46, 48, 49; and World Series (1968), 55, 63, 68, 293n48

Giles, Bill, 91, 118, 126, 159, 249; purchase of Phillies by, 246; release of Carlton by, 252–53

Green, Dallas: as farm director, 141–42; as manager, 232–33, 238–39; relationship of, with Carlton, 233, 238–39

Hemus, Solly, 15, 19, 22–23

Hochman, Stan, 138, 164–67, 217–19, 224–25, 231–32, 249

Hoefling, Gus, 183–85, 203–4, 239

Hoerner, Joe, 70, 95, 98, 103, 128, 135, 290n60

Hutton, Tommy, 94–95, 148

Jaster, Larry, 42, 43, 52, 290n51

Javier, Julian, 25, 26, 40, 47

Jenkins, Ferguson, 97–98

Johnson, Deron, 94, 96, 98, 119

Kaat, Jim, 189, 191–92, 197

K: A History of Baseball in Ten Pitches (Kepner), 64, 160

Kansas City Royals, 240–41

Keane, Johnny, 23, 40

Kelly, Ray, 98–99, 166

Kepner, Tyler, 64, 160, 182

King, Martin Luther, Jr., 16, 59–60

Koufax, Sandy, 54, 68, 69, 129–30, 269–70, 273

Kuhn, Bowie, 71–72

Landfield, David, 132–33

Lerch, Randy, 197, 220–22, 226, 229, 261–62, 264, 266

Lersch, Barry, 95, 100, 128

Lewis, Allen, 166, 168

Lonborg, Jim, 46, 47, 49, 197, 260–61, 264–65; and NLCS, 189, 191; and physical training, 184; pitching performance of, 150, 173,

188; on pitching to Bob Boone, 140; traded to Phillies, 132

Los Angeles Dodgers, 211–16, 227

Lucchesi, Frank, 89; fired by Phillies, 110–11; on Phillies acquiring Carlton, 85–86; and rebuilding Phillies, 89; relationship of, with McCarver, 103–6

Luzinski, Greg, 88, 94, 96, 99, 102; as All-Star selection, 180; hitting performance of, 120–21, 124, 127, 145, 150, 188, 197, 203, 226–27; and NLCS, 213–15; and trade rumors, 103

Lyle, Sparky, 239–40, 246

Maddox, Garry, 114, 156, 197, 198

Mainieri, Demie, 36–38

Major League Baseball (MLB): expansion of, 65–66; labor conflict in, 80–82, 84–85, 173, 175, 244

Marichal, Juan, 54, 68, 72, 99, 100

Maris, Roger, 45, 48–49, 51, 66

Maxvill, Dal, 30, 33, 37, 51, 66, 79–80, 297n62

McBride, Bake, 197, 198, 201

McCarver, Tim: as All-Star selection, 41, 45, 64; arm strength of, 148; boyhood of, 10–12; and Branch Rickey, 25, 26–27; as broadcaster, 242, 255–56, 324n92; career statistics of, 279–81, 321n26; as Carlton's personal catcher, 4, 68, 105, 163, 167–70, 173, 176–77, 193–94, 195, 223, 233, 319n50; on Carlton's pitching philosophy, 206–8; on Carlton's slider, 100, 159, 161, 162, 170, 182–83, 202, 256; as Carlton's spokesman, 201–2, 204, 218–19; catching ability of, 43, 51, 60–61, 97, 103, 176–77, 193–94, 206, 234–35; compared to Mickey Cochrane, 26; comradery of, 24, 43; and Ford Frick Award, 256; high school career of, 12–13; hitting performance of, 26, 30, 31, 39, 45, 70, 78, 104, 153–54, 162, 178–79, 205, 210, 223, 226, 235; humor of, 24, 104, 154–55, 178–79, 188, 195–97, 201–2, 209–10, 224–25, 229; injuries of, 39, 78, 233; leadership of, 60, 78; Minor League career of, 14–15, 20–21; and NLCS, 212, 215–16; on Phillies fans, 106; physical appearance of, 33; as player representative, 43,

McCarver, Tim (*cont.*)
106–7; on race, 59–60; reacquired by Cardinals, 153; relationship of, with Bob Boone, 210–11; relationship of, with Bob Gibson, 19–20, 58–61; relationship of, with Carlton, 2–4, 32–33, 61, 97, 138, 195–97, 210–11, 257; relationship of, with Frank Lucchesi, 103–6; relationship of, with Larry Christenson, xi–xii; signs with Cardinals, 13–14; speed of, 26; stubbornness of, 59, 61, 288n3; traded to Expos, 103–6, 153; traded to Phillies, 70–71, 158–59, 283n15; traded to Red Sox, 154–55; and World Series (1964), 29–31, 287n89; and World Series (1967), 48–50

McCracken, Julian, 260, 264

McGraw, Tug, 151, 174–75, 189; and colorful behavior, 209–10, 220–21; and NLCS, 190–91; and World Series (1980), 241

Miami Dade College, 36–38

Miller, Marvin, 81, 84, 106–7, 173

Money, Don, 94, 102, 108, 119, 126–27, 301n78

Montanez, Willie, 79, 94–98, 114–15, 118–19, 124, 150; relationship of, with Mike Schmidt, 142; traded to Giants, 156

Montreal Expos, 65, 107–8, 153, 244–45

Musial, Stan, 10, 15, 22–24, 26, 31

New York Yankees, 29–30, 53

Niblock, Doug, 267, 271

Oates, Johnny, 1, 157, 162–63, 175, 179–80

Owens, Paul, 1–2, 102; as general manager, 102, 117, 131, 143, 149; as manager, 110–11, 112–13, 115, 250–51, 301n78; and rebuilding Phillies, 88; relationship of, with Carlton, 115, 117, 148–49, 229–30; relationship of, with Danny Ozark, 137; and trades, 105, 151–52, 156–57, 201

Ozark, Danny, xi, 134, 209; criticism of, 168–69, 214–15; and Dodgers, 136; fired by Phillies, 232; and five-man rotation, 148–49; hired as Phillies manager, 135–36; and malapropisms, 136, 137; as Manager of the Year, 192; and NLCS, 191–92, 214–15; relationship of, with Carlton, 135–37, 145–46, 157–58, 203, 229–32; relationship of, with

McCarver, 228–29; relationship of, with Mike Schmidt, 141–42

Philadelphia Phillies: fans of, 86–87, 106; history of, 87; and Minor Leagues, 88–89, 94–95; and NLCS, 3, 188–92, 211–16, 227; payroll of, 169, 228; and Wheeze Kids, 249

pitching rotations: four-man, 51–52, 96–97, 128–29; five-man, 51, 137, 148–49, 291n2

Players Association, 43, 81, 106–7; and player salaries, 80–82, 84; and strike (1972), 84; and strike (1976), 175, 295n16

Quinn, John, 79, 100–101; fired by Phillies, 101–2; negotiating tactics of, 72, 80, 82–83, 85

Reed, Ron, 189, 191, 197, 222, 227, 241

reserve clause, 71–72, 73, 84–85

Reynolds, Ken, 95, 128

Rickey, Branch, 9–10; conflict of, with Bing Devine, 21–22, 28; and McCarver, 25, 26–27, 287n83; as pioneer, 284n4

Rippelmeyer, Ray, 115, 121, 138, 159, 201; on Bob Boone as catcher, 141, 159; on Carlton's slider, 92–93, 100, 159; on Larry Christenson, 143; on martial arts training, 203–4; retirement of, 232

Rose, Pete, 158, 189, 190, 228, 249

Ruthven, Dick: as All-Star selection, 181; pitching performance of, 150, 222, 227, 238; relationship of, with Carlton, 150–51; rookie year of, 145

Ryan, Mike, 78, 135, 137

Ryan, Nolan, 68, 77–78, 80, 251–52, 322n70

Sadecki, Ray, 24, 25, 40, 78

Scarce, Mac, 95, 121, 128

Schmidt, Mike, 88, 148, 206; as All-Star selection, 180; on Carlton's pitching, 206–8; hitting performance of, 150, 168, 169, 175, 178, 188, 197, 203; and NLCS, 190–92; and NLDS, 245; relationship of, with Carlton, 142–43; relationship of, with Danny Ozark, 141–42; rookie year of, 141–42, 145; and World Series, 241

Schoendienst, Red, 38, 40, 48–49, 74, 97, 125, 149

Seaver, Tom, 68, 101, 126, 223, 260, 262–63, 266, 268, 270, 273

Selma, Dick, 95, 100, 107, 128

Shannon, Mike, 29, 30, 40, 48, 105

Shenk, Larry, 96, 167, 248

Short, Chris, 95, 118, 119, 128

Simmons, Curt, 25, 28, 29, 30, 40, 128

Simmons, Ted, 70, 75–76, 77, 97

slider, 52, 61–62, 64–66, 92–94, 116, 159–61, 182–83

Stargell, Willie, 117, 161

Staub, Rusty, 101, 151

Stephenson, Dan, 246, 248

Steve Carlton and the 1972 Phillies (Morgan), 129

St. Louis Cardinals: history of, 9–10, 21–23, 51, 86–87, 284n3, 286n42, 289n27; and racial discrimination, 16–18; season of (1964), 27–31

Tata, Terry, 148, 190

Torre, Joe, 66, 73, 75, 78–79

Twitchell, Wayne, 95, 127, 145

Uecker, Bob, 24, 39

Underwood, Tommy, 156, 162–63, 164, 173

U.S. Supreme Court, 72, 84–85

Veterans Stadium, 89–91; and All-Star Game (1976), 180; attendance at, 126, 192; and bicentennial, 172; cost of building, 89–90; field dimensions of, 90; and NLCS, 190–91, 240–41; and NLDS, 243–45; opening of, 89; promotional events at, 118, 123; seating capacity of, 90; and World Series, 241–42

Vukovich, John, 94, 224–25

White, Bill, 16–17, 24, 25, 40

Wilson, Billy, 95, 128

Wise, Rick, 79, 80, 124–25; compared to Carlton, 86, 124; no-hitter of, 79; and salary dispute with Phillies, 80, 82–83, 297n53; traded to Cardinals, 82–83, 86, 298n80

World Series: in 1964, 20–31; in 1967, 46–50; in 1980, 241; in 1983, 252